Mike Meyers' CompTIA A+® Guide to Managing and Troubleshooting PCs Lab Manual

Sixth Edition

(Exams 220-1001 & 220-1002)

About the Authors

Michael Meyers is the industry's leading authority on CompTIA A+ and CompTIA Network+ certifications. He is the president and founder of Total Seminars, LLC, a major provider of PC and network repair seminars for thousands of organizations throughout the world, and a member of CompTIA.

Mike has written numerous popular textbooks, including the best-selling *Mike Meyers' CompTIA A+® Guide to Managing and Troubleshooting PCs, Sixth Edition (Exams 220-1001 & 220-1002)*, *Mike Meyers' CompTIA Network+® Guide to Managing and Troubleshooting Networks, Fifth Edition (Exam N10-007)*, and *Mike Meyers' CompTIA Security+® Certification Guide*.

Mark Edward Soper has worked with computers and related technologies for over 30 years, and specializes in technology education through training, writing, and public speaking. He is the author or co-author of 40 books on technology topics ranging from CompTIA A+ certification to Microsoft Windows, networking, and troubleshooting. Mark has also taught these and other topics across the United States.

Mark has CompTIA A+ and Microsoft MOS – Microsoft Excel 2013 certifications, and currently teaches Microsoft Office classes for University of Southern Indiana and Ivy Tech Community College. Mark blogs at www.markesoper.com.

About the Technical Editor

Chris Crayton (MCSE) is an author, technical consultant, and trainer. He has worked as a computer technology and networking instructor, information security director, network administrator, network engineer, and PC specialist. Chris has authored several print and online books on PC repair, CompTIA A+, CompTIA Security+, and Microsoft Windows. He has also served as technical editor and content contributor on numerous technical titles for several leading publishing companies. He holds numerous industry certifications, has been recognized with many professional teaching awards, and has served as a state-level SkillsUSA competition judge.

Mike Meyers' CompTIA A+® Guide to Managing and Troubleshooting PCs Lab Manual

Sixth Edition

(Exams 220-1001 & 220-1002)

Mike Meyers
Mark Edward Soper

New York   Chicago   San Francisco
Athens   London   Madrid   Mexico City
Milan   New Delhi   Singapore   Sydney   Toronto

**Mike Meyers' CompTIA A+® Guide to Managing and
Troubleshooting PCs Lab Manual, Sixth Edition (Exams 220-1001 & 220-1002)**

1 2 3 4 5 6 7 8 9   QVS   23 22 21 20 19

ISBN   978-1-260-45457-4
MHID   1-260-45457-6

Sponsoring Editor Tim Green	**Technical Editor** Chris Crayton	**Production Supervisor** James Kussow
Editorial Supervisor Janet Walden	**Copy Editor** William McManus	**Composition** Cenveo Publisher Services
Project Manager Anupriya Tyagi, Cenveo® Publisher Services	**Proofreader** Paul Tyler	**Illustration** Cenveo Publisher Services
Acquisitions Coordinator Claire Yee	**Indexer** Jack Lewis	**Art Director, Cover** Jeff Weeks

To students young and old who keep the faith that with hard work and diligence you will succeed.

–Mike Meyers

In memory of my dad, who sacrificed to make my dreams come true.

–Mark Edward Soper

Contents at a Glance

Contents

Acknowledgments

The crew at Total Seminars contributed mightily to this edition. Our Editor in Chief, Scott Jernigan, helped manage the flow of the textbook and provided direction for the accompanying lab manual. Michael Smyer and Ford Pierson provided stellar art, editing, and help with labs. Doug Jones and Dave Rush, fellow instructors at Total Seminars, added great feedback and support on the many labs in this book.

On the McGraw-Hill side, the crew once again demonstrated why McGraw-Hill is the best in show as a publisher. With excellent work and even better attitude, this book came together smoothly.

Our project manager, Anupriya Tyagi at Cenveo Publisher Services, rocked it, with great direction and follow-up on missing pieces. Our editorial supervisor, Janet Walden, and her excellent team were wonderful to work with. Quiet competence is totally *not* overrated and you and your team have it to spare. Thank you!

To the copy editor, page proofer, and indexer—Bill McManus, Paul Tyler, Jack Lewis—superb work in every facet. Thank you for being the best.

Finally, Mark thanks God for the opportunity to continue to share many years of training and experience with others, and thanks Mike for the chance to team up with him to bring the world the best CompTIA A+ certification training materials.

Additional Resources for Teachers

The answer keys to the lab manual activities in this book are provided along with resources for teachers using *Mike Meyers' CompTIA A+° Guide to Managing and Troubleshooting PCs, Sixth Edition (Exams 220-1001 & 220-1002)*. The Instructor Web Site provides resources for teachers in a format that follows the organization of the textbook.

This site includes the following:

- Answer keys to the Mike Meyers' Lab Manual activities

- Answer keys to the end-of-chapter activities in the textbook (available separately)

- Engaging PowerPoint slides on the lecture topics that include full-color artwork from the book

- Instructor's Manual that contains learning objectives, classroom preparation notes, instructor tips, a pre-test, a lecture outline, and an assessment quiz for each chapter

- Access to test bank files that allow you to generate a wide array of paper- or network-based tests, and that feature automatic grading. The test bank includes

  - Hundreds of practice questions and a wide variety of question types categorized by exam objective, enabling you to customize each test to maximize student progress.

  - Test bank files available for download in these formats: Blackboard, EZ Test, Word. Check with your sales representative for the availability of other cartridge formats.

Please contact your McGraw-Hill Education sales representative for details.

Chapter 1
Safety and Professionalism

Lab Exercises

Achieving CompTIA A+ certification is a great way to demonstrate to prospective employers that you have the appropriate technical skills to make you a worthy candidate for their workplace. But you have to demonstrate more than just technical skills to get hired by and succeed in an organization. You also need to demonstrate that you have the appropriate interpersonal skills to interact effectively with fellow employees and with clients. CompTIA recognizes the importance of interpersonal skills in the workplace and thus includes related questions on its CompTIA A+ certification exams to make sure you are prepared to show that you have the people skills to work well with others.

Face it: You're great at fixing computers and extremely interested in the latest gadgets, but do you have the people skills to land a job, keep a job, and climb the ladder of success? We've seen many talented young individuals who can fix just about anything but struggle in the area of how to communicate professionally with others; their impressive resume allows them to walk in the front door to a promising future…only to slink out the back door in disappointment after failing due to lack of people skills.

Whether you like it or not, people evaluate you based on how they perceive you. Developing and maintaining personal and professional workplace habits ensures that people perceive you as the IT professional that you are. This set of labs applies the information you learned in Chapter 1 of *Mike Meyers' CompTIA A+ Guide to Managing and Troubleshooting PCs*, with a focus on communicating properly, presenting yourself professionally at all times, and demonstrating your technical knowledge regarding safety. These labs will help you not only to pass the CompTIA A+ exam but also to develop skills that will serve you well throughout your career, whether in IT or another field.

The CompTIA objectives challenge you to conduct yourself in a professional manner while on the job. Objective 4.7 (Exam 220-1002) goes into detail to clarify how you should act on the job:

4.7 Given a scenario, use proper communication techniques and professionalism.

- Use proper language and avoid jargon, acronyms, and slang when applicable

- Maintain a positive attitude/project confidence

- Actively listen (taking notes) and avoid interrupting the customer

- Be culturally sensitive

    - Use appropriate professional titles, when applicable

- Be on time (if late, contact the customer)

- Avoid distractions

    - Personal calls

    - Texting/social media sites

    - Talking to coworkers while interacting with customers

    - Personal interruptions

- Dealing with difficult customers or situations

    - Do not argue with customers and/or be defensive

    - Avoid dismissing customer problems

    - Avoid being judgmental

    - Clarify customer statements (ask open-ended questions to narrow the scope of the problem, restate the issue, or question to verify understanding)

    - Do not disclose experiences via social media outlets

- Set and meet expectations/timeline and communicate status with the customer
  - Offer different repair/replacement options, if applicable
  - Provide proper documentation on the services provided
  - Follow up with customer/user at a later date to verify satisfaction
- Deal appropriately with customers' confidential and private materials
  - Located on a computer, desktop, printer, etc.

Many of the following labs will require you to have a partner, and your instructor will actually lead the classroom through a few of the labs, so buddy up.

 **30 MINUTES**

Lab Exercise 1.01: Safeguarding Your IT Future—Becoming a Professional

To safeguard your IT future, it is extremely important that you know how to carry yourself as a professional and keep your customers satisfied. As discussed in *Mike Meyers' CompTIA A+ Guide to Managing and Troubleshooting PCs*, good techs demonstrate professionalism in the workplace at all times.

Learning Objectives

In this lab, you will learn the proper way to dress for the workplace and present yourself in the workplace.

After completing this lab, you'll be able to

- Properly dress for the job and present yourself on the job
- Understand the do's and don'ts about cell phone usage on the job

Lab Materials and Setup

The materials you need for this lab are

- A PC with Internet access

Getting Down to Business

Choosing the proper way to dress and present yourself is extremely important in securing and maintaining a good job. Did you know that within the first 15 seconds of meeting someone, they form opinions of you based entirely on your appearance—your body language, your demeanor, your mannerisms, and how you are dressed? Once you have made that first impression, it is virtually irreversible, so you must be aware at all times of how you are being perceived and always maintain a positive and clean self-image.

Step 1   Based on your current knowledge of what it means to be a professional in the workplace, list three characteristics that show these qualities.

_____

_____

_____

Step 2   Go to www.mindtools.com/CommSkll/FirstImpressions.htm and read the article "Making a Great First Impression." Notice some of the characteristics you might have missed in Step 1. List three of them.

_____

_____

_____

Step 3   Read the article "Rules for Using Cell Phones at Work," by Dawn Rosenberg McKay, at www.thebalancecareers.com/rules-for-using-cell-phones-at-work-526258. Then, read the following scenarios and write a short explanation of what you would do next.

    A.   Your boss has specifically stated that you cannot use your cell phone on the job unless you are on break (away from your work space) or at lunch. Your father will be having surgery today, and you want to be informed right away about his status. What should you do?

_____

_____

_____

B. You're on the company phone with a client, attempting to walk her through various troubleshooting steps so that you don't have to travel to the client's location to fix the problem. Your personal cell phone suddenly rings (because you forgot to turn it off) and you can see on the caller ID that it's an old friend you have not talked to in a while. What should you do?

_____

_____

_____

C. Your boss just came in the office from a meeting with his boss and is extremely frustrated about issues that do not involve you. He speaks to you rather harshly and then abruptly leaves. The moment he leaves, you receive a phone call from a client who demands that you return his PC to him today and a text message you've been waiting for about a part for the client's computer that's due in. How should you react?

_____

_____

_____

 30 MINUTES

Lab Exercise 1.02: Avoiding the Rude Computer Technician Stereotype

Everyone is familiar with the stereotype of the rude technician so wrapped up in technology that he is unable to relate to the people around him. Sneering technobabble, a condescending attitude, and rude remarks have become traits that people expect to find in techs, and, all too often, the techs don't disappoint. In this exercise, you'll work with a partner first to role-play the part of the stereotypical rude tech and then to role-play a professional, well-behaved tech. In this way, you'll learn how you should and should not behave as a technician.

Learning Objectives

The plan is to have a classmate play the role of the client, and to have you play the role of the PC tech. You will work through the scenario live, just as if it were real.

At the end of this lab, you'll be able to

- Demonstrate proper communication skills
- Avoid distractions in the workplace

Lab Materials and Setup

The materials you need for this lab are

- A notepad and pen/pencil
- A clock with a second hand, or a timer
- A space to place chairs so that you can face your partner
- The *Mike Meyers' CompTIA A+ Guide to Managing and Troubleshooting PCs* textbook, for reference
- A PC with Internet access

Getting Down to Business

In this exercise, one person will act as the PC technician while the other will act as a customer sitting in a cubicle. As the PC tech, you will first try to emulate as many bad communication habits as possible while your partner, the customer, identifies and writes down those bad habits. Then, repeat the process, this time using proper communication skills. You will then trade roles and repeat the scenario.

Step 1   Create a scenario in which a customer would ask for technical support. For example, try "My computer is running slowly and all these Web pages keep popping up!"—a classic case of malware infection. The person playing the customer should act as if he or she is *not* technically savvy and is unable to answer any technical questions or understand any terms outside of what might be considered "common." What is considered "common" is up to the person playing the customer, so have fun!

Step 2   Between 1999 and 2001, the popular television show *Saturday Night Live* put on a series of comedy sketches called "Nick Burns, Your Company's Computer Guy." Many of these sketches are available online. Do a search for and watch a few of these humorous sketches to see actor Jimmy Fallon portray how insensitive a technician can be in his personal communications. Why are these sketches so funny? What does their popularity tell you about how techs are perceived by our society? Use these videos to get an idea of how to behave during the next step, and how never, ever to behave in real life.

Step 3   It's now time for the technician to do his thing in a timed scenario. Pretend the customer is sitting in a cubicle. Every computer has an "asset tag number," and the tech must confirm that number to make sure he is working on the right computer. After that, it's up to the tech! Be as rude as possible (but not so rude that a person normally would get fired), concentrating on the issues listed in Step 1 of this lab. Your goal is to try to get started working on the PC within three minutes.

As the customer, your job is to describe the problem and answer the tech's questions to the best of your ability. You want your computer fixed, but you won't get up until you have confidence in the tech. As the tech talks, jot down how he is rude or inconsiderate to you.

The scenario ends when either the tech is sitting at the customer's computer or three minutes have elapsed, whichever happens first.

Step 4   Discuss the issues that the customer wrote down. After a quick discussion, repeat the process, this time using good communication techniques. In most cases, the customer will quickly relinquish his or her seat and let you get to work.

The scenario ends when the tech is sitting at the customer's computer or three minutes have elapsed, whichever happens first.

Step 5   Repeat the entire process, this time trading roles. The person now playing the tech should attempt to come up with different ways to be inappropriate, within reason.

 15–40 MINUTES DEPENDING ON CLASS SIZE

Lab Exercise 1.03: Collecting Information Professionally

As Lab 1.02 pointed out in a comical way, there's a psychological aspect involved in providing good customer service. Yes, your goal is to extract from the customer the information that you need to solve the problem at hand. However, a good technician is able to get that information in a sensitive and customer-friendly manner, without making the client feel guilty or ignorant (even if they are, in fact, both).

Learning Objectives

In this lab, you will practice ways of phrasing technical questions and conveying technical information in a customer-friendly manner.

At the end of this lab, you will be able to

- Project a positive attitude when speaking with customers
- Elicit information from a client without blaming the customer for the problem

Lab Materials and Setup

The materials you need for this lab are

- A notepad and pen/pencil

Getting Down to Business

For every unfiltered thought you have in your head about a problem, there is a filtered, customer-friendly way of phrasing it. For example, instead of saying "What did you do to it?" you could say "Do you remember anything happening before the problem started?" Rephrasing the raw thought in a friendlier way can pay off in several ways. When customers don't feel accused or attacked, they are much more positive in their evaluation of your service, which can mean better ratings and reviews for you, as well as more business for your company. By putting a customer at ease you also may elicit more and better information from them, so you will have more facts with which to troubleshoot.

Some keys to eliciting feedback professionally are to

- Ask simple questions that focus on the problem without blaming anyone. For example:

  - Do you remember installing any software or changing any settings right before the problem started?

  - How long has this been going on?

  - Does it happen all the time, or intermittently?

- Don't ask questions about technical details that they do not need to know for their job. For example, don't ask whether they have the 32-bit or 64-bit version of Windows, or how much RAM their computer has. If you need that information, look it up yourself.

- Avoid making accusations. Don't accuse the user of breaking the computer, deleting a file, or changing a setting. Instead, make general inquiries such as "Did anything happen lately that might have caused files to be deleted or settings to change?"

- Help find a workaround. If a customer continues to do something that is causing problems with his computer, or with the network, help him find a way to achieve his goals without doing that thing; don't just tell him to stop doing that and leave him hanging.

- Leave the customer some dignity, even if that involves pretending not to know what he's been up to. Don't say "Stay away from the porn sites. I see them in your browser history, and that's why you have malware." Instead say "It looks like you have gotten into some malware. Certain websites can download malware to your computer when you click links on them."

Step 1   As a class or in small groups, recall some of the more outrageous things that were said in the student skits from Exercise 1.02. If your class did not do Exercise 1.02, brainstorm some things that a technician might say to a customer that might come off sounding rude or insensitive. Then brainstorm some ways you could rephrase them to sound kinder and more professional.

Step 2   Working individually, rephrase the following statements to be more customer-friendly and to elicit better information or cooperation from the customer.

A.   It's the same problem that I was here last week for, and I told you not to do that anymore. Why are you still doing it?

_____

B.   I need to get to that outlet. Move.

_____

C.   You've been using illegal file-sharing sites, haven't you?

_____

D.   None of my other users are having this problem; what are you *doing* to it?

_____

E.   What NIC model have you got?

_____

Step 3   As a class or in small groups, compare your answers from Step 1. Pick the top one or two favorite responses that represent the best customer service.

 **20 MINUTES**

Lab Exercise 1.04: Communicating Effectively

So, you want to be a successful IT technician but you have trouble communicating? One of the keys to professional communication is being able to listen well as duties are being assigned to you so that you can produce the results expected.

Learning Objectives

In this lab, you will practice professional communication with clients by role-playing scenarios with your classmates.

At the end of this lab, you'll be able to

- Communicate more effectively

- Help discern when it's best to talk and when it's best to listen

Lab Materials and Setup

The materials you need for this lab are

- Blank drawing paper and pencil

- A clock with a second hand, or a timer

- A sufficient number of folding chairs for all the students involved in the exercise

- The *Mike Meyers' CompTIA A+ Guide to Managing and Troubleshooting PCs* textbook, for reference

For the setup, arrange the chairs back to back in pairs around the room, with about five feet between each set of chairs.

Getting Down to Business

In this exercise, you'll listen as your partner speaks to you and you'll write down whatever he or she tells you under a tight timeline. The goal is to help you work under pressure while remaining professional at all times.

Step 1   Students should pair up. Each pair of students should designate one person to be the PC tech and the other to be the customer and then write their respective titles on the top of their papers.

Step 2   The instructor should start the timer and ask the designated customers to say the first five technology-related problems that come to mind; they have 20 seconds to do this. As the customers speak, their respective partner techs should write down what they say in the order stated. An example might be "system fails to boot, no wireless connection, printer not printing properly, no picture on the monitor," and so on.

 **STOP THE TIMER AT 20 SECONDS.**

Step 3   The PC techs write a brief solution to the five problems just mentioned by the customers. They have three minutes to complete this and must address the problems in the order received.

 **STOP THE TIMER AT 3 MINUTES.**

Step 4   The PC tech and customer groups face each other for one minute and share their information. Then, each pair presents their problems and solutions to the class, in turn. They have two minutes to present their solutions. The other groups should sit quietly and listen. After all groups finish, the instructor will give feedback to each group as to how they could communicate better. Students should be allowed to participate in the feedback as well.

 30 MINUTES

Lab Exercise 1.05: Integrating Safety into the Workplace

Demonstrating safety precautions at all times is one of the most important things you can do to protect yourself and your customers…and impress your employer. This mostly involves using common sense, but you should also make sure to carefully read and put into practice the safety guidelines provided in Chapter 1 of *Mike Meyers' CompTIA A+ Guide to Managing and Troubleshooting PCs*.

Many techs go into the field with the mind-set that safety is not that important, but it can save your life and the lives of others. The U.S. Department of Labor Occupational Safety and Health Administration's Web site at www.osha.gov is loaded with information for employers and employees to help them understand the importance of safety. It offers guidelines for electronics and computers/peripherals that we'll explore in this lab exercise.

Learning Objectives

In this lab, you will identify computer-related health and safety hazards in the workplace.

At the end of this lab, you will be able to

- Identify potential safety hazards affecting computer users and technicians
- Explain proper equipment-disposal procedures

Lab Materials and Setup

The materials you need for this lab are

- A school, office, or home environment with several PCs
- A notepad and pen/pencil
- A desktop PC with a case you can open for inspection

Getting Down to Business

In Chapter 1 of *Mike Meyers' CompTIA A+ Guide to Managing and Troubleshooting PCs*, in the section "Personal Safety," you learned about some of the physical hazards that computers present, not only for the technician but for end users. Once you start looking for these hazards in your daily working and living environment, you may wonder how you missed them before, and why other people don't seem to view them as a problem.

Step 1   First, let's look at safety from an end-user perspective. Walk through a school, home, or work environment where there are multiple computers, with a notepad and pen or pencil for taking notes. Note any instances of the following:

- Cables across paths where people walk
- Tangles of cables that could get caught and pulled as someone walks by, or that a family pet could get tangled in, if in the home
- Computer equipment operating in an area where there is no fire extinguisher that can handle electrical fires (Type ABC or, preferably, Class C)
- Notebook computers that get hot as they operate, with users resting the computers directly on their laps as they work

Step 2 Look for potential safety hazards specifically for PC technicians. Open a desktop PC's case and observe the following potential hazards, making notes as you go.

a. If the computer has been on recently, feel around (very cautiously, by hovering your hand rather than touching) for warm or hot components, such as heat sinks, cooling fins, and hot chips on the motherboard and video cards. If nothing is currently hot, identify the components you think would be heat hazards that a PC technician should avoid touching or brushing up against.

b. Look for sharp corners and rough metal edges. Many a technician has sliced open fingertips on the inside edge of a cheap PC chassis.

c. Look for parts sticking up that you could potentially catch a sleeve or jewelry on. Check the sleeves of your current outfit and any jewelry that you may be wearing; are you wearing anything that could catch?

d. Is the inside of the case very dusty, to the point where it would make you cough if the dust got stirred up and you weren't wearing an air filter mask? It's a good idea to carry a mask in your toolkit, in case you need to blow or shake the crud out of a PC. (Don't forget to close your eyes when you do that, or wear safety goggles.)

Step 3 (If Time Permits) Assign your environment a "safety grade" of A through F, depending on what you found. Write up a report of the major safety issues you identified and what you would recommend to fix them, or present the information as an oral report to the class.

 **30 MINUTES**

Lab Exercise 1.06: Taming Electrostatic Discharge

Imagine that you have an open container with a water-tight divider down the middle, and you have a large amount of water on one side and a small amount of water on the other side. What happens when you remove the divider? The water on the high side rushes into the low side to immediately equalize the level. That's the concept of equalizing potential.

Now imagine that it's happening with electricity. Object 1 has a 1000-volt electrical potential built up in it; Object 2 has none. Instead of a divider between them, you've got physical space keeping them apart. When the two objects physically touch, it's like removing the divider. Wham! All that voltage in Object 1 rushes over to Object 2, 1000 volts at once. That's known as electrostatic discharge (ESD).

Object 1 is a person wearing wool socks on a nylon carpet, and Object 2 is a delicate and expensive circuit board that is accustomed to receiving a nice steady 5 or 12 volts of power from a motherboard. It's just been shocked (literally) with a 1000-volt zap. From the human's perspective, nothing happened, but now Object 2 is dead.

That, in a nutshell, is why we care about ESD. In this lab, you will experiment with ESD and practice techniques for preventing it from damaging components.

Learning Objectives

In this lab, you will learn how ESD affects electronics and how to avoid ESD damage.

After completing this lab, you'll be able to

- Explain ESD
- Demonstrate an effective method to reduce the risk of ESD damage to PCs

Lab Materials and Setup

The materials you need for this lab are

- A PC with Internet access
- Presentation software, such as PowerPoint
- Antistatic mat and wrist strap
- A glass rod 8 to 12 inches long (try Zoro Tools at www.zoro.com) or a long test tube from the chemistry department, lab supply store, or Amazon
- Wool cloth: use a wool scarf, hat, or clean sock or get a sample wool square from a fabric store

Getting Down to Business

In Chapter 1 of *Mike Meyers' CompTIA A+ Guide to Managing and Troubleshooting PCs*, you read that ESD can cause permanent damage to some components and erase data on some storage devices. If you take this to heart and practice ESD safety measures as a PC tech early on, you will gain respect in the workplace and demonstrate that you care about your employer's investment.

Step 1   Use an Internet search engine such as Bing.com or Google.com to research ESD. Identify typical causes, environmental conditions that create ESD, and the types of damage to electronics and computers that can result from ESD. Find common ways to prevent ESD damage when working on computers. If possible, locate a video clip of someone wearing an antistatic wrist strap while working on a PC. Make sure you document your results and where you found your information.

Step 2   Compile the ESD research data into a presentation. Make sure that your presentation answers the following questions:

- What is ESD?
- How can ESD damage computer equipment?
- How does the flooring material in the room affect ESD?

- How does your choice of clothing and footwear affect ESD?

- How does an antistatic wrist strap work? To what do you attach the other end?

- How does an antistatic floor mat work?

- How does an antistatic plastic bag work?

Step 3   Do the following experiment, which shows firsthand how an antistatic mat and wrist strap can minimize the effect of ESD.

   a.   Hold one end of a glass rod in your hand, and rub the glass rod vigorously with wool cloth for one minute.

   b.   Put the cloth aside and, after asking permission, hold the rod close to the ear of a person with long hair. The static charge will attract the hair and pull it gently away from its owner.

   c.   Place an antistatic mat on the floor.

   d.   Wear the antistatic wrist strap, and attach the other end of it to the mat with the connecting cord that comes with the wrist strap.

   e.   Repeat Steps a and b.

   Notice that the hair is not as strongly attracted with the antistatic precautions in place. That's because the excess charge that would have built up on the rod was drawn through the wrist strap and into the mat, where it was evenly distributed and will slowly leak off to passing air and water vapor molecules.

 **30 MINUTES**

Lab Exercise 1.07: Understanding the Troubleshooting Methodology

CompTIA's best practice methodology to resolve problems is discussed in Chapter 1 of *Mike Meyers' CompTIA A+ Guide to Managing and Troubleshooting PCs* in the section "Troubleshooting Methodology." This methodology is useful for solving all types of computer problems, so it deserves to be part of your thought processes long after you have earned your CompTIA A+ certification.

Learning Objectives

In this lab, you will learn the troubleshooting methodology and practice how to apply it.

   After completing this lab, you'll be able to

- Identify the steps in the methodology

- Understand how to apply the methodology

Lab Materials and Setup

The materials you need for this lab are

- A PC with Internet access

Getting Down to Business

Here are the six steps in the troubleshooting methodology:

 Note

> **Always consider corporate policies, procedures, and impacts before implementing changes.**

1. Identify the problem
   - Question the user and identify user changes to computer and perform backups before making changes
   - Inquire regarding environmental or infrastructure changes
   - Review system and application logs
2. Establish a theory of probable cause (question the obvious)
   - If necessary, conduct external or internal research based on symptoms
3. Test the theory to determine cause
   - Once the theory is confirmed, determine the next steps to resolve problem
   - If theory is not confirmed reestablish new theory or escalate
4. Establish a plan of action to resolve the problem and implement the solution
5. Verify full system functionality and, if applicable, implement preventive measures
6. Document findings, actions, and outcomes

Step 1   You get a call from a user who says that she can't play music from a streaming service that she regularly listens to on her computer. Some of the steps you might follow include

A. Test your theory (audio muted in app).

B. Establish a theory (audio muted in app).

C. Identify the problem.

List these in order according to the troubleshooting methodology: _____

Step 2 After checking the streaming music app, you determine that the app's audio settings are not muted. List three questions you could ask the user to help determine what might be wrong.

_____

_____

_____

Step 3 After asking the user when the music stopped playing, you suspect the problem might be with the speakers or sound card. List two ways to test the speakers or sound card.

_____

_____

Step 4 You are unable to hear music from the computer speakers using sound files stored locally. However, you notice that the monitor has built-in speakers and is plugged into the HDMI port on the video display adapter. Asking the user when the display was installed would help to establish what?

_____

Step 5 You have determined that the problem started when the previous display was replaced with a new display with built-in speakers and HDMI connection (which carries sound and video information). The sound mixer was set to mute the old audio output but was not set to use the new speakers. After checking with IT, you determine that this is just one of three dozen identical displays that will be used for upgrades around the company. Write up a short paragraph identifying the problem and how to avoid it during the upgrade.

Lab Analysis Test

1. Your coworker Sara constantly takes personal calls on her cell phone even though she knows your employer has a rule banning personal use of the cell phone while in the workplace. Whenever she's on her cell phone, she does not answer her regular work phone, thus adding more work for you and others. How do you think you should handle this situation?

2. You just got a phone call from a PC repair company that wants to interview you today. It is dress-down day at your workplace, so you're wearing jeans and a T-shirt. Should you accept the offer to interview today or decline? Explain your answer.

3. You're the lead PC technician for a company and have been put in charge of two inexperienced technicians who know nothing about ESD. What steps will you take to educate them to ensure they use antistatic devices.

4. What is EMI and which components are particularly susceptible to it?

5. At what stage of the troubleshooting methodology do you establish a plan of action?

Key Term Quiz

Use the following terms to complete the following sentences. Not all terms will be used.

ABC	honesty
C	integrity
cell phones	outcomes
electrostatic discharge (ESD)	professional
findings	responsibility

1. A(n) _____ technician is one who not only possesses great technical expertise but also has good communication and people skills.

2. Documenting findings, actions, and _____ is step six of the troubleshooting methodology.

3. Antistatic wrist straps prevent _____.

4. When on the job, it is your _____ to follow the rules and guidelines set by the company regarding the use of _____.

5. The most effective fire extinguisher for electrical fires has a(n) _____ rating.

Chapter 2

The Visible Computer

Lab Exercises

Every competent tech knows the PC inside and out. Nothing destroys your credibility in the eyes of a client as quickly as not knowing the basics, like the difference between a graceful shutdown and a forced power down. The word "Oops!" doesn't go over well in the real world! In this chapter, you'll be poking and prodding a real PC. You'll begin by exploring the functions of a PC: input, processing, output, data storage, and network connection. Then you'll examine the typical user-accessible components—for example, what happens when you press the power button? The next lab takes you on a tour of common connectors. The chapter wraps up with labs that demonstrate the basics of the Windows 7, Windows 8.1, Windows 10, and macOS interfaces and labs that review the basics of Windows file management and Control Panel and Settings operations.

 **30 MINUTES**

Lab Exercise 2.01: Exploring the Functions and Components of a PC

Everything a computing device does falls into one of five categories: input, processing, output, data storage, and network connection. To troubleshoot PC problems successfully, you need a good understanding of these five processes and the components that are involved with each one.

Learning Objectives

In this lab exercise, you will familiarize yourself with the basic functions of a computer.

At the end of this lab, you'll be able to

- Define the five functions of computing devices
- Detail common components involved in each of these five functions

Lab Materials and Setup

The materials you need for this lab are

- A notepad and pencil, to create a five-column table

- Optional: Access to a working computer with a word processing or spreadsheet application installed to aid in creating the table

- The *Mike Meyers' CompTIA A+ Guide to Managing and Troubleshooting PCs* textbook, for reference

---

✔ **Hint**

Get used to taking notes and drawing pictures. Even after many years of repairing computers, from mainframes to tablets, we both still use a notepad to keep track of what we see and what we change. We recommend that you save your drawings and notes, as you'll find them useful in subsequent labs. If you have a tablet or a PC with Windows Ink support, consider making your notes and drawing pictures using your device and saving them as files you can edit later.

Getting Down to Business

In this exercise, you'll review, list, and define the various components involved in the PC's vital functions.

Step 1   Reread the "The Computing Process" section in Chapter 2 of *Mike Meyers' CompTIA A+ Guide to Managing and Troubleshooting PCs,* paying particular attention to the five stages described in the "Stages" section.

Step 2   For each of the following functions, write a definition and give a brief example:

Input:

_____

_____

Processing:

_____

_____

Output:

_____

_____

Data storage:

_____

_____

Network connection:

_____

_____

Step 3   Using the following table, list the components that operate in each of the five functional categories. Try to include as many components as you can; you might take a peek at some of the later chapters in the textbook to see if you can add any other components. Think about how each of the components contributes to the overall workings of the PC, and include as much detail about the component as possible.

Input	Processing	Output	Data Storage	Network Connection

Step 4   If you completed the table in the print book, you can review it later while finishing the rest of the lessons. If you made a table in your notebook or created an electronic version, make sure you keep

it nearby. As you work on later chapters, you'll want to update the table with additional components and extra details. The information in the table (and in your head) will expand as you develop a better understanding of how the components relate to the PC's "big picture."

 30 MINUTES

Lab Exercise 2.02: Examining User-Accessible Components

It's been one of those days. You walked into what should have been a simple job interview only to meet a very frantic IT manager dealing with a crisis of epic proportions. She doesn't even bother to interview you. Instead, she shuttles you out of her office, points down the hall, and says, "Go check Jane's PC—fourth cubicle on the left. Her PC's locked up and rebooting itself! I told her to turn it off until you get there. Don't change anything, and don't open it up. Find out if it will shut down, boot properly, and access the drives." Then the IT manager leaves to deal with her crisis, and you're on the spot.

This exercise looks at the many PC components that you can access without removing the case. Scanning the outside of the PC can help you track down any basic issues. Take your time, and jot down notes when you feel the need. Practice each step until you're confident you can do it on the job as a PC tech.

Learning Objectives

In this lab exercise, you will locate and describe the various user controls and built-in user-accessible devices of a PC system. You *will not* be opening the system case during this lab.

At the end of this lab, you'll be able to

- Recognize and manipulate user controls
- Describe the use of built-in user-accessible devices

Lab Materials and Setup

The materials you need for this lab are

- One fully functioning desktop computer system unit, with monitor
- A working *optical drive* (any drive that reads or records CD, DVD, or Blu-ray Discs)
- One readable data CD with files
- One keyboard
- One mouse or other pointing device
- A paper clip

Getting Down to Business

As a technician, you need to know how everything works on a PC. Let's start with the externally accessible functions. Make sure the computer is turned off.

Step 1   Before you can do much work with a PC, you need a functioning output device, such as a monitor. Check the monitor to see if it has power. If the monitor is not on, find the power button on the monitor and press it. You'll notice a small *light-emitting diode* (*LED*) on or near the monitor's power button. Record the color of the LED when the PC is turned off.

Color of the LED when the system is off: _____

Later in this exercise, we'll check the color of the LED when the PC is turned on. Stay tuned!

Step 2   Look at the front of your system unit. Locate the power button. Compare your button to the one shown in Figure 2-1. If you don't find a power button on the front, check the top of the computer.

Once you have located the power button on your system, make a note of its appearance. Is it in plain sight, or hidden behind a door or lid? Is it round, square, or some odd shape? Pressing the power button to start a PC when the electricity is off is known as a *cold boot* or sometimes a *hard boot*. Some systems (mostly older ones) also have a reset button, which you can use to restart a PC that is already on. This is also called a *warm boot*.

→ **Note**

Most PC manufacturers have stopped putting hardware reset buttons on PCs because they don't want to encourage that kind of reset anymore. It was fine to reset with a hardware button back in the days of MS-DOS, but in modern operating systems, such abrupt and unceremonious dumping of memory content can cause problems. Unsaved files may be open, both in applications and in the operating system itself. An abrupt restart that doesn't involve closing them in an orderly way can lead to file errors. It's better to use the Restart command in the operating system.

FIGURE 2-1   Recognizing the power button on the front of a PC

Describe your power button here (and reset button if you have one):

_____

_____

Sometimes software will lock up your system, in which case the only way to shut the system down is to force a *power down*. This requires that you press and hold the power button for four to six seconds.

Notice the LEDs on the front panel near the power button. The one nearest the power button (usually green) indicates that the PC is powered on, and it stays on all the time while the PC is running. The other LED (usually red) flashes when the hard disk reads or writes. You may also see additional LEDs on specific components, such as on the optical disc drive.

✔ Hint

Some systems have two power controls: a power switch located on the back of the case that controls the flow of electricity to the power supply, and a power button on the front that boots and shuts down the PC.

Step 3   Locate the external face of your system's optical drive. Most are designed to fit comfortably inside an available 5¼-inch slot (or drive bay). How many 5¼-inch drive bays does your PC have? Count both the slots that have components in them, like the optical drive, and the empty slots with blank faceplates. Are there any 3.5-inch external bays? These would be used for floppy drives, although most systems don't have floppy drives anymore.

Number of drive bays: _____

You'll see the front edge of the tray that opens to accept an optical disc. Once you've located this drive, notice that it also has a button in one corner. When the system is on, you can press that button to open or close the tray (see Figure 2-2).

FIGURE 2-2 An optical drive has a tray to hold optical discs.

Don't be tempted to force the disc tray to close by pushing it in. Always press the button on the front of the drive to close the tray or to eject a disc. Forcing the tray to close can cause the gears inside to become misaligned, so that the tray no longer closes properly.

Your system may have other devices installed, such as a Blu-ray drive, or a memory card slot. Each of these uses removable media; take care when inserting or removing the media. There may also be devices connected to USB ports, such as USB flash drives and external hard drives.

Step 4   Now it's time to prepare your system for the scenario outlined in the opening text.

Earlier, this exercise referred to the monitor power LED (light), as well as to the two LEDs near the power button. Now, let's watch them in action. Turn on your PC.

  A.   Color of monitor LED: _____

  B.   What is the status of the LED closest to the power button? Is it steady, flashing, or intermittent? What color is it?

  _____

  C.   What is the color and status of the other LED near the power button? Is it steady, flashing, or intermittent?

  _____

  D.   Press the eject button on the front of the optical drive. When the tray opens, carefully insert a disc. Press the eject button again to close the tray. If you haven't done this a lot, practice inserting and removing a disc until you feel comfortable with the process. When the optical drive closes, what is the status of its LED? Is it steady, flashing, or intermittent?

  _____

✖ **Warning**

Don't start any applications yet! Close any open applications or open windows before performing Step 5. You're going to force a "power down," and you do not want to corrupt any files.

Step 5   Now you're going to simulate a PC that has become nonresponsive and "locked up." Perform a forced power down as follows:

  a.   Press *and hold* the power button.

  b.   While continuing to hold the power button in, count out loud (one–one thousand, two–one thousand, three–one thousand…) until the system powers down and the screen goes blank.

  According to your count, how many seconds did it take for the screen to go blank? _____

✖ **Warning**

It is possible to configure Windows power management settings so that pressing the power button "normally" (that is, not holding it down) does something other than shutting down. For example, it might put it into Sleep or Hibernate mode. That's only for a regular push-and-release of the power button, though, not for this extended hold-down you're doing here. If you release the power button too soon in Step 5b, you might accidentally trigger whatever action is assigned by the OS to the power button. If that happens, just restart the computer and try again.

Step 6 After the system has been powered down for approximately one minute, do the following:

a. Press the power button and allow the system to boot.

b. Sign in normally, so that you are viewing the operating system desktop.

c. Open the file management utility (such as File Explorer or Windows Explorer on a Windows PC, or Finder in macOS), navigate to a list of drives on the local PC, and double-click the icon that represents the optical drive. This should enable you to view the contents of the disc that was inserted prior to the forced power down.

List some of the contents of the disc:

_____

_____

_____

d. Shut down the PC using the Shut Down command in the operating system. In Windows 7, select Start | Shut Down. In Windows 8/8.1, move the mouse to the lower right-hand corner of the desktop. Click the Settings (gearbox) icon that appears. From the Settings menu, click the Power icon and then click Shut Down. In Windows 10, select Start | Power | Shut Down. This performs a graceful shutdown of the system.

✔ **Hint**

If all the actions in Step 6 were successful, the system likely is stable and you can report to the IT manager that Jane's machine is back up and running. If any of the actions failed, you should issue the Restart command. (It's on the same menu as the Shut Down command in Step 6d.) After the system reboots, complete Steps 6b, 6c, and 6d once more. Sometimes, the forced power down leaves some of the files in a state of flux; restarting properly closes all open files before powering down. This should clear everything up and enable the computer to function properly.

Step 7   While the computer is turned off, take a paper clip and straighten it out, giving yourself a small handle to hold. Find the small hole on the front of your optical drive and insert the end of your paper clip. What happens?

 **30 MINUTES**

Lab Exercise 2.03: Recognizing External Connections

When you walk into a client's office, the first thing you might do is a quick visual assessment. What kind of computer is there, and what connections are possible? What kinds of external monitor connections can you hook up? What types of peripherals? An experienced technician should be able to take a port inventory at a glance.

Learning Objectives

In this lab exercise, you will identify, describe, and explain the functions of the external connections on a standard PC.

At the end of this lab, you will be able to

- Identify the external connectors on a PC and the related cables

- Explain the function of each external connection

Lab Materials and Setup

The materials you need for this lab are

- At least one fully functioning PC that's less than two years old (two or more systems is ideal, with one older than and one newer than two years old)

✖ Cross-Reference

Before you begin this lab, read the section "Computing Hardware" in Chapter 2 of *Mike Meyers' CompTIA A+ Guide to Managing and Troubleshooting PCs.*

Getting Down to Business

Now it's time to learn about all the external things that can be attached to a PC. This lab exercise steps you through identifying and understanding the functions of the various connectors.

✖ Warning

Shut off the power to your system and *unplug your PC* from the wall socket before you start the following exercise.

Step 1   Look at all those wires coming from the back of your PC! There's a power cable, a network cable, a keyboard cable, a mouse cable (or a wireless receiver for one or both), and maybe a few others, depending on your system. Fifteen years ago, each type of device used a different kind of connector, by and large. The printer used a parallel (LPT) port, the keyboard and mouse used PS/2 connectors, the monitor used a VGA connector, your digital musical keyboard used the MIDI port, and so on. Nowadays, however, many different device types have gone to the general-purpose USB interface. The keyboard, mouse, and printer that you use today are probably all USB, as are any special-purpose devices like musical devices or webcams. Monitors remain the exception because they require such high data transfer rates; a modern monitor is likely to connect via HDMI, Mini DisplayPort, or DVI.

Step 2   Unplug each of your PC's cables one at a time and practice plugging them back in until you get a feel for how each fits. You should not have to force any of the cables, though they may be firm. How is each cable held in place and prevented from coming loose? Is there a screw, clip, or some other fastener that holds the cable connector tight to the system? Is the connector keyed? What does it connect to? What is the shape of the connector on each end? Is it round, rectangular, D-shaped (Figure 2-3)? How many pins or holes does it have? How many rows of pins or holes?

✖ **Warning**

There are four different USB port standards that you may encounter on computing devices. The higher the standard number, the higher the maximum data throughput rate. Ports and connectors are color-coded: white is USB 1.1, black is USB 2.0, blue is USB 3.0 (aka USB 3.1 Gen 1), and teal is USB 3.1 Gen 2. USB C (Type C) connectors, which are smaller than traditional Type A connectors, might correspond to USB 3.0 (aka USB 3.1 Gen 1), USB 3.1 Gen 2, or Thunderbolt-3 (which can share the port with USB functions). There is basic backward compatibility, but if you connect a device that wants faster data throughput to a slower port, it won't perform to its top potential. As you disconnect and connect USB cables in Step 2, pay attention to the color of the port and the color of the little rectangular tab in the end of the connector that plugs into the port. USB port standards are covered in more detail in Chapter 10 of *Mike Meyers' CompTIA A+ Guide to Managing and Troubleshooting PCs.*

FIGURE 2-3 A VGA connector is an example of a D-sub connector.

Step 3   Is it possible to plug any cable into the wrong connector? If so, which one(s)? What do you think would happen if you plugged something into the wrong connector?

_____

_____

Step 4   Disconnect the cables listed in the upcoming table from the back of your PC and record some information about each in the columns provided. Keep in mind that the table was created for average PCs. Two blank rows are provided for any custom devices in your system (such as additional monitors, digital audio, and so on). If you don't have a particular connector, don't feel bad. Just write "N/A."

	Number of Conductors/Pins	**Name of the Port**	**Port Color**
Mouse			
Keyboard			
Monitor			
Printer			
Network			
Speaker			
Power			
External hard drive			

Once you complete this table, know it, live it, and love it. Every great technician should be able to identify these connectors at a glance.

Step 5   If you're working with someone else, play "Flash Cords." Have your partner hold up various cables, and try to guess what they connect to by looking at the connectors on the ends. Then switch roles and quiz your partner. Another really good way to learn the connector names is to have your partner sit behind the computer, while you reach around from the front, feel the various ports with your fingers, and call them out by name. Switch back and forth with each other until you both can easily identify all the ports by touch.

Step 6   Properly reconnect all the cables that you removed and prepare to turn on the system. If you have an On/Off button on the back of the system, be sure it is set to the On position. Make sure the monitor is turned on as well.

Step 7 Use these connector names to correctly identify the ports shown in the following table. (You will not use every name listed.) What is the name of each connector and what does it connect to?

PS/2	HDMI	USB	Serial	FireWire
RJ-45	RJ-11	1/8-inch audio	DVI	VGA
USB C	Mini DisplayPort	S/PDIF Optical	eSATA	S/PDIF Coaxial

A. _____	B. _____	C. _____
D. _____	E. _____	F. _____
G. _____	H. _____	I. _____
J. _____	K. _____	I. _____

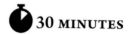 **30 MINUTES**

Lab Exercise 2.04: Navigating the Windows 7 Interface

Windows 7 debuted in 2009, and will be supported by Microsoft until January 14, 2020. Many people still use it, so you will likely run into it in tech support calls. Windows 7 features the classic desktop environment featured in previous Windows versions, including a Start menu for running programs, Windows Explorer for managing files, and Control Panel for adjusting settings.

This lab exercise is designed for students with limited or no experience with Windows 7. It provides a basic tour of the interface, including the Desktop, Aero, running an application, browsing the file system, and using a command-line interface.

Learning Objectives

The main objective of this exercise is to familiarize you with the interface of Windows 7.

At the end of this lab, you'll be able to

- Identify the components of the Windows 7 desktop interface

- Run an application in Windows 7

- Browse the file system in Windows 7

- Open a command prompt window and run a command

Lab Materials and Setup

The materials you need for this lab are

- A fully functioning PC with Windows 7 installed

Getting Down to Business

In this lab you'll fire up Windows 7 and perform a few basic tasks. Along the way you'll learn the correct terminology for various elements of Windows; this terminology will be important in later chapters' lab exercises, when you'll work in greater detail with these elements.

Step 1   Label the components in Figure 2-4 using correct Microsoft terminology. If you don't know the name of a component, leave it blank for now. You can come back here and complete your answers later if needed.

A   _____

B   _____

C _____

D _____

E _____

F _____

Step 2   Start up the Windows 7 PC, and sign in if prompted to do so. Then click the Start button to open the Start menu. (To close it again after completing this step, press ESC, click it again, or click away from it.)

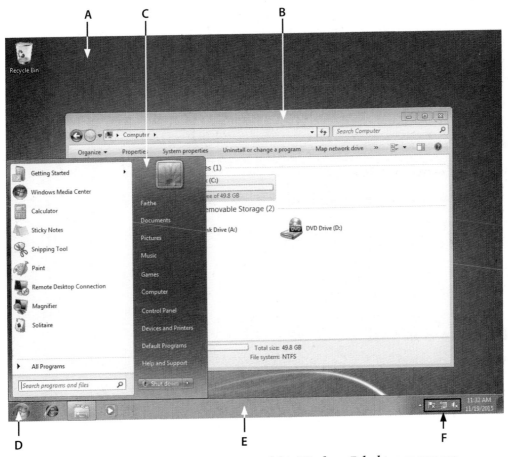

FIGURE 2-4 Label as many of the components of this Windows 7 desktop as you can.

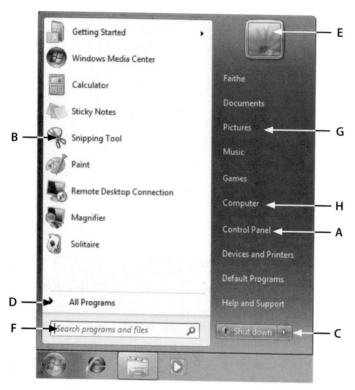

FIGURE 2-5 Key components of the Start menu

Figure 2-5 points out some of the key components of the Start menu. In the following table, draw lines to match each of the labeled components with its corresponding definition. If you don't know what one of the components does, experiment with it to find out.

Component		Description
A		Click here to make changes to the user account for the signed-in user
B		Click here to browse the local storage system
C		Click here to access one of the personal file libraries for the signed-in user
D		Click here to see a list of installed applications
E		Click here to find an application or file
F		Click here to open a menu from which you can choose to restart the computer or sign out
G		Click here to change system settings
H		Shortcut to a frequently or recently used application

Step 3 In the following steps you will open several applications, switch among them, and then close them in various ways.

- **a.** Click Start | All Programs | Accessories | Notepad.
- **b.** Click Start | All Programs | Accessories | Paint.
- **c.** Click the Internet Explorer shortcut icon on the taskbar.

    Now you have three applications open, each in its own window.

- **d.** Click each application's button on the taskbar to switch to that window in turn.
- **e.** Hold down the ALT key and tap the TAB key. Each time you tap TAB, a different thumbnail image is selected. When the thumbnail for the desired application window is selected, release the ALT key to switch to that window.
- **f.** Right-click the Notepad icon on the taskbar and choose Close window.
- **g.** Click the Close (×) button in the upper-right corner of the Internet Explorer window to close it.
- **h.** In the Paint window, click the File tab (the dark-blue tab near the upper-left corner) and click Exit on the menu that appears.

Step 4 The Aero interface is responsible for the semi-transparent, glass-like look of window frames in Windows 7, as well as some of the handy tricks and animations the taskbar does. If your display adapter doesn't support Aero, it can't be enabled. Because Aero consumes some system resources, people with less powerful computers sometimes turn it off for faster graphics performance.

Follow these steps to enable Aero (if possible):

- **a.** Right-click the Desktop and choose Personalize.
- **b.** Under the Aero Themes heading, click Windows 7 (or one of the other themes under that heading if you prefer). If your display adapter supports Aero, Aero features are enabled.
- **c.** Close the Control Panel window.

→ **Note**

To turn off Aero, select one of the themes that is *not* under the Aero Themes heading, such as Windows Basic.

Next, do an experiment with an Aero feature:

- **a.** Open Internet Explorer.
- **b.** Click New Tab in Internet Explorer so you have two Web pages open at once.
- **c.** Click the Minimize button in the upper-right corner of the Internet Explorer window to minimize the application window.

    d.   Point the mouse pointer at the minimized Internet Explorer button on the taskbar. Thumbnail images of each of the two tabs appear; you could click one of these to open the window and switch to that tab. This feature is called Aero Peek. If Aero isn't enabled, instead of these thumbnails you see a text list of the open tabs.

    e.   Close the Internet Explorer window.

Step 5   Windows 7's file manager is called *Windows Explorer*. You use it to browse files and folders on your local system and also on any network drives you might have access to. In Lab Exercise 2.07, "Managing Files and Folders in Windows," you'll review some basic file management techniques in Windows 10, which uses a similar utility called File Explorer. There are some minor differences between them, but they are basically the same application.

Follow these steps to open Windows Explorer and browse a few locations:

    a.   Click the Windows Explorer icon on the taskbar. The Libraries list opens. These are the personal folders for the logged-in user.

    b.   In the navigation bar on the left, click Computer. A list of the local drives appears.

    c.   Click Network. A list of any available network shared locations appears.

    d.   Click the Back arrow in the upper-left corner of the Windows Explorer window to return to Computer.

    e.   Close the Windows Explorer window.

Step 6   You'll use the command prompt in a lot more detail in Chapter 15's lab exercises, but for now you should at least be able to open and close that interface.

    a.   Click the Start button.

    b.   Type **cmd** and press ENTER. A command prompt window opens.

    c.   Type **dir** and press ENTER. A listing of the current folder's contents appears.

    d.   Type **exit** and press ENTER. The window closes. You could also close the window by clicking its Close (×) button.

 **30 MINUTES**

Lab Exercise 2.05: Navigating the Windows 8.1 Interface

Windows 8.1 is nobody's favorite OS. Microsoft intended it to be a hybrid of a desktop and tablet OS, suitable for both platforms, but ended up creating something that doesn't serve either platform very well. It's full of quirks and oddities, and people who upgraded to it from Windows 7 or earlier versions generally find it confusing and frustrating. Since Microsoft announced in 2015 free upgrades to Windows 10 for anyone running a legal copy of Windows 7 or 8/8.1, you probably won't run into many people using Windows 8.1 in the field.

Nevertheless, Windows 8.1 is fully covered in the current CompTIA A+ 220-1002 exam, so you'll need to be familiar with it. This lab exercise showcases the ways in which Windows 8.1 differs from Windows 7, and points out some of the less-obvious navigation and customization techniques that you may see on the exam. Keep in mind that when Windows 10 is used in Tablet mode, it closely resembles Windows 8.1.

> ➡ **Note**
>
> **You might encounter a few Windows 8 systems that have never been updated to Windows 8.1. Windows 8.1 is available as a free upgrade to Windows 8 through the Windows (Microsoft) Store for Windows 8. See www.maketecheasier.com/windows-8-vs-8-1-changed-pc-settings/ for a comparison of Windows 8 and Windows 8.1.**

Learning Objectives

The main objective of this exercise is to familiarize you with the interface of Windows 8.1.

At the end of this lab, you'll be able to

- Identify key components of the Windows 8.1 interface
- Run applications in Windows 8.1
- Manage pinned items on the Start screen
- Download new applications from the Windows Store app

Lab Materials and Setup

The materials you need for this lab are

- A fully functioning PC with Windows 8.1 installed

Getting Down to Business

In this lab you'll check out the Windows 8.1 Desktop and Start screen, its two main interfaces. You'll compare Modern (Metro) apps and Desktop apps, and learn how to start, exit, and switch among Modern apps. Finally, you'll learn how to customize the Start screen and how to install more apps from the Windows Store.

Step 1 Let's start at the front door of Windows 8.1: the sign-in screen. When you start Windows 8.1, you see a graphic with the current date and time. That's called the Welcome screen.

   a. Press any key or swipe upward to clear the Welcome screen and display a sign-in prompt.

   b. Type or select your user name, type your password, and press ENTER to sign in.

   c. The Desktop appears by default in Windows 8.1. If you see the Start screen instead, press the ESC key to clear it.

Here's a major change from earlier Windows versions: You can sign into Windows 8.1 with either a Microsoft account or a local account. A *Microsoft account* is tied to an e-mail address that has been registered with Microsoft; using a Microsoft account gives you access to online capabilities such as OneDrive (your free online storage cloud space). A *local account* exists only on that one PC, and isn't associated with anything online. In Chapter 13 you'll practice creating and managing accounts, including changing the account type.

Step 2   Next, you'll learn how to start and exit both Desktop and Modern apps in Windows 8.1, and how to view multiple Modern apps at once in a split screen.

When you boot into Windows 8.1, the Desktop appears by default (see Figure 2-6). It looks a lot like the Windows 7 Desktop (shown previously in Figure 2-4).

The main difference is that the Start button in Windows 8.1 doesn't open a Start menu (as shown for Windows 7 in Figure 2-5); instead it opens a full-screen affair called the Start screen, shown in Figure 2-7.

Follow these steps to experiment with the Windows 8.1 environment:

a.   Press the WINDOWS key. The Start screen appears. Then press ESC to clear it.

b.   Press the WINDOWS key again, and then click the Desktop tile on the Start screen to return to the Desktop.

c.   Click the File Explorer shortcut that's pinned to the taskbar. File Explorer opens. This is the equivalent of Windows Explorer in Windows 7 (covered in Lab Exercise 2.04).

d.   Press the WINDOWS key to open the Start screen, and then click the down arrow button at the bottom of the screen to open the Apps screen. This screen shows all the installed applications, of both kinds (Desktop and Modern).

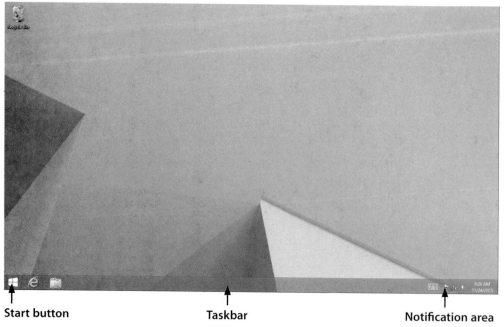

Start button   Taskbar   Notification area

FIGURE 2-6 The Desktop in Windows 8.1

FIGURE 2-7 The Start screen in Windows 8.1

e. Scroll to the right (use the scroll bar at the bottom) to locate Notepad, and click it to open Notepad.

f. Click the Close (×) button on the Notepad window to close it.

g. Click the Start button to reopen the Start menu.

h. Click Photo. The Photos app opens.

i. Position the mouse pointer at the top edge of the screen, so that the pointer turns into a hand icon.

j. Holding down the left mouse button, drag downward until the Photos app turns into a smaller image of itself; then drag to the left slightly until a divider appears in the middle of the screen. Release the mouse button to drop the Photos app into the left side.

k. Press the WINDOWS key to return to the Start screen, and click the Weather app. It opens side by side with the Photos app. See Figure 2-8.

l. Drag the divider line slightly to the right, so the Photos app takes up two-thirds of the screen.

m. Drag the divider all the way to the left, so that the Weather app takes up 100 percent of the screen.

n. Hold down ALT and press TAB (keep holding ALT). Notice that the Photos app doesn't appear in the thumbnail images of apps you can switch to. That's because Windows 8.1 has only one thumbnail for *all* of the Modern apps that are running. You have to switch between various Modern apps in a different way.

o. Move the mouse pointer to the upper-left corner of the screen. A thumbnail image appears.

p. Move the mouse pointer slightly downward, so that a bar of thumbnails appears. See Figure 2-9. The thumbnails here show one for the Desktop (if the Desktop is not active) and one for each individual Modern app that is running.

q. Click the Photos app to switch to it.

Drag the divider to change the relative sizes.

FIGURE 2-8 Two Modern apps side by side

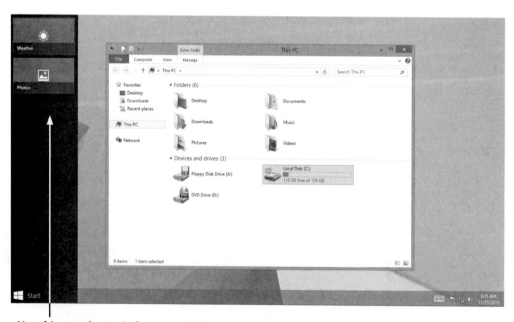

Use this panel to switch among Modern apps.

FIGURE 2-9 Modern apps appear in the navigation bar on the left when you point at the upper-left corner of the screen.

r. Move the mouse pointer to the top of the screen, so that the hand pointer appears. Then drag downward, all the way to the bottom of the screen. This closes the Photos app. The Start screen reappears.

s. Repeat Steps o through r for the Weather app to close it.

Step 3 The Start screen is like a bulletin board, on which you can pin anything you like. It comes with many items already pinned to it, but you have full control. Each item displays in a rectangular block called a *tile*. You can move, resize, add, and remove tiles.

a. Start at the Start screen. Click the Start button on the desktop to open it, if needed.

b. Right-click the Weather tile. A navigation bar appears along the bottom of the screen.

c. Click Resize. A pop-up menu appears.

d. Click Medium. The tile changes size, and other surrounding tiles shift to fill in the space if possible.

e. Click and hold down the left mouse button on the Weather tile for a few seconds. Then drag the Weather tile and drop it in a different spot.

f. Click the down arrow at the bottom of the Start screen to open the Apps list.

g. Right-click the Notepad application. Notice your choices at the bottom of the screen (see Figure 2-10). You can pin it to Start, pin it to the taskbar, open it, run it as an administrator, or open the location where the Notepad executable is located.

h. Click Pin to Start. The Start menu reappears with a tile for Notepad.

i. Right-click the Notepad tile and click Unpin from Start.

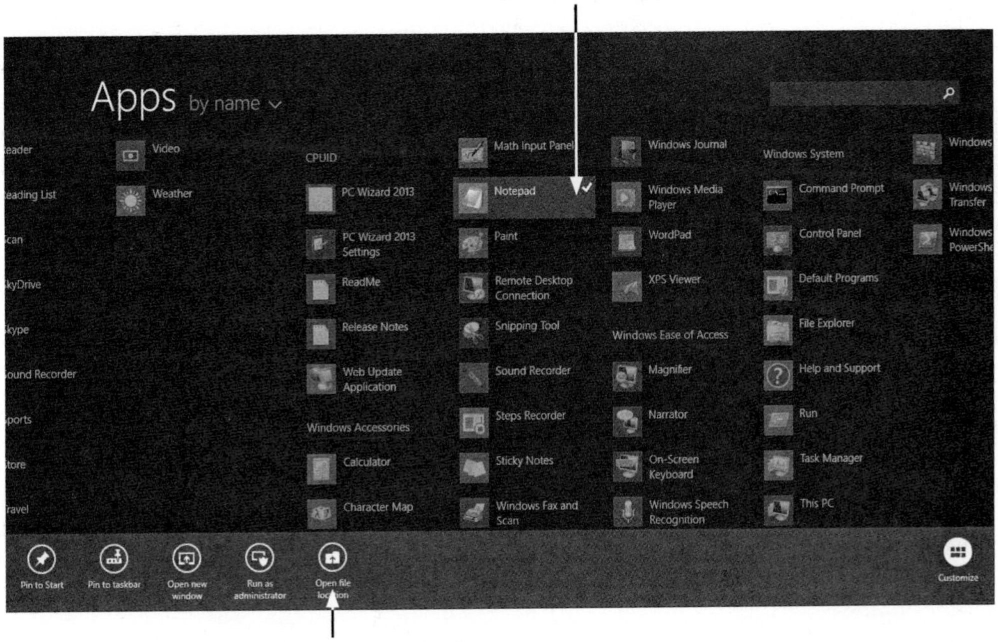

FIGURE 2-10 To manipulate a tile, right-click it and choose an action from the bar at the bottom of the screen.

Step 4   We'll wrap up our Windows 8.1 tour by checking out the Windows Store, from which you can install new Modern applications.

    a.   From the Start screen, click the Store tile. If you don't see a pinned Store tile, click the down arrow and select Store from the Apps list.

    b.   Browse the Windows Store. The interface changes periodically, so we can't tell you exactly what to select or click here. Locate a free app that interests you, and follow the prompts to install it.

    c.   Close the Store app.

    d.   (Optional) If you don't want to keep the app you downloaded, right-click its tile on the Start screen and choose Uninstall.

 **30 MINUTES**

Lab Exercise 2.06: Navigating the Windows 10 Desktop and Tablet Interfaces

Compared to Windows 8.1, Windows 10 provides a much better answer to the question, "How do you support both touch screen and mouse/keyboard users with a single operating system?" Windows 10 provides two different operating environments, Desktop mode and Tablet mode, to solve this problem. On most systems, Windows 10 boots into the default Desktop mode, which resembles a hybrid of the Windows 7 Start menu and the Windows 8.1 Start screen. However, on touch screen systems, it will usually boot into Tablet mode, which is similar to the Windows 8.1 default Start screen. Users with touch screens can switch between Desktop and Tablet modes and can specify which mode Windows 10 boots into.

This lab exercise demonstrates how to make the mode switch as well as some other new and improved features. Although Windows 10 is an example of Software as a Service (SaaS), with Microsoft pushing out new editions about every six to nine months, the instructions in this lab should work with any installed edition of Windows 10. As Microsoft's current desktop operating system, Windows 10 will also be used for many other labs in this and other chapters.

Learning Objectives

The main objective of this exercise is to familiarize you with the interface of Windows 10.

At the end of this lab, you'll be able to

- Identify key components of the Windows 10 desktop interface
- Switch between the desktop and tablet interfaces
- Identify key components of the Windows 10 tablet interface
- Run applications in Windows 10

Lab Materials and Setup

The materials you need for this lab are

- A fully functioning PC with Windows 10 installed

Getting Down to Business

In this lab you'll check out the Windows 10 Desktop and Tablet modes, its two main interfaces. You'll compare Desktop and Tablet menu systems, and learn how to customize the menus. Finally, you'll learn how to install more apps from the Windows Store.

Step 1 Let's start at the front door of Windows 10: the sign-in screen. When you start Windows 10, you see a graphic with the current date and time. That's called the Welcome screen.

   a. Press any key or swipe upward to clear the Welcome screen and display a sign-in prompt.

   b. Type or select your user name, type your password, and press ENTER to sign in.

   c. Depending upon the hardware in your system, the system might open to the Desktop or in Tablet mode (which resembles the Windows 8.1 Start screen).

As with Windows 8.1, you can sign into Windows 10 with either a Microsoft account or a local account. A *Microsoft account* is tied to an e-mail address that has been registered with Microsoft; using a Microsoft account gives you access to online capabilities such as OneDrive (your free online storage cloud space). A *local account* exists only on that one PC, and isn't associated with anything online. In Chapter 13 you'll practice creating and managing accounts, including changing the account type.

Step 2 Next, you'll learn how to run Win32 (Classic) apps such as those also included with older editions such as Windows 7 and Modern apps in full screen or windows.

When you boot into Windows 10 using a computer that does not have a touch screen, the Desktop appears by default (see Figure 2-11). It looks a lot like the Windows 7 and Windows 8.1 Desktop (shown previously in Figures 2-4 and 2-6 respectively).

The resemblance to Windows 7 and to Windows 8.1 is obvious when you click the Start button in Desktop mode (see Figure 2-12). The Windows 10 Start menu is split into two sections: the left section provides a scrollable alphabetical list of Windows 10 and third-party apps that have Start menu shortcuts, resembling the Windows 7 Start menu, and the right section is a scrollable panel of thumbnails for Windows 10 Universal (previously known as Modern) apps, resembling the Windows 8.1 Start screen. You can adjust the size of these thumbnails, reorganize them, turn off/turn on live tile previews, and add thumbnail shortcuts for both Universal and classic Windows apps to the right section.

Start button   **Taskbar**   **Notifications button**

FIGURE 2-11 Windows 10 in Desktop mode

Follow these steps to experiment with the Windows 10 environment:

a.   Press the WINDOWS key. The Start menu appears.

b.   Scroll down the left menu until the Windows Accessories folder appears.

c.   Click the down pointer next to the Windows Accessories folder to expand it.

d.   Click the Notepad shortcut to start it.

e.   If Notepad is in a window, maximize it by clicking the Maximize (single box) icon in the title bar.

f.   Press the WINDOWS key to open the Start screen, and then click the Photos app.

g.   Photos is a Universal app, but in Desktop mode, it can be placed in a window. Click the Window (two box) icon in the title bar to run it in a window.

h.   Click the Window icon in the title bar of the Notepad app.

i.   Drag the windows so they are next to each other. See Figure 2-13.

j.   Click the Photos app to make it the active app.

k.   Hold down the WINDOWS key and press the UP ARROW key. What happened to the Photos app window? _____

FIGURE 2-12 The Start menu screen in Windows 10 Desktop mode after scrolling down the left and right sections

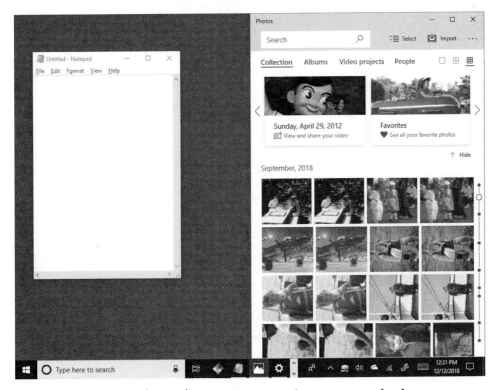

FIGURE 2-13 A Win32 (Classic) app and a Universal app next to each other

l. Click the Notepad icon in the taskbar.

m. Hold down the WINDOWS key and press the LEFT ARROW key. What happened to the Notepad app window? _____

n. Click the Photos app window. What happened to it when you clicked it? _____

Step 3 Next, you'll learn how to switch between Desktop and Tablet modes.

On a computer with a touch screen but no keyboard, such as a Windows 10 tablet or a convertible (2-in-1) device in Tablet mode, Windows 10 starts in Tablet mode (see Figure 2-14). You can also configure Windows 10 to start in Tablet mode even if you have a keyboard, through the Settings app (see Lab Exercise 2.09).

Follow these steps to switch between modes. The following steps assume that Tablet mode is off. The Tablet mode button toggles Tablet mode on and off.

a. Click or tap the Notification icon at the right end of the taskbar.

b. To turn on Tablet mode, click or tap Tablet mode. The Start menu tiles appear across the Windows 10 display.

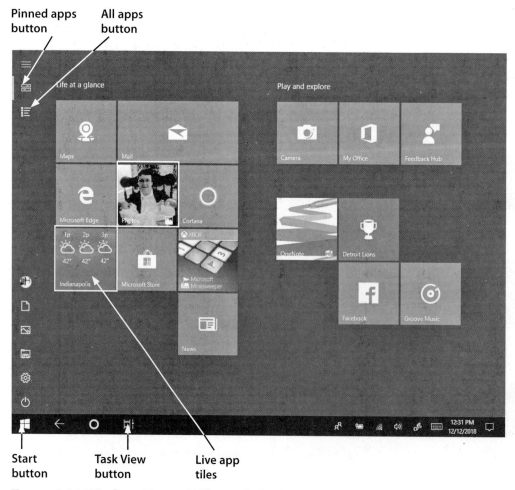

FIGURE 2-14 Windows 10 using Tablet mode displays tiles at all times.

c. Tap the Task View button to choose between running apps.

d. Tap Photos. Does Photos open in a window? _____

Does Photos have a Close (×) button? _____

e. To close Photos or other Universal apps in Tablet mode, use the same method as in Windows 8.1. (Need a refresher? Look at Step 2 in Lab Exercise 2.05.)

f. Tap the Task View button (it's to the right of the Search box on the Taskbar), then tap Notepad.

Can you switch Notepad to run in a window? _____

g. Close Notepad.

Step 4 In Tablet mode, finding apps is different than in Desktop mode. Follow these steps:

a. Tap the Start button if the Start menu is not visible.

b. Tap the All apps button.

c. Scroll down the list to the Windows Accessories folder. Tap it to expand the category (see Figure 2-15).

Figure 2-15 The All apps menu is full screen in Tablet mode.

   d.   Tap Windows Accessories again to collapse it.

   e.   Tap the Pinned apps button.

   f.   Tap the Expand button in the upper-left corner of the screen.

            What does the Settings icon look like? _____

   g.   Tap the Expand button again.

   h.   Switch back to Desktop mode.

 **30 MINUTES**

Lab Exercise 2.07: Managing Files and Folders in Windows

When you work as a computer professional, it's assumed that you know how file systems work and how to manipulate files and folders. This is basic-level stuff, so feel free to skip this exercise if you're already familiar with the procedures. But just in case you aren't up to speed, stick around. You're going to need this remedial lesson to keep up with the rest of the lab exercises in this book.

Learning Objectives

The main objective of this exercise is to familiarize you with file management under Windows. We'll use Windows 10 for this lab exercise, but all Windows versions are similar.

   At the end of this lab, you'll be able to

   •   Explain file structures and paths on Windows PCs

   •   Create, rename, and delete folders

   •   Create, rename, copy, move, and delete files

   •   Use the Recycle Bin

Lab Materials and Setup

The materials you need for this lab are

   •   A fully functioning PC with Windows 10 installed (or another Windows version if 10 is not available)

Getting Down to Business

In this lab you'll practice file and folder management by creating, deleting, renaming, moving, and copying files and folders. You'll need all these skills in a wide variety of situations, both as a technician and as an ordinary computer user.

   In Windows, as in most other computing environments, file storage is hierarchical. You start out on a volume (a drive letter), and within a volume are folders. Individual files can also be stored at the top level of

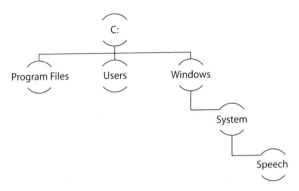

FIGURE 2-16 This folder tree illustrates the path C:\Windows\System\Speech.

a volume. Within a folder can be other folders, and within them other folders, and so on. When you write out paths, you typically write them with slashes, like this: C:\Windows\System\Speech.

This hierarchical structure is sometimes called a *folder tree* because when you map it out graphically it looks like the branches or root system of a tree (see Figure 2-16).

In the Address bar in File Explorer, the parts are separated by triangle arrows, like this:

This PC > Local Disk (C:) > Windows > System > Speech

It's basically the same thing as standard path notation, except the triangles offer an extra bit of navigation help, as you will see in Step 2.

Step 1 Familiarize yourself with the following key parts of the File Explorer window (called Windows Explorer in Windows 7), pointed out in Figure 2-17.

- **Navigation pane** The pane along the left side of the window; it offers shortcuts to commonly accessed locations.

- **Preview/Details pane** The pane along the right side of the window. It's optional; you turn it on/off on the View tab on the Ribbon, with the Preview Pane and Details Pane buttons. These two buttons are mutually exclusive; turning on one turns off the other.

- **Ribbon** The multi-tabbed toolbar across the top of the window.

- **Quick Access toolbar** The little collection of tools in the left corner of the window's title bar.

- **Address bar** The bar showing the path (address) of the active location.

- **Up button** Takes you up one level in the folder hierarchy. For example, if you're in C:\Files\January, it would take you up to C:\Files.

- **Back button** Takes you back to the last location you viewed.

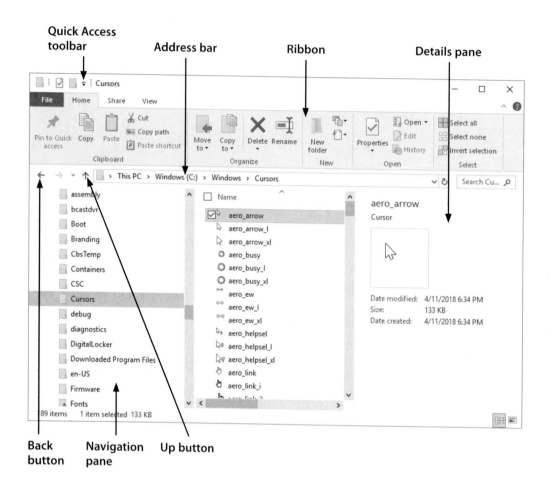

FIGURE 2-17 Parts of a file management window

Step 2   Follow these steps to get some practice moving between locations:

a.   Start File Explorer. One way is to click the File Explorer icon pinned to the taskbar.

b.   In the navigation pane, click This PC.

c.   Double-click the C: drive, double-click the Windows folder, and then double-click the Cursors folder.

d.   Click the first cursor listed.

e.   Check out the path in the address bar. (It should resemble the path in the address bar in Figure 2-17.)

f.   Click a down pointer to see a list of all the other folders at the same level as the folder to the right of the triangle, as shown in Figure 2-18.

g.   Click the Boot folder to navigate to it.

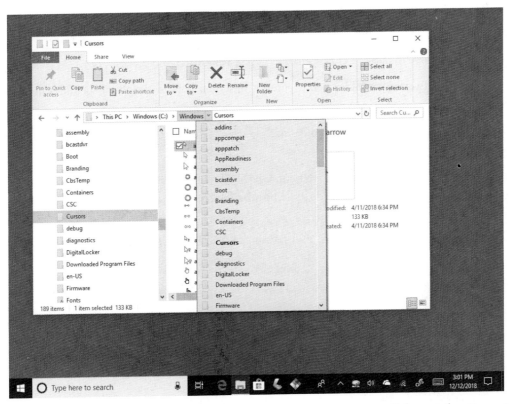

FIGURE 2-18 Click the down pointer in the address bar to see a menu of alternate locations at the same level as the folder to the right of the down pointer.

h. To see the path represented in traditional notation (with slashes), double-click in the address bar. Notice that the path is selected, so you could copy it to the Clipboard (CTRL-C) and then paste it somewhere if you wanted to (CTRL-V).

i. Click the Up arrow button to the left of the path. This takes you up one level, to C:\Windows.

j. Click the Back arrow button to return to C:\Windows\Boot.

k. Click This PC in the navigation pane, and then double-click the C: drive. You are now at the top level of the C: drive, also known as the *root directory* or *top-level folder*.

Step 3 Next you'll create two new folders, move one of them into the other, rename a folder, and create a new text file.

a. While viewing the root directory of C:, click the New folder shortcut on the Quick Access toolbar. A new folder appears. Type **Work** and press ENTER.

b. Here's another way to create a new folder. On the Home tab of the Ribbon, click New folder. Type **Play** and press ENTER.

c.   Drag the Play folder and drop it on the Work folder. It is moved into that folder, and becomes a subfolder of it.

d.   Right-click the Work folder and click Rename. Type **Everything** and press ENTER.

e.   Double-click the Everything folder to move into it, and then double-click the Play folder to move into it.

f.   Right-click an empty area in the Play folder and point to New, and then click Text Document. To name the file, type **Baseball** and press ENTER.

g.   Here's another way to create a new document. On the Home tab of the Ribbon, click New item, and select Text Document. To name the file, type **Football** and press ENTER.

Step 4   Now you'll copy a file, rename a file, move a file, and delete files and folders.

a.   Select the Baseball file and press CTRL-C, or click the Copy button on the Home tab. (You could also right-click the file and choose Copy. So many ways to copy!)

b.   Click Everything in the address bar to move to that folder. Then press CTRL-V to paste the copy.

c.   Right-click the Baseball file and choose Rename. Type **Basketball** and press ENTER. (You could also press F2 as a shortcut for the Rename command, or choose Rename from the Ribbon.)

✔ **Tip**

On some keyboards, the F2 key is preassigned to support a multimedia or laptop-specific function. On those keyboards, hold down the FN key and then press F2.

d.   Right-click the File Explorer icon on the taskbar and choose File Explorer on the menu that appears. This opens another File Explorer window.

e.   In the new File Explorer window, navigate to C:\Everything\Play.

f.   Drag-and-drop the Basketball file from C:\Everything (the original window) to C:\Everything\Play (the new window).

✔ **Tip**

The file is moved when you drag it because both locations are on the same drive. If they were on different drives, drag-and-drop would copy the file to the new location, rather than move it. To force a move, hold down SHIFT as you drag. To force a copy, hold down CTRL as you drag.

g.   In the C:\Everything\Play window, select the first file listed, and then hold down SHIFT and click the last file listed. Now all files are selected.

✔ **Tip**

Pressing SHIFT enables you to select contiguous files; pressing CTRL allows you to select noncontiguous files.

   h. Press the DELETE key. The files are moved to the Recycle Bin.

   i. In the Address bar, click C: to return to the top level.

   j. Select the Everything folder, and then on the Home tab of the Ribbon, click Delete.

   k. Close both File Explorer windows.

Step 5 As the final stop on the tour, you'll practice using the Recycle Bin.

   a. If Desktop icons aren't visible, right-click the Desktop and select View | Show desktop icons.

   b. On the Desktop, double-click the Recycle Bin icon to open the Recycle Bin.

   c. Select the Everything folder, and then on the Ribbon, click Restore the selected items.

   d. Right-click the Baseball file and choose Delete. Click Yes to confirm. Now this file is permanently gone and unrecoverable (unless you use a third-party data recovery tool).

   e. Right-click the Basketball file and choose Restore.

   f. Close the Recycle Bin window, and reopen File Explorer. Navigate back to the C:\ drive's root directory.

   g. Select the Everything folder.

   h. On the Ribbon, click the down arrow under the Delete button, and on the menu that appears, click Permanently delete. Click Yes to confirm.

   i. Close the File Explorer window.

 **30 MINUTES**

Lab Exercise 2.08: Using the Control Panel in Windows

The Windows Control Panel is another one of those things that you absolutely, positively need to be familiar with to be a competent technician. You'll be working with it in upcoming chapters extensively, so familiarize yourself with it now if you need to.

Learning Objectives

In this lab exercise, you'll familiarize yourself with the Control Panel. This knowledge will come in handy in later chapters when you'll be called on to open the Control Panel and navigate to a particular section of it. We'll use Windows 8.1 for this, but all Windows versions are similar.

At the end of this lab, you'll be able to

- Switch between views in the Control Panel
- Identify key customization settings
- Identify key system settings
- Identify key hardware settings
- Access the Administrative Tools

Lab Materials and Setup

The materials you need for this lab are

- A fully functioning PC with Windows 8.1 installed (or another Windows version if 8.1 is not available)

Getting Down to Business

In this lab you'll explore four key areas of the Control Panel: Personalization, System, Hardware, and Administrative Tools. Collectively these are the four areas where you will most often need to access utilities and adjust settings as a technician.

Step 1　We'll start by reviewing the basic navigation of the Control Panel and checking out the System category.

　a.　Open the Control Panel. The procedure depends on your Windows version:

- Windows 8.1: The easiest way is to right-click the Start button and choose Control Panel.
- Windows 7: Click Start and then click Control Panel on the Start menu.
- Windows 8: Display the Charms bar, click Settings, and then click Control Panel.
- Windows 10: The easiest way is to click the Cortana/Search window and type **Control Panel**, and then click it.

　b.　In the upper-right corner of the Control Panel window, open the View by drop-down list and examine the available viewing options. Click Category if it's not already selected. See Figure 2-19.

　　You can choose Category (the default, which is what we'll be using in this lab exercise), Large icons, or Small icons. The icons views are useful if you are trying to locate a particular utility or tool but you can't remember which category it is in.

　　Another way to locate a particular item is to search for it, as described next.

　c.　Click in the Search Control Panel box and type **mouse**. A list of all the settings that have to do with the mouse appears.

　d.　In the search results, under the Mouse heading, click Change mouse settings. The Mouse Properties dialog box opens.

Click here to change the view.

FIGURE 2-19 Choose a view of the Control Panel.

e. Click Cancel to close the dialog box.

f. Click the Back arrow in the upper-left corner of the Control Panel window to return to the Control Panel Home screen.

g. Click the System and Security heading.

h. Click the System heading. System information appears.

Notice the items in the navigation pane on the left (see Figure 2-20); some of them have a shield symbol next to them. These are items that will trigger User Account Control (UAC) intervention when you click them (unless UAC settings are adjusted so that doesn't happen).

✔ **Tip**

Notice that the address bar shows the path you have taken to get here. This is sometimes referred to as *breadcrumbs*. You can click any level listed in the address bar to return to it.

i. In the navigation pane, click System protection. Respond to the UAC box if it appears. You might need to type the sign-in information for an administrator user account if you are currently signed in as a standard user.

UAC shield

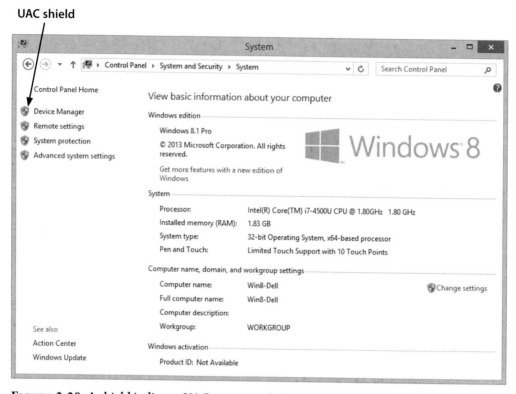

FIGURE 2-20 A shield indicates UAC restricts which users can adjust the settings.

j. Click through the tabs in the System Properties dialog box to see what's there; when you're finished, click Cancel.

k. Click Control Panel in the address bar to return to the top level of the Control Panel.

Step 2 Next we'll look at some hardware-related settings that are accessible from the Control Panel.

a. Click the Hardware and Sound heading, and check out the items available. From here you can add and remove printers, adjust sound and power options, and change the display settings.

→ **Note**

Display settings are split between Hardware and Personalization categories. In the Hardware category you'll find the settings that pertain to the screen resolution, icon size, and refresh rate. In the Personalization category are settings for screen colors and other appearance aspects.

b. Click the Sound heading. The Sound dialog box opens.

c.   Click through the tabs of the dialog box to see what's available. For example, if you were having a problem with a system that wasn't playing sound through its speakers, you might check the Playback tab here to make sure the expected sound device was selected. Click Cancel when finished.

Step 3   Now let's look at Personalization, the favorite category of most of the end users you will support. Here you can adjust how the desktop looks.

a.   In the navigation bar, click Appearance and Personalization to jump to that category. (Note that in Windows 10, Settings is used for most Appearance and Personalization options. See the next exercise for details.)

✔ **Tip**

Notice that there's a Display category under Appearance and Personalization that duplicates the one in Hardware and Sound. That's for your convenience, because it's easy to forget where those settings are stored.

b.   Click the Personalization heading. Personalization options appear. From here you can choose an appearance theme to apply by selecting one of the thumbnails in the center, or customize individual aspects of formatting by using the links at the bottom of the window, such as Desktop Background or Color.

✔ **Tip**

As covered in Lab Exercise 2.04, you can also get to Personalization by right-clicking the Desktop and choosing Personalize. That's a great shortcut to know for times when the Control Panel isn't already open.

c.   Click one of the themes to apply it.

d.   Click the Color hyperlink at the bottom of the dialog box.

e.   Click one of the colored squares to change the color of the window borders and taskbar.

f.   Click Cancel to reject the change.

g.   (Optional) Return your Personalization settings to your own preferences if desired.

Step 4 Administrative Tools is a collection of lesser-known and lesser-used utilities that are mostly reserved for technicians and power users. Since that (hopefully) describes you on both counts, you should know about them.

a. Click Control Panel Home in the navigation pane.

b. Click System and Security, and then scroll down to the bottom of the list and click the Administrative Tools heading.

c. Switch to Medium Icons view (as shown in Figure 2-21) so you can see things more clearly. To do so, click the View tab, and click Medium icons.

Most of the Administrative Tools are covered in upcoming chapters, so we won't get into them in detail here, but let's check out a couple.

d. Double-click Windows Memory Diagnostic. A window opens with a utility that allows you to check for memory problems. Click Cancel to close it.

e. Double-click System Configuration. This opens the System Configuration utility, also known as msconfig.exe.

f. Click through the tabs of this dialog box to see what's available. For example, you can set up a boot into Safe Mode from the Boot tab. Click Cancel when you're finished looking.

g. Double-click System Information. The System Information utility opens, providing detailed information about the hardware and software.

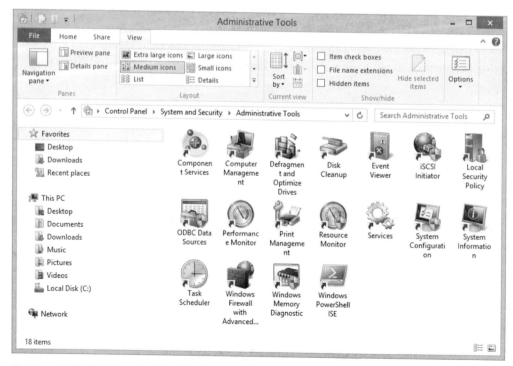

FIGURE 2-21 The icons in the Administrative Tools group

→ **Note**

If you are using Windows 7, you won't see System Information in the Administrative Tools. You can run it from the Start menu instead. Click Start, type System Information, and then click System Information in the search results that appear.

h.   Click the plus signs in the navigation pane to expand categories, and click categories to examine their content. Click Cancel when you're finished.

30 MINUTES

Lab Exercise 2.09: Using the Settings App in Windows 10

The CompTIA A+ 220-1002 exam objectives don't cover using the Settings app in Windows 10, but it's important for you to know that more and more of the functions previously included in Control Panel have migrated to Settings. This process has continued with subsequent releases of new Windows 10 versions. However, Settings still offers links to Control Panel functions for some tasks. In this exercise, you will learn how to access Settings to change Personalization options. If you have a computer with Tablet mode support, you will also use Settings to change how Windows 10 starts up.

Learning Objectives

The main objective of this exercise is to familiarize you with the Windows 10 Settings app.

At the end of this lab, you'll be able to

- Open the Windows 10 Settings app

- Move between categories

- Search for specific settings

- Configure Personalization options

- Configure Tablet mode (if available on your hardware)

Lab Materials and Setup

The materials you need for this lab are

- A fully functioning PC with the most recent edition of Windows 10 available to you installed (preferably version 1803 or later), preferably a PC with touch screen support.

Getting Down to Business

In this lab you'll explore the Windows 10 Settings app.

Step 1 We'll start by reviewing the basic navigation of the Settings app and checking out one of the categories.

    a. Open Settings. Click the Start button and then click the gearbox (Settings) button or right-click the Start button and then click Settings. The Settings app opens (see Figure 2-22).

        If you wanted to disable Wi-Fi or other wireless hardware, which category would you open?

        _____

    b. Click the icon for that category.

    c. Note that the screen is now split into two panes. The left pane shows submenus, and the right pane shows the current submenu selected.

        What is the name of your network? _____

    d. Click the Back arrow to return to the Settings home page.

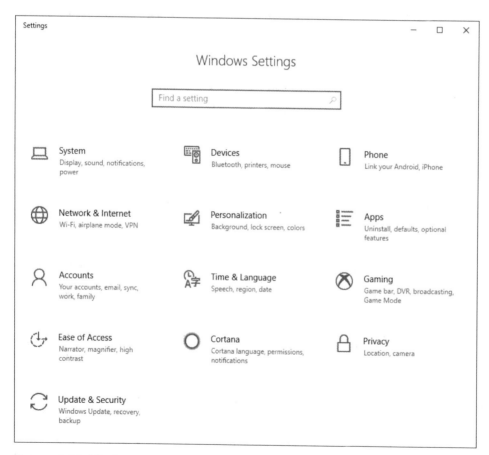

FIGURE 2-22 The Settings app in Windows 10

Step 2   Next, you'll find details about the version of Windows you are using.

    a.   Click the System category.

    b.   Scroll down to About and click it.

        What processor is installed in your computer? _____

        How much RAM is installed in your computer? _____

    c.   Scroll down until you can see the Windows edition. What is it? _____

        What version of Windows are you using? _____

        What is the OS build number? _____

    d.   Click the Home button to return to the main menu.

Step 3   Next, you'll learn how to use the Search tool in Settings to find specific settings.

    a.   Click in the Find a setting search box (above the categories).

    b.   Type **memory**.

    c.   Click the best match for memory diagnostics.

        According to the dialog box, what needs to happen before you can test your system's memory?

        _____

    d.   Click Cancel to close the dialog box.

    e.   Click in the Find a setting search box.

    f.   Type **Device Manager**.

    g.   Click the matching entry.

    h.   Close the Device Manager window.

Step 4   Next, let's see how to set Personalization options for the Desktop in Windows 10.

    a.   Click the Personalization category.

    b.   Personalization options appear. From here you can customize individual aspects of formatting by using the links at the left side of the window, such as Desktop Background or Color, or you can click a theme.

✔ **Tip**

As covered in Lab Exercise 2.04, you can also get to Personalization by right-clicking the Desktop and choosing Personalize. That's a great shortcut to know for times when Settings isn't already open.

c. Click Themes.

d. Click one of the themes to apply it.

e. Click the Color hyperlink at the bottom of the dialog box.

f. Click one of the colored squares to change the color of the window borders and taskbar.

g. (Optional) Return your Personalization settings to your own preferences if desired.

h. Click the Back arrow until the Windows Settings menu appears.

Step 5 (Optional)   Finally, if you have a touch screen, you can specify which mode your system starts in, Tablet or Desktop mode.

a. Click the System category.

b. Click Tablet mode on the left.

c. Open the When I sign in drop-down menu.

d. To force Desktop mode, choose it. To force Tablet mode, choose it. If you want Windows 10 to decide based on how your system is configured (for example, if a keyboard is attached or active), select the *Use the appropriate mode for my hardware* option.

e. To change whether Windows 10 will switch modes automatically, open the *When this device automatically switches tablet mode on or off* drop-down menu and select a preference.

f. To keep app icons visible on the taskbar, move the *Hide app icons on the taskbar in tablet mode* switch to Off.

g. You can also hide the taskbar in Tablet mode by moving the *Automatically hide the taskbar in tablet mode* switch to Off.

h. After viewing or choosing settings, click the Home button to return to the Windows Settings menu.

Lab Exercise 2.10: Getting Familiar with the macOS Interface

The CompTIA A+ 220-1002 exam objectives include some basic macOS features and functionality. You won't see a *lot* of questions on macOS, as the test is still pretty Windows-centric, but you should familiarize yourself with at least its basic operation. In this lab exercise, you'll poke around macOS a bit, figure out what features correspond to Windows features, and locate the macOS features listed in the 1002 exam objectives.

Learning Objectives

The main objective of this exercise is to familiarize you with the macOS operating system.

At the end of this lab, you'll be able to

- Understand the macOS desktop

- Use and customize the Dock

- Manage files with Finder

- Understand the Gestures, Spotlight, Keychain, and Boot Camp features

Lab Materials and Setup

The materials you need for this lab are

- A fully functioning PC with macOS installed (preferably High Sierra or later)

Getting Down to Business

In this lab you'll explore the macOS environment, and you'll locate and become familiar with the key macOS features that are covered on the 1002 exam.

Step 1   Boot into the macOS desktop environment. Use Figure 2-23 to orient yourself to the Desktop features listed next. Click each feature to check it out.

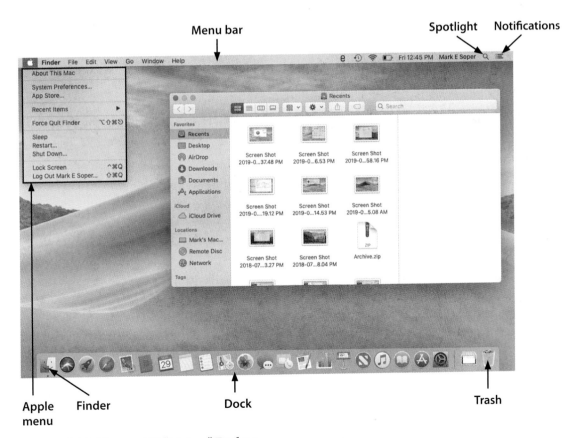

FIGURE 2-23 The macOS "Mojave" Desktop

✔ **Tip**

From the menu bar at the top, choose Help | New to Mac? Tour the Basics to see a tour of desktop features.

- **Apple menu**   Click the apple icon in the upper-left corner of the screen for a system menu from which you can select Sleep, Restart, Shut Down, and Log Out, among other options.

✔ **Tip**

From the Apple menu, you can select Force Quit, which exits a locked-up application. It's equivalent to shutting down an app with Task Manager in Windows.

- **Dock**   This is sort of like the pinned icons on the Windows taskbar. A running application is indicated by a dot under the app's icon. We'll look at the tools on the Dock in Step 2.

- **Menu bar**   A menu bar across the top of the Desktop provides access to the menu system for whatever program is active. If no program is active, it defaults to Finder (the equivalent of File Explorer in Windows). The first menu on the menu bar (after the Apple menu) is named for the application's name.

- **Spotlight**   The magnifying glass opens a Spotlight Search feature, which is equivalent to the Search box in File Explorer (CompTIA refers to this feature as Spot Light).

- **Notifications**   Click here to see a sidebar of timely information including the weather, your calendar, and any upcoming events. Windows 8.1 doesn't have anything that's a direct correlation to this, but Windows 10 has a Notifications feature that is very similar.

- **Trash**   This is the equivalent of the Recycle Bin in Windows; you can use it to retrieve deleted files and folders.

Step 2   Now let's look at how to launch an application, and find out what the Dock has to offer.

- **a.**   On the Dock, click the Launchpad button (the rocket ship). This shows the available applications in icon form, like on an iPad.

- **b.**   Click the Other icon. A subgroup of utility programs opens. Knowing where this subgroup is available will be handy for later use.

- **c.**   Click outside of the subgroup to return to the main screen of icons.

- **d.**   Drag the Calculator icon to the Dock and drop it there.

- **e.**   Click the Launchpad icon on the Dock again to close Launchpad.

- **f.**   Click and hold the Calculator icon on the Dock, click Options, and click Remove from Dock.

g. On the Dock, click the Safari button (the button that looks like a compass). The Safari browser opens.

h. Notice that the menu bar at the top of the screen changes to Safari menus. The first menu (after the Apple menu) is the Safari menu. Click Safari to open that menu. Then choose Quit Safari to close the application.

i. Click the Finder button on the Dock. The Finder window opens.

macOS uses rectangular window frames for content, just like Windows does. The main difference is in the positioning of the window control buttons. They're in the upper-left corner, rather than the upper right. The red button is Close; the yellow button is Minimize; and the green button is Maximize. See Figure 2-24.

Click the yellow button to minimize the Finder window. Note that in the Dock, the Finder window now has a black dot under it, indicating it is open.

j. Click Finder on the Dock to reopen its window.

k. Click the Finder window's Maximize button. The window fills the whole screen. Notice that the window's title bar (and window control buttons) disappears.

l. Move the mouse pointer to the top of the screen, bringing the title bar and window controls into view again.

m. Click the Maximize button again to restore the window to its previous size.

Step 3 Finder is the equivalent of File Explorer in Windows. You use it to browse the file system. So, while we're here, let's play with that a bit.

a. In the Finder window, click each of the icons in the Favorites list in the navigation pane to see what files appear in each of those areas. For example, click Applications to see what apps are installed, and click All My Files to see all your data files.

Here are a couple of ways to search.

- Click in the Search box in the upper-right corner of the Finder window. Click *This mac* for where to search, then type **time**. Search results appear showing all files that have the word "time" in their names. This might be a motley assortment, which might include various music clips and applications, all mixed together.

- Across the top of the Finder window are View buttons, as shown in Figure 2-25. Click each in turn to see how it changes the view.

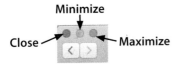

FIGURE 2-24 Window controls are in the upper-left corner in macOS.

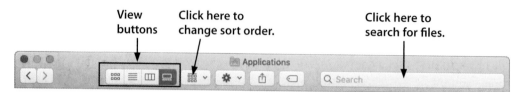

View
buttons

Click here to
change sort order.

Click here to
search for files.

FIGURE 2-25 Change the view of the current location with the View buttons in Finder.

b. Click the Spotlight icon (the magnifying glass) in the upper-right corner of the screen. The Spotlight Search box opens.

c. Type **time**. Search results appear in a single-column, well-organized fashion, neatly categorized. Click one of the results and a preview of it, or information about it, appears in the right pane. Figure 2-26 shows an example for Time Machine.

One important thing to know about Finder is that it doesn't show you *all* the files the way File Explorer does in Windows. It keeps nontechnical users safe by showing only the files it thinks you need to see, like your data files and your applications. Everything else is hidden. (Stuff like this is why newbies love Macs and most techies hate them.)

✔ **Tip**

At some point you may need to include hidden files in a search. To do so, open Terminal (open Finder, click Applications, double-click Utilities). In Terminal, type the following command and press ENTER: defaults write com.apple.finder AppleShowAllFiles YES. Then hold down the OPTION key, click and hold the Finder icon, and click Relaunch.

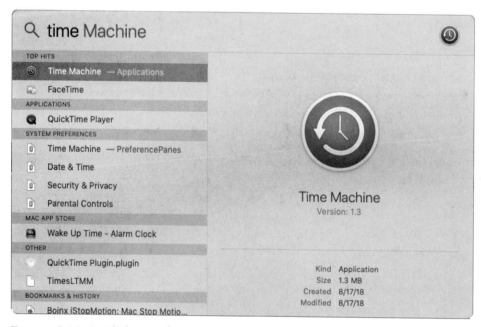

FIGURE 2-26 Spotlight Search provides categorized results.

Step 4   The Keychain feature (referred to as Key Chain by CompTIA) safely stores your Safari Web site user names and passwords, so you don't have to remember them or continually type them. It can also keep the accounts you use in Mail, Contacts, Calendar, and Messages up to date across all your Mac computers. When you set up your Mac initially, you are asked whether you want to enable the Keychain feature. If you chose not to, you can do so at any time as follows:

    a.   On the Apple menu, choose System Preferences | iCloud.

    b.   Scroll down to Keychain, and if there is not a checkmark beside it, click to place one. Enter your Apple ID password if prompted. Go through the process of getting approval for this device to use the app; you may need to use your iCloud security code or request approval from another device.

    c.   After Keychain has been enabled, close the iCloud window.

➜ **Note**

To access Keychain settings, open Finder, click Applications, double-click Utilities, and double-click Keychain Access.

Step 5   *Gestures* are shortcuts that you can perform to navigate using a touchpad or touchscreen. Here's a good way to learn about them:

    a.   From Finder, choose Help. Click the Search box and type gestures.

    b.   Click the *Use trackpad and mouse gestures* entry to see some of the common gestures.

    c.   To see all of the gestures, click the *Open trackpad preferences for me* link. The window opens behind the Help window. The Point & Click tab shows you how to perform a secondary click; the Scroll & Zoom tab shows you how to zoom in or out or rotate an object; the More Gestures tab shows you how to start some macOS apps and swipe between pages.

➜ **Note**

Secondary Click is analogous to right-click on a Windows PC. To secondary-click with gestures, press down with two fingers on the touchpad.

    d.   Try out the gestures if you have a touchpad or touch screen. Then close the help and System Preferences windows.

Step 6   iCloud is an online storage area, free to Mac users. It's equivalent to OneDrive in Windows. To access iCloud:

    a.   Open Finder.

    b.   In the navigation pane, click iCloud Drive.

You can drag-and-drop files to and from your iCloud drive (for example, from the Desktop).

Step 7   Boot Camp is a utility that helps you install Microsoft Windows on a Mac, and then switch between the two operating systems. Super handy! Especially since Windows lacks the corresponding ability. To use Boot Camp:

    a.   Make sure your Mac has hardware that will pass muster (CPU, RAM, and hard drive). Use the Mac's System Information app to check things out: click Finder, click Applications, double-click the Utilities folder, and double-click System Information.

    b.   Make sure you have a Windows disk image (ISO) file.

    c.   Run Boot Camp Assistant: click Finder, click Applications, double-click the Utilities folder, and double-click Boot Camp Assistant.

    d.   Work through the onscreen instructions to repartition your startup disk, download the needed software drivers, and install Windows.

Lab Analysis Test

    1.   Joe has just moved his PC to his new office. After hooking up all the cables, he turns on the system, and when it asks for his password, the keyboard will not respond. What could possibly be wrong?

    2.   Audrey has just returned to her desk after taking a break. She was only gone a few minutes, so she kept her PC on. Now the monitor is blank and the monitor LED is blinking a different color than usual. What might have happened?

    3.   Jeff has just upgraded from Windows 7 to Windows 10 and he is confused. He has started several Universal apps, but he can't figure out how to close them. How would you explain the process for closing a Universal app?

    4.   Michael wants to use the Event Viewer tool in Windows 10. Someone told him it's in Administrative Tools, but he doesn't know where that is. Walk him through the process of accessing the Administrative Tools folder.

    5.   Sally has just switched from Windows to macOS. She sees a few applications on the Dock, but thinks that there surely must be more applications installed than just those. Explain two different ways she could access a full set of installed applications.

Key Term Quiz

Use the following terms to complete the following sentences. Not all of the terms will be used.

click

Dock

double-click

File Explorer

Finder

FireWire

Keychain

light-emitting diode (LED)

Notification

optical drive

right-click

Windows Explorer

1. The macOS feature used to manage passwords is called _____.

2. A(n) _____ is a visible indicator to tell you that your PC is on or that your hard drive is active.

3. Remember to use the eject button on your _____ when closing the tray so you don't damage anything.

4. On a Windows 10 PC, the file management utility is _____; in Windows 7 it is called _____; and in macOS the equivalent utility is _____.

5. To move, resize, or delete pinned tiles on the Start menu in Windows 10, _____ the tile.

6. To switch between Desktop and Tablet modes in Windows 10, click the _____ area, then click the Tablet mode button.

Chapter 3

CPUs

Lab Exercises

Many PC users can perform simple installation and upgrade tasks, such as adding RAM or installing a new sound card. When it comes to the more complicated tasks, however, such as installing or replacing a CPU (central processing unit or microprocessor), wise users turn to the experts—this means you!

As a tech, you will install plenty of CPUs. Whether you're building a new system from scratch or replacing the CPU on an existing computer, it's your job to know the important characteristics of the CPU, match the CPU to compatible motherboards, and confirm that the CPU in the PC is running properly.

In this set of lab exercises, you'll identify current CPU types, form factors, and sockets. You'll then explore the specifications of the CPU with a freeware program known as CPU-Z. Finally, you'll learn how to remove and install a CPU.

It's time to find your antistatic wrist strap and get started with your exploration of CPUs!

 **30 MINUTES**

Lab Exercise 3.01: Identifying CPU Characteristics

There you are, innocently strolling down the hall at work, following the smell of freshly brewed coffee, when you're ambushed by Joe the accountant, brandishing a CPU packaged with a cooling fan. He wants to replace the CPU in his machine with this new one he bought on eBay, and he wants you to help him. When you're the resident computer tech geek, your coworkers will expect you to be able to deal competently with a situation like Joe's.

Staying on top of the many developments in CPU technology can be challenging, but it's also a necessary part of your job as a PC technician. By this point, you know that you can't just plug any CPU into any motherboard and expect it to work—you have to match the right CPU to the right motherboard. To accomplish this, you need to identify important CPU characteristics such as form factor, clock speed, and bus speed, as well as things like voltage settings, clock multiplier configurations, and cooling requirements.

Learning Objectives

In this lab, you'll practice identifying CPUs and CPU fan components.

At the end of this lab, you'll be able to

- Recognize the different kinds of CPUs

- Recognize different CPU fan attachments

- Identify the basic specifications of different classes of CPUs

Lab Materials and Setup

The materials you need for this lab are

- A notepad and pencil to document the specifications

- Optional: Access to a working computer with a word processing or spreadsheet application installed and access to the Internet to facilitate research and documentation of the CPU specifications

Getting Down to Business

In the following steps, you'll review your knowledge of CPU specifications, and then examine the CPU and fan attachment on a PC.

✖ Cross-Reference

Use Chapter 3 of *Mike Meyers' CompTIA A+ Guide to Managing and Troubleshooting PCs* to help fill in the specifications for each CPU in the following charts.

Step 1   A good tech not only will learn the specifications of different CPU chips, but also will master the use of reference tools such as the Internet, manufacturers' Web sites, product documentation, and reference books. A quick search of the Web or your motherboard manual will generally yield a full list of specs for a given CPU.

In the following table, see how many CPU chip features you can fill in given the maker and CPU type. Keep in mind that CPUs have very short production lives. If some of these CPUs have become obsolete, use the extra rows provided to add more modern processors to the assignment.

➜ Note

Some CPUs do not have an L3 cache; chip architects are split on the value of an L3 cache if the L2 caches are sufficiently large and speedy. Some Intel processors have unified Smart Cache in place of separate L2 and L3 caches.

Maker	CPU Type	Package	Max Clock Speed (GHz)	Wattage Consumption	L2 Cache	L3 Cache (or Smart Cache)	Number of Cores
AMD	Ryzen Threadripper 2950WX						
Intel	Core i5-7600T						
Intel	Core i9-9900X						
AMD	A12-9800 APU						

Step 2   Modern Intel CPUs are identified not only by general categories like i3, i5, i7, i9, Pentium, and Celeron, but also by microarchitecture, also called generation. While you will probably need to look up individual CPU model numbers to find out which microarchitecture each uses, you should have a good understanding of the approximate age of a particular architecture's code name.

Place the following Intel architectures in order from oldest to newest by assigning a number next to each one (1 being the oldest and 8 being the newest):

_____ Skylake

_____ Kaby Lake

_____ Broadwell

_____ Haswell

_____ Cascade Lake

_____ Core

_____ Coffee Lake

_____ Sandy Bridge

Step 3   Many users argue that Intel is better than AMD or vice versa. What do you think? Do some research and prepare a recommendation for selecting either an Intel processor or an AMD processor. Check multiple Web sites, read different articles online, check prices on processors with comparable performance, and then write a short comparison/contrast essay on which CPU manufacturer you think is better. Be sure to cite your sources!

_____

_____

_____

_____

_____

_____

_____

_____

_____

 **30 MINUTES**

Lab Exercise 3.02: Recognizing CPU Sockets

Now that you've identified Joe's purchase, you explain to him that you can't be sure it will work in his PC until you see his motherboard. CPU compatibility is determined by what the motherboard can support. Many motherboards enable you to upgrade the PC by replacing the existing CPU with a faster model of the same type. As a technician, your job is to make sure that the newer CPU has the same pin configuration as the motherboard. If you do not know where to begin, perform an online search for the maker of the motherboard. In many cases, you must replace the entire motherboard if you want to move up to a faster microprocessor.

Learning Objectives

In this lab, you'll identify various CPU sockets.

At the end of this lab, you'll be able to

- Recognize different kinds of CPU sockets
- Know which CPUs require which sockets

Lab Materials and Setup

The materials you need for this lab are

- A notepad and pencil to document the specifications

- Optional: Access to a working computer with a word processing or spreadsheet application installed and access to the Internet to facilitate research and documentation of the CPU socket specifications

This lab is more effective if you have access to different types of motherboards with different types of CPU sockets.

Getting Down to Business

In the following steps, you'll review your knowledge of CPU socket types.

Step 1   Draw a line connecting each CPU to its corresponding socket type. Choose the *best* match.

CPU		Socket Type
AMD Ryzen Threadripper 2950WX		AM4
Intel Core i5-7600T		LGA 2066
Intel Core i9-9900X		TR4
AMD A12-9800 APU		LGA 1151

Step 2   Identify the different socket types in Figure 3-1 and write the letter for each socket next to its name:

Socket AM4 _____   Socket TR4 _____

Socket LGA 1151 _____   Socket LGA 2066 _____

A   B   C   D

FIGURE 3-1 Identifying sockets

Step 3   Using the Internet as your guide, find and list three processor models that fit in the following sockets.

Socket AM4:

_____

_____

_____

Socket LGA 1151:

_____

_____

_____

Step 4   As a PC technician, you will sometimes encounter older motherboards and CPUs, and you'll need to be able to identify them and determine their approximate age and capability, as well as the socket type.

Suppose that you read the following model numbers on CPUs installed in motherboards. For each one, use the Internet to research its year of manufacture, socket type, and speed and enter the information in the table. Some of these sockets may be new to you if you have worked only with current systems, but compatibility differences between AMD and Intel CPUs are included on the CompTIA A+ 220-1001 exam, so you should have a basic familiarity with older as well as newer sockets.

CPU Model	Year of Manufacture (approximate)	Socket Type	Speed (in GHz)
Intel Pentium Processor E6800			
Intel Core i5-3450			
AMD Phenom II X6 1035T			
AMD A8-3850			
Intel Core i7-990X Extreme Edition			
AMD FX-4150			

30 MINUTES

Lab Exercise 3.03: Cooling Your CPU

Now that Joe has his processor, he needs to keep it cool, and since you've done everything else for him so far, you might as well make sure it's properly cooled, too! Someone new to the CPU cooling business might be tempted to think that CPUs come from the factory with a defined operating temperature. This isn't the case. The operating temperature depends tremendously on the way you cool the CPU. A far more reliable measurement is *power consumption*, the amount of power a CPU needs. CPU power consumption is measured in watts (W), with most desktop CPUs consuming in excess of 100 W. If you've ever tried to touch a 100-W light bulb, you can appreciate that this level of power consumption generates a tremendous amount of heat. If this heat isn't taken away from the CPU by some form of cooling, the CPU will begin to overheat. If the CPU gets too hot, it will automatically shut itself down to prevent permanent damage. You need to make sure that the cooling device included with Joe's CPU is the correct one for the microprocessor and is installed properly. Keep in mind that some CPUs are not shipped with a cooling device, so one must be purchased and installed.

Learning Objectives

In this lab, you'll identify the strengths and weaknesses of three CPU cooling options: OEM fan assemblies, third-party fan assemblies, and liquid cooling.

At the end of this lab, you'll be able to

- Determine the cooling needs of your CPU

- Decide which form of cooling to use for your needs

Lab Materials and Setup

The materials you need for this lab are

- Access to a working computer with Internet access

- A notepad and pencil to document the specifications

Getting Down to Business

The three most common types of CPU cooling are original equipment manufacturer (OEM) fans, third-party fans, and liquid cooling. Each of the following steps gives you an opportunity to investigate each of these options for a particular CPU.

Step 1   For the purposes of this exercise, pick out any single modern CPU as a sample CPU—you'll use this to find the proper cooling devices. Any CPU will work, but you'll find more options if you choose one that's readily available on popular online stores. If you're not sure which online store to use, check out www.newegg.com.

Individual CPUs are most commonly sold in what's known as a "retail box." This includes both the CPU and an OEM fan assembly.

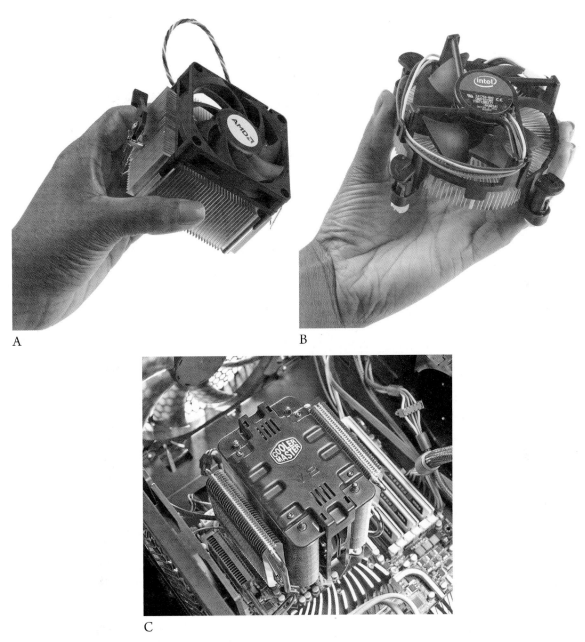

A

B

C

FIGURE 3-2 Comparing different CPU fans

Step 2 Many different types of fan assemblies can be attached to CPUs in many different ways. Describe the characteristics of the types of fans shown in Figure 3-2.

A _____

B _____

C _____

Step 3   Look online for third-party fan assembly solutions for the CPU you've chosen. Look for the following popular brand names and see what third-party fans each of these manufacturers offers for your CPU:

Antec, Arctic, Cooler Master, Thermaltake, Zalman

Document the name, model number, and price for one of the fan assembly solutions and list some of the benefits it offers:

Manufacturer: _____

Model Number: _____

Price: _____

Benefits:

_____

Step 4   Do some research on liquid cooling. What equipment would you need to liquid-cool your PC? (Water doesn't count!)

_____

_____

Why would anyone want to use liquid cooling?

_____

_____

Step 5   Using the same manufacturers listed in Step 3, try to find liquid-cooling options for your chosen CPU. Most liquid-cooling options are either bolt-on (they can be added to an existing case) or case-integrated (they are built into a system case).

Manufacturer: _____

Model Number: _____

Price: _____

Bolt-on or case-integrated? _____

 **30 MINUTES**

Lab Exercise 3.04: Exploring CPU Specifications with CPU-Z

Joe is very impressed with your knowledge and expertise—and he's relieved that the CPU he purchased on eBay happened to work out. You explain that not only did it work out, but he has really improved the performance of his system with the upgraded CPU. In fact, to further display the characteristics of the CPU Joe has just purchased, you download and run a utility known as CPU-Z from www.cpuid.com. This utility reads the specifications of different PC components from information embedded in those components. You launch the utility to display the parameters of the new CPU for Joe.

Learning Objectives

In this lab, you'll identify various CPU specifications.

At the end of this lab, you'll be able to

- Run the CPU-Z utility

- Recognize key characteristics of CPUs

Lab Materials and Setup

The materials you need for this lab are

- Access to a working computer with Internet access to facilitate downloading and running the CPU-Z utility

- A notepad and pencil to document the specifications

- Optional: A word processor or spreadsheet application to facilitate the documentation

This lab is more informative if you have access to different types of systems with different classifications of CPUs.

Getting Down to Business

In the following steps, you'll download a reference utility known as CPU-Z and use it to further explore the characteristics of the CPU.

Step 1   Sign in to a computer with Internet access and point your browser to the following Web site: www.cpuid.com. Follow the directions to download the current version of CPU-Z (the current version at this writing is 1.87). Unzip the file and launch CPU-Z. Don't mind any UAC warnings; this program is fine.

Step 2   The CPU-Z utility displays a number of tabs across the top of the window (see Figure 3-3). At this time, you are only concerned with the CPU and Caches tabs.

FIGURE 3-3 The CPU-Z utility

✔ **Hint**

Because of variations in CPUs, chipsets, BIOS, and motherboards, CPU-Z may not be able to display all of the information about your CPU. In some cases, the information may actually be erroneous. The CPUID Web site has good documentation on some of the common incompatibilities.

Using the data gathered by CPU-Z, record some of the pertinent information here:

Name: _____

Code Name: _____

Package: _____

Core Speed: _____

Multiplier: _____

Bus Speed: _____

L2 Cache: _____

L3 Cache: _____

→ **Note**

The code name is used by the manufacturers to refer to different revisions of a chip. For instance, the Core i7 line of CPUs has a number of revisions. Three of the more common ones are Haswell, Broadwell, and Skylake. The AMD FX processor line has also had revisions, including Zambezi and Vishera.

Step 3   If possible, launch CPU-Z on various machines to compare the characteristics of different CPUs. Save the utility for use in future lab exercises.

 **30 MINUTES**

Lab Exercise 3.05: Removing and Installing a CPU

Luckily for Joe, his motherboard is compatible with his new CPU. Now he expects you to play your "computer expert" role and install the new CPU in his PC. As a PC tech, you must be comfortable with such basic tasks. In this exercise, you'll familiarize yourself with the procedure; using your disassembled PC, you'll practice removing and reinstalling the CPU and fan assembly.

Learning Objectives

In this lab, you'll practice removing and installing a CPU and CPU fan assembly.

At the end of this lab, you'll be able to

- Remove and install a CPU safely and correctly
- Remove and install a CPU fan assembly safely and correctly

Lab Materials and Setup

The materials you need for this lab are

- An antistatic mat, or other static-safe material on which to place the CPU following removal
- An antistatic wrist strap
- Thermal paste
- A small slotted (flat-head) screwdriver

Getting Down to Business

Time to get your hands dirty! Removing and installing CPUs is one of the most nerve-wracking tasks that new PC techs undertake, but there's no need to panic. You'll be fine as long as you take the proper precautions to prevent ESD damage, and handle the CPU and fan assembly with care.

> **✖ Warning**
>
> **Be careful not to touch any of the exposed metal contacts on either the CPU or the CPU socket.**

Step 1   Put the wrist strap on your wrist, with the metal clip to the inside of your wrist and making good contact with your skin. Make sure the cable is connected to the wrist strap. Use the alligator clip on the cable to connect to a metal component on the computer. Then, shut down and unplug the computer.

Open your PC's case. If you've never done this before, you might feel a little nervous. That's okay. As long as you don't go unplugging things at random and breaking off bits of the motherboard, you shouldn't have a problem.

Each PC case is built differently, so each will be opened in its own way. Some use screws, and others use latches. Almost all cases have a removable panel on one side that you'll need to take off. Refer to the documentation that came with your PC or case for more information.

How do you open your particular case?

_____

_____

Step 2   Find your motherboard, the largest circuit board in your PC. Everything else should be connected to it. Somewhere in that mess of cables, cards, and drives is your CPU.

Determine whether the process of reinstalling and removing the CPU and fan assembly will be easier with the motherboard on an antistatic mat or installed in its case. You may find that it is easier to work with the stubborn fan assembly clamp used on some CPUs if the motherboard is secured in the case. The case may even have a removable motherboard tray to ease the installation process.

Step 3   In most cases, you'll have to remove the heat-sink and fan assembly before you can remove the CPU. (You may also need to unplug any cables in your way.) Before removing the heat-sink and fan assembly, be sure to disconnect the fan from the motherboard. Screw-down fans are easier to remove than clip fans. Screw-down fans require only that you unscrew the securing hardware. Some types of clip fans, found on many types of CPUs, require you to apply pressure on the clip to release it from the fan mount. You might need to use a small slotted screwdriver to do this (see Figure 3-4). Be careful!

Newer types of processors that use clip fans use a locking lever, as shown in Figure 3-5.

FIGURE 3-4 Using a screwdriver to remove a clip-type CPU fan from its mount

FIGURE 3-5 A clip-type CPU fan that uses a locking lever

✔ **Hint**

You'll discover that releasing a fan clip that does not use a locking lever takes way more force than you want to apply to anything so near a delicate CPU chip. Realizing this in advance, you can be sure to brace yourself and position the screwdriver carefully, to minimize the possibility of it slipping off and gouging something. Always use two hands when attempting this procedure.

The CPU and fan assembly will have thermal paste residue on the surfaces that were previously touching. You cannot reuse thermal paste, so you'll need to apply a fresh layer if you reinstall the CPU fan. Using a clean, lint-free cloth, carefully wipe the thermal paste residue from the CPU and fan assembly. If necessary, use 91 percent or higher denatured alcohol on your cloth. Then place the fan assembly on an antistatic surface.

✖ **Warning**

Reusing an OEM CPU fan on a different processor is not a good idea because the new processor will usually need more powerful cooling.

Step 4   Before proceeding, notice the CPU's orientation notches. All CPUs have some form of orientation notch (or notches). Remove the CPU. Start by moving the end of the zero insertion force (ZIF) lever a little outward to clear the safety latch; then raise the lever to a vertical position. Next, grasp the chip carefully by its edges and lift it straight up and out of the socket. Be careful not to lift the CPU at an angle—if it's a pin grid array (PGA) CPU, you'll bend its tiny pins. Land grid array (LGA) CPUs don't have pins, but you can damage the pins on the motherboard, so still be careful! As you lift out the CPU, make sure that the ZIF lever stays in an upright position.

Record your socket type: _____

Step 5   Now that you have the CPU chip out, examine it closely. The manufacturer usually prints the chip's brand and type directly on the chip, providing you with some important facts about the chip's design and performance capabilities. Note any markings that denote the processor manufacturer, model, speed, and so forth.

What is the CPU information printed on the chip package? _____

✖ **Warning**

Always handle a CPU chip like a fragile old photograph: very gently, holding it only by the edges. Make sure you take *complete* ESD avoidance precautions, because even a tiny amount of static electricity can harm a CPU!

Step 6 Reinsert the CPU with the correct orientation, lock down the ZIF lever, and reattach the fan. Now remove the fan assembly and the CPU again. Practice this a few times to become comfortable with the process. When you're finished practicing, reinsert the CPU for the last time. Be sure to apply a thin film of fresh thermal paste onto the square in the center of the top of the CPU before you place the fan. Now reattach the fan assembly. Don't forget to plug the fan back in!

Step 7 You may leave your CPU/fan assembly installed on the motherboard and place the motherboard on your antistatic mat. Optionally, if you reinstalled the motherboard in the case, you may leave it assembled.

Lab Analysis Test

1. James has an AMD FX-4100 CPU installed on his motherboard and has just bought a faster Intel Core i7 CPU from an eBay auction. He asks you to install the new CPU. What is your first reaction?

2. Joanna called you to say that ever since you installed her new CPU, the PC experiences intermittent problems when it runs. Sometimes it just quits or freezes up. What could possibly be wrong?

3. Theresa has an older computer that has an LGA 775 motherboard with an Intel Core 2 Quad 2.83-GHz processor. Can she install an Intel Core i7 2.93-GHz processor? Why or why not?

4. Lindsey runs CPU-Z on her system and notices that the processor's core speed is 2191.2 and the displayed multiplier is ×22. What is the speed of the system clock in Lindsey's machine? How would the industry display this system clock speed?

5. David currently has an older system with only two cores in the processor. David decides, since he is a power gamer, that he will upgrade to a system with a multicore CPU with at least six cores to improve the performance when playing his favorite game. Is a multicore processor likely to improve game-playing performance in this scenario? Explain.

Key Term Quiz

Use the following terms to complete the following sentences. Not all terms will be used.

AMD	multicore
code name	packages
CPU	water block
fan assembly	zero insertion force (ZIF)
Intel	

1. AM4, LGA 1151, and LGA 2066 are all types of CPU _____.

2. Both Intel and AMD have adopted the use of a(n) _____ to distinguish among revisions of their CPUs.

3. You often need to remove the _____ to get to a system's CPU.

4. To remove a CPU, you'll need to disengage the _____ lever.

5. A(n) _____ is placed directly over the CPU in a liquid-cooled system.

Chapter 4

RAM

Lab Exercises

One of the easiest and most cost-effective upgrades you can make to a PC is to add more memory. As such, you'll perform many RAM installations as a PC tech—get used to it.

RAM installation tasks include determining how much RAM the PC has installed, determining how much RAM the PC can support, determining what type of RAM it uses, and then physically installing the RAM on the motherboard. The following labs are designed to help you practice working with RAM by using visual recognition of the different types and packages and by walking you through the steps of installing RAM.

 14 MINUTES

Lab Exercise 4.01: Determining the Amount of RAM in a PC

While pummeling your fellow PC techs in *Far Cry New Dawn* over lunch, a coworker named Holly appears, clutching a stick of RAM she got from a guy on the fourth floor. She wants you to install it in her system. You tell her you have to check on some things first, including how much RAM her system can handle and how much it already has, before you can help her.

✔ **Hint**

> **High-end PCs usually come straight from the factory equipped with hefty amounts of RAM. Lower-cost PCs sometimes cut corners by skimping on RAM.**

Before installing any RAM, you'll need to determine how much RAM is already installed in Holly's PC, and then consult the motherboard book to determine how much RAM the system supports.

Learning Objectives

In this lab exercise, you'll use various methods to determine how much memory is currently installed in your system, and how much it is capable of holding.

At the end of this lab, you'll be able to

- Find RAM measurements
- Identify how much RAM is installed in a system
- Determine how much RAM a particular motherboard supports

Lab Materials and Setup

The materials you need for this lab are

- A working Windows PC

- A notepad and pencil

✔ **Hint**

> **If you're in a computer lab or you have access to multiple PCs, you should practice on as many different PCs as possible.**

Getting Down to Business

There are several ways to determine how much RAM is installed in a PC. First, you can check the RAM count during the boot process (some of the newer machines hide the RAM count, even if it's enabled in the BIOS). This tells you how much RAM the system BIOS recognizes during its check of the system. Second, you can check the amount of RAM that Windows recognizes from within the OS. Third, you can remove the PC case cover and physically examine the RAM sticks installed on the motherboard. Fourth, you can run a utility to determine the size of the sticks already installed in your system.

Step 1 Turn on your PC, and watch the display as the system goes through its startup routine, otherwise known as a power-on self test (POST). If it's an older system, you might see the RAM count as the initial POST is performed, as in Figure 4-1. If you do, make a note of it.

```
AMIBIOS(C)2010 American Megatrends, Inx.
ASUS P6T ACPI BIOS Revision 1303
CPU : Intel(R) Core(TM) i7 CPU 920 @ 2.67GHz
 Speed : 2.66 GHz

Press DEL to run Setup
Press F8 for BBS POPUP
Press ALT+F2 to execute ASUS EZ Flash 2
DDR3-1066MHZ  O
Initializing USB Controllers .. Done.
8183MB OK
USB Device(s) : 1 Keyboard, 1 Mouse, 1 Hub
```

FIGURE 4-1 Viewing a typical RAM count during boot-up

Many systems run through the startup routine quickly, so the RAM count might appear on the screen for only a few seconds, or not at all. When you see it, you can press the PAUSE/BREAK key (if your keyboard has one) or WINDOWS-PAUSE keys to pause the boot process so you have time to write down the number accurately. When you want the boot process to resume, press the ENTER key. This doesn't work on most newer PCs, though, so you might not be able to complete this step.

What is the RAM count number displayed on your monitor? _____

→ **Note**

You can also check the RAM amount from BIOS/UEFI firmware setup. After entering BIOS/UEFI setup, you should find the RAM count on the main screen there. BIOS/UEFI firmware is covered in Chapter 5.

Step 2   Use the following methods to determine the amount of RAM in a system from within any version of Windows.

- In Windows 7, open the Start menu, right-click Computer, and select Properties.

  In Windows 8.1, display the Desktop if it is not already showing (click the Desktop tile on the Start screen), and then right-click the Start button and choose System.

  The RAM count is under the System heading (see Figure 4-2). You can also see other useful information here, like the processor type, Windows edition, the product ID, and more.

  In Windows 10, open the Start menu, click Settings, click System, and click About. The memory size is listed under the Device specifications heading (see Figure 4-3).

- In Windows 7, click Start | All Programs | Accessories | System Tools | System Information. Or, alternatively, click Start, type **msinfo32**, and press ENTER.

  In Windows 8.1 or Windows 10, right-click the Start button and click Run. In the Run box, type **msinfo32** and click OK.

  In the System Summary, look for a value called Installed Physical Memory (see Figure 4-4). The amount of RAM will be listed in the displayed information.

How much memory is in your system? _____

If you were able to complete Step 1 to view the amount of RAM shown during the startup routine, what is the difference, if any, in the amount of RAM reported by Windows? _____

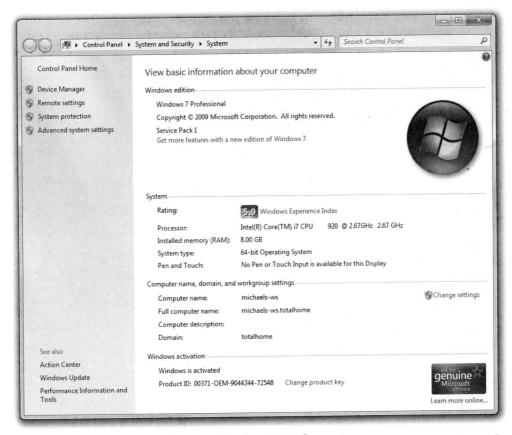

FIGURE 4-2 Viewing the RAM size in Windows 7 via Computer

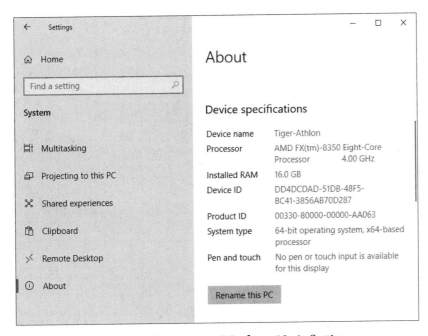

FIGURE 4-3 Viewing the RAM size in Windows 10 via Settings

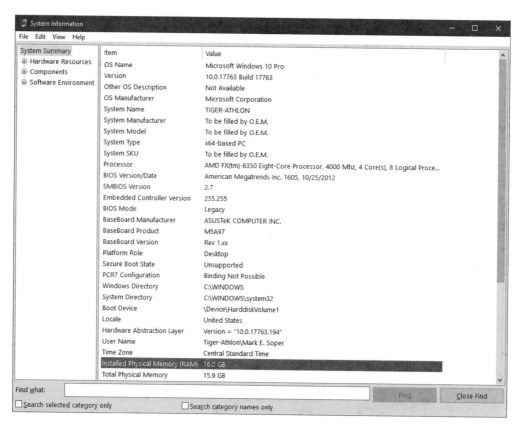

FIGURE 4-4 The System Information dialog box showing Installed Physical Memory

---

→ **Note**

If the numbers don't match, don't panic. There's a logical explanation. Entry-level PCs and laptops often have onboard display adapters (the display adapter is built into the motherboard). Manufacturers include little to no video RAM on the motherboard, so the display adapter must "steal" some portion of the system RAM to be able to handle today's intense graphic applications. If the amounts do not add up, then your system has probably allocated some of the system memory to handle your display adapter's needs.

Step 3   We'll save the last method for determining how much RAM is installed (looking inside your PC) for the next exercise in this lab. For the moment, let's talk about how to determine the maximum amount of RAM a system can support.

The amount of RAM you can install on a modern system depends on the limitations of the motherboard hardware. The motherboard has a limitation as to the amount of RAM it will accept. Neither the CMOS setup utility nor the OS can help you determine how much RAM a motherboard can handle. You can usually find this information in the system's motherboard manual, if you have it, or on the PC maker's or motherboard manufacturer's Web site.

Examine the documentation that came with your PC, or visit the manufacturer's Web site, to determine how much RAM you can install on the system.

What is the maximum amount of RAM that your system can support? _____

✱ Try This: Crucial System Scanner

On a Windows computer with Internet access, point your browser to the following Web site: www.crucial.com. Click the *I agree to the terms & conditions* **check box (after you read them) and click Scan Computer. The CrucialScan.exe file is then downloaded. Next, run CrucialScan.exe.**

The app uses your browser to display the total number of memory slots in the system, the current size of each module installed, the maximum memory capacity supported, if it uses memory channels (for example, 4 slots with 2 banks of 2 is a dual-channel system), and the sizes and speeds of compatible memory modules. If this does not correspond to the information you found earlier in the PC or motherboard documentation, what is the difference? _____.

 **30 MINUTES**

Lab Exercise 4.02: Identifying Types of RAM

Once you determine how much RAM is installed on Holly's PC, and how much her motherboard can handle, you conclude that there's room for more. "But," you explain to Holly, "this doesn't mean you can add that RAM stick you got, because not all RAM is the same." Having looked at the specs for her system, you know it takes 288-pin DDR4 SDRAM sticks. Holly thinks the stick she got is the right size, but you know it's 240-pin DDR3 RAM, so it won't fit. This is why they pay you the big bucks.

RAM comes in several standardized form factors, each compatible with specific types of systems. Modern desktop systems use full-sized dual inline memory modules (DIMMs) of various pin configurations (168, 184, 240, and 288). Laptop computers use scaled-down sticks called small-outline DIMMs, or SO-DIMMs (also called SODIMMs).

✱ Cross-Reference

For details on the various types of RAM found in modern systems, refer to the "DDR2," "DDR3," "DDR3L/DDR3U," and "DDR4" sections in Chapter 4 of *Mike Meyers' CompTIA A+ Guide to Managing and Troubleshooting PCs.*

The steps for identifying the different types of RAM are presented in this lab exercise.

Learning Objectives

In this lab, you'll examine and compare different RAM packages.

At the end of this lab, you'll be able to

- Recognize and differentiate between different kinds of RAM packages

Lab Materials and Setup

The materials you need for this lab are

- Demonstration units of various RAM packages (optional)

 Hint

It is helpful to examine the RAM configurations in multiple PCs, if you have them available. Having a laptop with removable RAM is a plus.

Getting Down to Business

Let's do a quick review of the types of RAM packages you'll see in modern PCs. Then you'll check your PC or motherboard documentation to determine the type of RAM it uses.

All modern PCs use some form of DDR memory for their system RAM. As was discussed in the textbook, DDR stands for *double data rate*, which means that for every tick of the clock, two chunks of data are sent across the memory bus. This has the effect of giving you twice the performance without increasing the clock rate.

Step 1   Another performance trick modern systems use to increase memory speed is multichannel architectures. This enables the memory controller to access more than one stick of RAM at a time, thus increasing performance. In effect, the 64-bit bus acts like a 128-bit bus (for dual channel), a 192-bit bus (for triple channel), or a 256-bit bus (for quad-channel). To use these multichannel architectures, you must install memory in identical pairs, triplets, or quads. Check your motherboard manual.

If applicable, specify whether your system supports dual-channel, triple-channel, or quad-channel memory: _____

What colors represent the different channels?

_____

Step 2   There are many different types of RAM. It's important for you to be able to distinguish the difference between all of them by knowing what they physically look like and what their defining characteristics are. For each of the following descriptions, identify the type of RAM by entering its name on the blank line preceding the definition.

A. _____ This type of RAM comes in 168-pin packages. It uses two notches to help guide the installation of the module: one near the center, and the other near an end. It was the first type of DIMM technology commercially available for PCs and usually had a speed rating of PC100 or PC133.

B. _____ This type of RAM doubled the speed by performing two processes during each clock cycle. It uses a 184-pin package. This style has one notch in it.

C. _____ Like its predecessor, it too performs two processes per clock cycle, but it takes it one step further by twice doubling the clock speed of the memory's input-output circuits. It uses a 240-pin package and has a single notch. It typically uses smaller memory chips than its predecessor.

If you are using a typical desktop system and it is relatively new (less than four years old), the motherboard will most likely support one of the following two types of RAM packages:

D. _____ If doubling the clock speed twice wasn't enough, this type of RAM doubles it three times. It uses a 240-pin package, like some other types, but don't let that fool you: it is completely incompatible with all other types of RAM. Not only is it different electronically, but the notch is in a different place.

E. _____ This type of RAM doubles the clock speed four times and uses a 288-pin package. The memory socket connectors are slightly curved.

Figure 4-5 illustrates DDR, DDR2, DDR3, and DDR4 memory sticks (markings have been removed). Match the picture ID (A, B, C, D) to the correct memory type.

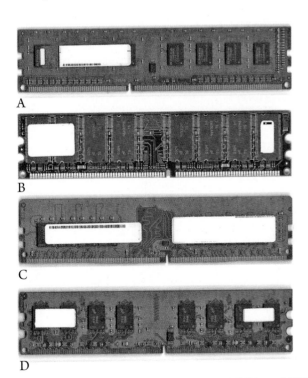

A

B

C

D

FIGURE 4-5 Identifying DDR, DDR2, DDR3, and DDR4 memory sticks

DDR _____

DDR2 _____

DDR3 _____

DDR4 _____

Step 3   In your PC or motherboard documentation, or on the manufacturer's Web site, locate the section listing the type of RAM your system uses.

What type of RAM does your system use? _____

What speed of RAM does your system need? _____

Step 4   Open your system case and make note of the following:

   A.   How many RAM slots does your motherboard have? _____

   B.   How many RAM slots are filled with RAM sticks? _____

   C.   Is your system set up to use single-channel, dual-channel, triple-channel, or quad-channel RAM? How could you find out?

_____

   D.   Standard RAM modules resemble the modules shown in Figure 4-5. However, some systems have modules that use heat sinks and fins to help dissipate heat (see Figure 4-6). This type of memory is typically easier to overclock (run at faster clock speeds) to improve performance and is frequently used in systems built for gaming. Check your system and note if it has any modules that resemble the one in Figure 4-6.

FIGURE 4-6   A high-performance DDR4 memory stick designed to dissipate heat

 30 MINUTES

Lab Exercise 4.03: Removing and Installing RAM

You've found a stick of RAM for Holly that works with her system, and now you have to install it. Although RAM installation is one of the simpler PC hardware upgrades, it's still important that you follow the correct steps and take all appropriate safety precautions.

Learning Objectives

In this lab, you'll practice removing and installing RAM.

At the end of this lab, you'll be able to

- Remove RAM safely and correctly
- Install RAM safely and correctly

Lab Materials and Setup

The materials you need for this lab are

- An antistatic mat or other static-safe material on which to place the RAM
- An antistatic wrist strap
- A notepad and pencil

✔ **Hint**

If you're in a computer lab or you have access to multiple PCs, you should practice on a variety of systems.

Getting Down to Business

Removal and installation procedures vary depending on the type of RAM your system uses. DIMMs snap into the RAM slots vertically, while SO-DIMMs (used by a few low-profile desktop and most all-in-one units) snap in at an angle (see Chapter 23 to learn more about installing and removing SO-DIMMs). The following steps describe the removal and installation procedures for DIMMs.

✖ **Warning**

Regardless of the type of RAM in your system, be certain to take measures to prevent ESD damage. Shut down and unplug the PC and place it on an antistatic mat. Strap on an antistatic bracelet and ground yourself. If necessary, remove any cables or components that block access to the system RAM before you begin.

FIGURE 4-7 Removing a DDR4 DIMM

PART I: REMOVE THE EXISTING RAM

Step 1   Open the PC case. Use whatever methods the case requires: some use screws, some use latches. Once the case is open, look for the RAM sticks on the motherboard, as in Figure 4-7. Locate the retention clips on either end of the RAM modules.

Step 2   Press outward on the clip(s) to disengage them from the retention slots on the sides of the RAM sticks.

Step 3   Press down on the clips firmly and evenly. The retention clips act as levers to lift the DIMM sticks up and slightly out of the RAM slots.

Step 4   Remove the DIMM sticks and place them on the antistatic mat or in an antistatic bag. Make note of the following:

How many pins does the RAM have? _____

Where are the guide notches located? _____

What information is on the RAM's label? _____

Step 5   While you have your system RAM out, this is a good time to check the condition of the metal contacts on both the RAM sticks and the motherboard RAM sockets. Dirty contacts are fairly rare. If you see this problem, use contact cleaner, available at any electronics store.

Are the contacts free of dirt and corrosion? _____

After you've examined your system RAM, inspected the motherboard RAM sockets, and ensured they are free of dirt and corrosion, reinstall the RAM as described next.

Part II: Install a DIMM

Step 1   Orient the DIMM so that the guide notches on the RAM module match up to the guide ridges on the RAM socket.

Step 2   Press the RAM stick firmly and evenly straight down into the socket until the retention clip or clips engage the retention notches on the ends of the RAM stick.

Step 3   Snap the retention clip or clips firmly into place.

Step 4   Repeat these steps to install other RAM modules as appropriate.

Part III: Complete the Installation

To finish a RAM installation professionally, specifically if you are on a production-level machine, follow these steps:

Step 1   Once the system RAM is in place, reattach any cables that you may have had to move, and plug in the system power cable. Do not reinstall the PC case cover until you've confirmed that RAM installation was successful.

Step 2   Boot the system and watch the RAM count (if displayed) to confirm that you correctly installed the RAM. If you don't see a RAM count, use one of the methods described earlier in Lab Exercise 4.01 to confirm the amount of RAM now installed.

✔ **Hint**

If the system has any problems when you reboot, remember that you must turn off the power and unplug the computer again before reseating the RAM.

 **30 MINUTES**

Lab Exercise 4.04: Exploring RAM Specifications with CPU-Z

Now that you have Holly's system up and running with double the memory it had before, you can take a moment to analyze the memory. You've already downloaded the utility CPU-Z from the Internet in Lab Exercise 3.04, "Exploring CPU Specifications with CPU-Z"; now you'll need to launch CPU-Z and examine the information on the Memory and SPD tabs.

Learning Objectives

In this lab, you'll identify various RAM specifications.

At the end of this lab, you'll be able to

- Recognize key characteristics of RAM

Lab Materials and Setup

The materials you need for this lab are

- Access to a working computer with the utility CPU-Z installed

- A notepad and pencil to document the specifications

This lab is more informative if you have access to different types of systems with different types of RAM.

Getting Down to Business

In the following steps, you'll explore the different characteristics of RAM.

Step 1   Launch the CPU-Z application.

Step 2   Navigate to the Memory tab. The CPU-Z utility displays the current statistics of the RAM installed, as shown in Figure 4-8.

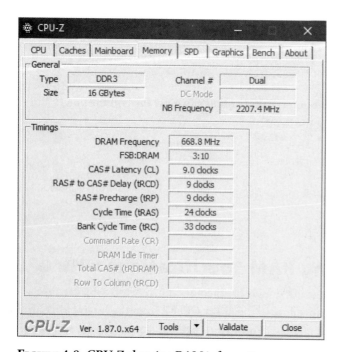

FIGURE 4-8 CPU-Z showing RAM information

Using the data gathered by CPU-Z, record the following information:

Type: _____

Size: _____

CAS# Latency (CL): _____

RAS# to CAS# Delay (tRCD): _____

RAS# Precharge (tRP): _____

Step 3 Click the SPD tab in CPU-Z.

Step 4 The SPD tab, shown in Figure 4-9, lists a number of technical bits of information about a particular stick of RAM. This information is contained on every RAM stick in a chip called the serial presence detect (SPD) chip.

Using the data gathered by CPU-Z, record the following information for each of the system's RAM modules:

	Module 1	**Module 2**	**Module 3**	**Module 4**
Slot #				
Module Size				
Max Bandwidth				
Manufacturer				

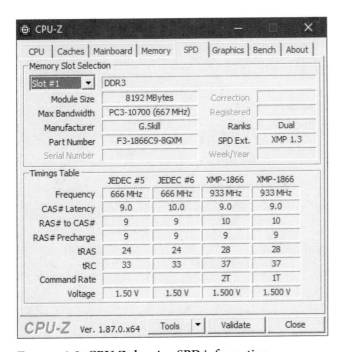

FIGURE 4-9 CPU-Z showing SPD information

✖ Cross-Reference

To review how the SPD chip works with the system, refer to the "Serial Presence Detect (SPD)" section in Chapter 4 of *Mike Meyers' CompTIA A+ Guide to Managing and Troubleshooting PCs.*

Step 4 If possible, launch CPU-Z on various machines to compare the characteristics of different types of RAM. Save the utility for use in future lab exercises.

Lab Analysis Test

1. Jarel wants to upgrade his memory on an older computer, and calls you for help. He knows that he's using DDR2 RAM and that his system clock is 333 MHz, but he isn't sure what type of DDR2 RAM sticks he should purchase. What DDR2 RAM would you recommend that he use?

2. Theresa's Windows 7 system has 1 GB of RAM. She adds another stick with 1 GB of RAM, but the RAM count still only shows 1 GB. What could be causing this?

3. John's system has 2 GB of PC4200 DDR3 SDRAM. He recently installed an additional 2 GB of DDR3 SDRAM that a coworker gave him. He tells you that his system now boots up correctly and shows the correct amount of RAM, but then it freezes after several minutes. He notes that if he removes the new RAM, the system runs fine. What could be a possible reason for this?

4. Kyle has a system that supports dual-channel architecture (there are two blue DIMM slots on the motherboard). The motherboard has space for three sticks of RAM, so Kyle installs three 4-GB RAM sticks. What will be the result?

5. Joe has recently purchased a pair of 4-GB DDR4 RAM sticks. He's replacing an older pair of DDR3 RAM but can't afford to replace the motherboard. Why won't this work?

Key Term Quiz

Use the following terms to complete the following sentences. Not all terms will be used.

168-pin DIMM	DDR4 RAM
184-pin DIMM	DIMM
240-pin DIMM	dual channel
288-pin DIMM	gigabytes (GB)
DDR SDRAM	SDRAM
DDR2 RAM	SO-DIMM
DDR3 RAM	SPD

1. DDR2 and DDR3 RAM both come in a(n) _____ package, but they are not pin-compatible, so they can't be interchanged.

2. A RAM module used in a laptop is called a(n) _____.

3. A component known as a(n) _____ chip provides additional information about an SDRAM module.

4. A stick of _____ looks a lot like a 168-pin DIMM, but it has 184 pins.

5. The technology that uses two sticks of RAM together to increase throughput is known as _____ architecture.

6. When purchasing RAM for a new motherboard, the motherboard manual says it uses 288-pin DIMMs. The user needs _____ modules.

Chapter 5
Firmware

Lab Exercises

Firmware is software stored in a chip. Every computer has at least one type of firmware, the BIOS. Basic input/output services (BIOS) provide the primary interface between the operating system's device drivers and most of its hardware. Although a modern BIOS is automated and tolerant of misconfiguration, a good PC technician must be comfortable with situations in which the BIOS may need some maintenance or repair.

A PC needs the BIOS to tell it how each basic component is supposed to communicate with the system. At the beginning of the PC revolution, many different manufacturers developed BIOS for PCs, but over the years the BIOS business has consolidated primarily to only three brands: AMI (American Megatrends, Inc.), Phoenix Technologies (which absorbed Award Software), and Insyde Software. All of these manufacturers provide a utility called the CMOS setup program (CMOS stands for *complementary metal-oxide semiconductor*, which is why everyone says "SEE-moss") that enables you to reconfigure BIOS settings for boot device order, amount of memory, hard disk drive configuration, and so on. Most of these configurations are automated, but as a PC tech, you're the one who people will call when "automatic" stops working!

As an example for the lab exercises in this chapter, suppose that the company you're working for is planning a mass upgrade from its current OS, Windows 7, to Windows 10. You've tested the upgrade process on a few lab machines and have found that systems with an out-of-date BIOS are having problems upgrading successfully. In preparation for the Windows 10 installation, you will upgrade outdated BIOSes. You're also aware that the prior IT manager did not use consistent CMOS passwords, so you may need to reset the passwords on a few machines.

The lab exercises in this chapter will teach you how to identify, access, and configure system BIOS and how to make and save changes to CMOS settings.

On newer systems, the BIOS is technically not the BIOS anymore, at least not in the same sense it always was before. Instead, it's the *Unified Extensible Firmware Interface (UEFI)*. It's a new name, and it has some advantages, but from the average technician's perspective, not much has changed. The BIOS and UEFI CMOS setup programs are not that different, and that's where you'll mostly be interacting with them. This book uses the term *firmware* generically to refer to both BIOS and UEFI in cases where there is no exam-relevant difference between them.

> ✖ **Cross-Reference**
>
> To learn more about how UEFI differs from traditional BIOS, see the "UEFI" section in Chapter 5 of *Mike Meyers' CompTIA A+ Guide to Managing and Troubleshooting PCs.*

 **10 MINUTES**

Lab Exercise 5.01: Identifying BIOS Firmware

Having received your orders to do the big OS upgrade, your first task is to check the BIOS types and versions on every machine in your office, and then look online to determine whether more recent versions are available.

The system BIOS is stored on nonvolatile memory called BIOS ROM. BIOS makers sometimes (but not always) label their BIOS ROM chips prominently on the motherboard. In this exercise, you'll look at three different ways to identify your BIOS ROM chip.

> → **Note**
>
> Insyde Software UEFI firmware is used primary by laptop vendors, which typically offer far fewer options in their CMOS setup menus than desktop vendors.

Learning Objectives

In this lab, you'll learn three ways to identify your BIOS.

At the end of this lab, you'll be able to

- Locate the BIOS ROM chip on the motherboard
- View BIOS information at startup
- Use a utility to view BIOS information

Lab Materials and Setup

The materials you need for this lab are

- A working desktop PC running Windows 7, 8.1, or 10
- An antistatic mat
- A notepad and pencil

Getting Down to Business

The first thing you'll do is remove your PC case cover and locate the BIOS ROM chip. Next, you'll make note of the BIOS information displayed during system startup.

> **✖ Warning**
>
> **Any time you take the cover off your PC, remember to unplug the power cord and follow all proper safety and ESD avoidance precautions.**

Step 1 Remove the case from your PC and locate the system BIOS ROM chip. Most older motherboards label their chip with the name of the BIOS manufacturer (see Figure 5-1), while most recent motherboards' BIOS chips display the name or logo of the flash chip's manufacturer, not the manufacturer of the BIOS code inside (see Figures 5-2 and 5-3).

Compare your system BIOS ROM chip to the ones in Figures 5-2 and 5-3. These chips are marked with the chip vendor, not with the BIOS code vendor. Look at the BIOS ROM chips in your system, read the chip's label *if you can*, and answer the following questions. If the BIOS chip has the chip manufacturer's information rather than the BIOS code vendor's information, answer the last question only.

Who made the BIOS? _____

What year was the BIOS written? _____

Record any other numbers on the label: _____

Does it look like you could easily remove the system BIOS chip, or does it look soldered to the motherboard? _____

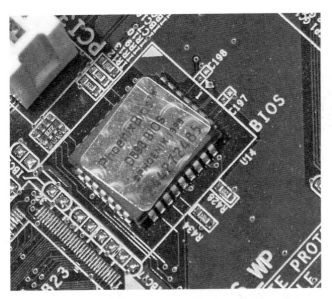

FIGURE 5-1 A typical BIOS chip (soldered in place) from an older system

Step 2 This next step may not work on newer systems, but give it a try. Replace the PC case cover, plug in the power cord, and start the system. Be sure the monitor is turned on. On older systems, you will see the BIOS information flash briefly on the screen at the very beginning of the startup process (from a cold boot, not when restarting). When that data appears on the screen, press the PAUSE/BREAK key or WINDOWS-PAUSE keys on the keyboard (if your keyboard has a PAUSE key). This suspends further operation until you press ENTER.

FIGURE 5-2 A typical socketed system BIOS ROM chip from a recent system

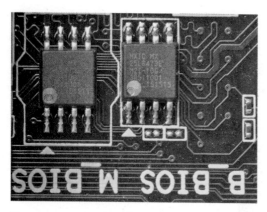

FIGURE 5-3 Dual surface-mounted BIOS ROM
chips from a recent system

Figure 5-4 shows an example of what you may see. At the top of the screen is the BIOS manufacturer's
name and version number. At the bottom of the screen is the date of manufacture and the product
identification number. You may also see messages letting you know what keys to press to get into boot options,
CMOS setup, and so forth.

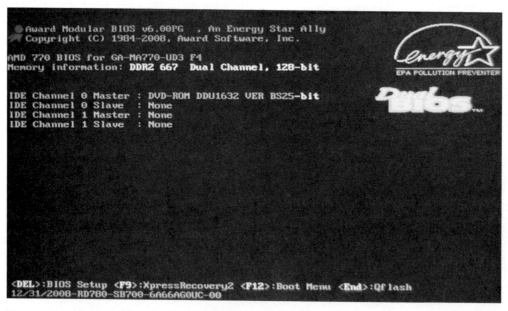

FIGURE 5-4 A typical boot screen on an older PC

On a newer PC, you might just see a logo from the PC manufacturer at startup, or some other equally unhelpful information. If that's the case for you, just move along to Step 3. Make note of the following information:

Who made the BIOS? _____

What version is the BIOS? _____

What year was the BIOS written? _____

✔ Hint

Not all BIOS display the same type of information. Some BIOS makers modify the BIOS to show nothing more than their logos during the boot process.

Step 3 Here's one more method for determining your BIOS information. This one works no matter the age of the PC; it just requires the System Information utility in Windows.

a. In Windows 7, click Start | All Programs | Accessories | System Tools | System Information. Or, alternatively, click Start, type **msinfo32**, and press ENTER.

In Windows 8.1 or 10, right-click the Start button and click Run. In the Run box, type **msinfo32** and click OK.

b. In the right pane, locate the BIOS Version/Date line and read the information there. Figure 5-5 shows an example. Write your BIOS information here:

_____

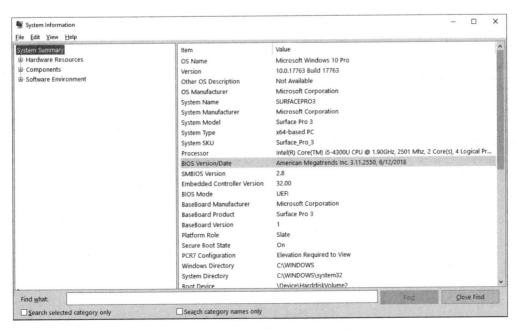

FIGURE 5-5 Check the BIOS version and date from System Information.

Step 4   Go online and find out whether a more recent version of the BIOS is available. Your first stop should be the PC maker's Web site. If it does not have this information available, try the motherboard manufacturer's Web site or the BIOS maker's Web site.

✖   **Warning**

If an update is available, do not download or install it now.

 15 MINUTES

Lab Exercise 5.02: Accessing BIOS Settings via the CMOS Setup Program

A BIOS has a number of configurable settings, such as boot order and security settings. You access them from a special setup program stored on a chip on the motherboard. This program is known by various names, such as the system setup utility, BIOS setup utility, UEFI/BIOS setup, or, most often, CMOS setup program (which is how we refer to it in this book). This setup program must be accessed from outside of the operating system. Depending on your computer and its operating system, you might do this when the PC is starting up by pressing a key, or you might issue a command in the operating system to tell it to reboot into that setup program.

➔   **Note**

Using the term "CMOS" to refer to the BIOS setup program is actually somewhat inaccurate on modern systems. CMOS refers to *complementary metal-oxide semiconductor*, which was a type of chip that stored custom BIOS settings on older systems. Today these settings are stored in the chipset, so there's no true CMOS chip anymore. But technicians have been calling it CMOS setup for so long that the name is ingrained.

Learning Objectives

In this lab, you'll go into the CMOS setup program and explore your BIOS configuration settings.

At the end of this lab, you'll be able to

- Enter the CMOS setup program and navigate its display screens

Lab Materials and Setup

The materials you need for this lab are

- A working PC whose BIOS settings you have permission to change

Getting Down to Business

In the following steps, you'll reboot your PC and access the CMOS setup program. The easiest way, if it's available to you, is to press a certain key at a critical moment as the PC starts up. Each BIOS maker has its own special way to do this, so how you go about it depends on which BIOS your system has installed.

If your system has UEFI Firmware and Windows 8 or later, you might not be able to enter CMOS setup by pressing a key at startup. Systems with Secure Boot enabled require an alternate method where users weave through a maze of Windows screens to convince the PC to restart itself and open CMOS setup.

Step 1   Watch carefully as the PC starts up for a message telling you what key or key combination to press to enter setup. The instant you see it, press that key or key combination. Usually it's one of these:

DELETE, ESC, F1, F2, F10, F12, CTRL-ALT-INSERT, CTRL-A, or CTRL-F1

If you hit it in time, CMOS setup loads. If you are too slow and the OS loads, shut down and try again.

If you don't see a message, or you aren't fast enough to read it, you can look up the key in the PC or motherboard documentation, or on the manufacturer's Web site. Alternatively, you can resort to trial and error with the preceding list of keys and key combinations.

Which key or key combination did you use to enter your CMOS setup program? _____

Step 2   If Step 1 didn't work out for you, and you have Windows 8 or later, you probably need to take a different route into CMOS setup.

Here's how in Windows 10:

- **a.**   Click Start.
- **b.**   Click Settings.
- **c.**   Click Update & Security.
- **d.**   Click Recovery.
- **e.**   Click Restart Now.
- **f.**   Click Troubleshoot.
- **g.**   Click Advanced Options.
- **h.**   Click UEFI Firmware Settings.
- **i.**   Click Restart.

Here's how in Windows 8.1:

a. From the Charms bar in Windows 8 or 8.1, click the Settings charm.

b. In the Settings pane, click Change PC Settings.

c. In the Settings app, click Update and Recovery.

d. In the navigation bar, click Recovery.

e. Under the Advanced Startup heading, click Restart Now.

f. At the Choose an Option screen, click Troubleshoot.

g. Click Advanced. (Do *not* click Refresh your PC or Reset your PC.)

h. At the Advanced Options screen, click UEFI Firmware Settings. The PC reboots and opens the CMOS setup program.

Step 3 Once you've entered the CMOS setup program, look at the screen and compare it to Figures 5-6 and 5-7, which show examples of two of the most popular BIOS types: Phoenix Tiano and AMI. The Phoenix Tiano BIOS shown in Figure 5-6 opens to an initial menu, whereas the AMI graphical BIOS shown in Figure 5-7, which is used by some Gigabyte motherboards, opens immediately into the MIT (Motherboard Intelligent Tweaker) screen. The BIOS in Figure 5-6 is typical of corporate-oriented systems, while the BIOS in Figure 5-7 is typical of motherboards designed for custom system builds. Although the screens for different CMOS setup programs may look different, they all contain basically the same functions.

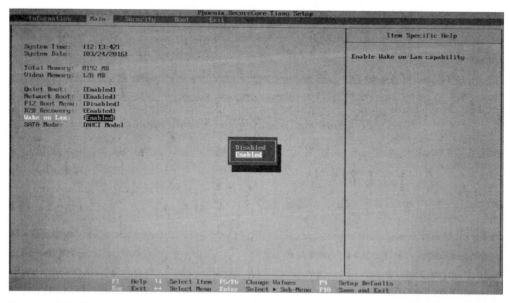

FIGURE 5-6 Phoenix Tiano text-based UEFI BIOS

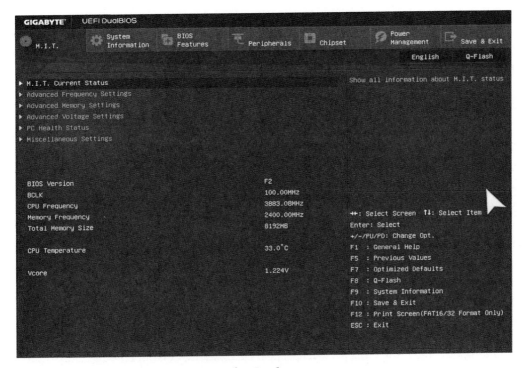

FIGURE 5-7 AMI graphical UEFI BIOS for Gigabyte

✖ Warning

Do not make any changes in BIOS settings during this lab exercise. You'll make changes in the next two lab exercises.

CMOS setup reports basic non-editable information about the system, such as the BIOS version, CPU type and speed, and amount of RAM. It also provides access to a whole host of settings you can change to affect the way the PC operates. For example, you can enable/disable onboard controllers for built-in components like video and network adapters, modify the settings for USB and SATA ports, and specify a preferred boot order for devices.

Step 4 Explore each screen and make notes about what each setting does. Navigation, like the method to enter the CMOS setup program, varies from maker to maker. Text-based BIOSes are navigable by keyboard only, but BIOS versions built for custom system builds or gaming uses, such as the AMI BIOS shown in Figure 5-7, have a graphical interface that supports mouse use. Look at the CMOS setup program screens to see how to navigate in your particular CMOS utility.

> ✔ **Hint**
>
> Usually the arrow keys and the PAGE UP and PAGE DOWN keys will select and change settings. Sometimes the + and – keys or the SPACEBAR will toggle settings. The CMOS setup program screen usually provides a key to the navigation and selection keys; refer to it as well.

While navigating through the different setup screens, pay particular attention to any password or security menu that enables you to configure administrator/supervisor passwords and user passwords. Do not make any changes at this time; just make a note of where you configure these passwords. You will configure a password in the next lab exercise.

Step 5   Following is a list of common settings found in the CMOS. Know that each BIOS arranges its settings differently. View every screen of your CMOS setup program to record these settings and their location:

- **System Information**   You'll see a brief description of the system, including processor model and speed, installed memory size, and BIOS version among other information.

  _____

- **Drives**   You'll see the installed drives listed. Hard drives are usually called Fixed HDD; optical drives are usually marked ODD (optical disk drive) or ATAPI. On older systems you might be able to change some settings for the drives, but on newer systems this information is read-only.

  _____

- **Onboard Devices/Peripherals**   These settings enable you to configure onboard devices such as your USB ports, SATA ports, and integrated network and video capabilities.

  _____

- **Performance/Chipset**   Found mostly on higher-end motherboards, this area enables you to tweak system timings for improved performance (also known as overclocking).

  _____

- **Security**   This section enables you to set administrator or system passwords. There might also be other security settings, such as Secure Boot configuration.

  _____

- **Boot Sequence**   This section enables you to define the order in which your system looks for boot devices.

  _____

- **PC Health/System Monitor**   This section informs you of current voltage levels and fan performance.

  _____

- **Power Management**   This section is used to configure power management settings.

  _____

Once you're done exploring, press ESC a couple of times until you get the message "Quit Without Saving (Y/N)?" Press Y, and then press ENTER. The system will boot into your operating system.

 **30 MINUTES**

Lab Exercise 5.03: Configuring and Clearing CMOS Setup Program Passwords

In many professional environments, the IT department doesn't want users to fool with any of the PC's settings, especially detailed items such as the BIOS settings. The IT manager may even devise a password to prevent entry to the CMOS setup program by unauthorized users. Unfortunately, in your organization, the IT manager has resigned and was not very thorough about documenting these passwords. Consequently, you are locked out of making changes because of CMOS setup passwords.

When a CMOS setup program has been password protected and its password has been subsequently lost, the typical way to clear the password is to shunt a jumper on the motherboard that clears either the password or the entire contents of CMOS.

Learning Objectives

In this lab, you'll learn how to configure CMOS setup program passwords and how to clear the contents of the password and CMOS using the onboard CMOS RTC clear jumper.

At the end of this lab, you'll be able to

- Set a password using the CMOS setup program
- Locate the CMOS RTC clear jumper on the motherboard
- Clear passwords and CMOS settings using the CMOS RTC clear jumper

Lab Materials and Setup

The materials you need for this lab are

- A working PC whose BIOS settings you can change, with access to the CMOS RTC clear jumper on the motherboard

- An antistatic mat/wrist strap

- A notepad and pencil

- A digital camera (optional)

→ **Note**

On some motherboards, a Clear CMOS button is located in the port cluster at the back of the computer.

Getting Down to Business

In the following steps, you'll reboot your PC and access the CMOS setup program using the method you learned in Lab Exercise 5.02. You will then navigate to the password or security menu and configure a CMOS setup program password. Then you'll verify the password by rebooting your machine and entering CMOS setup. Finally, you'll open the case and reset the CMOS settings by physically shunting the CMOS RTC clear jumper.

✖ **Warning**

Any time you remove the cover from your PC, remember to unplug the power cord and follow all proper safety and ESD avoidance precautions.

Step 1   Reboot your system and use the appropriate procedure to enter the CMOS setup program.

Step 2   Using your digital camera, take a readable photo of each screen in CMOS setup for later reference. If you don't have a digital camera, jot down the settings on paper or in a text editor on another computer. Turn off the flash to avoid screen glare.

Step 3   Navigate to the security or password menu (such as in Figure 5-8). Select the setup or supervisor password and enter a four- to eight-character password. Save changes and exit CMOS setup.

Record your password here: _____

The *supervisor* or *admin* password restricts access to the CMOS setup program so that only authorized personnel can change or modify BIOS settings. Organizations, especially schools, usually configure a supervisor password to keep curious users from causing system errors in CMOS setup.

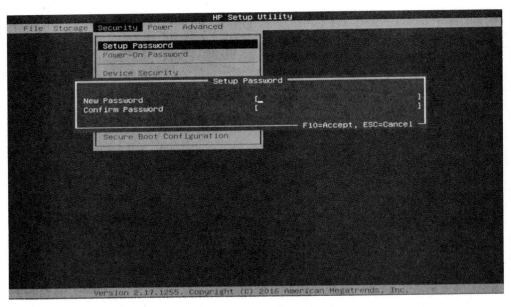

FIGURE 5-8 HP/AMI BIOS setup utility password setup

The *user* or *system* password restricts access to the PC itself, and is required every time the system boots (before an operating system is even loaded). This type of password is often used when an individual's PC is located in a public area. It provides protection from hacking activities that attempt to circumvent the security in the operating system by addressing the computer outside of it.

Many newer systems also have a *hard drive* or *HDD* password. Hard drive passwords prevent a user from accessing a particular hard drive unless they know the password.

Step 4 Reboot the PC and press the key or key combination required to enter the CMOS setup program. If you completed Step 3 correctly, you should be prompted to enter a password. Enter the password you configured in Step 3 and press ENTER. The main menu of the CMOS setup program will appear.

Discard changes and exit the CMOS setup program.

✖ Warning

The next step will erase all CMOS settings! While you are in the CMOS setup program, take the time to write down important settings such as the CPU settings (if any are configurable), boot order, and which integrated peripherals are enabled/disabled. If you haven't already done so, use your digital camera to take a picture of each screen of the CMOS setup program so you'll have something to refer to (turn off your flash to avoid screen glare). Although the system should run fine using the default settings, taking notes now will help you get back to any custom settings that may have been configured.

FIGURE 5-9 The CMOS RTC clear jumper on a motherboard

Step 5   Shut down the PC and unplug the power cord from the wall outlet. Remove the case from the PC and, referring to the PC or motherboard documentation, locate the CMOS RTC clear jumper. Follow the instructions included with the documentation and move the jumper (see Figure 5-9) to clear the CMOS.

A less elegant alternative to using the CMOS RTC clear jumper is to remove the onboard battery for at least 30 seconds, if your motherboard has one. Does your system have an onboard battery? Can it be removed easily? Check the motherboard documentation, or scout around for a battery visually. A coin-style battery (typically a CR2032 such as the one shown in Figure 5-9) is the most popular type on motherboards that have batteries.

Step 6   Replace the PC case cover, plug the system back in, and start the system. Press the appropriate key(s) to enter the CMOS setup program.

Were you prompted for a password? _____

Do you need to configure any of the other settings? _____

 **30 MINUTES**

Lab Exercise 5.04: Configuring BIOS Settings

If you find any issues when you examine the BIOS settings using the CMOS setup program, you'll need to reconfigure the settings.

You might also want to change some other settings if the previous exercise wiped out some custom settings that should be retained. If you are in a classroom lab environment, check with your instructor about this.

✖ Warning

> **Some settings, if configured incorrectly, can cause big problems. If you're not absolutely certain what a particular setting does, the best course of action is to leave it alone! If you have any doubts, you can always exit the CMOS setup program without saving.**

Learning Objectives

In this exercise, you'll access the CMOS setup program and navigate to find the various BIOS settings you would commonly need to modify.

At the end of this lab, you'll be able to

- Modify the settings in BIOS

Lab Materials and Setup

The materials you need for this lab are

- A working PC whose BIOS settings you have permission to change
- Digital photos of CMOS setup screens taken in Lab Exercise 5.03, if available

Getting Down to Business

In the following steps, you'll learn how to navigate to the CMOS setup program configuration screen that includes a feature called Bootup NumLock State. When this feature is turned on, as it usually is, the NUM LOCK key on your keyboard is turned on when the system starts.

✖ Cross-Reference

> **For more details about the features of CMOS setup programs, refer to the section "Typical System Setup Utility" in Chapter 5 of *Mike Meyers' CompTIA A+ Guide to Managing and Troubleshooting PCs.***

This feature is present on most BIOSes, even those with few configuration settings, and it is safe to change (unlike other options that could cause major issues if changed). Your CMOS setup program may vary, but most BIOS makers and versions should offer the same option.

➜ **Note**

If your system lacks this option, ask your instructor for a different BIOS setting you can change.

Step 1   Enter your CMOS setup program using the steps you learned in Lab Exercise 5.02.

Step 2   Using your notes and photos as a reference, navigate to the configuration screen that has the Bootup NumLock State option (see Figure 5-10). It is often under Boot Options, but not always. Some other typical configuration screens to check include Boot Settings Configuration, Boot Configuration, or Advanced BIOS Features.

Step 3   Select the Bootup NumLock State option and change it from On to Off (or Enabled to Disabled). Once again, your CMOS setup program's wording or appearance may be different.

Step 4   If needed, restore any custom CMOS settings that you wiped out doing the reset in Lab Exercise 5.03. Use the notes or photos you took in that lab as a guide.

Step 5   Save your change and exit the CMOS setup program. Usually, pressing F10 does this, but check the onscreen instructions to be sure. After you exit, the system will reboot automatically. You have just made a change to BIOS.

FIGURE 5-10 Finding the Bootup NumLock State (or whatever is the equivalent in your CMOS setup program)

The process you just followed is the same process you'll use for any changes you make to BIOS. Be sure to save the settings before exiting the CMOS setup program.

→ **Note**

The most common way to save CMOS settings is to select Save & Exit (or press the F10 key), then Y to confirm, and then press ENTER.

Step 6   Repeat Steps 1 through 3, but in Step 3 change Bootup NumLock State back to On (or Enabled). Then repeat Step 5 to save your change and exit the CMOS setup program.

Lab Analysis Test

1. Don bought a used computer at a garage sale, but it won't boot because someone has set a system password for it in CMOS setup. How can he gain access to the system if he doesn't know the password?

2. After running Windows 7 for a few years, Chris has decided to perform a clean install of Windows 10. After backing up his important files, he places the Windows 10 DVD in the optical drive and reboots his machine—but it just boots into Windows 7 like normal. What setting will he most likely need to configure in the BIOS to correct this situation?

3. Alex has just finished making changes to the CMOS settings and would now like to save these changes. Name two ways to save settings after making changes in the CMOS setup program.

4. Claire needs to get into the CMOS setup program for a PC, but no information appears at startup as to which key to press to do so. The PC has Windows 10 installed on it. What should she try?

Key Term Quiz

Use the following terms to complete the following sentences. Not all terms will be used.

AMI	DELETE key
Award Software	PAUSE/BREAK key
BIOS (basic input/output services)	Phoenix Technologies
BIOS ROM	Settings
CMOS (complementary metal-oxide semiconductor)	UEFI
CMOS setup program	WINDOWS-PAUSE keys

1. The system BIOS is stored on nonvolatile memory called _____.

2. Technicians configure the BIOS using the _____.

3. Press the _____ to suspend the boot process.

4. Almost all recent motherboards use _____ rather than a traditional BIOS.

5. In Windows 10, you can trigger entry into CMOS setup by using the _____ app.

Chapter 6

Motherboards

Lab Exercises

While the CPU, system RAM, power supply, hard drive, and all the other miscellaneous pieces of a typical PC are important, it is the motherboard that brings them together into a working whole. Every bit and byte of data that moves between devices passes through the motherboard's sockets and traces. Every component plugs into it, either directly or indirectly—a PC wouldn't be much of a PC without it. Replacing a motherboard is one of the most challenging tasks a PC tech will face.

Luckily, only a couple of circumstances require you to undertake this chore. The first is when the motherboard malfunctions or is damaged; modern motherboards aren't made to be repaired, so when they go bad, they must be replaced as a whole unit. The other is when you want to upgrade the PC to a more powerful CPU than its current motherboard supports. In either of these cases, you've got a bit of work ahead of you! Installing a motherboard requires more effort than any other type of installation—more preparation, more time performing the installation, and more cleanup afterward. Still, you shouldn't be intimidated by the prospect of replacing a motherboard—it's a common and necessary part of PC repair. In this chapter, you'll go through the process from start to finish.

In the following lab exercises, you'll research new motherboards, identify expansion slots, remove expansion cards, remove the motherboard from a working PC, and explore the motherboard's features. You'll then reinstall the motherboard, reinstall expansion cards, and use CPU-Z to discover all sorts of details. Finally, you will manage hardware with Device Manager.

 15 MINUTES

Lab Exercise 6.01: Researching New Motherboards

While the motherboard may be the backbone of a PC, all good upgrade efforts should begin with the CPU. Trying to pick out a motherboard and *then* a processor that goes with it is a little like buying a phone case before you've selected a phone model. How do you know it will fit? It's much less painful to work from CPU to motherboard, especially when your goal is to increase performance. Don't tie yourself down by doing it backward.

You need to make several choices when searching for a new CPU and motherboard. Ensuring compatibility is key. Once you've picked the latest and greatest processor from Intel or AMD, you need to find a motherboard that plays nicely with it: Match the socket type of the processor to the socket type of the motherboard. Make sure the socket is electrically compatible with the processor you want to use (some sockets have two versions that are physically the same but are made for different processors). Make sure the motherboard's form factor fits inside your case. And even after you've narrowed it down to that, you still need to pick a manufacturer and choose which features you want the motherboard to have.

Learning Objectives

In this lab, you'll become familiar with different motherboards and their compatibility with various processors and cases.

At the end of this lab, you'll be able to

- Recognize different motherboard form factors
- Understand considerations for upgrading a system with a newer motherboard

Lab Materials and Setup

The materials you need for this lab are

- A PC with Internet access

✔ **Hint**

As usual, if you have access to multiple systems, take advantage of it. It's most beneficial to have a variety of motherboards to study.

Getting Down to Business

The following steps will lead you through the process of determining which motherboard you need to obtain to update your client's systems. You'll also see that a motherboard is not an island unto itself, but one piece of the PC archipelago.

Step 1   Go to www.newegg.com (or another online PC component store) and search for a newer, faster processor. When selecting a new processor, be sure to keep track of important specifications so that you can refer to them when you need to pick out a motherboard. Record the following information:

Manufacturer: _____

Processor series: _____

Model #/clock speed: _____

CPU socket type: _____

Step 2   Search the online PC component store for a new motherboard. Keep in mind that the CPU's socket type must match the motherboard's socket type, otherwise they will be incompatible. You'll find several that are compatible, but for now, pick one and record the following information:

Manufacturer: _____

CPU socket type: _____

Form factor: _____

Expansion slots (number and type): _____

Step 3   The next step is to make sure that the new motherboard will work with the form factor of your client's system cases.

Current PC motherboards come in a few different styles, or *form factors*: ATX (Advanced Technology Extended), microATX, and mini-ITX, and proprietary form factors from companies such as Dell and Sony. Each motherboard form factor has a corresponding case it is compatible with, but some motherboards will fit in a case with a different form factor. ATX motherboards are what you find in most PCs on the market.

Your client's cases are all ATX. Is the motherboard you picked compatible? _____

Step 4   Look at a few different (but still compatible) motherboards. Compare their features. What makes them different? Does one have more expansion slots than the other? Does one have fewer RAM slots? Are there other features, such as support for NVIDIA's SLI (Scalable Link Interface) or ATI's CrossFire dual-graphics card technology, that would influence your choice? Using the motherboard you already selected, record the following information:

Number of memory slots: _____

Maximum memory supported: _____

Memory type(s) supported: _____

SATA ports: _____

Onboard video chipset: _____

Number of USB ports, types: _____

M.2 expansion slot: _____

Other features: _____

 15 MINUTES

Lab Exercise 6.02: Identifying Internal Expansion Slots

Unless you've got X-ray vision, the best way to examine expansion slots is to remove the PC case cover. In this exercise, you'll identify the type of expansion slots on your motherboard. Does your system use a slot for a graphics card (and if so, what kind?), or does it use onboard video? Check to see how many other expansion slots are available for adding a sound card and (if required) upgrading the graphics adapter.

> ✖ **Warning**
>
> **Remember to use proper safety and ESD avoidance procedures when working inside the PC case.**

Learning Objectives

In this exercise, you'll properly identify expansion slots and the basic features of each type of expansion technology.

At the end of this lab, you'll be able to

- Identify PCIe ×1 and PCIe ×16 expansion bus slots and component cards
- Identify PCI expansion bus slots and component cards

Lab Materials and Setup

The materials you need for this lab are

- A non-production PC
- A working PC (or more than one if possible)
- An antistatic mat
- A notepad and pencil
- A digital camera
- Optional: Some sample motherboards

Getting Down to Business

Shut down your PC and unplug the power cable. Place the PC on your antistatic mat, remove the PC case cover, and take a good look inside. Your aim is to determine what type of expansion slots your motherboard has, and what peripheral card components are currently installed.

Step 1   Although the standard PCI expansion slot is considered old technology and not many new cards use it, some motherboards include at least one PCI slot for backward compatibility. Here are the physical characteristics of PCI expansion slots:

- About 3 inches long

- Usually white in color (although modern motherboards may use bright colors like yellow or green to enhance the visual appeal of the motherboard)

- Offset from the edge of the motherboard by about 1 inch (see Figure 6-1)

Record the following information:

How many PCI slots are on your motherboard? _____

What PCI devices are installed on your system, if any? _____

Step 2   Next, locate the PCIe slots. Your motherboard will likely have several PCI Express (PCIe) slots, and they'll be different lengths depending on the number of lanes. PCIe ×1 slots are the everyday workhorses, and are used for a variety of expansion boards that have modest data throughput needs, like NICs or sound cards. They have the following characteristics:

- About 1 inch long

- Often brightly colored (blue and white being fairly common)

- Offset from the edge of the motherboard by about 1.25 inches

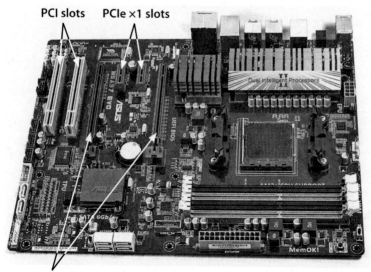

FIGURE 6-1   A motherboard with PCIe ×1, PCIe ×16, and PCI expansion slots

PCIe ×16 slots are used for boards with aggressive data throughput requirements: that is, primarily for video cards. They have the following characteristics:

- About 3.5 inches long

- Often brightly colored (blue and white being fairly common)

- Offset from the edge of the motherboard by about 1.25 inches

Figure 6-1 shows a modern motherboard with both PCI and PCIe slots. Compare the slots on this motherboard to those on your motherboard. Record the following information:

How many PCIe ×1 slots are on your motherboard? _____

How many PCIe ×16 slots are on your motherboard? _____

What version of PCIe is supported? _____ (this information may be marked on the motherboard, or listed in the motherboard or system documentation)

Are there any PCIe cards installed in the system? _____ If so, how many PCIe ×16? _____ ×1? _____ Others? _____

✖ Cross-Reference

For more detail about the PCI and PCIe buses, refer to the "Structure and Function of the Expansion Bus" section in Chapter 6 of *Mike Meyers' CompTIA A+ Guide to Managing and Troubleshooting PCs*.

Step 3 Does your motherboard have any riser cards? A riser card is used to enable two or more cards to fit into a single slot, or sometimes to enable a card to be mounted parallel to the motherboard to save space. Riser cards are seldom used on recent systems except in computers that use cube or other small form factor cases.

After you've completed your inventory of installed expansion bus devices, leave the cover off the PC in preparation for the next lab.

30 MINUTES

Lab Exercise 6.03: Removing Expansion Cards

In many situations, a PC that needs a motherboard replacement will have at least one expansion card installed. Removing expansion cards is fairly simple, although some cards require an extra step or two. This lab prepares your computer for the next lab, in which you will remove the motherboard itself.

Learning Objectives

In this lab, you'll remove expansion cards from inside a PC and inventory their functions and slot types.

At the end of this lab, you'll be able to

- Remove expansion cards safely and correctly
- Store them safely for reuse

Lab Materials and Setup

The materials you need for this lab are

- A working computer with at least one expansion card installed (PCIe ×16, PCIe ×1, and PCI if possible)
- A Phillips-head screwdriver
- An antistatic mat and antistatic wrist strap
- Antistatic bags for each card that will be removed
- A notepad, pencil, and a digital camera

Getting Down to Business

In this exercise, you'll physically remove expansion card devices from your PC. You'll then make note of any important information you can find on the device's label: device maker, version, and so on.

Shut down the system and unplug the power cable, placing the system on your antistatic mat. Once you remove the PC case cover and strap on your antistatic wrist strap, you're ready to start.

Step 1   Make a list of the expansion cards installed in your motherboard and note which slot each one uses.

✔ **Tip**

If you need PCIe or PCI cards for this exercise, check with a local electronics recycler. The cards need not be working.

Step 2   Take a picture of the cards and the internal and external cables attached to them, then disconnect the data cables from the cards. Some cards might use external data cables (such as video, USB, sound, or network), while others might use internal data cables.

Step 3   Remove the cards one at a time from your system. For each card, follow these procedures:

  a.   Be sure to disconnect any power leads going to the video or other cards (see Figure 6-2).

  b.   Remove the retaining screw and store it safely. If you are working with PCIe ×16 cards, you will need to release the latch holding them in place when removing them (see Figure 6-3).

  c.   Taking hold of the card by its edges, carefully and firmly pull it straight up and out of its slot.

FIGURE 6-2 This video card uses an 8-pin PCIe power connector.

✔ **Hint**

Some cards can be difficult to remove. If a card seems stuck, try rocking it back and forth (from front to back in the direction of the slot, not side to side).

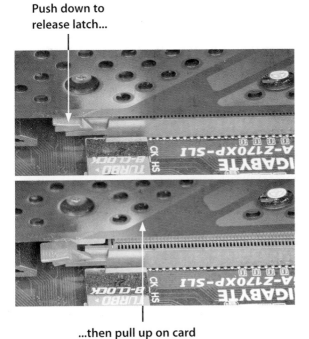

FIGURE 6-3 Releasing the latch to remove a PCIe ×16 video card

Step 4   Examine each of the cards you removed from your system and record the pertinent information.

If any of the cards have writing or labels on them, what information do these labels provide?

_____

_____

_____

If you can identify the manufacturer(s) of the cards, list each card and its manufacturer.

_____

_____

_____

If there are any version numbers or codes on the cards, list this information for each card.

_____

_____

_____

What kind of interface does each card use? List whether it is PCI, PCIe ×1, PCIe ×16, or something else. Figure 6-4 illustrates PCI, PCIe ×1, and PCIe ×16 slots and cards.

_____

_____

Step 5   After examining each card and noting which slot it was removed from, place each card in an antistatic bag for safekeeping. You will reinstall the cards in Lab Exercise 6.07.

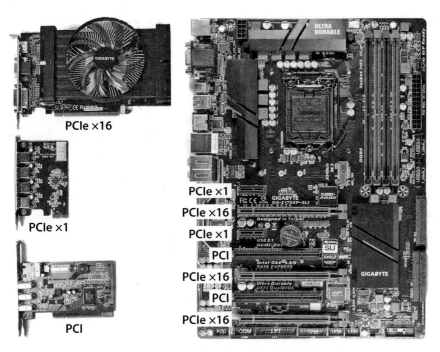

FIGURE 6-4 PCIe ×16, PCIe ×1, and PCI cards and slots

15 MINUTES

Lab Exercise 6.04: Removing a Motherboard

Techs will tell you that motherboard removal is the exercise that separates the geek from the meek and the true PC tech from the wannabe, but don't let that intimidate you! Motherboard removal is completely straightforward and simple.

Learning Objectives

In this lab, you'll remove your PC's motherboard.

At the end of this lab, you'll be able to

- Remove a motherboard safely and correctly

Lab Materials and Setup

The materials you need for this lab are

- A non-production or lab computer

- A Phillips-head screwdriver

- An antistatic mat and antistatic wrist strap

- A large antistatic bag

- A notepad, pencil, and a digital camera

Getting Down to Business

Take all precautions to avoid ESD. Remember those tools you learned about back in Chapter 1? Put on an antistatic wrist strap, clip it to your PC case, and dig in.

Start with your PC turned off. Disconnect everything, including the power cable, from the front and back of your PC. If you haven't already, open up your PC case using whatever method your case requires. Because you want to remove the motherboard from the case, you first need to disconnect (almost) everything from the motherboard. You've already learned how to remove RAM, CPUs, and expansion cards. We'll quickly outline how to disconnect the remaining cables.

Step 1   If you have any expansion cards installed, see Lab Exercise 6.03 for instructions on how to remove them.

Step 2   There will be several power, data, and signal cables attached to the motherboard. None of these are difficult to remove, though it may take a bit of force to disconnect a connector. Disconnect each cable until there are none connected.

✔ **Tip**

To remove the ATX main and ATX12V or EPS12V power connectors, push on the locking tab as you pull the connector out of the socket.

As you disconnect the wires that connect the front panel buttons and LEDs to the motherboard (see Figure 6-5), pay close attention to the connectors' locations. These connectors are tiny, and physically interchangeable, so it can be a challenge to put them back the same way they were before without notes.

FIGURE 6-5 Front-panel wires and headers on a typical motherboard

FIGURE 6-6 Removing screws securing the motherboard

Sketching the locations and orientations of the connectors on your notepad or taking pictures with your phone or tablet will make reassembly easier.

If the drives are installed in a way that will not impede access to the motherboard, you can leave them in place. Otherwise, remove them.

Step 3 Locate and remove the screws holding the motherboard to the frame of the case (see Figure 6-6). There are most likely six to nine screws. If paper washers are present, save them for reuse. Most systems may use metal supports called *standoffs* between the motherboard and the frame. Remove these if possible (sometimes they are built into the bottom of the case) and store them in a labeled container. Figure 6-7 illustrates a typical brass standoff installed in a case. Be sure to note their locations! If you install a different motherboard, some of them might need to be moved.

✖ Warning

> Remember to handle the motherboard as you would any printed circuit board: gently, by the edges, as if you were holding a delicate old photograph.

FIGURE 6-7 A motherboard standoff installed in a case

Step 4   Carefully remove the motherboard from the PC case and place it on your antistatic mat. If you are not going to do Lab Exercise 6.05 immediately after this one, place the motherboard inside a large antistatic bag to protect it. For additional protection, put the bagged motherboard inside a motherboard box. (It's a good idea to save boxes from motherboard installations to make this possible.) Be sure to remove the port cluster cover as well. You can push it back into the case from the rear of the system to remove it.

 15 MINUTES

Lab Exercise 6.05: Identifying Motherboard Features

At a glance, one motherboard pretty much looks like any other. Of course, as a PC tech, you know that many differences may exist: Two identical-looking motherboards can have completely different feature sets. Chipsets, bus speed, CPU socket type, and clock speed are just some of the important features that separate one motherboard from another. These differences aren't always obvious, but you can turn to your motherboard book to identify your motherboard's features, as described in the following steps.

Learning Objectives

In this lab, you'll become familiar with different motherboard features.

At the end of this lab, you'll be able to

- Recognize different motherboard features

- Identify the location of motherboard features

Lab Materials and Setup

The materials you need for this lab are

- A motherboard, such as the one you removed in Lab Exercise 6.04

- The motherboard book or online documentation for that motherboard

Getting Down to Business

In the following steps, you'll identify the location of key features on your motherboard.

 Hint

> If you're using the motherboard you removed in the previous lab, take this opportunity to clean any dust off of it, using canned air, before you begin.

FIGURE 6-8 Two examples of model number information printed on motherboards

Step 1 Note the location of the make and model information on the motherboards in Figure 6-8. Compare this to your motherboard and locate the manufacturer name and model number.

✖ Cross-Reference

For details on chipsets, refer to the "Chipset" section of Chapter 6 of *Mike Meyers' CompTIA A+ Guide to Managing and Troubleshooting PCs.*

What is the name of your motherboard manufacturer? _____

What is the model number of your motherboard? _____

What CPU socket do you have on your motherboard? _____

What type of chipset do you have on your motherboard? _____

Keep this information handy! Having the make and model of your motherboard readily available makes it easy to search the Web for drivers and updating the BIOS.

Step 2 Look for any charts or numbers printed on the surface of the motherboard.

Are there any jumper blocks? _____

What are some of the settings that can be configured using jumpers?

_____

_____

_____

Step 3 Find the following on your motherboard and note their locations (use Figure 6-9 as a reference):

System clock battery (if present): _____

BIOS: _____

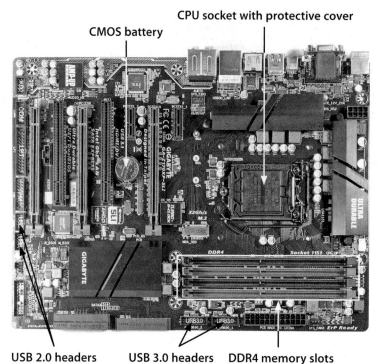

FIGURE 6-9 A typical late-model ATX motherboard

USB 3.0 headers (see Figure 6-10): _____

USB 2.0 headers (see Figure 6-11): _____

FireWire (IEEE 1394) headers*: _____

RAM slots (What type? How many? Dual-channel, triple-channel support, or quad-channel support?): _____

SATA connectors (How many?): _____

PATA (IDE) connectors*: _____

FDD connector*: _____

RAID (if present): _____

FIGURE 6-10 USB 3.0 header detail

FIGURE 6-11 USB 2.0 header detail

Graphics adapter support (onboard, PCI, PCIe? SLI or CrossFire support?): _____

M2 (M.2) SSD support: _____

Parallel port header*: _____

Serial port header*: _____

*Legacy port not common on current systems

 **30 MINUTES**

Lab Exercise 6.06: Installing a Motherboard

Now you get the real test of your tech skills: installing the new motherboard and reconnecting everything so that the computer works again! Don't be intimidated, though. Everything you need to install a motherboard (in your case, probably the motherboard you just removed in Lab Exercise 6.04) is right in front of you.

Learning Objectives

In this lab, you'll install a motherboard. You can use the motherboard and system you disassembled in Lab Exercise 6.04.

At the end of this lab, you'll be able to

- Install a PC motherboard and connect all of its associated components

Lab Materials and Setup

The materials you need for this lab are

- A working system from which the motherboard has been removed

- Components and cables previously connected to the removed motherboard

- The motherboard book or online documentation for the motherboard

- An antistatic mat and antistatic wrist strap
- A notepad and pencil

✔ **Hint**

When installing a motherboard, it's handy to use your notepad to check off assembly steps as you go along.

Getting Down to Business

Physically installing the motherboard itself is mostly a matter of being careful and methodical. The more complex part of the task is reattaching all the cables and cards in their proper places.

✖ **Warning**

Motherboards are full of delicate electronics! Remember to follow the proper ESD avoidance and safety procedures.

Step 1   Carefully place the port cluster cover for the motherboard at the cutout at the back of the case (see Figure 6-12), then line up the motherboard inside the PC case and secure it in place with the mounting screws (see Figure 6-13). Be sure to use the washers and plastic/metal standoffs, if necessary.

Figure 6-12 After the port cluster cover is in place, move the motherboard into place.

FIGURE 6-13 The first screw you install should be into a standoff at the back of the motherboard.

The metal standoffs in the case floor serve a dual purpose: they hold the motherboard off the floor and they serve as receptacles for screws that mount the motherboard in the case. If you are installing a different motherboard than the one you removed, you may need to reposition some of the metal standoffs to account for different screw hole positions in the new board.

✔ **Hint**

Make sure you use the tiny paper washers between the screws and the motherboard when provided. They serve an important purpose. With a metal screw coming so close to metal traces in the motherboard, there's potential for an electrical short under some conditions. (It shouldn't ever happen, but there can be that perfect storm of a trace being particularly close to a screw hole and a screw being slightly misaligned so that it's nearer that trace than it ought to be.) The washers help minimize that risk.

Step 2 Connect the front panel control wires to the motherboard, such as the connectors for the power button, front panel LEDs, and system speaker. Refer to the labels and your motherboard documentation for the proper connections.

Step 3 Connect all power cables to the drives, CPU fan, main motherboard, and so on. Refer to the sketch you made (or photo you took) in Lab Exercise 6.04 of the connections for the front panel LED and button connectors.

Step 4   Connect data cables to the drives, as well as the sound cable and USB connector dongles, if applicable. If you removed the RAM or CPU, reinstall them.

✖   **Warning**

CPUs that use ZIF (zero insertion force) sockets should be installed before the motherboard is reinstalled. Although no force is needed to install the CPU itself, the force needed to install the processor fan and heat sink could crack the motherboard if it is not properly supported in the case.

Step 5   Double-check all of your connections to make sure that they're properly seated and connected where they're supposed to be.

 30 MINUTES

Lab Exercise 6.07: Installing Expansion Cards

There are five steps to installing any expansion card device properly:

1.   Arm yourself with knowledge of the device before you install it. Is the device certified to run on the Windows OS that you're running? Is it compatible with your motherboard and other hardware? Look at the device's spec sheet on the box or on its manufacturer's Web site.

✖   **Warning**

Read the instructions that came with the device, and let those instructions supersede the general ones given here. A few devices want you to install their driver first, *before* installing the card. That can be the case if there is a known problem with using the driver that Windows automatically installs from its own driver set if no other driver is already present, for example.

---

2.   Remove the cover from your PC case and install the device. As always, follow all ESD avoidance and safety precautions and handle the card with care.

3.   Be sure to connect power to the card if needed. Some multiport USB 3.0/3.1, FireWire, and most PCIe video cards use a power connector.

4.   After restarting your computer, install device drivers for the component. Windows includes many drivers, and it may try to install a driver automatically when it detects the device, but that is not always the best driver to stick with. Visit the card manufacturer's Web site, download the latest

drivers for the card and your operating system, and then install the updated drivers. You can also install the card and then use Windows Update with Windows 7/8.1, which may find and download a copy of the latest driver from the manufacturer.

5. Verify that the device is functional.

The following exercise is a somewhat abridged version of this procedure; instead of installing a new device, you'll reinstall the expansion cards that you removed in Lab Exercise 6.03.

✖ **Cross-Reference**

To review the details of device installation, refer to the "Installing Expansion Cards" section in Chapter 6 of *Mike Meyers' CompTIA A+ Guide to Managing and Troubleshooting PCs.*

Learning Objectives

In this lab, you'll practice installing internal expansion cards.

At the end of this lab, you'll be able to

- Install expansion cards in a system correctly and safely

Lab Materials and Setup

The materials you need for this lab are

- At least one working Windows computer that has been disassembled
- The expansion card(s) removed from that computer
- Additional expansion card(s) (optional)
- A Phillips-head screwdriver
- An antistatic mat and wrist strap
- Antistatic storage bags
- A notepad and pencil

Getting Down to Business

After you install a motherboard, or if you are adding cards to an existing system, you will need to install expansion cards to provide features that are not present on the motherboard. You can also install expansion cards that provide more capability (faster networking, 3D video, and so on) than the motherboard's built-in ports.

Step 1   Reinstall into your system the expansion cards you removed. For each card, follow these procedures:

    a.   Check your notes to confirm where to reinstall the card. If you are installing a new card, look over the system to determine which slot is the best choice. Note that you can install a PCIe card into any PCIe slot that has the same or larger connector (for example, a PCIe ×1 card into a PCIe ×8 slot).

→ **Note**

If there are two or more PCIe ×16 slots, use the one nearest to the CPU socket for your primary (or only) video card. Use the additional slots for cards that will be configured for NVIDIA SLI or AMD CrossFire multi-GPU 3D (these slots actually support fewer PCIe lanes and will slow down cards that are not being used for SLI or CrossFire).

    b.   Align the card over its motherboard slot, making sure that the metal bracket is aligned properly with the case opening. Holding the bracket with one hand, place the heel of your hand on the top edge of the card and push the card firmly into the expansion slot.

    c.   Once the card is in the slot and the top of the bracket (also known as a flange) is flush with the case, replace the screw that holds the card in place. Don't be tempted to skip the screw! It keeps the card from working loose over time.

✖ **Warning**

After you have reinstalled all the expansion cards, take a look at the back of your system (where you can see input/output connections for the cards). Are there any openings where no cards are installed and a slot cover has not been used? It's very important to install slot covers wherever an expansion card is not installed. This ensures that air will flow properly through the computer case, keeping your critical components cool. It also keeps out large chunks of dust and hair that can impede airflow and retain heat inside the case.

Step 2   Replace the case cover on your PC, then plug the keyboard, mouse, and monitor back in, plug the power cable back in, and finally turn on the PC. Assuming you've done everything correctly, your system will boot up normally.

 **30 MINUTES**

Lab Exercise 6.08: Exploring Motherboard Features with CPU-Z

Now that you've completed the analysis and upgrade of your client's systems with new motherboards and CPUs where needed, you can verify some of the characteristics and features the motherboard manufacturer has promoted. You already downloaded the CPU-Z utility, so you can launch that to examine the information on the Mainboard tab.

✔ **Hint**

Over the years, motherboards have been called many names—and not just the bad names you might use when one doesn't work properly! Early motherboards were sometimes called the *planar board*. A motherboard can be referred to as the *system board*, *mainboard*, and sometimes just *board* or *mobo*. Regardless of the name, these terms refer to the large printed circuit board (PCB) used to connect all the components in a computer system.

Learning Objectives

In this lab, you'll identify various motherboard features.

At the end of this lab, you'll be able to

- Verify motherboard features

Lab Materials and Setup

The materials you need for this lab are

- Access to a working computer with the CPU-Z utility installed

- A notepad and pencil to document the specifications

- Optional: A word processor or spreadsheet application to facilitate the documentation

---

✔ **Hint**

This lab is more informative if you have access to different systems using various motherboards.

Getting Down to Business

In the following steps, you'll verify the features of your motherboard.

Step 1 Launch CPU-Z and navigate to the Mainboard tab. CPU-Z displays some of the key features of your motherboard, as shown in Figure 6-14.

Step 2 Using the data gathered by CPU-Z, record as much pertinent information as possible:

Manufacturer: _____   Southbridge: _____

Model: _____   BIOS brand: _____

Chipset: _____   Graphic interface version: _____

FIGURE 6-14 CPU-Z displaying motherboard information

Step 3   If possible, launch CPU-Z on various machines to compare the features of different motherboards.

✔ Try This: HWiNFO

Go to www.hwinfo.com and download and install HWiNFO. Launch HWiNFO. Close the System
Summary window and look at the main window. Click the Motherboard item in the left pane to
display detailed information in the right pane of the window.

Using this information, can you determine the integrated devices supported by your motherboard?
Does this correspond to the information in the PC or motherboard documentation? Open nodes in
the left pane for more information about your system. Use the Report menu to create a report.

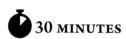 30 MINUTES

Lab Exercise 6.09: Managing Hardware with Device Manager

Windows is capable of utilizing a universe of peripherals and expansion cards—everything from modems to
TV tuners. Management of this massive collection of hardware in Windows is handled by Device Manager.

Device Manager provides a centralized location for dealing with all aspects of a computer's hardware. This includes a simple inventory of all installed devices, notification of malfunctioning devices, and the capability to install and update drivers.

This exercise will cover some of the more useful features of Device Manager.

Learning Objectives

In this lab, you'll use Device Manager to examine and update a system.

At the end of this lab, you'll be able to

- Use Device Manager to examine devices on your system, check for problems, and update drivers

Lab Materials and Setup

The materials you need for this lab are

- A working computer running Windows

- Access to the Internet

✔ **Hint**

As usual, if you have access to more than one system, take advantage of it.

Getting Down to Business

In this exercise, you'll use Device Manager to view the system resource settings on your PC.

Step 1 Do the following to open Device Manager.

a. Open the Control Panel in Windows.

b. Open Device Manager (see Figure 6-15). The procedure depends on your Windows version:

- Windows 7: System and Security | System | Device Manager

- Windows 8.1 and Windows 10: Right-click the Start button and click Device Manager

Step 2 Check for any missing devices, or devices marked with error icons (see Figure 6-16):

- A device marked with a black downward-pointing arrow on a white circle means that the device has been disabled.

- A device marked with a black "?" on a white circle means that Windows does not recognize the device. You might need to run the setup utility that came with the device to correct this problem.

- A device marked with a black exclamation point (!) on a yellow triangle means that there is a problem with the device or with its driver. The driver may be not installed, incorrect, or corrupted, for example.

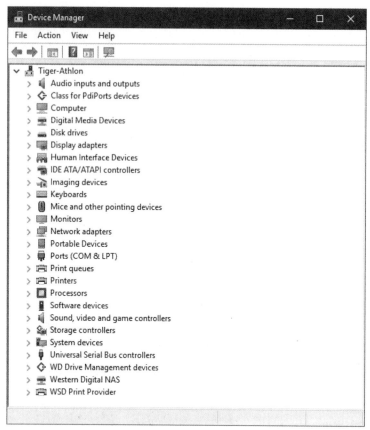

FIGURE 6-15 Device Manager in Windows 10

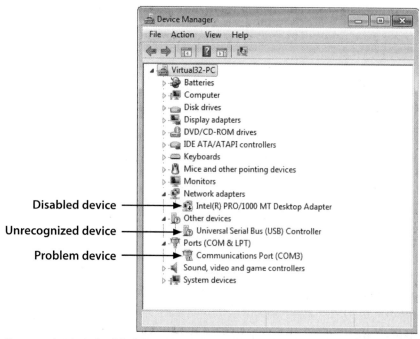

FIGURE 6-16 A disabled device, an unrecognized device, and a problem device in Device Manager (Windows 7; newer versions use similar icons)

If there is a problem with a device, double-click it to open its Properties dialog box, and then look at the status in the Device Status box. Click Cancel to close the dialog box when finished.

Step 3   Download and install the latest device drivers for each of your expansion cards. There are many methods you can use to accomplish this task, but the two that follow are the most common.

If your working PC is connected to the Internet:

a. Double-click the device to open its Properties dialog box, and click the Driver tab.

b. Click Update Driver. This opens a wizard that helps you find new drivers, as shown in Figure 6-17.

c. Click *Search automatically for updated driver software.*

d. Follow the prompts to install any newer drivers found.

If your working PC is *not* connected to the Internet, you'll need to download a driver using another PC and then transfer the downloaded file(s) to the PC that needs them using a USB flash drive.

a. Using a computer with Internet access, find and connect to the manufacturer's Web site.

b. Using the model number of the device, locate and download the correct driver for the operating system on the PC where the device is installed.

c. Save the driver to a USB thumb drive, remove the thumb drive from that system, and insert it into your working PC.

Most driver updates that you download nowadays come with their own setup program, and are downloaded as an executable file. If that's the case, then you just run the executable to install the driver update; you don't have to go through Device Manager.

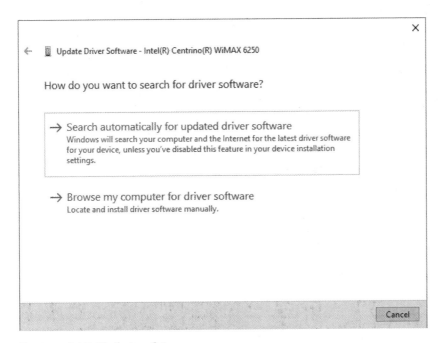

FIGURE 6-17   Updating drivers

In the odd case where you've downloaded bare driver files, and not an executable, here's how to install the update:

a.   Open Device Manager.

b.   Double-click the device that matches the expansion card you have installed.

c.   Click the Driver tab, and then click Update Driver.

d.   When prompted to connect to the Internet, choose *Browse my computer for driver software*, and follow the directions to locate and load the new device driver.

Lab Analysis Test

1.   Jonathan is building a system using an Intel Core i3 processor, and he's purchased a new motherboard from ASUS. He would like to use an old (but working!) ATX power supply he has lying around to power the system. Why might this *not* be a good idea?

2.   John has a system that uses a PCIe ×16 video card that has only one port. He wants to add another monitor. Can he add another PCIe ×16 display adapter? If so, what does he need to watch out for when purchasing and installing an adapter? If not, what could he do instead to get multi-monitor support?

3.   Dianne is trying to install an ATX motherboard in a new, empty ATX case. She tries to set it down in the bottom of the case, but it won't fit—the ports on the side are too low to poke out the back of the case, and she can't make the screws work at all. What has she forgotten?

4.   After Erik reassembled his PC and turned it on, he noticed that the green LED and the disk active LED never light up, but everything seems to work okay. What is the problem?

5.   You've installed a new PCIe ×1 NIC on Susan's Windows 10 system. The system starts up fine, but when you check Device Manager, you see a black exclamation point inside a yellow triangle beside the NIC icon. What is the problem?

Key Term Quiz

Use the following terms to complete the following sentences. Not all terms will be used.

ATX	mini-ITX
driver	PCI
expansion cards	PCI Express
lanes	PCIe
microATX	standoffs

1. The length of a PCIe expansion slot is directly related to the number of _____ it supports.

2. If a device isn't working properly, look in Device Manager to see whether there is a problem with its _____.

3. The _____ bus provides for ×1, ×2, ×4, ×8, and ×16 lanes of bidirectional communication, but in practice, most systems use only ×1 and ×16.

4. _____ are spacers that hold the motherboard slightly off the floor of the PC case.

5. One motherboard design, known for its lower power-consumption characteristics and small size, is called _____.

Chapter 7

Power Supplies

Lab Exercises

The power supply in a PC has two important functions: it converts the alternating current (AC) from the wall outlet to direct current (DC), and it supplies that direct current to the various components of the PC in varying voltages, stepping down the voltage as needed.

In a desktop PC, that big metal power supply box inside the case handles these functions, and parses out power to the components via sets of connectors and multicolored wires. In a notebook PC, the power transformation function is handled by the transformer block (the big black brick) built into the power cord, and the delivery of various DC voltages to components is handled through the motherboard or through tiny wires and connectors inside the case.

This lab focuses on the power supplies of desktop PCs, because they're more standardized (so we can make some assumptions about the system you are working with), and because most of the CompTIA A+ 1001 exam questions about power assume a desktop system.

As a PC technician, you need to be able to identify the connector types on a modern desktop power supply, along with their voltages. You should be able to test a connector wire-by-wire to ensure it is delivering correct voltages. You should also know how to remove and replace a power supply, and understand the factors involved in selecting a power supply for a new system or as a replacement.

Suppose a client calls you saying that her PC keeps locking up. After walking her through a few simple troubleshooting steps, you rule out a virus or a misbehaving application. This leaves hardware as the likely culprit, and in all likelihood, it's the power supply. In these lab exercises, you'll practice the procedures for measuring power going to the PC, testing the PC's power supply, selecting a replacement power supply, and swapping out the old for the new. You'll also do some research on power protection options, to help your client's PCs stay reliably powered.

✔ **Hint**

The CompTIA A+ certification exams show their American roots in the area of electrical power. Watch for power questions that discuss American power standards—especially ones related to household voltage (120 volts, 60 Hz) and outlet plug design. The exams will also typically refer to the power supply using the abbreviation PSU (power supply unit) or the acronym FRU (field replaceable unit). FRU can describe any component that would be replaced in the field by a technician.

 **30 MINUTES**

Lab Exercise 7.01: Measuring AC Voltage Levels

When troubleshooting a power issue, it's best to not make any assumptions, but to start from the wall outlet and ensure that it is delivering the correct voltage of AC power. If the wall outlet isn't working right, no amount of fiddling with the PC is going to help.

✖ **Cross-Reference**

For details on AC power from the power company, refer to the "Supplying AC" section in Chapter 7 of *Mike Meyers' CompTIA A+ Guide to Managing and Troubleshooting PCs.*

Learning Objectives

This lab exercise shows how to check power at its local source: at the AC wall outlet. This is where troubleshooting a power problem should begin.

At the end of this lab, you'll be able to

- Determine if the AC wiring is correct at a wall outlet
- Determine if the AC voltages are correct at a wall outlet

Lab Materials and Setup

The materials you need for this lab are

- An AC electrical outlet tester
- A multimeter

Getting Down to Business

Measuring the voltage coming from an AC outlet is a nerve-wracking task even for experienced techs! Sticking objects into a live power outlet goes against everything you've been taught since infancy, but when done properly, it's completely safe.

Use common sense and appropriate safety procedures. If you're not familiar with using a multimeter, please review the "Supplying AC" section in Chapter 7 of *Mike Meyers' CompTIA A+ Guide to Managing and Troubleshooting PCs* or ask your instructor for a demonstration.

Step 1   Look at Figure 7-1 and compare it to your electrical outlet.

A typical electrical socket has three openings: hot, neutral, and ground. The hot wire delivers the electrical power. The neutral wire acts as a drain and returns electricity to the local source (the breaker panel). The semi-rounded ground socket returns excess electricity to the ground. If your outlet doesn't have a ground socket—and outlets in many older buildings don't—then don't use it! Ungrounded outlets aren't appropriate for PCs.

✖ Warning

> Take all appropriate safety precautions before measuring live electrical outlets. In a classroom, you have the benefit of an instructor to show you how to do these exercises the first time. If you're doing these on your own with no experience, seek the advice of a trained technician, electrician, or instructor.

FIGURE 7-1 A typical AC electrical outlet

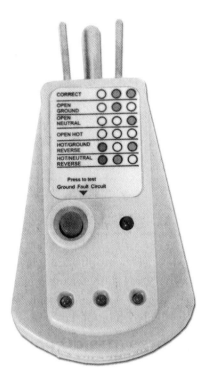

FIGURE 7-2 A circuit tester for AC electrical outlets

Step 2 Determine whether or not your electrical socket is "live." Do this with your electrical outlet tester. Plug your outlet tester (see Figure 7-2) into the electrical outlet or power strip where you plug in the PC. Look at the LED indicators. Are they showing good power? If the tester indicates that you have a missing ground or that the polarity is reversed, it's time to call in an electrician to rewire or replace the outlet.

Step 3 Now measure the voltage between the hot and neutral openings of the outlet. Start by setting your multimeter to AC voltage; do not proceed until you're sure you have done this correctly! If you aren't sure, ask your instructor for guidance. Referring to Figure 7-3, take the black probe and place it in the neutral opening (larger slot) of the wall socket. Make sure you have good contact inside the outlet. The metal probe tip must contact the metal connector inside the outlet.

Next, place the red probe inside the hot opening (smaller slot). Again, you must make good metal-to-metal contact. You may have to reposition the probes to get a good connection and proper reading for the AC circuit. Your reading should be somewhere between 110 and 120 V.

What is your reading? _____

Step 4 Measure the voltage in the hot-to-ground circuit. Place the black probe into the ground opening of the outlet, as shown in Figure 7-4. Make sure you have good contact. Then place the red probe into the hot opening. Move the probes around until you get a good reading for the AC voltage. Again, your reading should be in the 110- to 120-V range.

What is your reading? _____

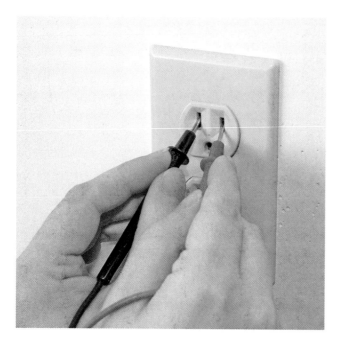

FIGURE 7-3 Multimeter probe locations when testing an AC outlet's hot-to-neutral circuit

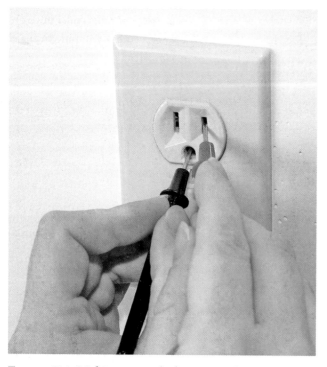

FIGURE 7-4 Multimeter probe locations when testing an AC outlet's hot-to-ground circuit

FIGURE 7-5 Multimeter probe locations when testing an AC outlet's neutral-to-ground circuit

Step 5   The last measurement you need to take is the voltage in the neutral-to-ground safety circuit. When the neutral wire is broken or missing, the ground wire is the only way for wayward electrons to depart safely. Any electricity on both the neutral and ground wires should have a direct path back to earth, so there should be no voltage between these wires.

Place the black probe into the ground opening of the outlet. Make sure you have good contact. Place the red probe into the neutral opening (refer to Figure 7-5). Move the probes around until you get a good reading for the AC voltage. You should get a reading of 0 V.

What is your reading? _____

Step 6   Measure another outlet in the same building, and repeat the previous steps. Are the readings similar? If the readings from your electrical outlets are outside of the ranges described, it's time to call an electrician. Assuming your reading is showing good power, go to the next exercise.

 **30 MINUTES**

Lab Exercise 7.02: Testing Power Supply Output

Once you've determined that the AC power going to your client's PC is good, you need to test whether the DC power traveling from the power supply to the rest of her system is good.

Learning Objectives

At the end of this lab, you'll be able to

- Identify the connectors of a PC power supply

- Measure the output of a PC power supply

Lab Materials and Setup

The materials you need for this lab are

- An ATX power supply

- A multimeter

- A PC power supply tester

- Optional: A working PC with an ATX power supply

Getting Down to Business

There are two ways to determine whether a power supply is providing the proper voltages to the components of the computer. One is the traditional method, using a multimeter to measure the actual voltages. Another method growing in popularity is the use of a PC power supply tester.

✖ Cross-Reference

For details on DC power from the power supply, refer to the "Supplying DC" section in Chapter 7 of *Mike Meyers' CompTIA A+ Guide to Managing and Troubleshooting PCs*.

METHOD 1: USING A MULTIMETER

In the following steps, you'll measure DC voltage coming from the PC power supply. The three places to measure power supply output are at the Molex power connectors, the SATA power connectors, and the motherboard power connectors. Molex power connectors plug into devices that need 5 or 12 volts of power. On older computers, these were used for PATA hard drives and PATA optical drives. SATA power connectors connect to SATA hard drives and optical drives. On most modern systems, the power supply will provide two motherboard power connectors: a main 24-pin P1 connector (old systems used a 20-pin P1 connector) and a smaller connector with 4 pins (P4) or 8 pins (EPS12V). Figure 7-6 shows a 24-pin P1 and a dual 4-pin power

FIGURE 7-6 Motherboard power connectors: P4 (left) and P1 (right)

connector; use one as P4 or use both on motherboards that use the EPS12V 8-pin power connector. (There may also be a 6-pin or 8-pin PCIe power connector that is used to power some video cards.)

You'll then plug the P1 power connector into a PC power supply tester and verify that the readings you measured with the multimeter are within tolerance. The power supply tester has LEDs that will glow green for each of the voltages that it passes.

✖ **Warning**

> **Although the power coming out of the PC power supply is considerably less lethal than that coming directly out of the electrical outlet, you should still take all appropriate safety precautions before taking measurements.**

To gauge whether or not a wire is delivering the correct voltage, you need to know what its voltage should be, obviously. Generally speaking, wire color indicates its expected voltage (note that some power supplies use the same color for all wires). Table 7-1 summarizes the most important wire colors to know. The positive voltages should be within 5 percent of their ideal voltage, and the negative voltages must be within 10 percent. Black (ground) wires should always be exactly zero.

✔ **Tip**

> **Negative voltages being out of tolerance are unlikely to cause any problems on a modern system, because most devices don't use them, so it's okay to skip testing the negative voltage wires in most cases. Some power supplies don't include –5-V wires.**

Wire Color	Ideal Voltage	Acceptable Tolerance
Black	0	0
Orange	+3.3 V	+3.135 V to +3.465 V
Red or Purple	+5 V	+4.750 V to +5.250 V
White	–5 V	–4.500 V to –5.500 V
Yellow	+12 V	+11.400 V to +12.600 V
Blue	–12 V	–10.800 V to –13.200 V

TABLE 7-1 Common Wire Colors and Their Voltages

✖ Warning

Some Dell systems use proprietary power supplies that use different pinouts than those shown in Table 7-1. Depending on the unit, it might be possible to use an adapter cable to enable a standard 24-pin ATX power supply to work (check www.moddiy.com or www.amazon.com), or the user might need to purchase a Dell-specific replacement.

Step 1   Make sure you can identify each of the connectors on a power supply, including its name, its appearance, and what it is used for.

Name: _____

Usage: _____

Name: _____

Usage: _____

Name: _____

Usage: _____

Name: _____

Usage: _____

Name: _____

Usage: _____

Step 2   Set the multimeter to read DC voltage. Find a Molex connector that's not being used for a device. If no Molex connectors are unused, turn the system off and disconnect the one from the optical drive, and then turn the PC back on. If your power supply is modular (one in which you can connect various combinations of power cables), but you don't have a Molex power cable connected, turn the system off, connect a Molex power cable, and turn the PC back on.

Do you have a free Molex connector? _____

If not, which device did you unplug? _____

Do you have a modular power supply? _____

Step 3 Referring to Figure 7-7, place the black probe into either one of the holes on the Molex connector that is aligned with a black wire. Now place the red probe into each of the other three holes of the Molex connector in turn, first the other black wire, then the red, then yellow, and record your findings. Refer to Table 7-1 to determine whether a reading was within tolerance.

Black wire to black wire: _____ V

Black wire to red wire: _____ V   Within tolerance? _____

Black wire to yellow wire: _____ V   Within tolerance? _____

✔ **Tip**

> If your power supply uses all black wires, look carefully at Figure 7-7. With the connector oriented as in Figure 7-7 (tapered edges of the connector upright), the leftmost wire from the front is the +12-V DC line. The next two lines as ground (GND). The rightmost wire from the front is the +5-V DC line.

Step 4 Measuring the voltage from the motherboard connector is a little trickier. Leave the power connector plugged into the motherboard, turn on the computer, and push the probes into the end of the connector that the wires run into. You must push the probe deep enough to touch the metal contact pins, but be careful not to push too deeply or you might push the pin out of the connector. This method of measuring power is sometimes referred to as back-probing.

Figure 7-7 Measuring the voltage on the +12-V line in a Molex connector

Push the black probe into the motherboard connector alongside any black wire, and leave it there. Insert the red probe into each of the other wires, and record your findings. Depending on your motherboard connector, you may not have all of these wires. Refer to Table 7-1 for the acceptable tolerance for each wire.

Black wire to red wire: _____ V   Within tolerance? _____

Black wire to yellow wire: _____ V   Within tolerance? _____

Black wire to purple wire: _____ V   Within tolerance? _____

Black wire to white wire: _____ V   Within tolerance? _____

Black wire to blue wire: _____ V   Within tolerance? _____

Many aftermarket power supplies today use a single wire color (usually black) for all wires. Use Figure 7-8 as a guide to back-probing power supplies that don't use color-coded wires. The connector diagrams provide the top view of each connector, illustrating how the wires are laid out after each connector is plugged into the motherboard.

✔ Hint

A single reading from a power supply may not be enough to pinpoint a power-related problem. Sometimes a power problem becomes evident only when the power supply is placed under a heavier-than-normal load, such as burning a CD or DVD. Also, some RAM-related errors mimic a failing power supply.

METHOD 2: USING A POWER SUPPLY TESTER

The other method to verify that the power supply is operating properly and supplying all the voltages within tolerance is to use a power supply tester. There are many styles of PSU testers on the market, so make sure you follow the specific directions included with your tester as you complete the steps.

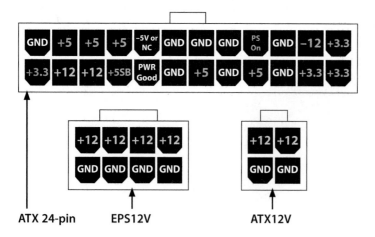

FIGURE 7-8 Standard pinouts and voltage levels for 24-pin ATX, ATX12V, and EPS12V connectors (top view)

Step 1   Starting with the P1 connector, follow the directions for connecting it to your specific PSU tester. Verify that all of the voltages provided through the P1 connector are acceptable (usually an LED will light to verify voltage present and within tolerance).

Did it light up or display an acceptable voltage? _____

✔ **Hint**

> When connecting and disconnecting the power supply connectors, always take care to insert the connector with the proper orientation. Most power connectors are keyed to make it difficult to install the connector backward, but if you use excessive force, you may be able to insert the connector improperly. This applies to powering the motherboard, plugging in devices, and even using the PSU tester.

Step 2   Now, depending on your tester and power supply, plug the 4-pin, 6-pin, or 7-pin auxiliary connector into the appropriate socket on the PSU tester and verify the voltages provided through this connector. Once they are verified, remove the connector from the socket.

Did it light up or display an acceptable voltage? _____

Step 3   Plug the Molex connector into the PSU tester and verify the voltages provided through this connector. Once they are verified, remove the connector from the socket.

Did it light up or display an acceptable voltage? _____

Step 4   Plug the SATA HDD power connector into the appropriate socket and verify the voltages provided through this connector. Once they are verified, remove the connector from the socket.

Did it light up or display an acceptable voltage? _____

Step 5   Finally, if your power supply has one, plug the mini floppy drive power connector (also known as the Berg connector) into the PSU tester and verify the voltages provided through this connector. Once they are verified, remove the connector from the socket and remove the P1 from the socket.

Did it light up or display an acceptable voltage? _____

 40 MINUTES

Lab Exercise 7.03: Choosing a Power Supply

Suppose you need to choose a power supply for a new system you are building, or replace the power supply in an existing system. You'll want to take the wattage requirements of the components into consideration when deciding which model to select, as well as the form factor (physical size), the number of connectors, and any special features.

Learning Objectives

At the end of this lab, you'll be able to

- Determine the total wattage requirements of the system

- Explain other factors involved in power supply selection

Lab Materials and Setup

The materials you need for this lab are

- A calculator (optional)

- A notebook, or a word processing or spreadsheet program in which to take notes

- A desktop PC (need not be working)

- A PC or mobile device with Internet connectivity

Getting Down to Business

One of the areas where PC manufacturers cut corners on lower-end systems is power supplies. High-end systems typically come with higher-wattage power supplies, whereas entry-level PCs typically have lower-wattage power supplies. You might not notice it until you add power-hungry components to the system, placing a heavier load on the power supply and causing an early failure.

Other features also factor into power supply selection, such as the number and type of connectors, multiple rails, and active power factor correction (active PFC).

In the following steps, you'll determine the wattage of the power supply on your system and calculate the power usage of your PC. Then you'll shop online to identify a replacement power supply that will meet the needs of the system.

Step 1   To determine the wattage rating of your power supply, remove the case cover and look at the label on the power supply (see Figure 7-9).

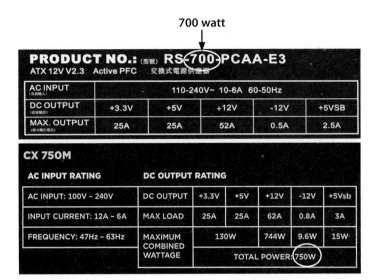

FIGURE 7-9 Typical ATX power supply ratings labels

Locate the watts rating. If you don't see a clear wattage rating as shown in Figure 7-9, or if you see something less evident, like the smaller "750W" marking on the label, the power supply rating may be hidden in the model number, which for the first power supply shown in Figure 7-9 is RS-700-PCAA-E3 (700 watt).

✔ **Hint**

All power supplies have a wattage rating. If it is not apparent on the power supply itself, search the Internet using the model number for reference.

What is the wattage of your power supply? _____

Step 2   When it comes time to replace a power supply, don't skimp on the wattage! As a general rule, get the highest-wattage replacement you can afford while maintaining compatibility with your system. Remember, the system will draw only the current it requires, so you will never damage a system by installing a higher-wattage power supply.

✖ **Warning**

Never replace a PC's power supply with one of lower wattage!

Use the following table to calculate the overall wattage needed for your system. Add the numbers for each component and determine the lowest and highest wattage requirements.

Component	Requirement	Voltage(s) Used
Video card • More powerful cards use more wattage. • Look up a card's power consumption at the manufacturer's Web site, and pay attention to which voltages it uses.	60 to 350 W	Depends on card, mostly 12 V on modern systems
PCIe expansion card	×1: 10 W ×4, ×7, and ×16: 25 W	3.3 V and 12 V
Solid-state drive	0.6 to 2.7 W	5 V
Hard disk drive	2.5" HDD 0.7 to 3 W 3.5" HDD 6.5 to 9 W	5 V and 12 V
Optical drive	SATA DVD 15 to 27 W SATA Blu-ray 25 to 30 W	5 V and 12 V
Case/CPU fans	0.5 to 6 W each	12 V
Motherboard (without CPU or RAM)	25–40 W	3.3 V and 5 V
RAM	(per stick) DDR1 (2.5 V) 5.5 W DDR2 (1.7 V) 4.5 W DDR3 (1.5 V) 3 W DDR4 (1.2 V) 2.4 W	3.3 V
CPU Visit the CPU vendor's Web site, or use tables at http://tinyurl.com/q9j73ow for exact number for your CPU. Examples: Intel Core i5-5257U Intel Core i7-6800K Intel Core i9-9900K AMD FX-8350 AMD Ryzen 7 1800X AMD Ryzen Threadripper 1950X	Varies, 55 to 150 W 28 W 140 W 95 W 125 W 95 W 180 W	12 V

Use the Expert version of the Extreme OuterVision Power Supply Calculator at https://outervision.com/power-supply-calculator as an additional resource. This calculator takes into account power usage by fans, liquid cooling, specific CPU models, specific video card/GPUs, and more.

If the highest total exceeds the power supply wattage rating, you may run into problems. When selecting a new power supply, you should multiply the load by a factor of 1.5. The multiplier provides a safety factor, allows the power supply to run more efficiently, and helps account for some devices drawing more power at startup. Many power supplies are more efficient at 30 to 70 percent of their full capacity rating. Thus, a 450-W PSU works best when only 135 to 315 watts are being used.

What wattage is appropriate for your system? _____

Step 3 Shop online to find a power supply with adequate wattage for your PC. Pay special attention to the 12-V rail, as this is likely where you will run into a shortfall on an inadequate power supply. Make sure the power supply you choose

- Uses active PFC

- Reaches at least 80 percent efficiency at up to 100 percent of rated load

- Is the appropriate form factor for the case

- Has enough drive connectors, of the correct types, to service all the system's drives, plus a few more for expansion

- Has the correct connectors to supply the motherboard's power needs, including any 12-V auxiliary connectors

➔ **Note**

Power supplies rated 80 PLUS are supposed to provide at least 80 percent efficiency at up to 100 percent of rated load. 80 PLUS Bronze-, Silver-, Gold-, Platinum-, and Titanium-rated power supplies provide even higher efficiencies. To learn more about 80 PLUS, go to www.plugloadsolutions.com/80PlusPowerSupplies.aspx. Keep in mind that 80 PLUS relies on vendor honesty, so check third-party test results for a specific 80 PLUS-rated power supply to make sure it lives up to its labeling.

Locate at least two different power supplies that will meet your needs. Write their specifications here.

Power Supply 1:

_____

_____

_____

Power Supply 2:

_____

_____

_____

 **30 MINUTES**

Lab Exercise 7.04: Replacing a Power Supply

Next to replacing the motherboard, the power supply is the most time-consuming component to replace, simply because of all those wires! Nonetheless, replacing the power supply is a simple operation, as described in this exercise. In a real-life situation you would replace the old power supply with the new one, but for this exercise you'll be removing the existing power supply and then putting it back in.

Learning Objectives

At the end of this lab, you'll be able to

- Replace a power supply

Lab Materials and Setup

The materials you need for this lab are

- A non-production PC with an ATX power supply

- A Phillips-head screwdriver

- A labeled container for holding screws

✔ **Hint**

> Depending on the design of your PC case, you may have to remove data cables or components before you can get to the power supply. Make certain that you have plenty of room to work inside the case!

Getting Down to Business

Replacing a power supply is one of the simpler PC repairs. First you disconnect the old one, including unplugging its connectors and removing it from the case. Then you secure the new one in the case and attach its wires to the components that need power.

Step 1   Shut down the system and remove the power cable from the back of the power supply. Then remove the power supply.

   a.   Disconnect the Molex, SATA, and mini connectors from your drive or fan devices, then unplug the P1 power connector from the motherboard.

   b.   Disconnect the P4 and/or other auxiliary connector(s) from the motherboard.

   c.   Unscrew the four screws holding the power supply onto the PC case (remembering to support it while you remove the last one), and remove the power supply from the case. Store the screws in the labeled container.

Was your power supply mounted to the top or bottom of your PC case? _____

Step 2   Take this opportunity to inspect and clean the power supply. Check for any rust or corrosion on the power supply casing or on any of the contacts. Inspect the wires for damage or frayed insulation. Use canned air (outside!) to blow dust and dirt out of the intake and exhaust vents.

✔ **Tip**

> Don't blow the dirt further into the power supply by pointing the air directly into a vent; angle the air so it blows the dirt away.

Step 3   Reinstall the power supply by performing the preceding steps in reverse order. If you had to remove data cables or other components to get at the power supply, be sure to reattach them.

When you've finished reinstalling the power supply, have your instructor or a knowledgeable tech sign off on it here: _____

 **20 MINUTES**

Lab Exercise 7.05: Understanding Power Protection

You've successfully fixed your client's power-problem-plagued PC (say that five times fast), but now you've noted that she has nothing in the way of power protection for her system, nor do any of her coworkers. None!

When you mention this to her, she tells you that her boss never really saw the point of spending money on surge protectors, uninterruptible power supplies, or any of "that stuff." With a straight face, she asks, "Do those things really do any good?"

Now it's your task to sell the boss on the idea of power protection. To do this, you must explain the types of power problems that lurk in the bushes just waiting to pounce on unwary users without power protection, and suggest precautions that they can take to prevent power-related damage.

Learning Objectives

At the end of this lab, you'll be able to

- Explain the need for power protection
- Explain the types of power protection available for a PC

✖ Cross-Reference

For details on power protection, refer to the "Protecting the PC from Spikes and Sags in AC Power" section in Chapter 7 of *Mike Meyers' CompTIA A+ Guide to Managing and Troubleshooting PCs.*

Lab Materials and Setup

The materials you need for this lab are

- A working PC

Getting Down to Business

Too often, PC users take for granted the electricity that powers their system. After all, there's not much you can do about the electricity, is there? Not so! Armed with the knowledge of the types of power conditions that can affect your PC, you can best determine what precautions to take.

Step 1 Describe the following types of power conditions and the types of damage they can cause.

Power spike:

Brownout:

_____

_____

Blackout:

_____

_____

Step 2   Describe the following types of power protection equipment.

Surge suppressor:

_____

_____

Online uninterruptible power supply (UPS):

_____

_____

Standby UPS:

_____

_____

Lab Analysis Test

1. Your client calls you and says that her PC is unusually quiet and keeps rebooting for no apparent reason. What should you ask her to check?

2. Athena lives in an area where the power is often interrupted. She bought a good surge protector strip, but that does not seem to help. What does she need to prevent her system from shutting down unexpectedly?

3. Your assistant technician calls you and says he suspects a bad power supply in one of your client's systems. He said the multimeter readings are 12.4 volts for the +12-V rail and 4.15 volts for the +5-V rail. What should he do?

4. One of your clients has a basic, older PC with a 300-W power supply. He wants to upgrade to a high-end video card, and has found one that will fit in the same slot as his existing card on the motherboard. What concerns would you have about this, and how would you suggest he proceed?

5. Approximately how many watts would the power supply for this system need?

   - AMD Ryzen 5 2600X CPU

   - 16-GB DDR4 RAM (2 sticks)

   - Solid-state drive

   - Blu-ray optical drive

   - AMD Radeon RX 580

6. Research the video card's specifications from question 5. What type of PCI Express supplementary power connector(s) would the power supply be required to have in order for this card to work in the system?

Key Term Quiz

Use the following terms to complete the following sentences. Not all terms will be used.

3.3 V	P4
5 V	P7/P9
12 V	power sags
20-pin P1	power spikes
24-pin P1	power supply
EPS12V	UPS
Molex connector	

1. The ATX 12-V 2.0 power supply plugs into the motherboard using the _____ connector(s).

2. PC devices with motors, such as hard drives and optical drives, usually require _____ of DC electricity from the power supply.

3. The 8-pin connector that provides additional 12-V power to the motherboard is the _____.

4. A surge protector prevents damage from _____ in the voltage.

5. For the best protection against power problems, connect your PC to a(n) _____.

Chapter 8
Mass Storage Technologies

Lab Exercises

Goodbye jumpers! Hard drives used to be a lot more complicated to install and configure than they are today. Nowadays, the dominance of the SATA interface and solid-state storage technology makes mass storage fairly quick to install and usually painless to configure. The CompTIA A+ 1001 exam objectives reflect the sea change in mass storage, removing the bugaboo of IDE and SCSI settings and CMOS configuration of drives that used to plague both certification candidates and on-the-job technicians and adding the new M.2 form factor for SSDs.

Every tech must know how to connect, configure, maintain, and troubleshoot hard drives of all types. In this chapter's labs, you will practice installing internal SATA hard drives, determine if a system supports M.2 SSDs, and select an appropriate external hard drive for a system. You'll do some research to compare solid-state drives and magnetic hard drives, explore RAID options, and troubleshoot problems with hard drive installations. Finally, you'll install several hard drives in preparation for a RAID lab in the next chapter. You'll work with the software aspects of all hard drives—partitioning, formatting, and running drive utilities—in Chapter 9.

 60 MINUTES

Lab Exercise 8.01: Installing Serial ATA Hard Drives

If you've been working around PCs for many years, you probably recall the configuration hell that was parallel ATA (PATA), the interface that hard drives used for decades. Masters, slaves, cable select, jumper tables, red lines on ribbon cables, 40-wire versus 80-wire cables, CMOS setup...ugh. Fortunately, there's none of that mess with SATA.

Installing SATA hard drives is a simple matter of plugging in the data and power cables to the drive and then attaching the other end of the data cable to the SATA controller card or motherboard connection. In this lab exercise, you'll practice taking out a drive and putting it back in again.

Learning Objectives

This lab is designed to introduce you to the three current flavors of internal SATA and walk you through the straightforward installation.

At the end of this lab, you'll be able to

- Explain key features of SATA 1.0, SATA 2.0, and SATA 3.0

- Install a SATA hard drive

Lab Materials and Setup

The materials you need for this lab are

- A PC with an onboard SATA host adapter and a SATA hard drive

Getting Down to Business

To start, you'll review the features and specifications of SATA; not all SATA drives are created equal, and it pays to know what you have (and what you want to have). Then you'll remove and reinstall a SATA drive.

✖ **Cross-Reference**

> **To help in answering the following questions, reference the "SATA" section in Chapter 8 of**
> *Mike Meyers' CompTIA A+ Guide to Managing and Troubleshooting PCs.*

Step 1   Using your reference materials, review the features and specifications of SATA hard drive technology. Then answer these questions:

A.   What is the speed of data transfer for SATA 1.0 drives? _____

B.   What is the speed of data transfer for SATA 2.0 drives? _____

C.   What is the speed of data transfer for SATA 3.0 drives? _____

D.   What is the speed of data transfer for SATA 3.2 (SATAe) drives? _____

E.   What is the maximum length of a SATA cable? _____

F.   How many wires are in a SATA cable? _____

G.   How many drives can a single SATA cable support? _____

Step 2   It's time to get working with some SATA drives. Shut down your system and remove the system cover, following proper ESD avoidance procedures.

FIGURE 8-1 Removing the SATA data cable

Step 3 Disconnect the data cable(s) from the SATA hard drive(s), as shown in Figure 8-1. Grasp the cable as closely as possible to the connector on the drive and pull, rocking the connector gently from side to side.

Disconnect the power supply from the SATA drive(s) by unplugging the SATA connector(s).

Step 4 Now look at the motherboard connections and note the orientation of the connectors. Disconnect the data cables from the motherboard, being careful but firm. Grasp the cable as closely as possible to the connector on the motherboard and pull, rocking the connector gently from side to side.

Lay the cables aside for later reinstallation.

Step 5 Look at the SATA connectors on your motherboard (see Figure 8-2). Depending on the motherboard, they might face upward or stick out from the front edge of the motherboard, or both.

How many SATA connectors do you see on your motherboard? _____

FIGURE 8-2 The SATA connectors on a motherboard

FIGURE 8-3 Some high-performance systems have SATAe ports.

Look closely at your motherboard and see if you can find writing on the board next to the SATA connectors. Are the interfaces grouped into pairs? Are any of them dedicated to special configurations such as RAID? Do you have any SATAe (SATA Express) ports (see Figure 8-3)? A SATAe port can be used with a single SATAe storage device or with two SATA storage devices.

If your motherboard has any SATAe connectors, how many does it have? _____

Step 6   Remove the hard drive from the system, note the type of screws you removed, and store the screws for safekeeping. Be sure to use proper ESD procedures when removing the drive from your system.

Because of the variety of cases, caddies, bays, slots, and so on, it's not possible to give detailed instructions here on how to remove the drive from your particular system. Look closely for caddy releases or retaining screws. Close inspection and a little logic will usually make it clear how to remove the drive. Make notes of how the drive comes out; you'll have to reinstall it later.

Step 7   With the hard drive out of the system and on a static-free surface, ground yourself, pick up the drive, and examine it carefully.

Note its dimensions; it should measure about 6" × 3.5" × 1". The bottom of the drive contains the hard drive controller, and the top of the drive is normally labeled with the drive's specifications.

Write down all the information on the label. Be sure to include the manufacturer and the model number for future reference.

_____

_____

_____

Leave the system case off to verify that everything is working properly and to facilitate later exercises.

Step 8   Power up the PC and boot into Windows. Windows should start normally. If it doesn't, turn to Lab Exercise 8.05, "Troubleshooting Hard Drive Installations."

 30 MINUTES

Lab Exercise 8.02: Choosing External Hard Drives

In the not-so-distant past, external hard drives were not commonly used for everyday operations because the interfaces available for them were not fast enough to compete with internal HDD interfaces. External hard drives were used primarily for storing backups and dumping data off of the internal hard drives. Nowadays, however, newer and faster external interfaces are available that make external hard drives a more attractive option.

In this lab exercise, you will research the options available for a customer who would like an external hard drive, and make a recommendation.

Learning Objectives

This lab explores the differences between various external hard drive interfaces and the ports they use.

At the end of this lab, you'll be able to

- List the possible interfaces for an external hard drive

- Identify the port required for each interface and determine whether a particular PC has that port

Lab Materials and Setup

The materials you need for this lab are

- A computer with Internet access

Getting Down to Business

Your customer wants to store a collection of high-definition videos on an external hard drive and be able to play clips directly from that drive without transferring them back to his PC. In order to do that, you know that he will need a drive interface that's fairly high-speed, so that there won't be any playback delays. You'll research the external drives available and their prices and interfaces; then you'll take a look at his computer to find out which interfaces he already has. If the port needed isn't present, you'll recommend a controller card to add that port.

Step 1   First, let's rate the current external hard drive interface options in terms of their maximum speeds. Complete Table 8-1, gathering the specs as needed from online research and/or from *Mike Meyers' CompTIA A+ Guide to Managing and Troubleshooting PCs.*

Interface	Maximum Throughput/sec
eSATA based on SATA 2.0	
USB 2.0	
USB 3.0 (aka USB 3.1 Gen 1)	
USB 3.1 Gen 2	

TABLE 8-1 External Hard Drive Interfaces

→ **Note**

What about a USB Type-C port? Depending upon the system, a USB Type-C port might support USB 3.1 Gen 1/USB 3.0 or USB 3.1 Gen 2 speeds. Check system documentation to see which speed it supports.

→ **Note**

What about Thunderbolt ports? Thunderbolt ports are standard on recent macOS computers, but are rare on Windows PCs. Thunderbolt port support must be built into a PC's motherboard, so you cannot retrofit a Thunderbolt port to a system that doesn't have motherboard support for it. Thunderbolt 1 runs at 10 Gbps (the same speed as USB 3.1 Gen 2) and Thunderbolt 2 runs at 20 Gbps. Both use the same physical connector as Mini DisplayPort (mDP), but the ports are not interchangeable. Thunderbolt 3 runs at 40 Gbps, using the same physical connector as USB Type-C. Thunderbolt cables are usually identified with a single lightning-bolt icon.

Step 2   Circle and label the photos that represent the three fastest interfaces from Step 1. These are the ports you will look for on your client's PC.

A. _____

B. _____

C. _____

D. _____

E. _____

Step 3   You check your client's PC and find that he has only USB 2.0 ports on his PC. You therefore recommend that he install a controller card with the needed port to give him the fastest performance. Which type of port will you add to his system? Before finishing this step, move ahead to Step 4 and verify that drives are available to connect to the fastest interface. If not, look at the fastest interface for which drives are available, and recommend that one. Write your answer here:

Step 4   Using a site such as www.newegg.com or www.frys.com, get prices for at least two different external hard drives that use the interface you chose in Step 3, and for a suitable controller card. Write your findings here:

_____

_____

_____

_____

 30 MINUTES

Lab Exercise 8.03: Comparing Solid-State Drives and Magnetic Hard Drives

Mechanical hard disk drives (HDDs) store data magnetically and have moving parts, but solid-state drives (SSDs) use _nonvolatile_ memory—memory that retains data even when it's not powered on—to store data and emulate a hard drive. Most common uses of SSDs have been in what are called flash drives or thumb drives, but now PC users are installing SSDs as their primary storage in desktops and laptops. Because SSDs have no moving parts, they are tougher, quieter, and faster than hard disks. The main drawback is the price; SSDs currently cost much more than their mechanical counterparts with similar capacities. In this exercise, we are comparing drives using the SATA form factor. In Lab Exercise 8.04, we will look at SSDs that use the M.2 form factor.

Learning Objectives

This lab explores the differences between solid-state drives and magnetic hard drives and is designed to help you recommend drives to clients as the need arises.

At the end of this lab, you'll be able to

- Explain solid-state drives

- Explain magnetic hard drives

- Discern which one will be best for your clients

Lab Materials and Setup

The materials you need for this lab are

- Access to a PC system and the Internet

- A solid-state drive and a magnetic hard drive

Getting Down to Business

In this scenario, your boss has asked you whether it is worth the money to replace the magnetic HDDs in all the office computers with SSDs. Rather than just giving her a yes or no answer, you've decided to prepare a quick spreadsheet for her that compares not only the costs but also the performance differences, power-saving benefits, and differences in reliability.

Step 1 Find information about three SATA form factor drives, all with the same capacity if possible, and all from the same manufacturer if possible: one SSD, one hybrid drive, and one magnetic hard drive. (Seagate is a good choice if you don't have a preference.) At the manufacturer's Web site, review the spec sheet on each drive and compile the following information:

Manufacturer: _____

Capacity: _____

	Model	Price	Seek Average Read (ms)	Average Data Rate Read (all zones) (MBps)	Power (W), Typical Operation	Predicted Annualized Failure Rate (AFR)
SSD						
Hybrid (SSHD)						
HDD						

Step 2 Based on your gathered data, what do you think of your boss's idea to replace all the office's HDDs with SSDs? Write a paragraph explaining your decision, to accompany your spreadsheet. Be prepared to share your data and conclusion with the class.

 **30 MINUTES**

Lab Exercise 8.04: Choosing an M.2 SSD

In the previous lab exercise, you looked at SSDs that connect via SATA interfaces. Many recent desktop motherboards and laptops feature the M.2 (also known as the NGFF, or New Generation Form Factor) connector for use exclusively with SSDs.

In this lab exercise, you will research the options available for a customer who would like to use an M.2 SSD and make a recommendation.

Learning Objectives

This lab explores the M.2 SSD interface and the drives available for it.

At the end of this lab, you'll be able to

- Determine if a particular computer supports an M.2 SSD

- Specify a range of drive capacities that will fit into the computer

Lab Materials and Setup

The materials you need for this lab are

- A computer with Internet access

- A computer (or motherboard) with an M.2 interface (optional but highly recommended). If you don't have access to one, choose a particular model from online specifications and use it as the basis for your research.

Getting Down to Business

Your customer wants to install an M.2 SSD for use as a boot drive for Microsoft Windows, and, if possible, for storage of a typical software load (office suite, Web browser, photo editor). You will need to determine if an M.2 connector is available, if it is already in use, and the specifics of the slot. Afterward, you can research available drives.

Step 1   Shut down your system and remove the system cover, following proper ESD avoidance procedures, and determine if the computer has an M.2 connector. An example of an M.2 connector that is not being used is shown in Figure 8-4.

Does your computer have an M.2 connector? _____

Is it being used? _____

Step 2   If an M.2 drive is installed (see Figure 8-5), examine it to determine its make (brand), model, and capacity. If an M.2 drive is not installed, complete Steps 3 and 4 first and then enter data from one of the drives you found online.

If your system has an M.2 drive installed, what brand is it? _____

What model? _____   What capacity? _____

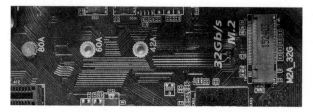

FIGURE 8-4 A typical M.2 connector on a late-model desktop computer

FIGURE 8-5 A 250-GB M.2 drive installed on a late-model desktop computer

Step 3   If an M.2 drive is not installed, examine the socket to determine what form factors of modules it supports. Look at Figure 8-4 again. Notice the screw holes (and screw) to the left of the M.2 port. This connector can handle 42A, 60A, and 80A M.2 modules. An M.2 SSD is mounted by sliding the power and data connector end into the socket at an angle, rotating it to be parallel to the motherboard, and screwing it into place with the provided screw.

If your motherboard has an M.2 socket but no drive, what screw holes are available for mounting an M.2 drive? _____

→ Note

A drive that is long enough to be secured with a screw in the 80A hole uses the 2280 (22-mm wide, 80-mm long) form factor. A drive designed to be secured using the 60A hole uses the 2260 form factor. A drive designed to be secured using the 42A hole uses the 2242 form factor.

Step 4   Using a site such as www.newegg.com or www.frys.com, get prices for at least two different M.2 SSDs in the largest form factor supported by the computer or motherboard. Provide pricing for 512 GB, 256 GB, and 128 GB (or similar capacities). Use searches such as M.2 2260 SSD or M.2 2280 512 GB. Record your findings here:

_____

_____

_____

_____

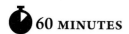 **60 MINUTES**

Lab Exercise 8.05: Troubleshooting Hard Drive Installations

Hard drives are pretty simple to install now that most of them are SATA, as you saw in Lab Exercise 8.01. However, mistakes do happen, and in this lab exercise you'll learn some ways to straighten things out. You'll also see how to check whether Windows sees a drive—even if it's not partitioned yet—and you'll experiment with SATA's hot-plugging capabilities.

Learning Objectives

This lab shows some techniques for checking your work if a newly installed hard drive doesn't behave as expected.

At the end of this lab, you'll be able to

- Troubleshoot hard drive installation problems

- Determine whether Windows recognizes a drive, even if it is not partitioned

- Understand SATA's hot-plugging capabilities

Lab Materials and Setup

The materials you need for this lab are

- A PC with SATA interfaces and Windows installed

- An additional SATA hard drive (magnetic or SSD) in addition to the PC's boot drive

Getting Down to Business

It might seem odd to mess up a hard drive installation deliberately, but you can't hurt anything, so give it a whirl. Seeing how the PC responds to mistakes when you know specifically what's wrong can help you when you run into similar situations later in the field.

Step 1   You must have a properly functioning PC for this lab to be effective, so verify first that you have a system up and running with one or more hard drives installed, bootable to Windows.

Step 2   Power down the system and disconnect it from power. Disconnect the data cable for the hard drive used to boot the system, then reconnect the power cable and power up the system. Describe the result:

It is difficult to imagine not connecting the data cables to hard drives, but many times to add RAM or new devices, we must disconnect the cables to gain access to the component. It is easy to miss reconnecting one of the cables after installing the new device.

Disconnecting the cable also simulates a broken SATA cable. These cables are somewhat delicate, and can fail after a sharp crease or a crimp from the system case. If you're having unexplained problems with your drive, check the cables prior to replacing the drive.

Step 3 Rest the palm of your hand on the hard drive. If it's a magnetic HDD, you may be able to feel a very mild vibration from the platter-spinning motor. (You won't feel that on an SSD, of course.) You might also hear the drive motor if you listen very closely.

Step 4 Power down the system and disconnect it from power. Then put the data cable back on properly. Then disconnect the drive's power cable, reconnect the computer's power cable, and try booting again. Describe the result:

Same thing, wasn't it? The drive needs *both* the power and the data cable in order to function. In the absence of either, a total failure to launch results. The difference is that without the power cable, you don't hear the drive spinning up nor feel it vibrate.

Step 5 Power down the PC, disconnect its power cable, and reconnect the drive's power cable.

Step 6 Connect an additional SATA drive to the system, with both data and power cables. You do not have to mount it securely in the case, as you'll be removing it after this exercise. Reconnect power to the computer and restart it.

Step 7 Boot into Windows, and check in Windows Explorer/File Explorer to see if the newly installed drive appears there with a drive letter. (Look in Computer or This PC, depending on the Windows version.) If the drive is unpartitioned, it won't appear there, even if it's installed correctly.

Step 8 Use Disk Management to see if the drive is recognized. Follow these steps:

   a. Start Disk Management:

   - Windows 7: Click Start, and in the Search box, type **diskmgmt.msc** and press ENTER.

   - Windows 8.1: Right-click the Start button and click Run. Type **diskmgmt.msc** and press ENTER.

- Windows 10: Click in the Search box on the taskbar. Type **diskmgmt.msc** and press ENTER. Or, right-click the Start button and select Disk Management.

b. In the bottom section of the window, look at the list of disks (see Figure 8-6). Each physical disk appears on its own line (Disk 0, Disk 1, and so on).

c. Verify that each of the installed disks appears.

d. Close the Disk Management window.

Step 9   With Windows still running, disconnect the SATA data cable from the additional drive (not the boot drive). What happened?

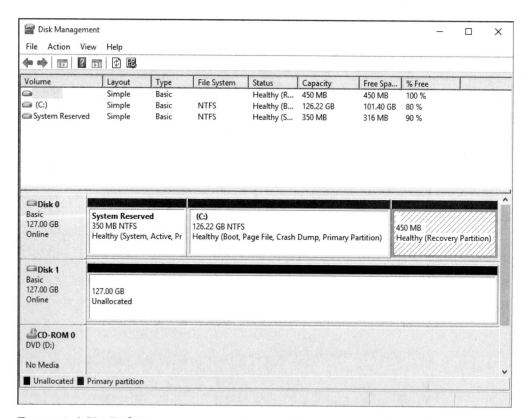

FIGURE 8-6 Use Disk Management to make sure all drives are correctly installed.

Step 10 Plug the data cable back in. Does Windows see the drive again?

Step 11 Disconnect the additional drive (the non-boot drive) and set it aside. You do not have to shut down the PC to do this. Then close up the case.

> ✖ **Cross-Reference**
>
> **Windows won't redetect the SATA drive if AHCI mode is not enabled in the BIOS or UEFI firmware. For more information, reference the "AHCI" section in Chapter 8 of** *Mike Meyers' CompTIA A+ Guide to Managing and Troubleshooting PCs.*

**30 MINUTES**

Lab Exercise 8.06: Configuring a Hardware RAID

A RAID offers some performance and/or data safety benefits compared to using a single physical hard drive. To review these benefits and the types of RAID, refer to the "RAID" section in Chapter 8 of *Mike Meyers' CompTIA A+ Guide to Managing and Troubleshooting PCs.* (I'm going to assume here that you've read all that and are familiar with the concepts.)

In this lab, you'll install more hard drives in a PC, and then you'll check out its CMOS setup to see whether the motherboard has an onboard RAID controller. If it does, you'll enable that controller. (If not, that's okay too, because doing the drive installation part of this lab will help you prepare for the software RAID lab coming up in Chapter 9.)

Learning Objectives

In this lab, you will install additional hard drives in an existing system. You will then access your motherboard's RAID controller to configure a RAID array. If the motherboard doesn't have a RAID controller, you'll set the system aside to be used in Lab Exercise 9.05, "Implementing Software RAID 0 with Disk Management," in Chapter 9.

At the end of this lab, you'll be able to

- Install multiple hard drives
- Configure a hardware RAID array

Lab Materials and Setup

The materials you need for this lab are

- A working PC with Windows 7 or later installed. Ideally the motherboard should include a RAID controller, but you can still do some of the steps if it does not.

- At least two additional (preferably three or four) hard drives

---

✖ Warning

When you create a hardware RAID array on many systems, all of the drives in the array are reformatted, causing existing data on the drives to be overwritten. Make sure your system (Windows) drive does not have any important files—and make an image backup of the drive or be prepared to reinstall Windows if this exercise overwrites the drive's contents. Use blank drives (or drives that can be reformatted) for the additional drives.

Getting Down to Business

You know that you should always take the proper antistatic precautions when opening the system case and working with the delicate components inside. Take those precautions now, and get ready to install a few extra hard drives into your system in preparation for setting up a RAID. In this exercise, you'll make sure these drives are recognized by the system; in the next chapter's labs, you'll configure them.

✔ Hint

For many of the exercises in the next chapter, it is very important that you have a working system with Windows 7 or later. Obviously, you will need to keep the system partition and boot partition intact (usually these are the same partition, and are the first partition on the first hard drive of the system) with the operating system running. Even if you have available space on the first hard drive, it is much cleaner if you can install at least two additional hard drives. That way, you can partition, format, and convert to dynamic disks to your heart's content, without the worry of losing data (or the operating system).

Step 1   Install the additional drives. Refer to Lab Exercise 8.01, "Installing Serial ATA Hard Drives" as needed.

Step 2   Boot into Windows, and use Disk Management to check that the new drives are recognized. Refer to Step 8 in Lab Exercise 8.05, "Troubleshooting Hard Drive Installations," if you need help doing that. Troubleshoot as needed, starting with Step 1 of that exercise, if all is not well.

To complete the rest of this lab exercise, your motherboard must support RAID. Check your motherboard manual to ensure the motherboard supports RAID, or poke around in CMOS setup to see if there are any RAID settings. If not, that's okay; you'll still configure a software RAID setup in the next chapter.

Step 3

    a. Enter the CMOS setup program. Refer to Lab Exercise 5.02, "Accessing BIOS Settings via the CMOS Setup Program," in Chapter 5 as needed.

    b. Locate the setting that enables the RAID controller and enable it. Refer to Lab Exercise 5.04, "Configuring BIOS Settings" in Chapter 5 as needed.

    c. Save your changes and exit the CMOS setup program.

Step 4   Watch the boot screens. A new screen should appear now that you have enabled RAID in CMOS. If the screens go by too fast, press the PAUSE/BREAK key or WINDOWS-PAUSE keys (if you have one) to pause the screen during boot-up. To enter the RAID setup utility, press the key combination required by your motherboard, similar to the key you press to enter CMOS.

Which button must you press to enter your RAID setup utility? _____

Step 5   Once you are in the RAID setup utility, practice setting up different styles of RAID that your motherboard supports. Every configuration screen is different. As in the CMOS setup program, each setting should have an explanation to help you figure out what to do. Because you are using hard drives with no important data (right?), feel free to experiment. Disconnect drives once you have set up a particular RAID, such as RAID 0, 1, 5, or 10. What are the results?

_____

_____

_____

Step 6   Once you have completed the RAID configurations, return to the CMOS setup program and reset it to the original settings.

Lab Analysis Test

    1. When selecting a new hard drive, what are the factors influencing your choice of HDD versus SSD?

    2. What type of external hard drive interface would you recommend for someone who wants a low-cost backup drive?

3. If you want to install an SSD without using up a SATA port or drive bay, what drive interface should you look for?

4. The second SATA hard drive on your company's server has just died. You have a replacement drive, but it's critical that the server remain up and functioning. Can you replace the second hard drive without shutting down the server?

5. Sean would like to create a new RAID 5 volume on a PC that already contains a single hard drive. What is the minimum number of hard drives he will need to add to this system, assuming he doesn't want to make changes to the system drive?

Key Term Quiz

Use the following terms to complete the following sentences. Not all terms will be used.

data cable	RAID
Disk Management	SATA
HDD	SATAe
hybrid	SSD
M.2	

1. A(n) _____ uses memory chips to store data and has none of the moving parts of traditional hard drives.

2. The acronym _____ refers to a traditional hard disk drive that stores data magnetically on platters.

3. An internal drive interface that is backward-compatible with SATA is known as _____.

4. In order to implement a hardware _____, enable the onboard controller on the motherboard for that capability.

5. A great way to determine whether a new drive is installed and configured correctly is to run the _____ utility in Windows.

Chapter 9
Implementing Mass Storage

Lab Exercises

Once you've installed a new drive on a PC and it has been recognized by the system, you have two more steps to complete before you can start storing data: partitioning and formatting.

✔ **Hint**

The tasks of partitioning and formatting have really become automated into the installation of the operating system (and the tools included in the operating system). Many of the steps are now completed in sequence, blurring the line between partitioning and formatting. Make sure you're clear on the distinction between partitioning and formatting, because you must do them in the proper order. As you learned in Chapter 9 of the textbook, partitioning is the process of electronically subdividing a physical drive into one or more units called partitions. After partitioning, you must format the drive. Formatting installs a file system onto the drive that organizes each partition in such a way that the operating system can store files and folders on the drive.

In the early days of DOS, Windows 3.*x*, and Windows 9*x*, your hard drive had to be partitioned and formatted before you could run the installation setup routine. Windows now incorporates these disk-preparation steps into the installation routine itself. However, it's still important for you to be able to perform these tasks from scratch as part of your basic PC tech repertoire.

You have a number of tools at your disposal for performing partitioning and formatting tasks. If you are working with a fresh hard drive, you need to get to these tools without necessarily having an operating system installed (this may be the first disk in the system, and you are preparing it for the OS installation). The first of these tools is the Windows installation media. A number of third-party utilities are available for partitioning and formatting, such as Avanquest's Partition Commander, EaseUS Partition Master, and the open source Linux tool GNOME Partition Editor, affectionately known as GParted. These specific tools are beyond the scope of the CompTIA A+ exams; however, a good tech should develop skills in the use of these tools because they often have features not available in Windows' built-in partitioning utility.

Once you have an operating system up and running, you should have some type of partitioning and formatting tool that you can run from the GUI. Windows uses a tool known as the Disk Management utility, which you worked with in Chapter 8. Disk Management enables you to create, modify, and format partitions. You can also format partitions from File Explorer/Windows Explorer (although you can't make changes to partitions from there).

After looking at how to create and format partitions using the Windows installation media and the live CD of GParted, you'll start up Windows to look at how to accomplish these tasks using the built-in tools. Next, you'll use the Disk Management utility to convert basic disks to dynamic disks and implement a RAID 0 stripe set. Windows 8 and later include an alternative method of implementing RAID-like disk manipulation, like combining spaces from multiple drives; we'll look at how that works in this chapter. Then you'll practice performing regular hard drive maintenance and troubleshooting tasks.

✔ Hint

The following exercises walk you through the basic management of hard drive storage available on your system. If you have only one drive installed, you will need to install the operating system after the first few exercises to perform the later exercises. In Lab Exercise 8.05, "Troubleshooting Hard Drive Installations," you installed additional hard drives into a machine with Windows installed. I recommend that you use this machine for all of the implementation labs (being careful not to partition or format the first drive, which should contain the operating system). Not only will this enable you to practice creating and deleting partitions and formatting and reformatting those partitions, it will also enable you to verify the partitions and file systems with the Disk Management tool in Windows.

 **30 MINUTES**

Lab Exercise 9.01: Creating and Formatting Partitions with Windows Installation Media

After physically installing drives, as you did in Chapter 8, you are only halfway there. To make that storage space available, you must then partition each drive into usable space (even if only one partition uses all of the available drive space) and then format each partition with a file system.

In this lab, you will use the Windows installation media to partition and format hard drives in your system. You will be left with blank partitions, one of which needs an operating system. In the labs for Chapter 11 you will complete the process of installing the operating system.

✖ Cross-Reference

For more details about partitioning and formatting drives with a Windows installation disc, refer to "Partitioning and Formatting with the Installation Media" in Chapter 8 of *Mike Meyers' CompTIA A+ Guide to Managing and Troubleshooting PCs*.

Learning Objectives

In this exercise, you'll use the Windows installation media to partition a hard drive and format the partition for use.

At the end of this lab, you'll be able to

- Set up a primary partition on a hard drive
- Format the partition with the NTFS file system

Lab Materials and Setup

The materials you need for this lab are

- Windows 7, 8.1, or 10 installation media, such as a bootable CD, DVD, or flash drive
- A PC with the following:
  - An operating system already installed on its primary hard drive
  - At least one additional hard drive, already installed, that is either empty or contains nothing you want to keep

✖ **Warning**

Partitioning and formatting a hard drive destroys any data on it! Practice this lab using only drives that don't store any data you need.

Getting Down to Business

In this exercise, you'll start the system by booting from the Windows installation media (you will have to configure your system CMOS to boot from the optical drive or, if available, a USB device). You'll partition a portion of one of the hard drives and format it with the NTFS file system, as if you're preparing to install the operating system.

Step 1   Enter the CMOS setup program and configure the boot order, selecting the optical drive (or, if necessary, a USB device) as the first boot device. Also make sure that the setting called "Boot Other Device" (or something similar) is enabled; otherwise, your system may not recognize the optical drive as a bootable drive.

✖ **Cross-Reference**

Refer to Lab Exercise 5.02, "Accessing BIOS Settings via the CMOS Setup Program," if you need help getting into CMOS setup.

Step 2   Place the Windows installation media in the optical drive tray (or connect it to a USB port if it's a bootable flash drive) and boot the machine. When you see the message to press any key to boot from the CD/DVD, do so, so that the Windows Setup program runs.

Step 3   Work through the initial screens of the Windows Setup utility:

a.   Set your language and regional preferences on the first screen, and then click Next.

b.   Click the large Install Now button.

c.   Setup will ask for a product key. If using Windows 7, you do not need to enter one right now. Click Next to move on. If using Windows 8.1, you must type the product key before clicking Next. With a first-time installation of Windows 10, you must type the product key. However, if you have previously installed Windows 10 on this computer, click I don't have a product key.

d.   (Windows 7 only) Pick the edition you wish to install. Your product key will only activate the edition that you purchased. Click Next to continue.

e.   Agree to the license agreement on the next screen and click Next.

f.   Click Custom install (Windows 7) or Custom: Install Windows only (Windows 8.1/10).

Step 4   At this point, the screen displays the installed drives and any partitions and/or file systems that have been configured on the drives prior to this session. In Figure 9-1, for example, you see these items:

- **Drive 0 Partition 1: System Reserved**   This is the hidden system partition for the currently installed operating system.

- **Drive 0 Partition 2**   This is the main partition where the current operating system resides (in other words, the C: drive).

- **Drive 1, Drive 2, and Drive 3**   These are three blank physical hard drives, with no partitioning or formatting yet.

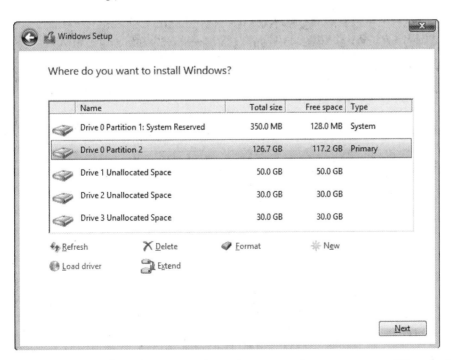

FIGURE 9-1   Windows Setup provides an inventory of your current partitions and drives.

Step 5   If any partitions exist on the drives you have installed to practice this lab (and the data on these drives is expendable), delete them at this time (so you can re-create them in the next step).

To delete a partition:

   a.   Select the partition.

   b.   (Windows 7 only) Click Drive options (advanced).

   c.   Click Delete.

   d.   At the warning message, click OK. The partition will be returned to unpartitioned space.

Step 6   To create a partition on one of the empty drives, follow these steps:

   a.   Click the desired drive.

   b.   (Windows 7 only) Click Drive options (advanced).

   c.   Click New.

   d.   In the Size field, enter the desired size of the partition you want to create (see Figure 9-2). For example, type 51200 for a 51.2-GB partition.

   e.   Click Apply. *Primary* now appears in the Type column for that drive.

Step 7   Next, format the partition:

   a.   Click Format.

   b.   If a warning appears, click OK. The partition is quick-formatted.

Step 8   (Optional) If you want to practice deleting a partition, do the following:

   a.   With the drive still selected, click Delete.

   b.   A warning appears; click OK.

   c.   Repeat Steps 6 and 7.

FIGURE 9-2 Set the desired size for the new partition.

Step 9   Do not continue Windows Setup. Instead, remove the Windows installation media from the system and reboot. Allow the already-installed copy of Windows to start normally.

Step 10   Use the Disk Management tool in Windows to verify the partition you created. If you need help using Disk Management, refer to Step 8 of Lab Exercise 8.05, "Troubleshooting Hard Drive Installations."

 30 MINUTES

Lab Exercise 9.02: Creating and Formatting Partitions with GParted

As a competent tech, you might need to partition and format a machine before installing an operating system and deploying it to a user. To accomplish this task, it might be easier to use a standalone partitioning/formatting tool such as the open source GNOME Partition Editor (GParted). GNOME is one of many GUI-based distributions available for the Linux operating system. GParted uses a basic, bootable version of GNOME with disk management tools built in. This method is somewhat beyond the scope of the CompTIA A+ exams (although the latest version does cover some basic Linux commands), but the skills and techniques you will practice in this lab are valuable to a real-world tech and can help you gain a deeper understanding of partitioning and formatting hard drives.

✔ Tip

Many techs, and specifically techs employed by the IT departments of small to large businesses, often use one of the popular drive-imaging tools such as Acronis True Image (free versions are available from Seagate and Western Digital for use with their drives), Macrium Reflect Free Edition, or AOMEI Backupper. Drive imaging is used to roll out the operating system and applications on multiple machines expediently. This method creates the partition and copies the OS, applications, and user profiles onto the file system that was used to make the image, all in one step.

In this exercise, you will use the live CD of GParted to partition and format one of the additional hard drives installed in your lab system. If you are working in a classroom setting, the instructor should be able to provide copies of the GParted live CD to you for this exercise. Alternatively, you could jump ahead to Lab Exercise 11.07, "Installing Ubuntu Linux," where you will create a live CD by burning a CD with an ISO image.

✖ Cross-Reference

For additional details about the GParted live CD, refer to the "Third-Party Partition Tools" section in Chapter 9 of *Mike Meyers' CompTIA A+ Guide to Managing and Troubleshooting PCs*.

Learning Objectives

In this exercise, you'll use the GParted live CD to partition a hard drive and format the partition for use.

At the end of this lab, you'll be able to

- Set up primary and extended partitions on hard drives
- Format the partitions with various file systems

Lab Materials and Setup

The materials you need for this lab are

- A PC with the following:
    - An operating system already installed on its primary hard drive
    - At least one additional hard drive, already installed, that is either empty or contains nothing you want to keep
- A GParted live CD or live USB thumb drive
    - The GParted website is https://gparted.org. It contains a number of methods to create the live CD, but we recommend that you use the Tuxboot tool because it enables you to automatically download the GParted image and will easily create a CD or, if you prefer, a USB drive. Head over to https://sourceforge.net/projects/tuxboot/ and download the Tuxboot tool (Tuxboot has both a Windows version and a Linux version).
    - This lab refers to a live CD, but feel free to instead make a bootable USB drive—just adjust as needed.

✖ **Warning**

Partitioning and formatting a hard drive or USB flash drive destroys any data on the drive! Practice this lab only on drives that don't store any data you need.

Getting Down to Business

In this exercise, you'll start the system by booting from the GParted live CD. (You will have to configure your system CMOS to boot from the CD.) You'll then partition a portion of one of the hard drives and format it with the file system of your choice.

Step 1 Enter the CMOS setup program and configure the boot order, selecting the optical drive as the first boot device. Also make sure that the setting called "Boot Other Device" (or something similar) is enabled; otherwise, your system may not recognize the optical drive as a bootable drive.

✖ **Cross-Reference**

Refer to Lab Exercise 5.02, "Accessing BIOS Settings via the CMOS Setup Program," if you need help getting into CMOS setup.

Step 2   Place the GParted live CD in the optical drive tray and boot the machine. GParted displays an introduction screen, as shown in Figure 9-3.

✔ **Tip**

If your PC won't boot to the GParted live CD, try turning off Secure Boot in CMOS setup temporarily.

Press ENTER to boot; GNOME Linux should begin to load. It may take a few minutes to load. If GParted doesn't load after several minutes, and gives you a bunch of error messages, try running it in one of its alternative modes, like Failsafe mode. Use the menu on the opening screen (shown in Figure 9-3) to experiment to see if you find something that works.

As the system loads, you will be queried a number of times for settings related to boot options, language, keyboard, and screen depth and resolution. Unless told to do otherwise by your instructor, select the defaults for these settings by highlighting OK and pressing ENTER.

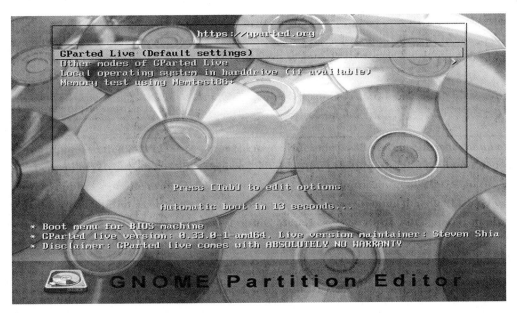

FIGURE 9-3 The GNOME Partition Editor opening screen

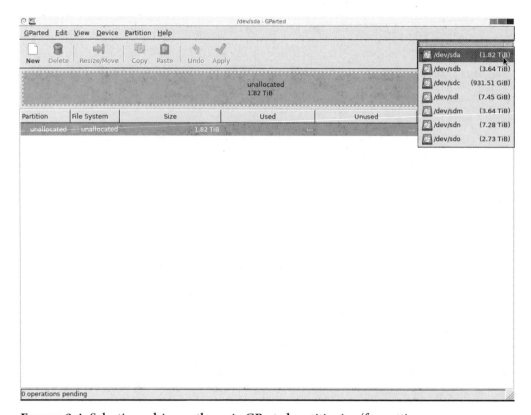

FIGURE 9-4 Selecting a drive on the main GParted partitioning/formatting screen

GParted should finish booting and arrive at a graphical screen displaying various menu items, icons, and the current drive focus with strange Linux names such as /dev/hda1, /dev/hda3, and so forth. Notice the item at the far right of the menu bar; here, you can click the drop-down arrow to select which physical drive the GParted screen is focused on (see Figure 9-4).

Step 3   Now change the focus to one of the empty drives installed on your system. In Figure 9-4, it is /dev/sda, but on your system it might be labeled as /dev/hdb or /dev/hdc in the drop-down list of hard drives.

✔ **Hint**

> If you are using the machine that you configured in Lab Exercise 8.05, "Troubleshooting Hard Drive Installations," Windows has been installed on one of the drives in the system (most likely the first drive). When GParted first launches, the screen focus will be on this drive and the label will probably read /dev/hda1. Make sure that you select one of the drives that has been set up to be partitioned and formatted, or you'll find yourself reinstalling Windows.

The screen now focuses on the drive you've selected and shows any partitions and/or file systems that have been configured on that drive prior to this session. If any partitions are displayed, highlight the partition, right-click, and select Delete.

Step 4   GParted requires that you commit any changes that you make to the partitions on the disk, so after deleting the partition, you must click the Apply button to apply the settings and actually delete the partition.

When you click Apply, GParted applies the pending operations. You should now have a drive visible with all of the available space denoted as unallocated space.

Step 5   Select the unallocated space, right-click, and select New. Then follow these steps in the Create new Partition dialog box (see Figure 9-5):

a.   Enter the size of the partition in megabytes into the New size field; either type a number or use the up and down arrows to select a size. For the purposes of practice, anywhere in the range of 4000 MB (4 GB) to 9000 MB (9 GB) is a good size for the partition.

b.   Select Primary Partition or Extended Partition; primary is a good choice for the initial partition on the drive.

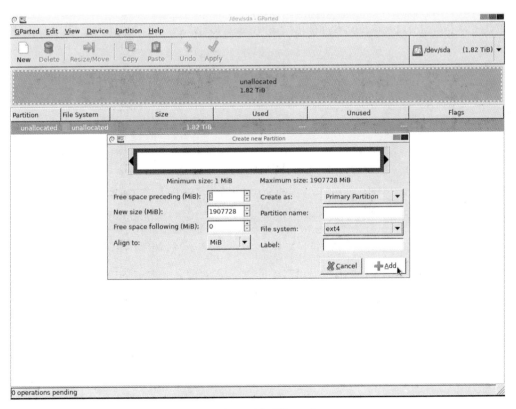

Figure 9-5 Preparing to create a partition with GParted

c. Select the NTFS file system.

d. Click the Add button. The new partition with the formatted file system should appear on the screen.

e. Click Apply to create the formatted partition. A message box will pop up, asking you to confirm that you want to apply the pending operations. Click Apply again, and then watch as the Applying pending operations dialog box appears, shows you the status of the operation, and then disappears.

f. Click Close.

Congratulations! You should now have a drive with a formatted partition visible in the main screen (see Figure 9-6).

✔ **Tip**

Some versions of GParted have problems creating an NTFS partition. If you are unable to create an NTFS partition with GParted, use this workaround: Select ext4 as the file system (refer to Figure 9-5) and add it. After the partition is created, right-click the partition, click Format to, and choose ntfs as the format type. GParted will format the partition as NTFS and Windows can use it.

Step 6 There is one last step, which depends on whether you plan to use this partition to boot the machine with an OS (active partition) and which file system you have selected.

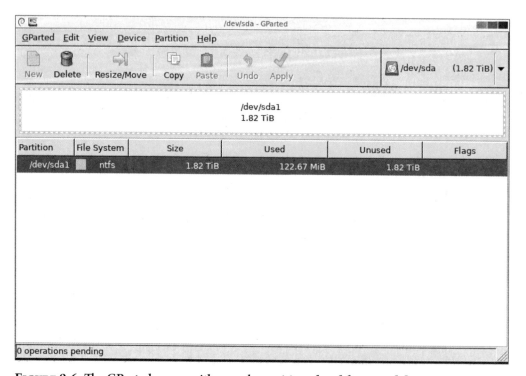

FIGURE 9-6 The GParted screen with a newly partitioned and formatted drive

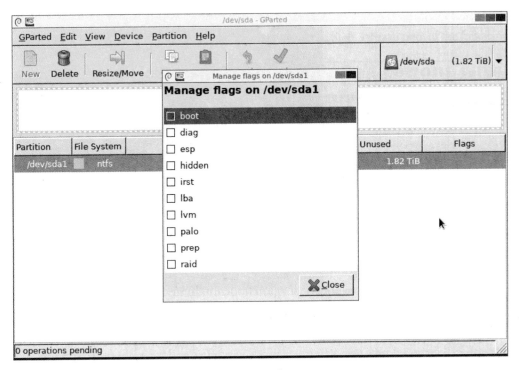

FIGURE 9-7 The Manage flags window in GParted

With the partition highlighted, right-click the partition and select Manage Flags. A small window appears in which you'll see a number of flags that you can set (see Figure 9-7). Many of these apply to operating systems other than Windows, but one of them must be set if you are to use the partition in Windows: boot. This flag must be set if the partition is to be the active partition in the system (this is usually the first partition on the first hard drive in the system).

Set the appropriate flags for your partition and file system and close the Manage flags window. Notice that you will not have to apply changes, as the settings take effect immediately.

Step 7   Reboot the machine and allow Windows to boot. You can then use Disk Management to verify the partition(s) you have created with GParted.

Step 8   Practice deleting, creating, and formatting different combinations of partitions and file systems to become comfortable with the GParted program.

Step 9   Remove the GParted disc from your drive and reboot into Windows.

✖ **Warning**

If you turned off Secure Boot in CMOS setup, you may need to reenable it before Windows will boot normally.

 **30 MINUTES**

Lab Exercise 9.03: Using Windows Tools to Create and Format Partitions

Windows includes tools that let you create, modify, and format partitions "on the fly" from within Windows. One of these utilities is called Disk Management.

✖ Cross-Reference

For details about creating and formatting partitions using Disk Management, refer to the "Disk Management" section in Chapter 9 of *Mike Meyers' CompTIA A+ Guide to Managing and Troubleshooting PCs.*

This lab exercise assumes that you want to create a partition on one of the empty drives installed on the Windows lab system and then format that partition with a file system. Disk Management will enable you to format the partition right away; however, you can also use another Windows utility that you should be intimately familiar with by now: Computer (or This PC, depending on the Windows version). Follow the steps in this lab exercise to create and format a new partition.

✔ Hint

Each version of Windows can read from and write to the FAT16, FAT32, and NTFS file systems. However, only old versions of Windows, up to Windows XP, can be installed to a FAT16 or FAT32 partition—Windows Vista and later must be installed on an NTFS partition.

Learning Objectives

In this exercise, you'll use the Disk Management program to partition a hard drive and format the partition with a file system.

At the end of this lab, you'll be able to

- Set up a primary, active partition on a hard drive
- Set up an extended partition and logical drives in that partition
- Format partitions with various file systems

Lab Materials and Setup

The materials you need for this lab are

- A PC with the following:

  - Microsoft Windows 7 or later installed

  - At least one additional hard drive (preferably two or more), already installed, that is either empty or contains nothing you want to keep

---

✖ Warning

Partitioning a hard drive destroys any data on it! Practice this lab only on drives that don't contain any data you need.

Getting Down to Business

The steps for partitioning drives and formatting partitions in each version of Windows are very similar.

Step 1 Start Disk Management, and verify that all the physically installed hard drives appear. To start Disk Management:

- Windows 7: Click Start, and in the Search box, type **diskmgmt.msc** and press ENTER.

- Windows 8.1: Right-click the Start button and click Run. Type **diskmgmt.msc** and press ENTER.

- Windows 10: Click in the Search box on the taskbar. Type **diskmgmt.msc** and press ENTER.

Step 2 If the Initialize Disk dialog box appears (and it will for any drives you have added to the system), click OK to initialize the disk with the default partition style (MBR). See Figure 9-8.

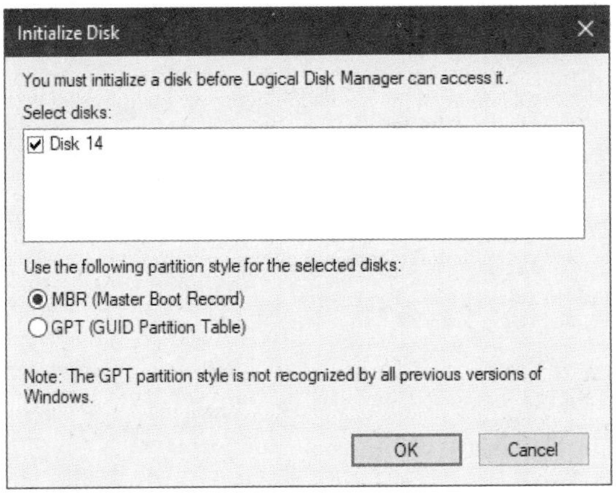

Initialize Disk ✕

You must initialize a disk before Logical Disk Manager can access it.

Select disks:

☑ Disk 14

Use the following partition style for the selected disks:

◉ MBR (Master Boot Record)
○ GPT (GUID Partition Table)

Note: The GPT partition style is not recognized by all previous versions of Windows.

OK   Cancel

FIGURE 9-8 Initialize any newly added disks.

Step 3   If there are any existing partitions on the empty drives, highlight the partitions and either right-click and select Delete Volume or simply press DELETE. Click Yes to confirm.

Step 4   Run the New Simple Volume Wizard to create a new partition, as follows:

a.   Right-click an unpartitioned section of drive space and choose New Simple Volume. The New Simple Volume Wizard opens.

b.   Click Next to begin.

c.   To create a single partition out of all the space, leave the Simple volume size in MB setting at its default. Or, to use only part of the space, decrease the value as needed. See Figure 9-9.

d.   Click Next.

e.   At the prompt for assigning a drive letter, leave the default assignment, or choose a different letter from the drop-down list (see Figure 9-10). Then click Next.

f.   You are then asked whether you want to format the volume. See Figure 9-11. At this point you could save time by allowing the wizard to format the volume for you, but for this lab, we'll save that for later so that you can learn an alternate formatting method.

g.   Click Do not format this volume, and then click Next.

h.   Click Finish.

Notice at this point that the information for the partitioned-but-not-formatted disk reports that it is in RAW format, rather than the usual NTFS reported for others.

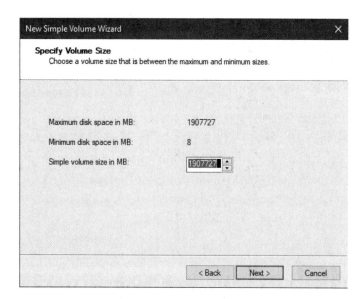

FIGURE 9-9 Specify the size of the partition.

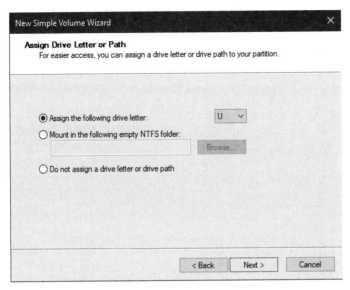

FIGURE 9-10 Choose the drive letter to assign.

Step 5 You're about to learn an alternate method for formatting drives; generally speaking you'll use this method only to format removable media, such as USB thumb drives, but we're going to use it for a hard drive just for practice.

    a. Minimize the Disk Management window.

    b. Open the file management tool: either File Explorer (Windows 8 and later) or Windows Explorer (Windows 7).

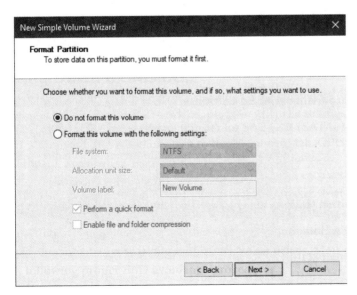

FIGURE 9-11 Choose whether to format the partition now, and with what file system.

→ **Note**

When you attempt to open the file management tool, you might see a prompt asking if you want to format the unformatted drive. If you see that prompt, skip Steps c and d.

---

c. Navigate to the top level of the local drive hierarchy by clicking Computer (or This PC) in the navigation pane on the left.

d. Double-click the unformatted drive. A dialog box asks if you want to format the disk.

e. Click Format Disk. The Format Local Disk dialog box opens (see Figure 9-12).

f. Confirm the settings in the dialog box.

✔ **Tip**

Make sure you understand what each of those settings is (Capacity, File system, Allocation unit size, Volume label, and Quick Format). Refer to Chapter 9 of *Mike Meyers' CompTIA A+ Guide to Managing and Troubleshooting PCs* as needed.

---

g. Click Start.

h. At the warning dialog box, click OK. Then wait for the drive to be formatted.

i. When the formatting completes, click OK to confirm.

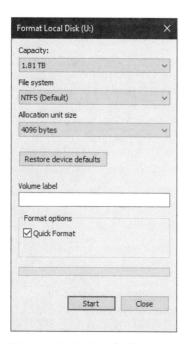

FIGURE 9-12 Use the Format Local Disk dialog box to format the new drive.

Step 6 Switch back to the Disk Management utility. Note that the drive now appears formatted; it has NTFS listed as its file system.

Step 7 Practice deleting, creating, and formatting different combinations of partitions and file systems to become comfortable with the Disk Management utility. When you finish up, all of the empty disks in your practice PC should be partitioned with a single partition per physical drive and formatted using the default settings for an NTFS file system volume.

 **30 MINUTES**

Lab Exercise 9.04: Converting Basic Disks to Dynamic Disks with Disk Management

As you learned in Chapter 9 of *Mike Meyers' CompTIA A+ Guide to Managing and Troubleshooting PCs*, there are many advantages to using dynamic disks. For example, you can extend one volume into another, to combine two physical disks into a single pool of storage, and you can implement software-based RAID. In this lab you will convert your two blank disks into dynamic disks.

> ✖ **Cross-Reference**
>
> **To learn more about dynamic disks, refer to the "Dynamic Disks" section in Chapter 9 of *Mike Meyers' CompTIA A+ Guide to Managing and Troubleshooting PCs*.**

Learning Objectives

In this exercise, you'll use the Disk Management utility to convert basic disks to dynamic disks.

At the end of this lab, you'll be able to

- Convert basic disks to dynamic disks

Lab Materials and Setup

The materials you need for this lab are

- A PC with one of the following Windows versions already installed:
    - Windows 7 Professional, Ultimate, or Enterprise
    - Windows 8 or 8.1 Pro
    - Windows 10 Pro
- Additional hard drives on the PC that are partitioned (one partition per drive) and formatted (NTFS) that contain nothing you want to keep

Getting Down to Business

As you learned in Chapter 9 of *Mike Meyers' CompTIA A+ Guide to Managing and Troubleshooting PCs*, there are many advantages to using dynamic disks. One of those is the ability to set up a software-based RAID, as you will learn in Lab Exercise 9.05. In this lab, you will prepare for that upcoming lab by converting two basic disks to dynamic disks.

→ **Note**

The entire physical disk will be converted from basic to dynamic; you can't convert individual partitions separately.

Step 1 Open the Disk Management utility, as in the previous lab exercise.

Step 2 Delete the existing partitions on the disks to be converted. This is not necessary in order to convert to a dynamic disk; you can retain a disk's existing partitions and data when converting. However, we are doing so in this exercise because it will simplify the next exercise.

  a. Right-click a partition and choose Delete Volume.

  b. Click Yes to confirm.

  c. Repeat Steps a and b for each remaining partition on each of the disks to be converted to dynamic disks.

Step 3 Convert each of the empty disks to dynamic disks:

  a. Right-click at the left end of the bar representing one of the disks in the bottom of the window, opening a shortcut menu (see Figure 9-13). This shortcut menu is for the entire physical disk, not any one partition.

  b. Click Convert to Dynamic Disk.

  c. In the Convert to Dynamic Disk dialog box, the checkbox for the selected disk is already marked. Select the checkbox for the other disk(s) you also want to convert at the same time.

  d. Click OK.

  e. Click Convert.

  f. A warning message appears that you will not be able to start installed operating systems from any volume on the disks. That's okay, since they are all blank.

  g. Click Yes to confirm.

After the disks have been converted, they appear with "Dynamic" in their names in Disk Management. Leave Disk Management open for the next lab exercise.

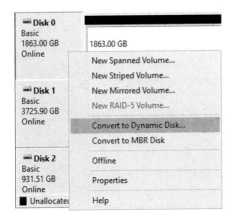

FIGURE 9-13 Right-click the disk to be converted and choose Convert to Dynamic Disk.

 **30 MINUTES**

Lab Exercise 9.05: Implementing Software RAID 0 with Disk Management

It's finally time to flex your RAID muscles. In this lab exercise, you'll use the dynamic disks you prepared in the previous exercises to create a software-based RAID 0 stripe set using two disks.

➜ **Note**

Software-based RAID is not ideal; if you have the equipment available, hardware-based RAID is better. You learned how to create a hardware-based RAID in Lab Exercise 8.06, "Configuring a Hardware RAID," and you will revisit the skill in Lab Exercise 11.07, "Installing Ubuntu Linux."

Learning Objectives

In this exercise, you'll use the Disk Management program to configure a RAID 0 striped volume.

At the end of this lab, you'll be able to

- Create and configure a RAID 0 striped volume

✖ **Cross-Reference**

Additional information on RAID 0, 1, and 5 may be found in the "Dynamic Disks" section in Chapter 9 of *Mike Meyers' CompTIA A+ Guide to Managing and Troubleshooting PCs.*

Lab Materials and Setup

The materials you need for this lab are

- A PC with the following:

- One of these Windows versions already installed:

    - Windows 7 Professional, Ultimate, or Enterprise

    - Windows 8 or 8.1 Pro

    - Windows 10 Pro

- Two additional hard drives that have been converted to dynamic disks (in Lab Exercise 9.04)

✖   Warning

The steps in this lab will destroy any data on the disks. Practice this lab only on disks that don't contain any data you need.

Getting Down to Business

At this point, you should have two dynamic disks, each with no partitions (volumes) on them. Each of them should show its space as Unallocated in Disk Management. From here, complete the following steps.

Step 1   Right-click at the far left end of the bar representing one of the disks in the bottom part of the Disk Management window. A shortcut menu appears (see Figure 9-14). Click New Striped Volume.

Figure 9-14   Right-click one of the disks to be involved in the RAID and choose New Striped Volume.

Step 2 Work through the New Striped Volume Wizard, as follows:

a. In the New Striped Volume Wizard, click Next.

b. Select the second disk to be included in the RAID, and then click Add to move it to the Selected list. Now there are two disks listed there: the original one you chose in Step 1, and the second one you added. See Figure 9-15.

c. Click Next. You are prompted to assign a drive letter.

d. Choose a different drive letter if desired, or leave the default selection.

e. Click Next.

f. Leave the default formatting option selected (NTFS). Select the Quick Formatting option to save time.

g. Click Next.

h. Click Finish. You now have a striped volume.

If the two drives were not the same capacity, you will notice in Disk Management that only a part of the larger drive was used for the RAID, to match the capacity of the smaller drive. The rest of the space shows as Unallocated.

Step 3 Look in File Explorer/Windows Explorer for the new drive. Notice that its capacity is the combined capacity of the two drives if they are the same size, or double the capacity of the smaller of the two drives if they were different sizes.

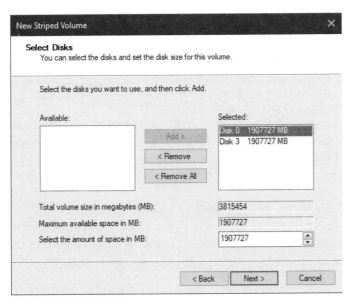

FIGURE 9-15 Add the second disk to be included in the RAID.

Step 4   If desired, delete the volumes and practice deleting and creating various sizes of striped volumes using various file systems. Can you format a striped volume with FAT? Why or why not?

_____

_____

Step 5   Finish up by deleting all the volumes from the two blank drives and converting them back to Basic disks. To do so:

   a.   Right-click the striped volume on one of the disks and choose Delete Volume.

   b.   At the confirmation box, click Yes. Notice that the volumes that were shown on both physical disks are now gone; they were actually a single volume.

   c.   For each of the drives that still shows as Dynamic, right-click at the far left end of its bar and choose Convert to Basic Disk or Convert to MBR.

 **60 MINUTES**

Lab Exercise 9.06: Maintaining and Troubleshooting Hard Drives

Of all the devices installed in a PC, hard drives tend to need the most attention. Maintaining and troubleshooting hard drives is one of the most common tasks you'll undertake as a PC tech, but also one of the most important.

Windows includes three important drive maintenance tools that can help correct storage errors and improve performance:

- **Error checking**   This GUI tool checks for storage errors, such as two files both claiming the same cluster or an orphan cluster that no file claims. It can also check the surface of the HDD for any unreadable or unwriteable areas, and mark those areas as off-limits. The command-line utility that performs the same duties is called chkdsk. This utility is only for magnetic HDDs, not SSDs.

- **Optimize Drives**   This tool (known as Disk Defragmenter in Windows 7) relocates stored files so that all the clusters for a particular file are stored contiguously. Doing so modestly improves disk seek times because the read/write head doesn't have to jump around picking up data from all over the place. (As you can probably deduce, this isn't of any use on SSDs.)

- **Disk Cleanup**   This tool works at the Windows system level, rather than the disk level. It identifies files that are unnecessary, like temporary files and setup files for applications you have already installed, and offers to delete them for you, saving disk space.

Learning to use these utilities is useful, both for the CompTIA A+ 1002 exam and for your everyday work in the field. However, they're not essential tools like they were a decade or more ago. Technologies have advanced to the point where disk errors are uncommon (and usually automatically fixed by the OS before you even know they exist). Optimizing offers only very minor performance improvements on modern drives, and hard drive capacities are so gigantic that saving a bit of disk space is usually not that important. So, learn these, but don't spend hours tinkering with them.

Learning Objectives

This lab provides practice in running several essential disk utilities.

At the end of this lab, you'll be able to

- Use Error checking to scan for and fix physical errors on the hard drive
- Use the Disk Defragmenter or Optimize Drives utility to reorganize the hard drive's file structure
- Use the Disk Cleanup utility to reclaim wasted disk space

Lab Materials and Setup

The materials you need for this lab are

- A fully functioning Windows PC

Getting Down to Business

If you're getting obvious disk-related errors (such as error messages indicating that your disk has bad clusters or cannot be read), or if files are missing or corrupt, a disk check is in order. You might also run a disk check when you acquire a used system, to make sure all is well with the hard drives. It's also a good idea to do a disk check after a serious system crash or after removing a virus infection.

You'll know that it's time to optimize a hard drive when it seems to be taking longer for large files to open or for Windows to start. Another sign that your drive needs optimization is excessive disk activity, or disk "thrashing." The hard disk LED flashes when the disk is operating, and you might hear the drive's mechanical parts moving as well, as the actuator arm moves in and out to pick up data from clusters.

Step 1   Skip this step if you don't have a magnetic hard drive to check.

To scan a hard drive for physical problems, open This PC (or Computer) and right-click the hard drive's icon. Select Properties, and then select the Tools tab, shown in Figure 9-16. Click Check (or Check now) to start the Error checking utility.

In Windows 7, you can opt to fix file system errors automatically, scan for and attempt to recover bad blocks, or both. See Figure 9-17. When you've made your selections, click Start.

FIGURE 9-16 Disk Properties Tools tab

✔ **Hint**

The Error checking utility must have *exclusive* access to the drive to finish scanning it. If you have services or applications running in the background, the utility will halt. In most cases, the utility will ask you if you want to check the hard disk for errors the next time you start your computer. This is common in Windows 7, but in Windows 8 and later Microsoft seems to have figured out how to run the check without restarting, so you seldom see that warning anymore.

FIGURE 9-17 Error checking in Windows 7

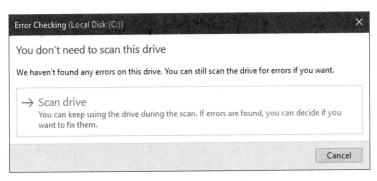

FIGURE 9-18 Error Checking dialog box in Windows 10

In Windows 8, 8.1, and 10, you don't see the options shown in Figure 9-17. Windows lets you know whether it thinks you need to scan the drive, and offers to let you scan it anyway (even if no errors have been detected yet) by clicking Scan drive. See Figure 9-18.

Step 2 Skip this step if you don't have a magnetic hard drive to optimize.

To launch Disk Defragmenter, click Defragment now (Windows 7) or Optimize (Windows 8 and later) on the Tools tab.

For Windows 7, in the Disk Defragmenter dialog box (see Figure 9-19), you have a choice: click Analyze disk to examine the disk to see if a defragmenting operation is needed, or simply click Defragment disk to start the process without first analyzing the disk.

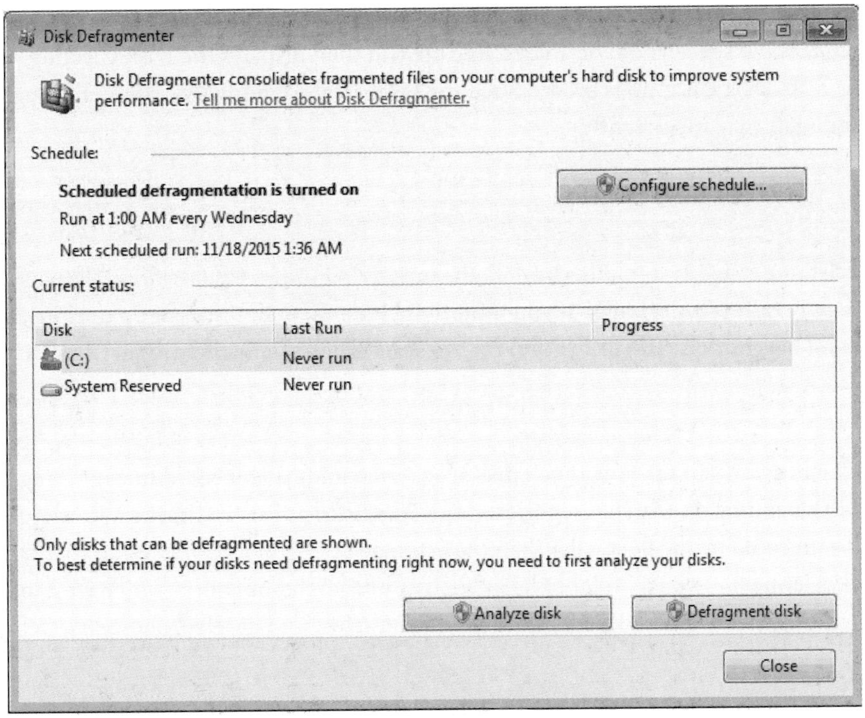

FIGURE 9-19 Disk Defragmenter in Windows 7

> **➜ Note**
>
> Notice the Configure schedule button in Figure 9-19. You can use that to set up defragmentation to occur automatically if it is not already configured to do so.

In Windows 8 and later, the utility is called Optimize Drives, but it's otherwise the same as in Figure 9-19. You have the same basic choices: Analyze and Optimize, and you can click Change settings to schedule optimization.

Step 3   Next, let's look at the Disk Cleanup utility. Unlike the other two tools discussed in the previous steps, this utility doesn't operate at the disk level; it works within Windows itself, getting rid of unneeded files that may be causing the hard disk to fill up. You would run this utility if you were running out of hard disk space.

> **✔ Tip**
>
> Because Windows uses hard disk space for virtual memory, if you don't have much empty hard disk space, the size of your paging file may be decreased, which can in turn cause performance problems with Windows. That's why a system that is running out of disk space often appears to run more sluggishly than normal. Disk Cleanup is one way to correct such a problem; another is simply to move off some of the stuff stored on that drive to another drive for archiving.

To use Disk Cleanup, click the General tab in the drive's Properties dialog box, and then click Disk Cleanup. Disk Cleanup calculates the space you'll be able to free up, and then displays the Disk Cleanup dialog box, shown in Figure 9-20. Disk Cleanup is pretty much the same in all Windows versions, although the specific file categories it targets may vary slightly.

> **✔ Tip**
>
> Disk Cleanup doesn't list unneeded system files by default, such as Windows Update files that have already been installed and crash error reports. If you want to include them in the cleanup options, click the Clean up system files button. The utility will then rescan and present a new report screen.

Near the top of the dialog box you can see how much disk space (maximum) you could free up using Disk Cleanup. But look carefully! Depending on which categories in the *Files to delete* list are checked, the actual amount of disk space you'll gain could be much smaller than the estimate at the top. Keep in mind that Disk Cleanup might recommend deleting files you'd prefer to keep, such as Image Thumbnails; if you have a lot of picture files (like I do), rebuilding them could take a lot of time. As you select and deselect choices, watch this

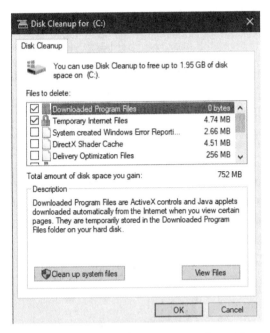

FIGURE 9-20 Disk Cleanup in Windows 10

value change. Disk Cleanup can remove Recycle Bin files and temporary Internet files, and can also compress old files. When you're ready to clean, click OK and let Disk Cleanup do its thing.

Step 4   We'll finish up this lab by running the command-line version of the Error checking program, chkdsk. This is a venerable command from the days of DOS, but it still works today.

One important thing to note about chkdsk is that if you run it without any switches, it doesn't make any changes. It literally "checks" for errors but it doesn't fix them. To fix errors, you must run it with the /f switch. (Presumably f stands for "fix.")

Try the following to see chkdsk in action:

a.   Open a command prompt window. In Windows 7, click Start, type **cmd**, and press ENTER. In Windows 8.1 or 10, right-click the Start button and choose Command Prompt (Admin).

b.   Type **chkdsk** and press ENTER. An error check begins; you can watch it count down as it operates. This may take several minutes.

c.   If any errors were found, repeat using the /**f** switch (or better yet, run the graphical Error checking utility as in Step 1).

d.   Close the command prompt window.

Lab Analysis Test

1. Name at least two indicators that you should perform maintenance on your hard drive.

2. What is the command-line version of the Windows Error checking utility?

3. Amanda argues that a hard drive must be formatted before you can set up the partitions. Samantha says the drive must be partitioned first. Who is correct, and why?

4. Kyle is running out of disk space on his hard drive on a Windows 7 Professional system. He has installed and configured a third hard drive in the system to increase the total storage. He is planning on converting his current drive to dynamic storage and extending the storage space to the newly installed drive (also dynamic storage). Pablo argues that the conversion is destructive and that Kyle would not be able to extend the volume anyway. Is Kyle going to be able to make this work?

5. Sean has created a RAID 0 array using three drives on a Windows 10 Pro system. After running the system for a couple of years, he arrived at work one day to find one of the three drives had failed. He thought that if only one drive failed, he would still be able to access his data. What facts about RAID 0 did Sean misunderstand?

Key Term Quiz

Use the following terms to complete the following sentences. Not all terms will be used.

basic disk	Error checking
chkdsk	format
defragmentation	GParted
Disk Cleanup	partition
Disk Management	volumes
dynamic disk	Windows installation media

1. To partition and format a hard drive when no operating system has been installed, you may use either _____ or _____ to boot the system and run disk setup utilities.

2. Use a(n) _____ tool to fix noncontiguous file clusters on a hard drive.

3. The _____ tool enables you to partition and format drives in Windows.

4. Microsoft supports two types of storage configurations now; the _____ uses partitions, whereas the _____ uses _____.

5. If your hard drive is running out of free space, you should use the _____ utility.

Chapter 10

Essential Peripherals

Lab Exercises

Peripherals are essential to customizing a desktop or laptop computer for specific tasks. This chapter provides a variety of exercises to help users troubleshoot, maintain, or install important types of peripherals.

USB ports are the most versatile ports for adding peripherals ranging from printers and webcams to mice, keyboards, and external drives. Keeping USB ports working properly is a vital task in a USB-dominated world.

Because of the wide variety of USB port types and USB flash drives, finding the fastest drive and port combinations takes more than simply looking at rated speeds. In this chapter, you learn how to evaluate USB port and device performance.

Keyboards have many openings for dirt, dust, and liquids, all of which can adversely affect how keyboards work. Depending upon the keyboard type and replacement cost, cleaning a dirty keyboard can be a cost-effective method for returning a high-quality keyboard to active service. Pointing devices can also be affected by dust interfering with their optical sensors, but a more critical issue is proper configuration.

Although computers have included built-in sound support for many years, gamers and sound editing specialists need higher-quality audio. The processing of adding a new sound card also includes disabling the existing sound hardware.

 **30 MINUTES**

Lab Exercise 10.01: Troubleshooting and Benchmarking USB

Universal serial bus (USB) has become the expected standard port for a wide variety of peripheral devices, from basic keyboards and mice to high-end external drives, image scanners, and webcams.

Most people take USB ports for granted—that is, until they don't work right for some reason. "Not working right" could mean not working at all, or it could mean operating at a slower speed than anticipated. In this lab exercise, you will learn how to troubleshoot problems with a USB port, including benchmarking it to make sure it is transferring data at a rate commensurate with the USB standard it is supposed to conform to.

Learning Objectives

This lab teaches you some troubleshooting and benchmarking techniques for USB devices and ports.

At the end of this lab, you'll be able to

- Troubleshoot problems with USB devices and ports

- Benchmark a USB storage device running on a specific port

Lab Materials and Setup

The materials you need for this lab are

- A Windows system

- A USB flash drive

- The USB Flash Benchmark utility, available from http://usbflashspeed.com/static/FlashBench.zip

- A USB 3.0 card reader

- A USB flash memory card compatible with the card reader (such as an SD or microSD card)

Getting Down to Business

In this lab exercise you will simulate troubleshooting for a variety of problems involving USB devices, including not being recognized, not being adequately powered, and not performing at expected data transfer rates.

Step 1 You connect a USB flash drive, and Windows ponders it for a minute or two. At long last, a message appears such as *USB Device Not Recognized*. Now what? In earlier days of USB devices, this was actually pretty common. Many USB devices therefore came with a disc containing the needed driver. Nowadays, you don't see that so much, because most USB devices work smoothly with the generic USB devices and controllers on the average system.

When that dreaded error occurs, here are some steps to take to troubleshoot. Walk through these now, in preparation for needing them later. In the column on the right, jot down notes about why each of these steps might help, based on what you know about PCs, Windows, and USB. Refer to Chapter 10 of *Mike Meyers' CompTIA A+ Guide to Managing and Troubleshooting PCs,* as needed.

Try This		Why Would This Help?
a.	Disconnect and reconnect the device.	
b.	Try a different USB port.	
c.	Try the device in a different computer.	
d.	Reboot.	
e.	Check the device manufacturer's Web site for drivers.	
f.	Check for motherboard driver or firmware updates, and install if any are found.	
g.	Use Device Manager to check your USB controller.	
h.	Use Device Manager to check your USB device.	

Step 2   Many USB devices are *bus-powered*; they draw the small amount of electricity they need from the USB port. USB keyboards and mice are like that, for example, as are USB flash drives. And that's fine, in most cases. On most motherboards, a USB host adapter supports only a couple of ports. Most external devices use somewhere between 100 and 200 mA (milliamps) apiece, and most host adapters deliver 500 mA, so a single host adapter has no trouble supporting them.

A problem can crop up, though, when you connect multiple bus-powered devices to USB ports that are themselves piggybacked on other bus-powered devices. You can nest USB hubs up to seven levels deep on a single port, so it is possible for a single port on the computer to end up supporting several dozen USB devices. Even if each device is just drawing a little bit of power, you can quickly run into a situation where there is insufficient power from the port to power all the devices if the externally connected USB devices and hubs don't have their own power supplies. You might see a Windows error message telling you that the device has insufficient power, or the device might simply not work right (or at all), especially when another device on the same host controller is also drawing power.

Even if you have only a single USB bus-powered hub, you can run out of power very quickly. USB bus-powered hubs deliver only 100 mA of power to each port, so a device that draws more than 100 mA will fail.

Follow these steps to check out the power usage of the devices plugged into your USB ports:

a.   Open Device Manager:

- In Windows 8.1 and Windows 10, right-click the Start button and choose Device Manager.

- In Windows 8, open the Search charm, enter **device manager**, and click the matching app.

- In Windows 7, open the Control Panel, navigate to System, and then click Device Manager.

b.   Double-click the Universal Serial Bus Controllers category to expand it.

c.   Double-click one of the Generic USB Hub or USB Root Hub entries to open its Properties dialog box.

d. Click the Power tab. The Hub information section shows the total power available, and the Attached devices section shows which devices are connected already and how much power they require.

e. To see all USB devices, you might need to repeat Steps 1c and 1d. Figure 10-1 shows an example from Windows 10 in which installed devices are connected to two generic USB hubs.

f. For each of the entries in the Universal Serial Bus Controllers category in Device Manager that has a Power tab in its Properties dialog box, record the following information:

Device Name	Total Power Available	Devices Attached	Power Required for Each Attached Device

g. In the chart, identify each of the devices in the Devices Attached column. You might be surprised to find out what devices are attached to the motherboard's USB bus. For example, a laptop's touch screen might be connected to a generic USB hub.

h. Close all open windows, including Device Manager, when you are finished.

Step 3 USB storage devices are fairly reliable in general, but they do have one Achilles' heel: if you unplug the device from the PC in the middle of a write operation, you get corrupted files. To prevent

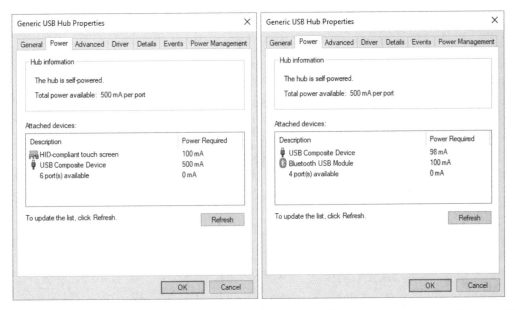

FIGURE 10-1 Device Manager reports the total power available and power required for each USB hub.

this, Windows offers the Safely Remove Hardware tool, which waits until the USB drive finishes its write operation and then shuts down the communication on that port and lets you know it is safe to disconnect the drive. Communication will not resume on that port until the device is disconnected and reconnected.

Follow these steps to try out the Safely Remove Hardware tool:

a.   Connect an external USB drive to the PC.

b.   Write a file to it.

c.   In the notification area, click the Safely Remove Hardware icon (shown in Figure 10-2). If the icon is not visible, click the up arrow in the notification area (refer to Figure 10-2).

d.   On the menu that appears, click the Eject command for the connected device.

e.   Try accessing the connected device. What happens?

_____

f.   Disconnect and reconnect the device. Then try accessing it again. What happens?

_____

Step 4   Not all USB ports are created equal. There are four different USB port standards that you may encounter on computing devices. The higher the standard number, the higher the maximum data throughput rate. Ports and connectors are color-coded: white is USB 1.1, black is USB 2.0, blue is USB 3.0/USB 3.1

FIGURE 10-2   Click this icon in the notification area to remove a USB drive safely (Windows 10 version shown).

Name	Standard	Maximum Speed
Low-Speed USB	USB 1.1	1.5 Mbps
Full-Speed USB	USB 1.1	12 Mbps
Hi-Speed USB	USB 2.0	480 Mbps
SuperSpeed USB	USB 3.0/USB 3.1 Gen 1	5 Gbps
SuperSpeed USB 10 Gbps	USB 3.1 Gen 2	10 Gbps

TABLE 10-1 Data Transfer Rates per USB Standard

Gen 1, and teal is USB 3.1 Gen 2. There is basic backward compatibility, but if you connect a device that wants faster data throughput to a slower port, it won't perform to its top potential. Table 10-1 provides the maximum speeds for each type, although you won't see these top speeds in real-life usage.

The real-life transfer rate is determined by whatever is the bottleneck point among these factors: the standard that the port supports, the standard that the drive supports, the limitations of the hardware, and the sizes of the files being transferred (larger files transfer faster than smaller ones). Generally speaking, USB 2.0 is adequate for flash drives, but SSDs and external hard drives will benefit from USB 3.0 or 3.1.

Follow these steps to benchmark the real-life performance of a flash drive:

a. Identify the USB ports available to you on the PC you're working with. Choose the fastest port available if there are different port standards (for example, both USB 2.0 and 3.0 ports). Connect your flash drive to the port.

b. If you didn't install it earlier, download the USB Flash Benchmark utility from http://usbflashspeed .com/static/FlashBench.zip. Unpack its ZIP file and run the utility (Flashbench.exe).

c. In the USB Flash Benchmark window, open the Drive drop-down list and choose the flash drive.

d. Click the Benchmark button to begin the test. Wait for the test to complete.

Figure 10-3 shows an example of the completed test for a typical USB 2.0 flash drive, and Figure 10-4 shows an example for a typical USB 3.0 flash drive. The top line represents read speed, and the bottom line write speed. The numbers along the bottom of the chart represent different file sizes; notice that the larger file sizes (toward the left end) produce the fastest results.

What was the best transfer rate for a 16-MB file? _____

Flash drive name, model #, rating: _____

What was the best transfer rate for a 2-KB file? _____

Flash drive name, model #, rating: _____

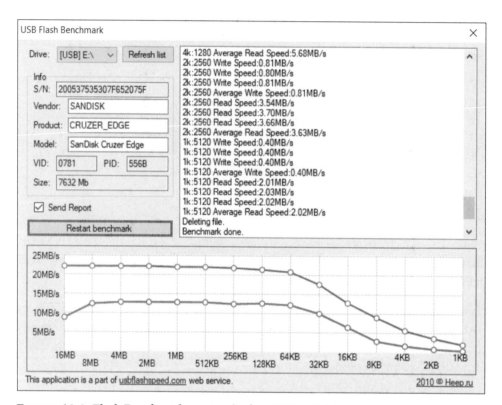

FIGURE 10-3 Flash Benchmark test results for a USB 2.0 drive

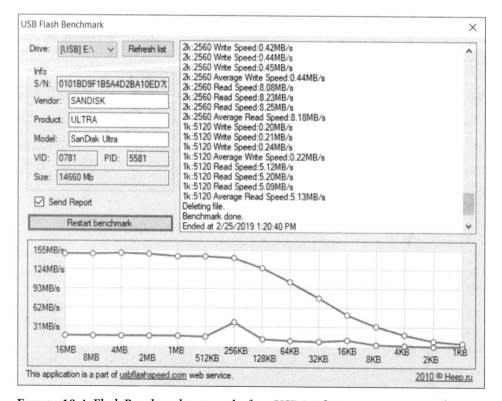

FIGURE 10-4 Flash Benchmark test results for a USB 3.0 drive

e. (Optional) If available, test other USB flash drives, and/or different USB ports on your PC, to see if the results vary. If you want to test USB flash memory cards, use a USB 3.0 card reader and a USB 3.0 port. How did the results vary, if at all?

_____

_____

 **30 MINUTES**

Lab Exercise 10.02: Disassembling and Cleaning a Keyboard

Keyboards are plentiful and common, and a new basic keyboard is very inexpensive. Even with cheap keyboards, users tend to get attached to these devices over time—and in the case of an expensive keyboard with lots of extra buttons and features, the user may have both a financial *and* an emotional attachment! For these reasons, it's important that you learn to play "Dr. Keyboard," fixing these devices when they break.

Learning Objectives

This lab teaches you how to clean and perform simple repairs on a standard keyboard.

At the end of this lab, you'll be able to

- Repair stuck keyboard keys
- Dismantle and clean a keyboard

Lab Materials and Setup

The materials you need for this lab are

- A Windows system
- As many "throw-away" keyboards as possible (functional keyboards that you won't mind throwing away at the end of this lab; connection type is unimportant as long as they're usable by a Windows system)
- A medium-sized flathead screwdriver
- Compressed air
- A lint-free cloth

✔ **Hint**

Try to avoid using older (pre-2004) laptop keyboards, as many older laptop keyboards used a delicate type of scissors key connector that would shatter if pried off.

Getting Down to Business

In this exercise, you'll dismantle one or more keyboards, cleaning up the keyboard components in the process, and then reassemble the device(s) and test for functionality.

Step 1   Disconnect the keyboard from the Windows system. Try prying off two or three keys using the flathead screwdriver (see Figure 10-5). Include more difficult keys such as the SPACEBAR, ENTER/RETURN, and a key from the center of the keyboard such as the letter G. Inspect the bottom of the key and the key post that it sits on—how much dirt is there? Reinsert the keys, making sure they are snapped all the way down.

Step 2   Test the keyboard by installing it into a Windows system. If any of the keys you removed aren't working, double-check that they're properly snapped in. Shut down the system and remove the keyboard. Repeat this process until all keys are working.

→ **Note**

What should you do if you break a key? That depends on the keyboard. If you've broken a key on a $10–30 "throwaway" model, don't worry about it. Just recycle it unless you have a spare nonworking keyboard you can cannibalize for parts. However, if you break a gaming keyboard that uses Cherry or similar mechanical switches, there are replacement key switches and keytops available from many third-party vendors. If a classic IBM/Lexmark/Unicomp buckling-spring keyboard has a broken key, check with Unicomp for a replacement at www.pckeyboard.com.

FIGURE 10-5   Removing the CTRL key with a screwdriver

Step 3   Insert the nozzle of the compressed air under a key and start blasting away. If the keyboard is really old or looks dirty, you may want to do this outside! Did you see any dust or crumbs come out?

Step 4   Completely dismantle the keyboard. Most keyboards have a number of screws underneath that you must first remove to begin this process. Inspect the screws—are they different sizes? Keep track of which screw goes into which hole.

Step 5   The inside of the keyboard will have a number of plastic contact templates (see Figure 10-6). Remove these, keeping track of their relation to each other so you can reassemble them. Wipe down each template with the lint-free cloth dampened with water. If you run into serious dirt, add a bit of mild detergent and repeat until the keyboard is clean.

✖ Warning

All keyboards have small circuit boards inside as well. Don't get them wet!

Step 6   After allowing everything to dry, reassemble the keyboard and test it on a Windows system. If the keyboard is not working properly, dismantle it and try again.

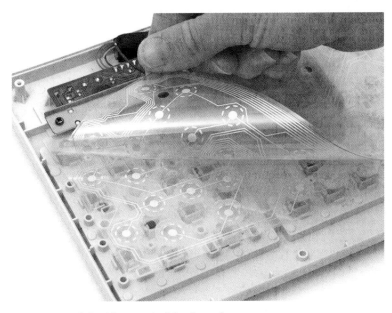

FIGURE 10-6 Inside a typical keyboard

 **30 MINUTES**

Lab Exercise 10.03: Troubleshooting and Adjusting a Pointing Device

The humble pointing device—that is, the mouse, trackball, touchpad, or whatever it is that moves the mouse pointer onscreen—is another component that is easy to ignore when it's working. It's only when it starts acting up that it draws our attention. In this lab exercise, you'll learn some of the most common things that go wrong with pointing devices and how to fix them. You'll also learn how to make adjustments to the pointing device's settings in Windows.

Learning Objectives

This lab teaches you the basics of troubleshooting pointing device problems and adjusting pointer settings.

At the end of this lab, you'll be able to

- Troubleshoot common pointing device problems

- Adjust pointing device settings

Lab Materials and Setup

The materials you need for this lab are

- A working computer system running Windows

- One or more pointing devices, either built-in (such as a touchpad on a laptop) or external (such as a mouse or trackball)

Getting Down to Business

When a pointing device acts up, it is generally in one of these ways:

- The pointer doesn't move at all.

- The pointer moves along only one axis (up/down or left/right).

- The pointer is erratic and jumps around all over the screen.

- The pointer doesn't move the way you prefer it to, or doesn't recognize double-clicks consistently.

The following steps look at each of these conditions.

Step 1 If the pointer doesn't work at all when you operate the device, follow along with these steps to troubleshoot. (Go ahead and work through these steps even if your pointing device is fine, just for the practice.)

a. Check that the device is securely connected to the correct port on the computer. If it's a USB mouse or USB wireless mouse receiver, it can go into any USB port. On a very old computer with a PS/2 mouse, it must be connected to the mouse port (green). It won't work if it's connected to the keyboard port (also PS/2, but purple). A combo PS/2 port (green/purple) can be used with either a PS/2 mouse or PS/2 keyboard.

b. If the mouse is wireless, make sure the batteries are working. Replace the batteries with fresh alkaline or lithium batteries (rechargeable batteries produce a lower voltage and are not suitable for most mice). After replacing the batteries, re-pair the mouse with the receiver.

c. Open Device Manager (see Lab Exercise 10.01 for details).

d. Double-click the Mice and other pointing devices category to expand it. (You might also look in the Human Interface Devices category for your pointing device. It may appear in both categories.)

e. Look for your mouse there. It shouldn't have any special symbols on its icon (like a question mark or exclamation point).

✔ **Tip**

You might have more than one mouse listed in this category, especially if you are working with a laptop with its own built-in pointing device and also using an external mouse. To differentiate, double-click an entry and see if the Location field on the General tab provides any helpful information.

---

f. Double-click the mouse to open its Properties dialog box and confirm a device status of *This device is working properly* as in Figure 10-7. If so, great. Close all dialog boxes and close Device Manager. You're done here. If not, proceed to the next step.

If there's a problem with the device, try updating its driver. To do so:

g. In the device's Properties dialog box, click the Driver tab, and then click Update Driver.

h. Click Search automatically for updated driver software.

i. Follow the prompts that appear to install a newer driver or to confirm that the best driver is already installed. Then click Close twice to finish up.

If the device still isn't working, try removing it from Device Manager and letting Windows redetect it, as follows:

j. From Device Manager, select the device (single-click, not double) and then click the Uninstall button on the toolbar. Respond to any confirmation boxes that appear.

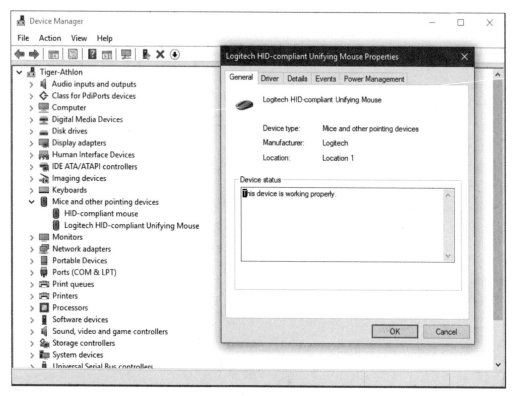

FIGURE 10-7 Device Manager and the Properties box for a mouse.

   k.   On the toolbar, click the Scan for Hardware Changes button to refresh the list of installed devices. Your pointing device should be redetected and its driver reinstalled.

If it still doesn't work after all this, the device itself is probably physically dead/broken.

Step 2   Next, let's say that the pointer is moving when you move the device…sort of. It only moves in certain ways (like only up and down), or it stops and starts or takes a lot of movement for the arrow to travel a short distance. These are all classic symptoms of a dirty device.

Clean up the device as best you can; some devices are easy to disassemble, while others are a solid chunk of technology with no visible entryway. Remove any clumps of dirt, hair, or lint that may be blocking the sensors or preventing the wheels or rollers on a trackball from turning freely. Use canned air to blow out lint from anywhere you can't reach.

Here are some tips:

- Disconnect the device from the PC before cleaning it if possible.

- Use alcohol and cotton swabs to get inside any cavities or chambers where there are sensors or rollers.

- You shouldn't need to use any hand tools to get inside the device to clean it. If it doesn't disassemble easily with just your fingers, you shouldn't attempt to get inside it.

Step 3   A pointer that's sluggish and works intermittently is usually a hardware issue, as discussed in Step 2, but a pointer that's manic and crazy, jumping around all over the place when you move the mouse, that's a software issue. More specifically, that's usually a problem with the display adapter. Follow these steps to see if you can straighten that out:

a.   Reboot. A lot of times this clears up the problem.

b.   If rebooting didn't help, update the driver for the display adapter. Use the same basic process as for updating the pointing device driver in Step 1, or go to the adapter manufacturer's Web site and download a driver update directly.

Step 4   If the pointer is moving—but not to your liking—you can adjust its operation in the Mouse Properties in the Control Panel. Here's how to do that:

a.   Open the Control Panel.

b.   Click in the Search Control Panel box and type **mouse**. In the search results, click Change mouse settings. The Mouse Properties dialog box opens.

✔ **Hint**

The interface you see for mouse controls in Windows depends on the type of pointing device; some pointing devices install their own driver software that supersedes the default Mouse Properties in Windows.

---

c.   Click through the tabs in the dialog box, making changes as desired. For example, you can

- On the Buttons tab, drag the Speed slider to adjust the double-click speed
- On the Pointer tab, change the appearance of the pointers
- On the Pointer Options tab, adjust the pointer speed

d.   Click OK. Then close all open windows.

 **30 MINUTES**

Lab Exercise 10.04: Installing Sound

Sound cards aren't as common as they once were, because most motherboards include onboard sound these days. If you don't mind the default sound card's capabilities, you don't have to fuss with adding another one. Nevertheless, high-end audiophiles can be extremely picky about their sound card specifications, and may prefer to research and purchase a top-of-the-line model.

Let's say you have a client who is one of those people who really cares about the sound card. The first task on the agenda is to do a little research on sound cards and choose a few that meet the needs of this project. There are a number of different sound chips, and the "card" can be anything from the onboard sound capability of a mid-priced system to professional multichannel (input/output) devices used in recording studios. After you assemble a few candidates, you will select a sound card and then install, configure, and test that card. For the purpose of completing this lab, it is perfectly acceptable to use any working card, or an onboard sound device if that's what you have available.

Learning Objectives

This lab teaches you the basics of installing and configuring a sound card.

At the end of this lab, you'll be able to

- Identify features of sound cards

- Remove and install a sound card and associated devices (speakers and microphone)

- Configure a sound card

Lab Materials and Setup

The materials you need for this lab are

- A working computer system running Windows

- A removable sound card, microphone, and speakers properly installed and functioning (the sound drivers must either be part of the operating system in use or be available on disc or online)

✖ Warning

Different versions of Windows handle the drivers differently, to say the least. You should have a current driver for your sound card handy, just in case Windows decides it cannot remember your sound card when you go to reinstall!

Getting Down to Business

This lab will step you through removing, researching specifications for, installing, and configuring a sound card.

✖ Cross-Reference

For more information on sound cards, review the "Sound Components" section in Chapter 10 of *Mike Meyers' CompTIA A+ Guide to Managing and Troubleshooting PCs*.

Step 1 Take a moment and look up the specifications of your current sound card online. You can find out the sound card make/model by looking in Device Manager or in System Information.

Then look up the specs for at least two other sound cards, such as higher-end models by ASUS and Creative (Sound Blaster). Record in the following chart your current sound card specs and the specs for two other sound cards.

	Current Sound Card	Sound Card 1	Sound Card 2
Manufacturer and Model			
Slot Type			
Output Signal-to-Noise Ratio (A-Weighted) (Front-out)			
Frequency Response (–3 dB, 16-bit/44.1-KHz input)			
Output THD+N at 1 KHz (Front-out)			
Chipset			
Analog Output			
Analog Input			
Digital I/O			
Special Features			
Compatible OSs			

✔ **Tip**

THD+N means total harmonic distortion plus noise. The way it's calculated is complicated and not important to know. Lower THD+N values mean more accurate sound reproduction.

Step 2 Now that you've seen some of the relevant specifications, the next step is to practice removing and reinstalling the sound card.

> ✔ **Hint**
>
> This lab assumes that you have a removable sound card, not onboard sound. If all you have to work with is a system with onboard sound, go into the CMOS setup utility and turn off the onboard sound. Make what observations you can and resume the exercise with Step 3. When the time comes in the second half of Step 3 to reinstall the sound card, just go back into CMOS and enable the onboard sound again.

a.   Shut down your system properly. Unplug the power cord.

b.   Remove the case cover from your system and locate the sound card (see Figure 10-8).

What type of slot does the card use? _____

c.   Disconnect any cables that are attached to the sound card (both internal and external), take out the screw that secures the sound card to the case, and then carefully remove the card. Make sure you're properly grounded before you touch the card!

What sort of internal connectors does the card have? _____

What sort of external connectors does it have? _____

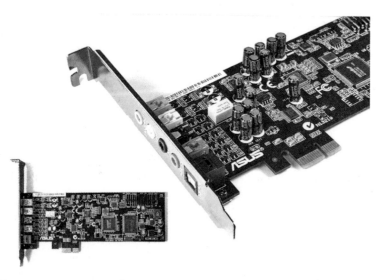

FIGURE 10-8 A typical sound card

    d.   Find the name of the card manufacturer and search that company's Web site for information on your specific model. This information is also available in the documentation for the card, if you still have it around.

    What is the brand name of the sound-processing chip? _____

    What is the brand name of the sound card? _____

    What is the model? _____

    Is the name on the chip different from the name of the manufacturer of the card? (For example, the chip might have *ESS* printed on it, while the board is marked *Creative Labs*.) _____

Step 3   With the card out of your system, turn on the machine and let it boot to the Windows Desktop. Then go to Device Manager and see if your sound card is still listed.

Did Windows automatically remove the device when the card was removed? _____

    If the sound card is still listed, highlight its icon, right-click, and select Uninstall.

    Save your changes and shut down your system properly.

    The next steps will confirm that the device has been removed:

    a.   Reboot your system, go to Device Manager, and confirm that the sound device is no longer listed.

    b.   Shut down your system and disconnect the power cord. Insert the sound card in the slot where you originally found it, secure the card to the case using the screw you removed, and reconnect all the cables.

    c.   Reboot the system. When plug and play (PnP) kicks in, your system should recognize that you have added a card.

    Windows will now locate the software drivers for the new hardware you installed. In fact, unless you uninstalled them, the drivers should still be on your system.

Step 4   Return to Device Manager. Find your device and open the Drivers tab and confirm that Windows installed the same drivers in the system. If necessary, use the driver disc to reinstall the correct drivers.

Step 5   To check the driver installation, use the DirectX Diagnostic Tool.

    a.   Start the DirectX Diagnostic Tool:

- In Windows 7, click Start, type **dxdiag** in the Search field, and press ENTER.

- In Windows 8.1, click Start, type **dxdiag**, and then click dxdiag in the search results.

- In Windows 10, click in the Search box on the taskbar, type **dxdiag**, and then click dxdiag in the search results.

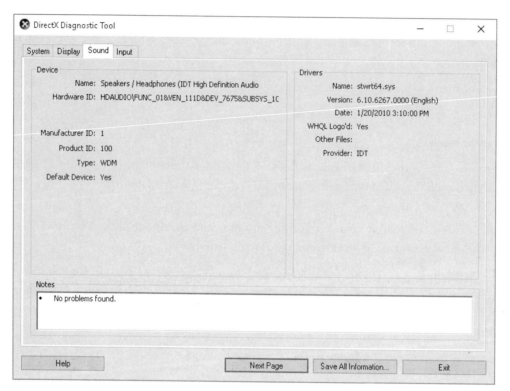

FIGURE 10-9 Using the DirectX Diagnostic Tool

    b. Click the Sound tab in the utility window and examine the information displayed about your sound card and drivers. See Figure 10-9.

    c. Click Exit to close the utility.

Step 6 To confirm that sound is working properly, start by ensuring that the speakers are powered and connected, and that the volume is set at a comfortable level.

Make sure your speakers are plugged into the proper jack on the sound card.

Is the speaker pair plugged into a working AC outlet, or does it have good batteries? _____

Is there a volume adjustment knob on your speakers? _____

If you have a volume knob, adjust it to the middle position.

To check the volume, play a sound file with your preferred audio player (Windows Media Player or a third-party app).

Step 7 Now suppose that your sound system is working, but your speakers sound a little rough. Are they "blown" out because they were overdriven with poor adjustments? You can go to the Audio Check website site and test the response of your speakers at different frequencies:

www.audiocheck.net/index.php

These tests will help you confirm whether your speakers can still handle all the frequencies they are designed to handle. Note any speaker issues that you discovered.

 **30 MINUTES**

Lab Exercise 10.05: Installing Optical Drives

Optical drives include all the drives that accept shiny round discs, including CD, DVD, and Blu-ray Disc (BD). Optical drives typically are internally installed, fitting into a 5.25-inch drive bay in a desktop case, and externally accessible once they are installed. Most full-size "tower" desktop cases have optical drives installed, although with the rise of downloadable apps, many small form factor systems (and most laptops) no longer include optical drives.

SATA interfaces are commonly used for optical drives in desktop computers as well as hard drives, although some very old computers might have IDE (also known as PATA or ATAPI) optical drives. In this lab, we are looking at SATA optical drives.

✖ Cross-Reference

If you are not familiar with IDE drive configuration, review the section "PATA" in Chapter 8 of *Mike Meyers' CompTIA A+ Guide to Managing and Troubleshooting PCs* **as needed.**

Learning Objectives

In this lab, you'll remove and inspect an optical drive, and then reinstall the drive.

At the end of this lab, you'll be able to

- Remove and install an optical drive safely and properly
- Identify the physical features of an optical drive

Lab Materials and Setup

The materials you need for this lab are

- A working computer with Windows and an optical drive of some type installed

Getting Down to Business

Removing an optical drive is almost too easy. The only real secret here is to remember which cable you removed and how the cable ends were oriented—you've got to make sure you can put it back!

Step 1 Properly shut down your system. There are so many different ways that drives are held into system cases that it would be impossible to list all of the various carriers, caddies, bays, and so on that might be used to hold your drive. Using whichever method is appropriate, remove the cover from the PC case so that you can access the screws on both sides of the drive. Using proper ESD procedures, perform the following steps to remove the drive from your system:

    a. Unplug the connections. First unplug the SATA power connection from the back of the drive, and then disconnect the SATA data cable from the drive.

    b. Using a Phillips-head screwdriver, remove the screws holding the drive in place. Notice that the screws are small-threaded screws—the same type you encountered when you removed and installed a hard drive.

✔ **Hint**

Some optical drives are held in their bays by rails. Simply squeeze the rail toggles (sticking out of the front) and remove the drive by pulling it forward.

Step 2 Inspect the optical drive. Look at the front of the drive. Do you see a tiny hole near the edge of the tray door? Most drives have such a hole (see Figure 10-10). You can take a straightened-out paper clip and push it into this hole to release the tray. This is handy in case you accidentally leave a disc in the drive when you remove it from the system. Go ahead and push a straightened-out paper clip into the hole to eject the tray.

Look at the back of the drive. You should see two areas for connections:

- The SATA power connection
- The connection for the SATA data cable

Step 3 Reinstall the optical drive into your system. Figure 10-11 shows a properly installed SATA drive.

FIGURE 10-10 A typical optical drive with a manual tray-ejector hole

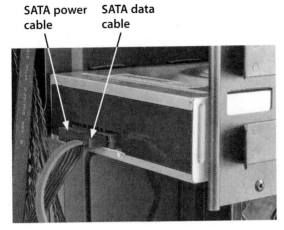

SATA power cable   SATA data cable

FIGURE 10-11 Viewing a properly installed SATA optical drive

Now answer these questions:

Did you fasten the drive using the correct screws or rails? _____

Is the data cable connected properly? _____

Is the power plug fully inserted? _____

Step 4   Leave the cover off the system and boot the PC to the Windows Desktop.

Step 5   Select Computer/This PC. Notice if the drive's icon is present. If so, all is well. If not, repeat Steps 2 and 3. The most common problem when installing hardware is a loose connection, so recheck your cable ends and try again. Replace the PC cover once the drive is recognized in Windows.

Lab Analysis Test

1. Mark loaned his computer to a co-worker, and when he got it back, the mouse pointer was moving slowly. He had to drag the mouse all the way across the mouse pad to get it to move just a few inches onscreen. Describe how you would troubleshoot and fix this problem.

2. Don has a wireless keyboard and wireless mouse. When he tries to enter CMOS setup as his computer starts up, he can't do it, because the wireless keyboard isn't recognized until later in the boot process. What do you suggest he do?

3. Donna installed a new sound card in a system that already has built-in sound on the motherboard. She unplugs the speaker from the built-in sound port on the PC and plugs it into the speaker port on the new sound card. Then she boots into Windows. She turns up the volume, but hears no sound. What should she do?

4. Rita just shut down her system after ripping a music CD to cloud storage. Unfortunately, she forgot to eject the optical drive tray before shutting down her system. She cannot log back onto her system until tomorrow morning because of account restrictions. What can she do to remove the disc before going home?

5. Jeff wants to buy a DVD rewriteable drive to add to his old PC, as an additional drive (not removing his old optical drive). His motherboard supports both SATA and PATA. What should he consider in choosing an interface?

Key Term Quiz

Use the following terms to complete the following sentences. Not all terms will be used.

2.0	PCIe slot
3.0	recalibrated
analog	sound
cleaned	updated
digital	USB
drive bay	

1. If you connect an external USB 3.0 hard drive to a USB _____ port, it will probably work but data transfers will be very slow.

2. You can check _____ drivers with the DirectX Diagnostic Tool.

3. When a trackball will only move the pointer up/down, it probably needs to be _____.

4. A high-quality sound card has a variety of ports, including both _____ and _____ inputs and outputs.

5. An optical drive would typically fit into a 5.25-inch _____ in a desktop case.

Chapter 11

Building a PC

Lab Exercises

Picking the right PC is a very personal choice, but the number of PCs available can make the search overwhelming. CompTIA, in its infinite wisdom, has decided to break down and categorize the different types of computers that users can choose from. Depending on the type of work that a user does, you need to be able to point them to a PC that can fill that role. Think of it as being similar to picking out an automobile. Some people need a truck with four-wheel drive and a huge bed for hauling equipment, while others need a small, compact car for city driving. In this chapter, we'll research a few different types of computers using the Internet and explore their differences.

As a PC technician, you'll spend a lot of time installing and upgrading operating systems. For this reason, it's important that you become familiar with the tasks involved; otherwise, you might find yourself in a tight spot when Windows won't install on the laptop that your boss needs for a presentation this afternoon.

A number of different operating systems are in use today, including Apple macOS, several different flavors of Linux, and of course the Microsoft Windows family. Generally speaking, you won't likely do any clean installs of macOS because Macs come with it preinstalled and free updates are automatically downloaded whenever they become available. Therefore, this chapter focuses mostly on Windows and Linux.

Just about anyone can install software if everything goes right and no problems come up during the process; plenty of people with minimal software knowledge have upgraded Windows without the slightest incident. Even an experienced technician may have problems, though, if the system has incompatible expansion cards, broken devices, or bad drivers. As a PC technician, you'll need to handle both the simple installations—the ones with only new, compatible components—and the more complex installations on older and more problematic systems.

Installing and upgrading Windows requires more than just popping in the installation disc and running the install program. You need to plan the installation thoughtfully, check for component compatibility, and thoroughly understand the installation options and how to configure them. Good planning up front will give you the best chances for a successful installation or upgrade.

Be sure to have everything you need before you start, from the installation disc to the discs containing your device drivers. Remember the old adage, "Measure twice, cut once." Believe me, it's no fun to start over on an installation or upgrade if you mess it up! Do it right the first time—you'll be glad you did.

 **30 MINUTES**

Lab Exercise 11.01: Building a Thick Client

A *thick client* is a PC that is equipped to run and store applications locally—in other words, a good old-fashioned PC. Techs rarely use the term "thick client" except when comparing it to its smaller sibling, the *thin client*. When building a thick client, you must consider all the tasks the machine will be asked to perform, and select components that will support those tasks adequately. In this exercise, we're not interested in a fancy PC (that'll come in Lab Exercise 11.02), but something basic that will run Windows, Office, and standard business applications and connect to a network.

Learning Objectives

In this exercise, you'll research what it takes to create a standard thick client.

At the end of this lab, you'll be able to

- Find parts for a standard thick client by using the Internet

Lab Materials and Setup

The materials you need for this lab are

- An Internet-capable PC for research

Getting Down to Business

Here is a list of criteria your PC must meet to qualify as a thick client for this lab exercise:

- Runs the latest Windows operating system
- Runs standard desktop applications such as Microsoft Office and Google Chrome
- Network connectivity
- Storage (SSD or HDD)
- Monitor
- Keyboard and mouse

Step 1   Open a Web browser and visit a Web site from which you can purchase computer parts. Suggestions include

- www.newegg.com
- www.tigerdirect.com
- www.cdw.com

Your instructor will set a price limit for you. You don't want to make a high-end gaming machine—at least not yet! If this is a self-guided course, then set a limit of $650. That should keep you in the realm of the thick client.

Step 2   Shop for the parts listed in the following table and complete the other columns for each component you choose.

Part	Model/Version	Web Site	Price
Motherboard			
CPU			
RAM			
Hard drive			
Optical drive			
Power supply			
Case			
Mouse			
Keyboard			
Monitor			
Windows OS			
Video card (optional)			

Step 3   Add up all the prices for your parts.

Grand total: _____

If you went over budget, find less expensive parts for your components, use a motherboard with built-in video instead of a separate video card, and try to cut some corners to make that perfect thick client computer.

 **30 MINUTES**

Lab Exercise 11.02: Building a Gaming PC

In Lab Exercise 11.01, you priced the parts for a standard thick client computer. Now let's have a little more fun and see what we need to build a gaming PC. Everything will be very similar to the previous exercise when picking out your parts, but with a special twist: your PC will need to be able to handle some of the most hardware-intensive applications on the market.

Learning Objectives

In this exercise, you'll research what it takes to create a gaming PC.

At the end of this lab, you'll be able to

- Find components for a gaming PC by using the Internet

Lab Materials and Setup

The materials you need for this lab are

- An Internet-capable PC for research

Getting Down to Business

Creating a gaming computer takes all the knowledge you gained from creating a thick client, plus the following additional requirements to make it a gaming PC:

- Runs the latest Windows operating system
- (If assigned) Specs meet or exceed the minimum requirements for a particular game assigned by instructor
- Powerful CPU (high clock speed and at least four cores)
- Network connectivity
- Storage (SSD or HDD)
- 24-inch monitor
- Keyboard and mouse

- High-capacity RAM

- High-end graphics card with a powerful GPU

- High-definition sound card

- High-end cooling system (air or liquid)

Step 1   Open a Web browser and visit a Web site from which you can purchase computer parts. Suggestions include

- www.newegg.com

- www.tigerdirect.com

- www.cdw.com

Just like in the previous lab exercise, the instructor will set a price limit for you. If this is a self-guided course, then set a limit of $1500. In a perfect world, you would have an unlimited budget to get all the highest-end components in the world, and while it's always fun to be a dreamer, we want to show you a realistic, everyday gaming machine.

Step 2   Shop for the parts listed in the following table and complete the other columns for each component you choose.

Part	Model/Version	Web Site	Price
Motherboard			
CPU			
After-market CPU cooler (air or liquid)			
RAM			
Hard drive			
Optical drive			
Power supply			
Case			
Mouse			
Keyboard			
Monitor			
Windows OS			
Video card(s)			
Sound card			
Speaker/headphones			

Step 3   Fill in the following table with any additional parts you might need to purchase, such as fans, lights, or fans with lights!

Part	Web Site	Price	Quantity

Step 4   Now, add up all the prices for your parts.

Grand total: _____

Did you go over the price limit of $1500 or the price set by your instructor? If you went over your budget, maybe you need to get some lower-capacity RAM or let go of a graphics card, if you went with an SLI or CrossFire setup. Do what you need to do to fall within the price limit.

Step 5   Now, let's take a look and see if the power supply you chose will actually power your computer. There are many power supply calculators online that will show you how much wattage you need to power your components, and you did some manual calculations in Chapter 7, "Power Supplies" on your own. But for now, we'll go an easier route: go to http://outervision.com/power-supply-calculator. Fill in the calculator with your gaming PC's specifications.

How much wattage does the power supply you chose supply? _____

Is that amount enough for your gaming rig? _____

If so, how much wattage do you have left over? _____

 **20 MINUTES**

Lab Exercise 11.03: Verifying Operating System Requirements

Your client has asked you to upgrade his operating system to Windows 10. He's currently running Windows 7 Professional 64-bit, and everything works fine. But is his system capable of running Windows 10? In this lab, you'll learn how to find out.

Learning Objectives

You'll review how to assess a system's hardware configuration and how to look up OS requirements online.

At the end of this lab, you'll be able to

- Use System Information to assess a system
- Look up Windows version requirements online
- Check for Windows 10 hardware and software compatibility by starting (but not completing) the Windows upgrade

Lab Materials and Setup

The materials you need for this lab are

- A PC running Windows 7
- Internet access
- Installation media for Windows 10

Getting Down to Business

Before spending money on an OS upgrade, it's important to assess the system to be upgraded to determine whether the new OS will work with it. First we'll check a system for its basic specs and compare them to the requirements for Windows 10. Then we'll use the Windows 10 installation media to check for potential problems.

Step 1   In Windows 7, open System Information and gather information about the system:

   a.   Click the Start button.

   b.   Type **System**.

   c.   Click System Information in the results that appear.

   d.   Complete the following table using the information you gather.

Component	Where It's Located in System Information	Specs
Processor speed	System Summary/Processor	
Memory	System Summary/Installed Physical Memory (RAM)	
Free hard disk space	Components/Storage/Drives/Free Space	
Graphics card	Components/Display/Name	

Step 2   Look up Windows 10 system requirements online and record them here:

Component	Specs
CPU speed	
Amount of RAM	
Free hard disk space	
Graphics card	

Step 3   For Step 3, we are going to start the Windows 10 upgrade process and stop it before it is complete. Early in the process, Windows 10 checks for incompatible programs and hardware.

→ **Note**

You might also find the Windows 10 Upgrade Assistant (also known as Windows 10 Update Assistant), which checks your system hardware, to be useful. Get it from https://www.softpedia.com/get/System/OS-Enhancements/Windows-10-Upgrade-Assistant.shtml. The Windows Compatible Hardware List can be searched for certification information by product type and vendor. Find it at https://partner.microsoft.com/en-us/dashboard/hardware/search/cpl.

If you want to find out what business software vendors and specific apps are reported as working with Windows 10, go to https://developer.microsoft.com/en-us/windows/ready-for-windows#/.

You'll start the upgrade process from within Windows 7. Insert the Windows 10 Setup DVD or connect a thumb drive with installable Windows 10. You can also navigate to the Windows 10 ISO file and open it with Windows Explorer. If it doesn't automatically run, do the following:

    a.   Click Windows Explorer on the taskbar, and click Computer in the navigation pane.

    b.   Double-click the DVD or USB thumb drive to browse its contents.

    c.   Double-click the setup file or right-click it and select Run as administrator (see Figure 11-1).

    d.   If UAC prompts you, click Yes.

Step 4   Next you are led through a series of interactive prompts in which you enter data and make choices.

    a.   When asked whether or not you want to download the latest updates for installation, choose the second option, Not right now. Then click Next. Ordinarily, you would agree to do this, but it can take a long time to complete this download, so you don't need to bother right now.

    b.   At the License terms screen, click Accept.

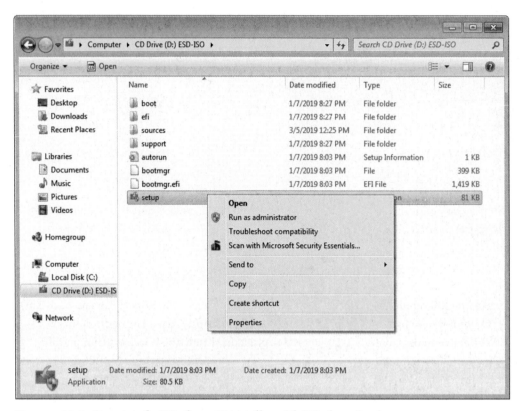

FIGURE 11-1 Opening the Windows 10 installer with Windows Explorer

c.   At this point, the Windows 10 installer checks for software or hardware issues. If it doesn't find any issues, it displays the Installing Windows 10 dialog box. Click Cancel and confirm your choice. If it finds any issues, the What needs your attention dialog box appears (see Figure 11-2).

If any apps should be uninstalled before upgrading to Windows 10, make a note of which app(s) and what the installer instructs you to do (for this exercise, do not click Confirm):

_____

_____

_____

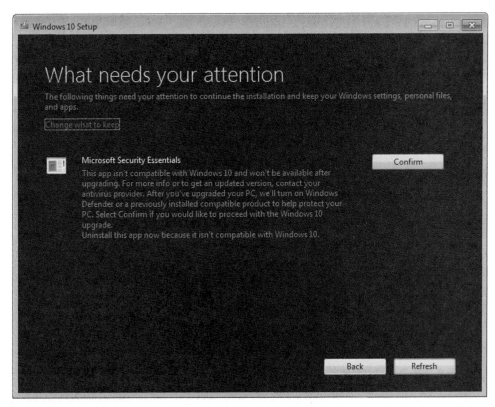

FIGURE 11-2 The What needs your attention dialog box displays apps and hardware that are not compatible with Windows 10.

If any hardware devices need updated drivers, make a note of which device(s) and what the installer instructs you to do (again, do not click Confirm):

_____

_____

_____

d. Click the Close button (×) in the upper-right corner of the What needs your attention dialog box to exit Windows 10 Setup, and then confirm your choice to exit.

Step 5 Based on the results you collected, do you think that Windows 10 will run on this PC without any major problems? Explain.

_____

_____

_____

➔ **Note**

When you upgrade to a new version of Windows on a computer, the process usually preserves your existing files, settings, and apps. However, bugs in the upgrade process (such as the one that briefly affected upgrades to Windows 10 Version 1809 when it was first released) could cause data files to be lost. For safety, back up data before upgrading to a new version of Windows or other operating systems. If you want to move apps, settings, and data from one computer to another, you can use Windows Easy Transfer to move them between Windows 7 and Windows 8.1. However, Windows Easy Transfer is not available on Windows 10. If you want to move apps, settings, and data from a Windows 7/8/8.1 computer to a Windows 10 computer, Microsoft recommends commercial tools such as LapLink PCmover or Zinstall.

 60 MINUTES

Lab Exercise 11.04: Performing a Clean Installation of Windows 10

Your boss has traditionally ordered new workstations already assembled and loaded with the latest Windows OS version. She recently decided that with her great in-house techs, she should be buying PC parts from a wholesaler instead and having you and your team build the systems. You've enjoyed choosing the various hardware components and building these custom machines, but now it's time to bring your creations to life! You need to load Windows 10 Professional onto these new machines that have never seen the light of day.

Learning Objectives

You should complete at least one clean Windows installation, both for the experience and to prepare for questions asked on the CompTIA A+ exams.

At the end of this lab, you'll be able to

- Install a Windows operating system on a blank hard drive

Lab Materials and Setup

The materials you need for this lab are

- A working PC with a blank hard drive, or with a hard drive that you can write to without negative consequences

- A Windows 10 installation disc or USB thumb drive (these instructions are based on Windows 10 version 1809; a different Windows 10 version might have slightly different steps)

Getting Down to Business

In this exercise, you'll be putting an operating system onto a hard drive that doesn't currently have one. Even if the hard drive has an operating system on it, doing a clean installation will format that drive and erase all its data, so be sure you've backed up any important files!

Step 1   Prepare the PC by doing the following, taking proper ESD avoidance procedures:

   a.   If there are any other hard drives in the PC that have working operating systems, disconnect them, so that when the PC boots, it finds only the blank hard drive you are using for this exercise. Doing this helps ensure that you don't accidentally wipe out your old OS while doing this clean install.

   b.   Insert the Windows 10 DVD in the optical drive. (You might need to power the PC on to get the tray to eject.) Or, connect the Windows 10 USB drive to a USB port.

Step 2   Begin the installation process as follows:

   a.   If necessary, enter CMOS setup and change the boot sequence so the DVD or USB thumb drive is the first boot device (see Chapter 5 for details). You can change this setting later.

   b.   Reboot the PC. If prompted, press any key to boot from the DVD. Wait for the Windows Setup screen to appear.

   c.   Choose your preferred language, time and currency format, and keyboard or input method (see Figure 11-3).

   d.   Click Next.

   e.   Click Install Now.

Step 3   Follow these steps to work through the user-interactive portion of the install, including choosing the drive on which to install and creating the partition:

   a.   Enter the product key if you are installing Windows 10 for the first time on this computer and click Next. If you are reinstalling Windows, or don't have a product key, click I don't have a product key, choose the version of Windows you are installing (Windows 10 Pro in this example), and click Next.

   b.   At the license terms screen, select the I accept the license terms checkbox and then click Next.

   c.   Click Custom: Install Windows only (advanced) to do a clean installation (see Figure 11-4).

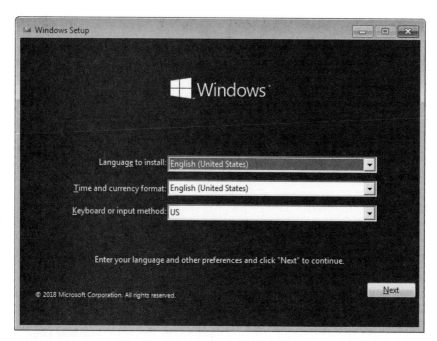

FIGURE 11-3 Language selection screen

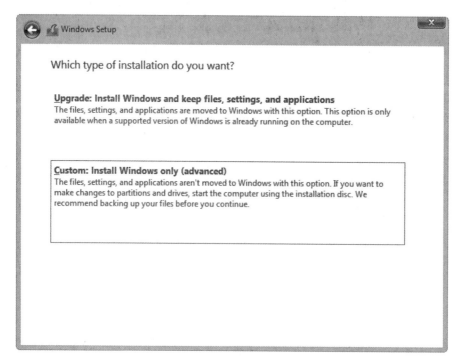

FIGURE 11-4 Installation selection

d. When prompted to choose where you want to install Windows, choose the blank drive (which should be your only choice if you disconnected all other drives in Step 1). Then click Next.

e. Wait for Windows 10 to install itself. It's going to take awhile (30 minutes or so), so this is a good time for a stretch break. The PC may restart itself one or more times; this is expected, so let it do its thing. Eventually it finishes, and prompts you to configure your system and set up a user.

Step 4   The following steps configure your system:

a. When prompted, confirm or select the region, then click Yes.

b. Confirm or select the keyboard layout, then click Yes.

c. When prompted to add a second keyboard layout, click Skip.

Step 5   These final steps set up a user account. (The PC must have at least one, and it must be an Administrator account.)

a. Click Set up for personal use (if you're setting up the computer for a company at work, choose Set up for an organization—the steps will be different), then click Next.

b. If you already have a Microsoft account, enter the e-mail, phone number, or Skype ID associated with that account and click Next. Otherwise, click Create account to set up a new Microsoft account, or click Offline account to set up a local account. In this example, we will set up a local (offline) account.

c. Click No to continue with an offline account.

d. Enter the user name and click Next. This user will be the system's administrator.

e. When prompted, type a password for your user account that you can remember. Click Next.

f. Retype the password, and click Next.

g. Select a security question, enter an answer, and click Next. Repeat until all three security questions have been selected and answered.

h. Skip the Cortana personal assistant by clicking Decline.

i. Skip activity history by clicking No.

➜ **Note**

If you use a Microsoft account, you will find it more useful if you enable these options.

j. Scroll down and view privacy settings. You can individually select privacy settings. To save time in this exercise, click Accept to use all defaults.

k.   When prompted to select Edge web browser options, you can set up your browser, try search, or click Get Started. Close the browser window.

l.   Windows 10 is ready for use.

 **60 Minutes**

Lab Exercise 11.05: Upgrading from Windows 7 to Windows 10

A client running Windows 7 decides to modernize by moving to a more recent OS. He asks you to upgrade his system to Windows 10. You agree to upgrade the system for him.

Learning Objectives

You need to perform at least one complete upgrade, both for practice and to prepare for questions asked on the CompTIA A+ exams.

At the end of this lab, you'll be able to

- Upgrade an operating system

> **✖ Cross-Reference**
>
> **To refresh your memory about the ins and outs of performing a Windows upgrade, read the "Installing and Upgrading Windows" section in Chapter 11 of *Mike Meyers' CompTIA A+ Guide to Managing and Troubleshooting PCs.***

Lab Materials and Setup

The materials you need for this lab are

- A working Windows 7 PC with a hard drive that you can write to without negative consequences, and with hardware compatible with Windows 10 (see Lab Exercise 11.03, "Verifying Operating System Requirements"). Make sure Windows 7 is activated.

- A Windows 10 installation disc or USB flash drive

Getting Down to Business

As with the preceding lab exercise, you'll need quite a bit of time to complete this lab exercise; most of that time will be spent waiting for Windows to install files. The exercise will walk you through upgrading a Windows 7 system to Windows 10. Depending on the systems and software licenses you have available, you may not be able to do this lab exactly as it's laid out here. The important thing is that you actually perform a Windows upgrade, to see the questions that are asked during the installation, and to become familiar with the process so that you're prepared for the CompTIA A+ certification exams.

Step 1 You'll start the upgrade process from within Windows 7. Insert the Windows 10 Setup DVD or USB thumb drive. If it doesn't automatically run, do the following:

a. Click Windows Explorer on the taskbar, and click Computer in the navigation pane.

b. Double-click the optical drive to browse its contents.

c. Double-click the setup file.

d. If UAC prompts you, click Yes.

Step 2 Next you are led through a series of interactive prompts in which you enter data and make choices.

a. When asked whether or not you want to download the latest updates for installation, choose the second option, Not right now. Then click Next. Ordinarily, you would agree to do this, but it can take a long time to complete this download, so you don't need to bother right now.

b. At the License terms screen, click Accept.

c. If there are software or hardware issues, a What needs your attention dialog box appears, as described in Lab Exercise 11.03. If an app should be uninstalled, open the Windows 7 Start menu, go to Control Panel, and uninstall it. Click Refresh to make sure it is removed. Click Confirm to continue.

d. At the Ready to install dialog box, *Install Windows 10* and *Keep personal files and apps* should both be checked. To change this information, click *Change what to keep* and choose what you want to keep. To continue, click Install.

e. Settle in to wait for about 30 minutes as Windows is upgraded. The PC will restart several times; don't interfere.

Step 3 At long last, Windows prompts you for some settings, as follows:

a. You are prompted to log into Windows 10. Your user name and password are the same as in Windows 7.

b. At the Choose privacy settings dialog, click Accept. (There's no need to customize them for this lab, although you might want to do so in the field.)

c. When prompted to select Edge web browser options, you can set up your browser, try search, or click Get Started. Close the browser window.

d. Windows 10 is ready for use.

 15 Minutes

Lab Exercise 11.06: Post-Installation Tasks: Drivers and Updates

As a tech, you will run into countless well-meaning, industrious, but ultimately hopeless customers who have taken their OS installation into their own hands, only to find that some critical piece of hardware doesn't work properly post-installation. Because of this, you absolutely must become well versed in the art of finding and installing hardware drivers and Windows updates.

Imagine, then, that you have a friend who has been happily using an older version of Windows on his custom-built PC for a few years. The PC recently grew unstable, so your friend decided to do his own migration to a newer version (let's say Windows 10), which seemed to go pretty well. Now, however, his wireless networking card doesn't work. And his graphics card seems to be acting kind of funny. And he can't hear any sound. And … you get the picture. Because you're an excellent tech, you instantly recognize the problem, and you graciously let him know that the problem is a result of his not properly following up his Windows installation with the appropriate driver installations. Then, of course, you offer to help him out.

> ### ✖ Cross-Reference
>
> To review the process of installing drivers and updates, refer to the "Post-Installation Tasks" section in Chapter 11 of *Mike Meyers' CompTIA A+ Guide to Managing and Troubleshooting PCs.*

Learning Objectives

In this exercise, you'll learn how to finish up an installation by installing hardware drivers and operating system updates.

At the end of this lab, you'll be able to

- Find and install the correct hardware drivers for your operating system
- Install updates to the operating system

Lab Materials and Setup

The materials you need for this lab are

- A working PC running Windows 10
- Internet access
- A notepad and pencil
- Possibly a second PC and a USB flash drive

Getting Down to Business

After installing a new operating system, the housekeeping tasks to perform include getting Windows updates, checking drivers (and downloading/installing drivers if needed), and checking/reinstalling applications.

Step 1   First things first: can the PC access the Internet? If Windows was able to identify your network adapter well enough to install a usable driver for it, then you're good to go, and you can skip this step. But if you aren't connected, here's the process to follow:

   a.   Check the notification area to see whether there are wireless networks available; you might need to connect to one, even if you were automatically connected to it before the upgrade. If there are wireless networks available, then your wireless network adapter is working, and you don't have to worry about a driver for it right now.

   b.   Open Device Manager and check that the needed driver is installed for your network adapter. Work through the procedure in Lab Exercise 6.09, "Managing Hardware with Device Manager," to troubleshoot device issues as needed.

If you need to download a driver for your network adapter to get it to work, you have a thorny problem: how do you get to the Internet if your network adapter isn't working? You have two choices:

   •   Make a note of the model of network adapter you have, and then use another PC to go to the Web site for the device maker and download the needed driver to a USB drive. Then insert the USB drive into the PC that needs the driver and run the setup program for the driver.

   •   If it's a wireless adapter that isn't working, see if you can temporarily connect via Ethernet to your broadband modem or router.

Step 2   Once you have Internet access, run Windows Update to make sure your copy of Windows is current. Doing so may also update drivers, so doing this first may clear up problems you're having with specific devices in some cases.

To run Windows Update in Windows 10:

   a.   Click Start | Settings | Update & Security | Windows Update.

   b.   Click Check for updates.

   c.   Windows 10 displays any available updates and starts installing them (see Figure 11-5). You can use your computer while updates are being downloaded and installed.

   d.   Click Change active hours. Sometimes, an update requires a restart of Windows 10. Windows 10 won't restart during active hours (8 A.M.–5 P.M. is the default). Change the active hours if a computer will be used at different times. Click Save to save changes.

Step 3   Once you've got your operating system updated, check the various hardware devices to make sure everything is functioning, and install drivers as needed.

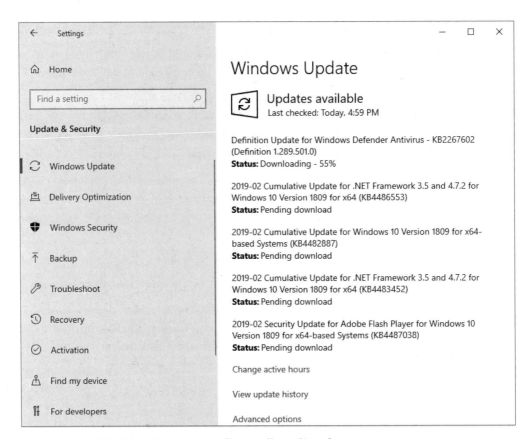

FIGURE 11-5 Windows 10 automatically installs updates for you.

If it's a brand-name PC, like a Dell, you might be able to go to the Support site for the maker, enter your model and serial number (for example, Dell uses a special number called a Service Tag), and access a customized page containing the drivers you need for your exact hardware. Score! Do that if possible.

On a custom-built PC, you have to track down drivers for each component separately, because they each have a different manufacturer.

First, check Device Manager to get an idea about what drivers you should be looking for. Refer to Lab Exercise 6.09, "Managing Hardware with Device Manager," to recall how to do this.

In Device Manager, look for any entries with special icons next to them (down arrows, exclamation points, or question marks) that indicate they are not working properly or disabled. If a device seems to be functioning, you can probably leave it be. There might be a newer driver available for it, but it likely won't do anything different if you aren't having a problem with the device.

In some cases a component's name may appear generically, like Video controller (VGA compatible) or Ethernet controller; this means Windows was unable to identify the specific model. Installing a driver will clear that up. This problem is rarer than it used to be, because each successive version of Windows and each generation of hardware have gotten better at talking to each other.

✔ **Tip**

If you have a lot of unknown system devices in Device Manager, several of them probably pertain to your motherboard's chipset. If you can find your motherboard's chipset drivers, most of these unknowns will go away, so concentrate on finding your motherboard drivers first, and the expansion cards second.

Faced with an unknown device or a missing or nonworking driver, try the easy route—see if Windows can figure out the driver situation itself:

a. Right-click the device in Device Manager and choose Update Driver Software.

b. Click Search automatically for updated driver software.

c. Follow the prompts to see whether a driver (or a better driver) is available, and install it if possible.

If that didn't work, you'll need to download the drivers from the appropriate Web site manually, and then install them yourself, either with their installation program or through Device Manager.

To find the drivers, you'll need to know the model name or number of your devices. If Device Manager doesn't tell you, you have to go on a sleuthing mission. First, check the documentation that came with the PC (if available) to see if there's a list of specs. If that's not available, shut down your computer, open the case (following proper ESD avoidance procedures), and look at the motherboard, graphics card, and any other expansion cards the PC may have, like sound cards, TV tuners, and so forth. Often, these parts will have a manufacturer and model number on them somewhere, such as Gigabyte GA-X99-UD4P written on your motherboard, or NVIDIA GeForce GTX 1060 on your graphics card. You can also use an app such as CPU-Z or GPU-Z to see what hardware you have.

Write those things down and then open a search engine, such as Google, and search for each of them. If you can find the manufacturer, just go to its Web site, look up your product, and follow the link to download drivers.

Sometimes, you're not lucky enough to get a manufacturer or model number, but just about every device out there should have a sticker with some sort of part number or serial number on it. Usually, doing a quick Google search for that number and the word "driver" will get you the results you need. Finding drivers can be pretty frustrating, but keep searching and you're almost guaranteed to find what you're after.

Step 4 After you help Windows recognize and enable all the hardware, here's a final checklist of things that complete an upgrade:

- Reinstall any applications that didn't carry over with the upgrade.

- Set up additional local user accounts as needed.

- Test-run all important applications to make sure they still work. Check for updates to installed applications as needed to correct any problems.

- Set up legacy applications to run in Compatibility mode as needed if they are not compatible with the new OS.

- Check any important network shares to make sure they still function.

 **60 Minutes**

Lab Exercise 11.07: Installing Ubuntu Linux

Although the CompTIA A+ 1002 exam is mostly Windows-focused, exam candidates should also become familiar with Linux basics, including how to acquire, install, and use a basic graphical Linux environment and run Linux command-line commands.

To get started toward that goal, this lab exercise guides you through downloading and installing Ubuntu Linux, one of the most popular and user-friendly distributions. You'll use this Linux platform to complete a Linux lab in Chapter 15, "Working with the Command-Line Interface."

Learning Objectives

In this exercise, you'll learn how to acquire, download, and install Ubuntu Linux.

At the end of this lab, you'll be able to

- Download and install Ubuntu Linux on a PC

Lab Materials and Setup

The materials you need for this lab are

- A working Windows PC with Internet access

- A PC with a blank hard drive on which to install Linux

  - At least 6.6 GB of free space on the drive

  - Access to an Internet connection (preferred but not essential)

- One or both of the following:

  - A writeable DVD drive and blank DVD disc

  - A USB flash drive containing nothing you want to keep

No spare PC on which to install Linux? Look ahead to Chapter 22, "Virtualization," to learn how you can install Linux in a virtual machine on another PC. (If you go that route, you might need to burn an optical disc for the install, because USB drives sometimes don't work in virtual environments. However, some virtualizers can create a "virtual DVD" from an ISO file.) Alternatively, you can boot from the Ubuntu Linux CD or USB flash drive and choose Try Ubuntu to gain access to the Ubuntu interface without committing your hardware to it. You can also install Ubuntu Linux alongside your existing OS; the installation program asks whether you want to do that if it finds an existing OS during the setup process.

Getting Down to Business

Linux is a free, open source operating system that is flexible, works on multiple platforms, and is surprisingly robust for something that costs nothing. It's based on UNIX, and was invented by Linus Torvalds. (The name Linux is an amalgamation of Linus and UNIX.)

Linux itself is just a command-line operating system, but there are many add-ons and support packages available for it that add GUI capability. Some are free; some aren't. One of the most popular free packages (called *distros*, which is short for distributions) is Ubuntu Linux. That's the distro you'll work with in this lab exercise. The CompTIA A+ exam objectives do not mention a specific distro; the coverage of Linux on the 1002 exam is generic, and mostly limited to command-line operations.

Step 1   First, you'll need to download Linux.

   a.   Go to www.ubuntu.com.

   b.   Click Download, then click the green button under Ubuntu Desktop to download the latest version for your system (64-bit Windows).

→ Note

If you need a 32-bit version of Ubuntu, go to www.ubuntu.com/download/alternative-downloads, scroll down to the "Past releases and other flavours" section, and click the Past releases link. Click Ubuntu 16.04.6 LTS (Xenial Xerus) and click the 32-bit PC (i386) desktop image.

---

   c.   Make a note of the location of the download. You'll need that in Step 2.

Step 2   If you have a favorite ISO burner, use it to burn the downloaded file to an optical disc. Make sure you use your burning software's ISO option, and don't just transfer the file to the disc like a normal file; otherwise the disc won't be bootable.

If you would prefer to make a bootable USB flash drive, consider using Tuxboot. It's a handy little free utility that will create a bootable USB flash drive.

Here are the steps for making a bootable USB flash drive out of your Ubuntu Linux ISO file:

   a.   Download Tuxboot from http://sourceforge.net/projects/tuxboot. Run it to open its window.

   b.   Attach your USB flash drive to the PC.

   c.   Click the Pre Downloaded option button.

    d.   Click the … button to browse for the file. Select your Linux ISO file and click Open to return to the Tuxboot window.

    e.   Open the Type drop-down list and choose USB Drive.

    f.   Open the Drive drop-down list and choose the letter of your USB flash drive. Figure 11-6 shows the application at this point.

    g.   Click OK to burn the ISO file to the USB flash drive, making it bootable.

    h.   Wait for the utility to write the ISO file to the USB flash drive. Then shut down the utility.

Step 3   You have a choice at this point: you can try Linux without installing it, or you can install it. We highly recommend installing it, if you have the hardware available, because you'll need it for other labs later in the book.

    a.   Boot the PC on which you plan to install Linux from the bootable media you created in Step 2.

    b.   At the Welcome screen, you'll see a choice of Try Ubuntu and Install Ubuntu. Click Install Ubuntu.

    c.   At the Preparing to install Ubuntu screen, click Continue.

    d.   Wait for the installation to complete.

If time permits, play around with the Ubuntu Linux desktop environment, and explore some of the icons along the left side of the screen. You'll use Linux in upcoming labs.

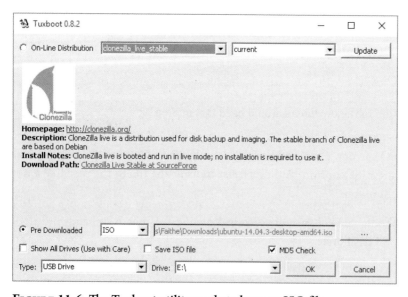

FIGURE 11-6 The Tuxboot utility ready to burn an ISO file

Lab Analysis Test

1. Bruce wants to build a computer that specializes in audio/video editing. What can you tell him about that type of workstation that makes it unique?

2. Natasha is trying to decide if she should have thin clients or thick clients attached to the network. Explain the similarities and differences between thin and thick clients.

3. Phyllis wants to do an upgrade installation from Windows 7 Professional (32-bit) to Windows 10 Pro (64-bit). Will she be able to? Why or why not?

4. Michael wants to move his files and settings from a Windows 8.1 PC to a Windows 10 PC. What tool can you recommend that he use to do that?

5. Jess wants to try out Ubuntu Linux, but she doesn't have an extra PC to spare. What are her options?

Key Term Quiz

Use the following terms to complete the following sentences. Not all terms will be used.

10	product key
activation code	thick client
clean	thin client
home server PC	upgrade
live CD	Windows Easy Transfer
phone number	

1. A(n) _____ is a type of computer that connects to a server on a network. It offloads much of the processing to the server. In many situations, this computer doesn't even have a hard drive.

2. When installing Windows, you may be prompted for a(n) _____ to verify the authenticity of your copy of Windows.

3. You can start with a blank hard drive to perform a(n) _____ installation of Windows.

4. The Windows _____ installation program will check your system to see if there are any problems making the upgrade from Windows 7 or 8.1.

5. You can use a(n) _____ to try Ubuntu Linux without installing it.

Chapter 12

Windows Under the Hood

Lab Exercises

While Windows is arguably one of the most accessible operating systems available, Microsoft doesn't plaster your desktop with every single feature and option. In fact, certain options are well hidden so that less technically inclined users don't break anything. As a PC tech, of course, you'll be the one digging up these options and understanding how they work. These labs are designed to look a bit more "under the hood" and expose you to a few of these more hidden tools. The Registry rests at the heart of Windows, storing everything there is to know about your computer. The Task Manager utility enables you to control programs, processes, services, and more. While all of these tools hide under the hood, they are key to controlling how Windows functions.

 **30 MINUTES**

Lab Exercise 12.01: Editing the Windows Registry

The Registry stores everything about your PC, including information on all the hardware in the PC, network information, user preferences, file types, and virtually anything else you might run into with Windows. The hardware, software, and program configuration settings in the Registry are particular to each PC. Two identical PCs with the same operating system and hardware can still be remarkably different because of user settings and preferences. Almost any form of configuration done to a Windows system results in changes to the Registry.

> ✖ **Warning**
>
> When changing the Registry, proceed with great care—making changes in the Registry can cause unpredictable and possibly harmful results. To paraphrase the old carpenter's adage: consider twice, change once!

Learning Objectives

Most of the common tools used to modify the Registry are contained in the Control Panel or Settings, depending upon the version of Windows you use. When you use the Display applet to change a background, for example, the resultant changes are added to the Registry. The Control Panel applets or Settings options are what you should normally use to configure the Registry. However, there are times—a virus attack, perhaps, or complete removal of a stubborn application—when direct manipulation of the Registry is needed. In this lab, you'll familiarize yourself with the Windows Registry and the direct manipulation of the Registry using the regedit command.

At the end of this lab, you'll be able to

- Access the Registry using regedit

- Export, import, and modify Registry data subkeys and values

- Define the function of the five top-level Registry keys

Lab Materials and Setup

The materials you need for this lab are

- A working computer running Windows 7 or higher

Getting Down to Business

A technician needs to know how to access the Registry and modify the configuration based on solid support from Microsoft or other trusted sources. As mentioned in the Learning Objectives, your main interface to the Registry is the Control Panel or the Settings app. Changes made through the applets in the Control Panel or menu selections in Settings result in modifications to the Registry settings. To see what's going on behind the scenes, though, you'll explore the Registry directly in this exercise using the regedit command.

> ✖ **Cross-Reference**
>
> **For more details on the Windows Registry and working with regedit, refer to the "Registry" section in Chapter 12 of *Mike Meyers' CompTIA A+ Guide to Managing and Troubleshooting PCs.***

Step 1 You almost never need to access the Registry directly. It's meant to work in the background, quietly storing all the necessary data for the system, updated only through a few menus and installation programs. When you want to access the Registry directly, you must use the Registry Editor (regedit).

To edit the Registry directly, follow these steps:

a. Start the Registry Editor. To do so:

- Windows 7: Click Start, type **regedit**, and press ENTER. If a UAC prompt appears, click Yes.

- Windows 8.1/10: Right-click the Start button and select Run. Type **regedit** and click OK. If a UAC prompt appears, click Yes.

b. Note the five main subgroups or root keys in the Registry (see Figure 12-1). Some of these root key folders may be expanded. Click the minus sign by any expanded folders. Do a quick mental review— do you know the function of each Registry key? You should!

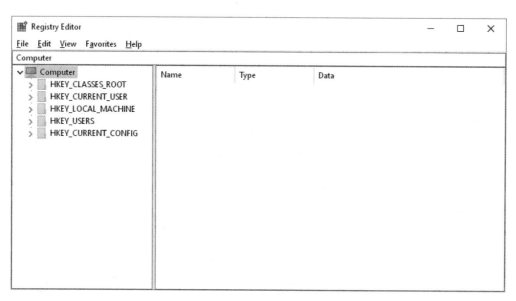

FIGURE 12-1 Viewing the five main subgroups of the Windows Registry

c.   Now test your knowledge of the Registry. Referring to the textbook as necessary, match the listed keys with their definitions by writing the definition letter next to the corresponding key:

HKEY_CLASSES_ROOT: _____

HKEY_CURRENT_USER: _____

HKEY_LOCAL_MACHINE: _____

HKEY_USERS: _____

HKEY_CURRENT_CONFIG: _____

   A. Contains the data for non-user-specific configurations, and includes every device in your PC and those you've removed

   B. Contains the personalization information for all users on a PC

   C. Contains additional hardware information when there are values in HKEY_LOCAL_MACHINE such as two different monitors

   D. Defines the standard class objects used by Windows; information stored here is used to open the correct application when a file is opened

   E. Contains the current user settings, such as fonts, icons, and colors, on systems that are set up to support multiple users

Step 2 Before we go any further, you should back up the Registry key that you're going to modify, in case something goes wrong. Follow these steps to back up HKEY_CLASSES_ROOT:

a. Select HKEY_CLASSES_ROOT in the left pane of the Registry Editor.

b. Choose File | Export to open the Export Registry File dialog box.

c. Type a name for the key file, and choose a location where you'll be able to find it again. Then click Save.

✔ **Tip**

To back up the entire Registry, select Computer instead of HKEY_CLASSES_ROOT in Step 2a.

Step 3 As a tech, you will frequently want to open a file in Notepad to see what it contains. The trouble is that not all text files have a .txt extension, and some files that you might want to peek inside with Notepad need to retain their file associations with other applications, such as log files with a .log extension. Here's a nifty Registry tweak that adds the command "Open in Notepad" to the right-click menu of all icons:

a. Expand the HKEY_CLASSES_ROOT key by double-clicking it. Notice that there are more subkeys underneath it, some of which have subkeys of their own, and so on.

➜ **Note**

You're probably used to Windows Explorer or File Explorer, where the folders you see in the navigation pane on the left are mirrored in the content pane on the right. Registry Editor doesn't work that way. The folders you see on the left are called *keys*. The settings you see on the right are *values* of various types within the selected key.

---

b. In the left pane, double-click the * key to expand it, and then click shell.

c. Right-click shell, point to New, and click Key, creating a new key. Name it **Open with Notepad**.

d. Right-click the Open with Notepad key, point to New, and click Key, creating a new key. Name it **Command**.

e. With the Command key selected in the left pane, double-click Default in the right pane to open the Edit String dialog box. In the Value data text box, type **notepad.exe %1** and then click OK. Figure 12-2 shows the key at this point.

f. Right-click any icon on the Desktop (if you don't have icons on the Desktop, open File Explorer/Windows Explorer and right-click a file) to confirm that the Open with Notepad command appears on its shortcut menu.

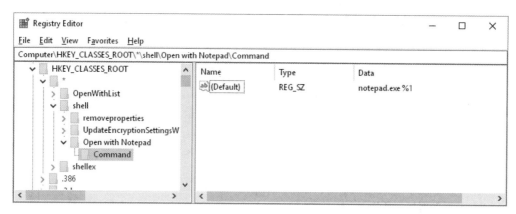

FIGURE 12-2 A new key has been created.

Step 4   Now you'll delete the keys you just added—because, come to think of it, being able to open every file in Notepad is probably not a good feature to leave enabled permanently on an end-user's PC. There's too much potential for trouble there.

    a. In the left pane, click Open with Notepad to select it.

    b. Right-click Open with Notepad and choose Delete. A confirmation box appears.

    c. Click Yes.

Step 5   Step 3 likely went pretty well for you, but what if it didn't? What if you accidentally deleted the entire * key and all its subkeys? You might gasp in horror at that thought, but it happens. People make mistakes all the time like that.

So let's restore that backup of HKEY_CLASSES_ROOT that you made in Step 1, to make sure everything is back the way it was.

    a. Make sure that HKEY_CLASSES_ROOT is selected in the left pane.

    b. Choose File | Import.

    c. Select the file you exported in Step 1.

    d. Click Open.

    e. A warning message will probably appear that not all data was successfully written to the Registry. That's normal, because Windows is running and some keys are in use. Click OK.

    f. Close the Registry Editor window.

✔ **Hint**

The Web site www.winhelponline.com/blog/misc-registry-fixes-for-windows-10-7-8-xp-vista/ offers a number of working Registry fixes. Not all edits are suitable for all versions of Windows, though. Be cautious, and back up before making any changes.

 **30 MINUTES**

Lab Exercise 12.02: Using the Task Manager

All Microsoft operating systems include a utility that enables you to view all of the tasks running on your system. Since the days of Windows NT, Windows has used the Task Manager to accomplish this. The Task Manager is arguably one of the most important troubleshooting utilities included in Windows. The Task Manager enables you to start, view, and end tasks. You can also see the resources being used by each running task. This lab exercise will show you how to best use the Task Manager, as well as introduce you to a third-party tool that makes the Task Manager look like a child's toy by comparison.

Learning Objectives

In this lab, you'll learn how to use the Task Manager and Process Explorer to work with running applications and processes.

At the end of this lab, you'll be able to

- Locate and use the Task Manager
- Download and run Process Explorer

Lab Materials and Setup

The materials you need for this lab are

- A working computer running Windows 7 or later
- An Internet connection

Getting Down to Business

Your friend Max just bought a new computer. He's loaded it up with new games and applications, but after he finished installing everything, he noticed his computer slowing down. He has no idea what could be causing this and needs help! Assist Max by using the Task Manager and a third-party tool called Process Explorer.

Step 1 Opening the Task Manager can be done in a variety of ways on a Windows computer. Try each of the following:

- Press CTRL-ALT-DEL and then click Task Manager

→ **Note**

If you are on a PC with the Welcome screen disabled, you will need to use CTRL-SHIFT-ESC.

- Press CTRL-SHIFT-ESC
- Right-click the taskbar and select Start Task Manager (Windows 7) or Task Manager (Windows 8.1/10)

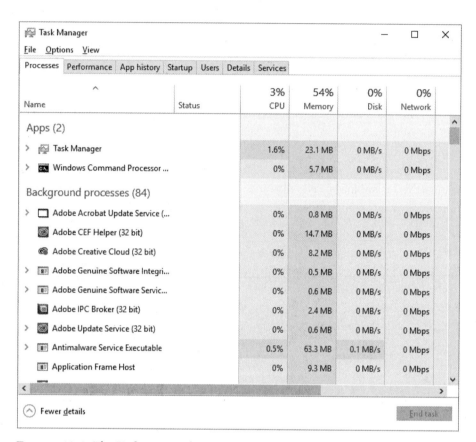

FIGURE 12-3 The Task Manager's Processes tab in Windows 10

Step 2   In Windows 8.1/10, the Task Manager opens in a simplified view by default that contains only a list of running programs. You can optionally click More details to enter a tab-based environment with many more details, as shown in Figure 12-3. Running applications appear on the Processes tab, under the Apps heading. This list should include all open applications on your taskbar.

In Windows 7, the Task Manager opens to the Applications tab, which also shows the open applications. See Figure 12-4.

  a.   With the Task Manager still open, open Notepad.

  Notepad should now be listed as a task in the Task Manager. In Windows 8.1/10, if an application is behaving normally, you won't see any entry at all in the Status column on the Processes tab. This is good—we like it when applications (or tasks) are running. If you ever see an application listed as Not Responding, the application is having issues. In Windows 7, the Status column should list applications as Running.

  b.   With Notepad selected in the Task Manager, click End Task. Describe the results.

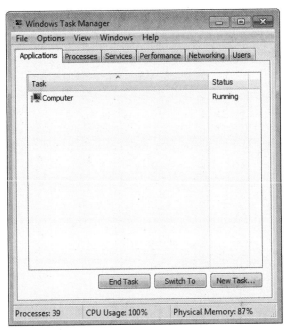

FIGURE 12-4 The Task Manager's Applications tab in Windows 7

Step 3 Sometimes, using the End Task button doesn't end the task. The application might not respond and won't close. When this happens, you must dig a bit deeper and find the errant processes to shut down.

a. Open Windows Media Player.

b. Open the Task Manager (if it is not already open). You should now see Windows Media Player listed in the running applications on the Processes tab (Windows 8.1/10) or the Applications tab (Windows 7).

c. Right-click the Windows Media Player task and select Go To Details (Windows 8.1/10) or Go To Process (Windows 7). This opens the Details tab (Windows 8.1/10) or the Processes tab (Windows 7) with the appropriate process selected.

d. Record the process that is associated with Windows Media Player as well as how much memory is allocated to it.

Process name: _____

Mem Usage: _____

e. Right-click the process name and click End Process or End Process Tree. Describe what happens.

→   **Note**

If you ended the process and Windows Media Player didn't go away, then you ended the wrong process. Whoops!

Step 4   With the Task Manager open, click the Performance tab. This is another great area for troubleshooting and diagnosing a Windows PC. You'll notice that you can monitor the CPU and RAM usage from this tab.

a.   Record the overall physical memory percentage: _____

- Windows 8.1/10: Click Memory in the left pane, and then view the percentage listed next to the memory amount, as shown in Figure 12-5.

- Windows 7: The Physical Memory value is shown in the bottom-right corner of the Task Manager window.

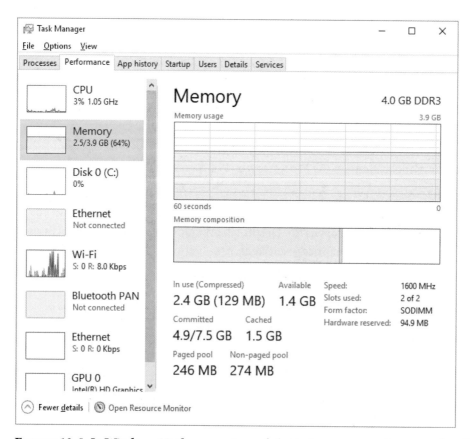

FIGURE 12-5 In Windows 10, the percentage of physical memory use is reported under Memory in the left pane.

    b. Open 15 instances of Microsoft WordPad. Record the new physical memory percentage:

    _____

    c. Close all 15 instances of Microsoft WordPad.

Step 5 Back to Max's problem in our scenario: his system is slowing down, and he doesn't know why. The Task Manager can help pin down the application or process that is hogging the resources.

    a. On the Processes tab, click the CPU column heading to sort the running processes according to amount of CPU time used. The items near the top of the list are using the most. If one process is a big chunk (like 40 percent or more), it's probably the one causing the problem.

    b. Click the Memory heading to sort the processes according to amount of memory used. Look at the biggest memory hogs as a potential cause of the slowdown problem.

Step 6 Next, we'll use an alternate tool to examine the inner workings of the OS: Process Explorer. This tool has far better capabilities than the Task Manager.

    a. Open a Web browser and search for **Process Explorer**. Clicking the first search result should take you to the Microsoft Windows Sysinternals site's Process Explorer's page (see Figure 12-6). There might be a newer version than shown here by the time you are reading this.

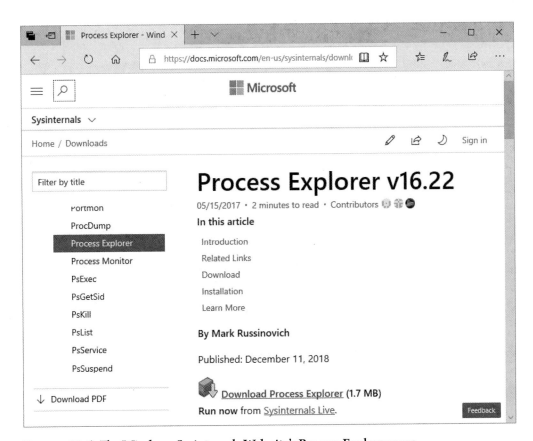

Figure 12-6 The Windows Sysinternals Web site's Process Explorer page

b. Download the latest version of Process Explorer. Once downloaded, extract the contents of the zipped archive to a folder on your desktop or another location of your choosing.

c. Open the folder with the extracted files. If you are using a 64-bit version of Windows, run the program **procexp64.exe**. For a 32-bit version of Windows, run the program **procexp.exe**. Either way, Process Explorer should look familiar. Think of Process Explorer as a super-advanced Task Manager.

d. Look around the Process Explorer application (see Figure 12-7). Notice that certain processes branch off of other processes.

e. Let's say there's a process you're not sure about. Process Explorer can help you find out about it. To try this out, right-click RuntimeBroker.exe and select Search Online. Give a detailed description of RuntimeBroker.exe:

_____

_____

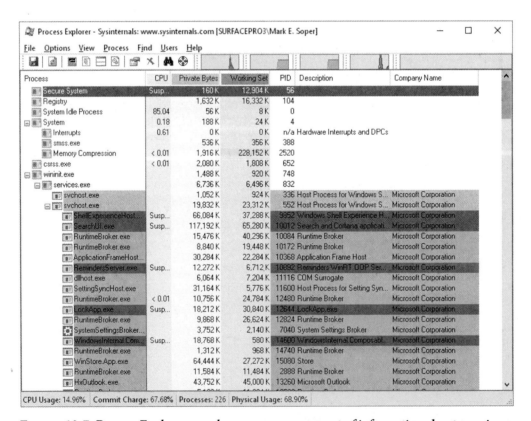

FIGURE 12-7 Process Explorer reveals an enormous amount of information about running apps and processes in Windows.

→ Note

If the Search Online feature fails to work, try using a different browser as your default. In Windows 10, go to Settings | Apps | Default apps, click Web browser, and select from the installed web browsers on your system. In Windows 7 and 8.1, open the Programs Control Panel applet and choose Default Programs | Set your default programs to make this change.

Step 7   Take some time to become more familiar with Process Explorer. You'll see that it's more powerful than the Task Manager. You can even use Process Explorer to replace the traditional Task Manager when you press CTRL-ALT-DEL.

a.   In Process Explorer, click Options | Replace Task Manager.

b.   If you want to undo the replacement of the Task Manager, just repeat the previous step.

c.   Close out of all the open windows and programs to finish the exercise.

 **20 MINUTES**

Lab Exercise 12.03: Working with Services

Windows handles many routine operations through services, which are subroutines of code that process data from multiple applications. The Print Spooler is one classic example; it handles print job spooling for printing from all applications. User Management is another service, managing who is signed in and what privileges they have.

When a service fails to start or malfunctions, the corresponding capability in Windows is impacted. Sometimes all that's needed to restore a service's functionality is to restart it, or stop it and then restart it. In this lab exercise, you'll explore the Services applet, and stop and start a service.

Learning Objectives

In this lab, you'll learn how to use the Services applet in Windows.

At the end of this lab, you'll be able to

- Browse a list of services

- Stop and start a service

Lab Materials and Setup

The materials you need for this lab are

- A working computer running Windows 7 or later

Getting Down to Business

When Gordon tries to print, no printers are available, even though he knows that there are several printers his computer can normally access. You suspect that the Print Spooler service may have stopped for some reason. You'll investigate using the Services applet, and restart Print Spooler if needed.

Step 1   Open the Control Panel and browse to System and Security | Administrative Tools. Then double-click Services to open the Services applet.

Step 2   Locate the Print Spooler service, and double-click it to open its Properties dialog box. Check the Service status: it should read Running, as in Figure 12-8.

Step 3   Now you'll experiment with stopping and starting Print Spooler.

    a.   Click Stop. The status now appears as Stopped.

    b.   Open Notepad, and try to print something (File | Print). What happens?

FIGURE 12-8 The Print Spooler service's Properties as shown in Windows 10

    c. Return to the Print Spooler Properties dialog box and click Start. The status now appears as Running.

    d. Switch back to Notepad and try printing again. What happens?

    _____

    e. Click OK to close the dialog box.

Step 4 Maximize the Services window, and widen the Description column so you can read the descriptions more clearly. Scroll through the list of services to discover what other Windows features are services, and might possibly need to be stopped or started as part of your troubleshooting of a system.

Lab Analysis Test

    1. Sally says that her computer runs slowly and that it doesn't respond like it used to. How could you use the Task Manager to check out the problem?

    2. Describe the function of the Registry and explain why someone would edit it.

    3. What can you do before making a Registry edit to protect your system in case you make a mistake?

    4. What Windows utility would you use to troubleshoot a Windows service that isn't running but should be?

    5. John wants to access the Task Manager so he can end some processes. What are the three ways he could open it?

Key Term Quiz

Use the following terms to complete the following sentences. Not all terms will be used.

HKEY_CLASSES_ROOT	Process Explorer
HKEY_CURRENT_CONFIG	regedit
HKEY_CURRENT_USER	Registry
HKEY_LOCAL_MACHINE	service
HKEY_USERS	Task Manager

    1. The Registry contains all the configuration data and can be accessed directly using _____.

    2. The _____ is a built-in Windows tool used to start and end processes.

3. The _____ app can be downloaded and used to provide very detailed information about Windows processes.

4. _____ is the Registry key that stores the plug-and-play information about your computer.

5. Print Spooler is an example of a Windows _____.

Chapter 13

Users, Groups, and Permissions

Lab Exercises

Users, groups, and permissions are intrinsic to every Windows computer. The challenge to users and groups is that so many techs only think of them in an enterprise network context. But not every computer is a part of some vast corporate network. Not everyone logs on to a domain and manipulates multiple file servers to carry out their business. Sometimes, a system stands alone. And lest you take pity on this lonely PC—or worse, ignore it entirely—you must still think about its security. Even without a network, a single computer contains plenty of vital data. Without taking the necessary security precautions, your data could easily be stolen or destroyed by anyone else who uses that computer. This is why user accounts, permissions, and encryption in Windows are so important.

As a PC tech, you may be called upon to set up a new user account. But simply adding a new user is just the beginning. You will need to keep in mind what sort of powers or permissions you want each user to have—do they need to be able to install new software, or is just being able to open and edit files enough?

But sometimes, the general set of abilities granted by each type of user account isn't specific enough—maybe certain files or folders should be accessed only by certain users, or groups of users. Then there are the files that should only be seen or touched by you, with access granted by your password alone. Or the opposite—maybe you need to share some folders so that everyone on that PC can get to them. This chapter will show you how to implement these security features in Windows so that a single system can have multiple users working with and sharing files securely.

 15 MINUTES

Lab Exercise 13.01: Managing Users in Windows

Any time you access a PC that is not part of a Windows domain, you do so through either a local user account or a Microsoft account. A lot of home PCs have only one user, and on older versions of Windows there might not even be a password, so this process becomes transparent. But that setup would be a disaster for the workplace, because everyone would be able to go through everyone else's bank records, e-mail messages, personal photos, and so on. Having local user accounts or Windows accounts provides a means of authentication—making sure that Steve *is* Steve—and authorization—allowing Steve to only perform specific actions.

Learning Objectives

In this lab, you'll practice creating and managing new users.

At the end of this lab, you'll be able to

- Create and manage a new local user account
- Work with user groups

Lab Materials and Setup

The materials you need for this lab are

- A PC running Windows 7, 8.1, or 10

Getting Down to Business

Your client is a small business in which four employees share one computer. They each need their own user account so that they can keep their personal data private and so that they stop accidentally deleting everything while logged on as an administrator. Adam is the only one with enough knowledge of computers to have a more powerful account. Carol, Dale, and Betsy need more limited accounts, because they aren't tech savvy and could easily break something.

This exercise works with any version of Windows, but for the sake of instruction, the steps will be repeated for Windows 7, Windows 8.1, and Windows 10. Do as many of the steps as you have Windows versions available for.

✖ Cross-Reference

For more information on users and groups, refer to the "Managing Users in Windows 7," "Managing Users in Windows 8/8.1," and "Managing Users in Windows 10" sections in Chapter 13 of *Mike Meyers' CompTIA A+ Guide to Managing and Troubleshooting PCs.*

Step 1   Follow these steps to create a new user account for Dale in Windows 7:

    a.   Make sure to sign in as an administrator, so that you can create the user account. Then click Start | Control Panel. Under the link to User Accounts and Family Safety, click the link Add or remove user accounts.

    b.   Click Create a new account.

    c.   Type in a new account name. Standard user should already be selected. Click Create Account.

    d.   Select Dale's user account from the Manage Accounts screen. Click Create a password. Type in a memorable password, confirm it, and then create a password hint to remind yourself in case you forget. Click Create password.

Step 2   Windows 8.1's process is quite different, because of Windows 8.1's ability to use both Microsoft accounts and local accounts. If you use a Microsoft account, you are led through the process of setting up an e-mail address if you don't already have one you want to use, and you're led through registering that e-mail address as a Microsoft account if it isn't already.

Follow these steps to create a new account for Betsy in Windows 8.1:

    a.   Make sure to sign in as an administrator, so that you can create the user account. Then from the Charms bar, click Settings, and click Change PC Settings.

    b.   In the Settings app, click Accounts in the navigation bar.

    c.   Click Other Accounts in the navigation bar.

    d.   Click Add an Account.

At this point you have several options. Make your selection, and then follow the prompts to complete the process:

- Enter an e-mail address for the account to set up. Use this method to create a Microsoft account with an existing e-mail address. The steps that follow will vary depending on whether that e-mail address has previously been registered as a Microsoft account.

- Click Sign up for a new email address. With this method you can create an Outlook.com or Hotmail.com address to use as the sign-in account for Windows.

- Create a local-only account by clicking Sign in without a Microsoft account. Use this method if you want complete privacy for this account and you don't mind missing out on the online benefits of a Microsoft account, such as automatic connection to OneDrive storage and synchronization of personalization preferences across devices.

Step 3   Windows 10's process differs from that of Windows 8.1 by adding the ability to use a phone number instead of an e-mail address in the latest release, but like Windows 8.1, Windows 10 offers the ability to use both Microsoft accounts and local accounts. If you use a Microsoft account, you are led through the process of setting up an e-mail address if you don't already have one you want to use, and you're led through registering that e-mail address as a Microsoft account if it isn't already.

Follow these steps to create a new account for Carol in Windows 10:

a. Make sure to sign in as an administrator, so that you can create the user account. Then, click Start.

b. Click Settings.

c. In the Settings app, click Accounts.

d. Click Family & other users.

e. Click Add someone else to this PC.

At this point you have several options. Make your selection, and then follow the prompts to complete the process:

- Enter an e-mail address for the account to set up. Use this method to create a Microsoft account with an existing e-mail address. The steps that follow will vary depending on whether that e-mail address has previously been registered as a Microsoft account.

- Click I don't have this person's sign-in information. With this method you can create an Outlook.com address to use as the sign-in account for Windows, use a telephone number instead of an e-mail address, or add a user without a Microsoft account.

Now that you have standard users created, your client decides that he really needs another administrator besides Adam. Upgrade each of the accounts you created to Administrator status.

Step 4 In Windows 7, follow these steps to upgrade Dale's account, which you created in Step 1, to Administrator status:

a. As usual, make sure your account is set to Administrator. Click Start, right-click Computer, and select Manage.

b. On the left side of the screen, select Local Users and Groups. On the right side, double-click Groups, and then double-click Administrators.

c. In the Administrators Properties dialog box, click Add. Type the user name in the *Enter the object names to select* box, and then click Check Names. Click OK.

d. Click OK in the Administrators Properties dialog box. Find the name of the group that the user had been in previously, most likely Users. Double-click it to open the Properties dialog box.

e. Find the user name in the list, click it, and then click Remove. Click OK. Now the user Dale is an administrator.

Step 5 In Windows 8.1, follow these steps to upgrade Betsy's account, which you created in Step 2, to Administrator status:

a. From the Charms bar, click Settings, and then click Change PC Settings.

b. Click Accounts in the navigation pane.

    c.   Click Other Accounts in the navigation pane.

    d.   Click Betsy's account, and then click Edit.

    e.   Open the Account Type drop-down list and choose Administrator.

    f.   Click OK.

    g.   Close the Settings app. Now the user Betsy is an administrator.

Step 6   In Windows 10, follow these steps to upgrade Carol's account, which you created in Step 3, to Administrator status:

    a.   Click Settings.

    b.   Click Accounts.

    c.   Click Carol's account.

    d.   Click Change account type.

    e.   Select Administrator from the drop-down menu.

    f.   Click OK.

    g.   Close the Settings app. Now the user Carol is an administrator.

 15 MINUTES

Lab Exercise 13.02: Defining NTFS Permissions

Now that you've learned how to set up authentication, it's time to talk about authorization—what a user can do with files, folders, or any other resource. Granting NTFS permissions is a powerful and complex tool that allows you to define precisely who can do what on a system. Depending on your needs, this can quickly become a complicated and sticky web of overlapping settings that you don't want to deal with. But it's important to know how to define these permissions so that each user has the specific powers and limitations he or she requires. It's best to start thinking about it one folder at a time: who can open it, and who can edit it?

Learning Objectives

In this lab, you'll use NTFS permissions to define which users can access specific files and folders.

At the end of this lab, you'll be able to

- Set up NTFS permissions for files and folders

Lab Materials and Setup

The materials you need for this lab are

- A PC running Windows 7 Professional/Ultimate/Enterprise, Windows 8.1 Pro, or Windows 10 Pro on an NTFS partition

Getting Down to Business

Now that your client has a set of user accounts for his employees, he wants to set up a folder on the C: drive for everyone to use. But there's one text file he doesn't want Dale to touch—he doesn't even want Dale to be able to open it, let alone make any changes. He's asked you to set up the file with the right permissions so that Dale can't access the file.

Setting up permissions for files and setting up permissions for folders are very similar procedures. In this exercise, you'll work with setting up permissions for a text file, but the same procedure will also work with folders.

Step 1 If you haven't done so already, create an account for Dale on your computer using Lab Exercise 13.01. Make sure Dale *isn't* an administrator and that the account you are signed in with *is*. If you made Dale an administrator in Lab Exercise 13.01, change his account back to standard user now.

If you are working in Windows 8.1 or Windows 10, create an account for Dale now in Windows 8.1 or Windows 10, and make it a local (non-Microsoft) account. You won't need Dale's account to be a Microsoft account, and there's no reason to assign an e-mail address to it.

Step 2 Using Windows Explorer (Windows 7) or File Explorer (Windows 8.1/10), create a new folder at the top level of the C: drive and name it **Work**.

Step 3 Open the Work folder you just created. Right-click an empty area in it and select New | Text Document. Name the new document **Private**.

Step 4 First, you'll add Dale to the list of users for which you can set permissions.

   a. Right-click the Private file and select Properties.

   b. Click the Security tab, and then click Edit. This opens a more detailed version of the tab you were just looking at. Listed should be several users and groups, but Dale probably isn't listed.

   c. To add Dale, click Add. Type **Dale** in the *Enter the object names to select* box (see Figure 13-1) and click Check Names. Click OK.

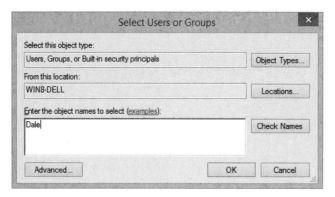

FIGURE 13-1 The Select Users or Groups applet

Step 5   Now that Dale is on the list, you can set his permissions.

   a.   Select Dale from the list of Group or user names. The bottom half of the window shows a list of permissions for Dale.

   b.   Check the Deny box next to Read.

   c.   Click Apply.

   d.   A dialog box will pop up explaining how this will change the permission of this file and how it could affect other files. Choose Yes.

Step 6   Now you'll try accessing that folder as Dale.

   a.   Sign out of the administrator account and sign in as Dale.

   b.   Go back into Windows Explorer/File Explorer and open the Work folder you created. Double-click the Private file.

If all goes well, Notepad should open, but Windows should deny you (Dale) access to the text file. Congratulations! You just set a permission!

 10 MINUTES

Lab Exercise 13.03: Sharing Files and Folders

There are plenty of times when delving into specific NTFS permissions is overkill. Sometimes, you just want to share a folder, one that everyone can freely add to, edit, and so on. Windows makes it easy to share a folder with multiple local user accounts. Most versions even come with a folder set up for this purpose, like Public Documents. But one shared folder isn't always enough.

Learning Objectives

In this lab, you'll use sharing in Windows to set up a folder that can be accessed by all users.

At the end of this lab, you'll be able to

- Set up a shared folder

Lab Materials and Setup

The materials you need for this lab are

- A PC running Windows 7 Professional/Ultimate/Enterprise, Windows 8.1 Pro, or Windows 10 Pro

Getting Down to Business

In the previous lab, you created the Work folder on the C: drive of your computer. But the only account that has complete control of that folder is the one used to create it. Your client wants to make sure that every user on that system has full access to the contents of that folder. The easiest way to accomplish that is to use the Share feature of Windows.

Step 1 Navigate to the C: drive in Windows Explorer/File Explorer. If you haven't already done so (Lab Exercise 13.02), create a Work folder in the root folder of the C: drive. Then right-click the folder and select Share With (Windows 7/8/8.1) or Give access to (Windows 10). Select Specific people. The File Sharing dialog box opens.

Step 2 From the drop-down menu, select Everyone, and then click Add.

Step 3 In the list of Names and Permission Levels, open the Permission Level drop-down menu for the Everyone group and select Read/Write. Click Share.

Step 4 In the File Sharing dialog box, a message appears that your folder is shared. Click Done.

 **10 MINUTES**

Lab Exercise 13.04: Encrypting Important Data

So far, you've gone through several methods of securing data on a machine accessed by multiple users. But these features don't secure the data itself as much as put a wall around it to keep people out. The data inside is (as of yet) defenseless. If a system has two administrator accounts, and one administrator sets up file permissions to keep the other out, the second administrator has the power to undo those permissions and access the data—unless you activate encryption.

When you encrypt a file, it becomes absolutely secure from everyone else but you or, more specifically, your password. If you were to lose your password, or an administrator were to change it for you, that data would be lost forever, because that password is *the only way* to get it back. So be careful!

Learning Objectives

In this lab, you'll use encryption to protect sensitive data.

At the end of this lab, you'll be able to

- Use the Encrypting File System in Windows

Lab Materials and Setup

The materials you need for this lab are

- A PC running Windows 7 Professional/Ultimate/Enterprise, Windows 8.1 Pro, or Windows 10 Pro

Getting Down to Business

Your client has several personal documents that she keeps copies of on her computer at work. But she isn't the only administrator on that system, so to fully secure the data, she wants it to be encrypted.

Thanks to the Encrypting File System (EFS) introduced with NTFS, encrypting files in Windows is simple. Be warned, however, that if you lose access to the user account that you used to encrypt the files, you will lose those files forever!

✔ **Hint**

The Home editions of Windows, such as Windows 7 Home Premium, do not include a utility to encrypt data. If you need encryption, third-party applications are available, but it may be more economical, not to mention safer for your data, to simply upgrade to a professional edition of Windows.

Step 1 First, you'll encrypt a folder.

a. In Windows Explorer/File Explorer, navigate to the top level of the C: drive, so that the Work folder is visible. You created the Work folder earlier in this chapter.

b. Right-click the Work folder and select Properties.

c. Next to the Attributes checkboxes, click the Advanced button.

d. At the bottom of the Advanced Attributes dialog box, check the box for Encrypt contents to secure data (see Figure 13-2).

e. Click OK to close the Advanced Attributes dialog box.

FIGURE 13-2 The Advanced Attributes dialog box

f. Click OK to close the Work Properties dialog box. A Confirm Attribute Changes dialog box appears. The default setting here is Apply changes to this folder, subfolders, and files.

g. Click OK to accept the default setting. Notice that the Work folder's name now appears in green text, indicating the encrypted status.

Step 2 Next, you'll back up your encryption key. This is optional, but it doesn't take long, and you'll be very glad you did so if you can't get into your encrypted folders at some point.

a. Click Start, and then type **certmgr.msc**. When that utility appears in the search results, click it to open it.

b. In the navigation pane, double-click Personal, and then click Certificates.

c. In the main pane, click the certificate that shows Encrypting File System in the Intended Purposes column. If there is more than one, you should back up all of them.

d. Open the Action menu, point to All Tasks, and click Export. The Certificate Export Wizard runs.

e. Click Next. Click Yes, export the private key, and then click Next again.

f. Click Personal Information Exchange, and then click next.

g. Mark the Password checkbox. Type the password you want to use, confirm it, and click Next.

h. In the File name box, type the name you want to use for the export file. You can type the entire path in that box, or you can click Browse, navigate to a location, type a filename, and then click Save.

i. Click Next, and then click Finish.

j. At the message stating the export was successful, click OK.

> → **Note**
>
> **You don't practice it in this lab, but you should know how to restore a certificate. Repeat Steps 2a–b, and then with Certificates selected in the navigation pane, choose Action | All Tasks | Import. Then work through the Certificate Import Wizard.**

Step 3   Now switch to another user, even another administrator. Navigate back to the folder that you just encrypted. Try opening it. What happens?

 10 MINUTES

Lab Exercise 13.05: Configuring User Account Control

Starting with Windows Vista, Microsoft introduced users to a new feature called User Account Control (UAC). User Account Control was designed to put controls in place to stop malicious code from spreading on a computer. UAC ensures that important changes cannot be made to a Windows computer without the permission of an administrator. When it debuted with Windows Vista, users were less than enthusiastic about this new feature. Many turned the feature off almost immediately because of how invasive it was. With Windows Vista, UAC could either be on or off—there was no middle ground. Starting with Windows 7, Microsoft fixed this and has enabled users to choose four distinct levels of how UAC presents itself.

Learning Objectives

In this lab, you'll learn the effects of the different UAC settings.

At the end of this lab, you'll be able to

- Understand the effects of User Account Control

Lab Materials and Setup

The materials you need for this lab are

- A PC running Windows 7 or later

Getting Down to Business

You have a client who has had numerous problems with malware infections, due to the questionable nature of the Web sites he visits. Rather than convincing him not to visit such Web sites, you have decided to simply bump up his UAC settings so that he will be notified before any changes are made to his system.

Step 1   First, let's see what User Account Control looks like and the different settings it offers in Windows 7 and higher.

   a.   Open the Control Panel and view the System and Security section.

   b.   In Windows 7/8.1, under the Action Center heading, click the Change User Account Control settings link. In Windows 10, under the Security and Maintenance heading, click Change User Account Control settings.

   c.   You should now be in the User Account Control Settings window. There is a four-notch slider, and the default setting is the next-to-highest setting, as shown in Figure 13-3.

   d.   Drag the slider to each of the other positions, and read the description that appears for each one.

   e.   Drag the slider to the highest setting, and then click OK.

   f.   At the User Account Control prompt, click Yes to confirm.

Step 2   Now let's explore the effect of cranking up the UAC setting to its highest level.

   a.   Click Control Panel Home to return to the top level of the Control Panel.

   b.   Click System and Security.

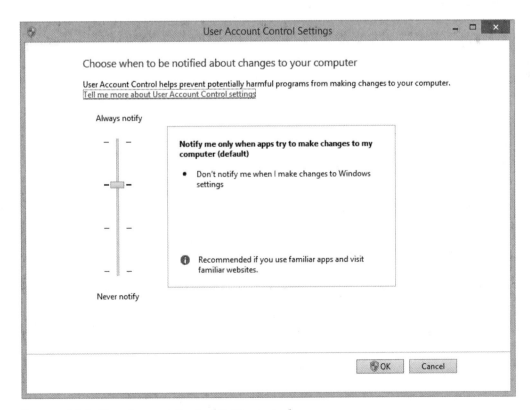

FIGURE 13-3 User Account Control Settings window

    c.   Click any of the options that have a shield next to them; these are items that require you to check in with UAC. Describe what happens:

_____

    d.   At the UAC prompt, click No to not allow the activity. Describe what happens:

_____

Step 3   Return the UAC setting to the default (the second-from-highest setting).

Step 4   Answer these questions:

    A.   This exercise was designed to help you become more familiar with UAC. Why do you think this feature is useful in modern computing?

_____

_____

    B.   Which level of User Account Control best fits your needs as a user and why?

_____

_____

 **10 MINUTES**

Lab Exercise 13.06: Using BitLocker To Go

BitLocker To Go, available in Windows 7 and later, enables you to encrypt flash drives and other similar devices using a technology similar to that of BitLocker, its utility for encrypting entire hard disk drives. Enabling BitLocker To Go password-protects access to the removable drive. Whenever the drive is connected to a different computer, BitLocker To Go prompts for the assigned password.

Learning Objectives

In this lab, you'll learn how to use BitLocker To Go.

At the end of this lab, you'll be able to

- Use BitLocker To Go to encrypt a flash drive

- Manage BitLocker To Go settings

Lab Materials and Setup

The materials you need for this lab are

- A PC running Windows 7 Enterprise or Ultimate, Windows 8.1 Pro, or Windows 10 Pro

- (Optional) A PC running Windows 7 Home Starter, Home Basic, or Home Premium, Windows 8.1 Home, or Windows 10 Home

- A USB flash drive

Getting Down to Business

Nikki works for a company that has highly sensitive data stored on its servers. The network administrator is concerned about possible data theft when users like Nikki take work home on a flash drive. He wants to train Nikki and users like her to use BitLocker To Go so that lost flash drives won't be readable by any stranger who picks them up.

Step 1   First, you'll use BitLocker To Go to encrypt the flash drive on your Windows 7 or later PC.

   a.   Connect a USB flash drive to the PC.

   b.   Open the Control Panel and go to the System and Security section.

   c.   Select BitLocker Drive Encryption. If you don't see that option, you don't have a suitable version of Windows. By default, BitLocker is turned off, as shown in Figure 13-4.

   d.   Click the down arrow next to the USB drive to expand its options, and then click Turn on BitLocker. This will begin the BitLocker To Go wizard (see Figure 13-5).

   e.   Check the Use a password to unlock the drive checkbox.

   f.   Enter (and reenter) a password that will later unlock the drive.

   g.   BitLocker To Go also has another way of unlocking the drive besides a password. What is the other method of unlocking the drive?

   _____

   h.   Click Next. This screen asks you where you want to store the recovery key in case you forget the password. What options are available for storing the recovery key?

   _____

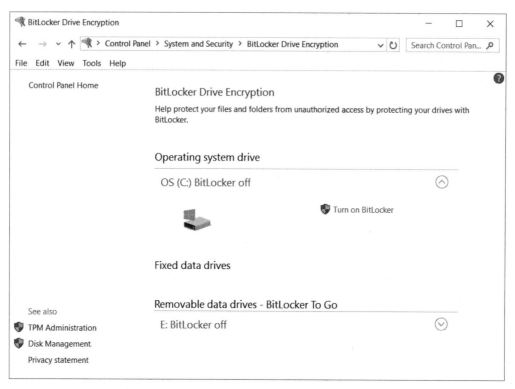

FIGURE 13-4 BitLocker Drive Encryption applet

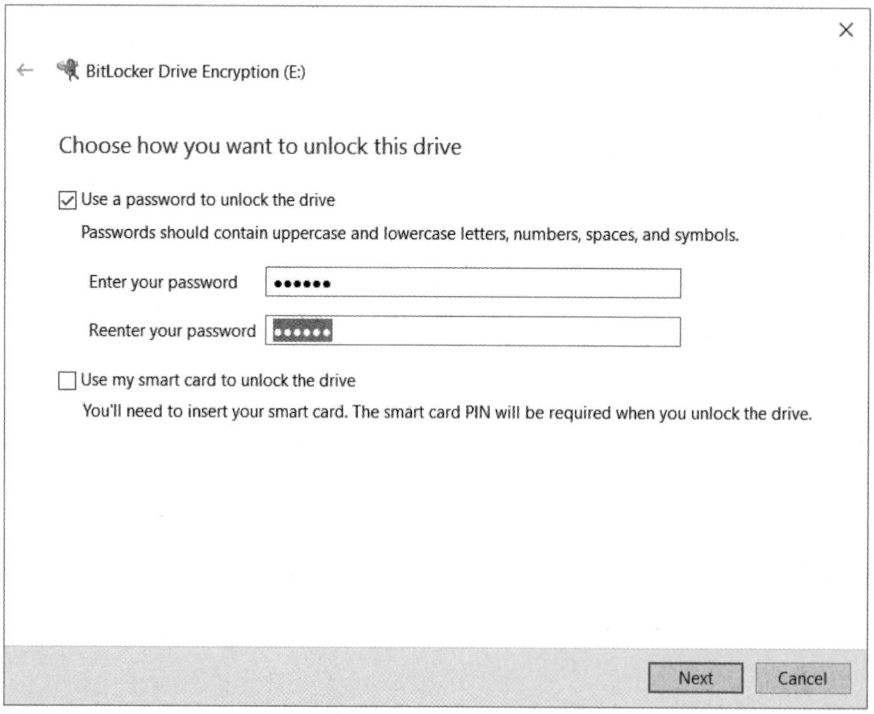

FIGURE 13-5 BitLocker To Go wizard

i.   Choose Save to a file, confirm the filename and location, and click Save. (Remember this location; you'll need it in Step 3.) Click Next.

j.   If prompted, choose how much of your drive to encrypt. (This option may not be available, depending on the Windows version.) You can choose to encrypt used disk space only or encrypt the entire drive.

k.   If you are running Windows 10, choose which encryption mode to use. Windows 10 introduced a new disk encryption mode that is incompatible with older versions of Windows. Choose Compatible mode unless *all* the machines on which you will use the drive are running Windows 10. Then click Next.

l.   Click Start encrypting. This can take a while, depending on the size of the flash drive.

m.   Upon completion, you will receive a message stating that the drive has been encrypted. Click OK or Close, depending on the version of Windows in use.

Step 2

a.   Open Windows Explorer/File Explorer and view Computer/This PC. What is different about the flash drive's appearance now?

_____

b.   Try opening and working with your flash drive. It should work and act like any other flash drive.

Step 3   To test what happens when you connect to your PC a flash drive encrypted using BitLocker To Go, you'll need to disconnect it from your PC, then reconnect it.

a.   Remove your flash drive from the computer.

b.   Wait a minute and then reinsert your flash drive into the computer.

    c. Look in Windows Explorer/File Explorer. How does the icon look different now for the flash drive?

_____

    d. You might be prompted with a BitLocker Drive Encryption window to supply your password. If not, double-click the flash drive's icon to open a password prompt.

    e. Do one of the following, depending on the Windows version:

- Click I forgot my password.

- Click More Options, then click Enter recovery key.

    f. Open the recovery text file you saved in Step 1 using Notepad, and copy the Recovery Key value to the Clipboard. Then paste it at the prompt for the recovery key and click Unlock.

    g. You can also automatically unlock the drive on this computer from now on. When might you check the option?

_____

    h. Click Unlock or Turn on auto-unlock, depending on the Windows version. You now should be able to read and write to the drive on this particular PC without any problems.

Step 4 You can manage a BitLocker To Go drive's settings from the Control Panel.

    a. Return to BitLocker Drive Encryption in the Control Panel. The available options for managing the drive's security settings are listed to its right. List the options you see:

_____

_____

_____

    b. Close the Control Panel.

➜ **Note**

Although you cannot manage the settings on a BitLocker To Go–encrypted drive using Home editions of Windows 7, 8.1, or 10, you can open the drive and read/write files if you know the password or have the encryption key.

Step 5 Now you'll decrypt the drive, restoring it to its unprotected state.

    a. Return the USB flash drive to the PC you used to encrypt it.

    b. Right-click the drive in Windows Explorer/File Explorer and choose Manage BitLocker. The BitLocker section of the Control Panel reopens.

    c. Next to the flash drive, click Turn off BitLocker. A warning appears.

    d. Click Turn off BitLocker and wait for the drive to be decrypted.

 **30 MINUTES**

Lab Exercise 13.07: Setting File Permissions in Linux

In Linux, like in Windows, each file or folder has its own permissions that govern who may do various things to it (read it, change it, and so on). Because Linux is based on UNIX, an OS with robust and very configurable security settings, Linux also brings a lot of power and flexibility to file security. Examining and changing these permissions makes for an excellent reason to explore the Linux command line, which you'll need to know about for the CompTIA A+ 1002 exam.

Learning Objectives

In this lab, you'll learn how to change file permissions in Linux.

    At the end of this lab, you'll be able to

- View permissions
- Change permissions

Lab Materials and Setup

The materials you need for this lab are

- A PC running Linux (any version, Ubuntu preferred)

Getting Down to Business

You want to store some files on a Linux PC that you share with several other users, but you want those files to be private, so that no other users can access them. You will create a new folder and two new files, and then set permissions on the folder that will keep others from using it.

Step 1 First you'll need to fire up Linux and get to a command prompt by running the Terminal application. The exact steps depend on your distro; in Ubuntu Linux you can press CTRL-ALT-T for a terminal window, or click *Search your computer and online sources* and start typing **terminal** until you see the program, and then click it. Terminal opens up in the Home folder for the signed-in user.

Step 2   Next, to get your bearings, you'll list the files in the current location, and then enter the Documents folder.

    a.   Type **ls** and press ENTER. You see a list of files and folders in the current location. The blue items are folders; the white items are files.

    b.   Open the Files application in the Linux graphical user interface (GUI) for your distro, and browse to the Home folder. To do this in Ubuntu Linux, open the Files application and click Home in the places bar. Keep this window open just so you can keep an eye on what's happening in a familiar GUI.

    c.   Switch back to the terminal window, type **cd Documents**, and press ENTER. Notice that the command prompt changes to show /Documents. See Figure 13-6.

Step 3   Next, you'll make a new folder, and enter it.

    a.   Type **mkdir Private** and press ENTER.

✔ Tip

If you are following along in the GUI, switch over to the Files app and look inside the Documents folder there. You'll see the Private folder you just created.

---

    b.   Type **cd Private** and press ENTER.

    c.   Check out the results in the Files GUI window.

Step 4   In the Private folder, you'll now create a new text file, just to have something to work with. There are many ways to create a new file, including using an application in the GUI, but we're going to do a quick-and-dirty method here.

    a.   In the terminal window, type **cat > sample.text** and press ENTER.

    b.   Type **This is private stuff** and press ENTER.

    c.   Press CTRL-D to exit the file and return to the prompt.

```
🔴🟡🟢  faithe@faithe-Virtual-Machine: ~/Documents
faithe@faithe-Virtual-Machine:~$ ls
Desktop    Downloads        Music      Public     Videos
Documents  examples.desktop Pictures   Templates
faithe@faithe-Virtual-Machine:~$ cd Documents
faithe@faithe-Virtual-Machine:~/Documents$ ▮
```

FIGURE 13-6 A Linux terminal window showing the result of the ls command and the cd Documents command

```
faithe@faithe-Virtual-Machine: ~/Documents/Private
faithe@faithe-Virtual-Machine:~/Documents/Private$ ls -l
total 8
-rw-rw-r-- 1 faithe faithe 22 Dec  7 13:25 another.txt
-rw-rw-r-- 1 faithe faithe 22 Dec  7 13:23 sample.txt
faithe@faithe-Virtual-Machine:~/Documents/Private$ 
```

FIGURE 13-7 Two files in the Private folder, with details shown including their permissions

Step 5   Now you'll copy that file so you have two files to work with.

  a.   Type **cp sample.text another.text** and press ENTER.

  b.   Type **ls** and press ENTER to confirm that there are now two files in the Private folder.

  c.   Check out the results in the Files GUI window.

Step 6   Next you'll examine the default permissions on the files you just created.

In the terminal window, type **ls –l** and press ENTER. This shows more details about each file, including its permissions. See Figure 13-7.

Let's take a moment to review what those permissions mean. Each file's permissions appear like this:

-rw-rw-r--

(Ignore the – at the beginning; that just means it's a file, folder, or shortcut.)

That leaves three groups of three characters each: r, w, and x (read, write, and execute, respectively).

If one of the characters is not present in one of the groups, a dash stands in for it. The three groups, from left to right, are Owner, Group, and Everyone. So, to break that down:

  - **Owner**   Read and Write (no Execute, in this case not because the owner is not entitled, but because it's not an executable file)

  - **Group**   Same as Owner in this case

  - **Everyone**   Read, but not Write or Execute

What is this "group" that the permissions reference? You can assign a folder or file to a group, such as adm (administrators), so that users who belong to that group have enhanced permissions that not everyone has. You can change the group with the chown (which is short for *change owner*) command. This lab exercise doesn't cover changing the group via the command line, but there are instructions for doing so in the section "Permissions in Linux and macOS" in Chapter 13 of *Mike Meyers' CompTIA A+ Guide to Managing and Troubleshooting PCs*. You'll also see how to do it from the GUI in Step 7.

Step 7   Next you'll limit the permissions on the Private folder to just the Owner (that's you). But first, a reminder of how permissions are assigned with the chmod (which is short for *change mode*) command.

When using chmod, the permissions for Owner, Group, and Everyone are assigned using a single numeric value. It's determined by adding up the following:

- Read: 4

- Write: 2

- Execute: 1

If the Owner has a permission of Read and Write but not Execute, then the Owner's permission is 6. If Everyone has a permission of 4, then Everyone can Read but not Write or Execute.

By this measure, the numeric values of the permissions for the files you created in Step 3 are 664. If you were setting permission for a folder called Extra with chmod so that the Owner has all permissions and nobody else has any, the numeric values would be 700, and the command would look like this:

```
chmod 700 Extra
```

a.   Type **cd ..** and press ENTER to move up one level in the file hierarchy.

b.   Type **ls –l** and press ENTER to see what the current permissions are for the Private folder. It appears as drwxrwxr-x. The "d" at the beginning means it's a directory.

c.   What are the current permissions for this folder?

Owner: _____

Group: _____

Everyone: _____

d.   What are the numeric values for these permissions? (Remember: Read =4; Write =2, Execute =1.)

Owner: _____

Group: _____

Everyone: _____

e.   Suppose you want the Owner to have all permissions, the Group to have Read and Execute only, and Everyone to have no permission at all. What would the numeric values be for that?

Owner: _____

Group: _____

Everyone: _____

f.   At the command prompt, type **chmod 750 Private** and press ENTER.

g.   Type **ls –l** and check the permissions for the Private folder. If they do not match what you indicated in Step e, how do they differ?

h. Enter the Private folder from the command prompt and change the permission on sample.txt to remove the Write ability from the Group. Write the command that you used:

Step 8 Now that you've seen the arduous, long way around with the command prompt, you're going to see how much easier it is using the Files GUI window that's available in most Linux distros. We'll use Ubuntu here as the example.

a. In the Files application, navigate to the Private folder.

b. Right-click sample.text and click Properties.

c. In the Properties dialog box, click the Permissions tab.

d. Open the Group drop-down list. You can choose which group you're assigning permissions for here.

e. Click adm. (That's the administrators group.)

f. Open the Access drop-down list for that group and choose Read and write. See Figure 13-8.

g. Click the Close button.

FIGURE 13-8 Setting permissions is much easier via the GUI.

Lab Analysis Test

1. Jonas has an administrator account and sets up the permissions for a folder on the C: drive to deny anyone else from accessing it but himself. If another administrator account was created, would the folder still be secure? Why or why not?

2. Reginald needs to set up a folder that can be seen by the administrator and two standard users, but can be edited only by the administrator. How would he make this work?

3. Nina created several user accounts in Windows 7 for her family, but forgot to give each of them passwords. List the steps to take to add a password to a user account in Windows 7.

4. What makes EFS a great security feature in Windows?

5. Suppose you want to make the file Free.text available for both reading and writing to everyone in Linux. (You would not set Execute permission because it is not an executable file.) What command would you use at the command prompt to set this permission?

Key Term Quiz

Use the following terms to complete the following sentences. Not all terms will be used.

administrator   limited user

authentication   NTFS permissions

cd   standard user

chmod   Trusted Platform Module

chown   User Account Control (UAC)

group

1. A(n) _____ cannot install software or delete system files.

2. Typing your user name and password is a means of _____.

3. _____ are used to define specific rules for which users and groups can and cannot access files and folders on the local PC.

4. _____ prevents a program from running unless a user authorizes it to.

5. The _____ command can be used to change the group to which a folder belongs in Linux.

Chapter 14

Maintaining and Optimizing Operating Systems

Lab Exercises

Imagine that your company has just acquired a small architectural firm, including its mixed group of computers. One of the principals of the firm informs you that they haven't really had any IT support to speak of in a few years. You visit the office and determine that most of the computers are about five years old. They were good machines when they were purchased, and as long as the hardware is not failing, they should be more than adequate for a year or two more. The architects do complain that their machines are running slowly and that it's affecting productivity. You would like to avoid a complete rollout of new PCs and Macs, since you're looking at a replacement expense of tens of thousands of dollars. Consequently, you decide it would be worthwhile to spend a day trying to figure out if anything can be done to make the machines run faster.

After checking out a few of the systems, you determine that most could definitely benefit from additional memory, but that's not the only issue—none of the systems have been updated in over three years! Even though most operating systems are optimized when they're installed, time and use can alter that fact significantly. It's important, therefore, to be able to take what you know about navigating and manipulating the Mac and Windows environments and put that knowledge to work figuring out what needs to be fixed, updated, or improved. Sometimes a simple tweak is all it takes to make a sluggish system run like it's fresh out of the box.

One of the first tasks is to make sure that all of the systems have the latest operating system updates. Before you do that, however, it's recommended that you back up all of the data on the systems, as this can be a pretty major upgrade. You'll analyze the machines to make sure nothing unwanted is loading at startup, such as third-party adware or toolbars, and remove any unwanted applications you find. You will also help systems run better in the future by scheduling routine maintenance tasks to run automatically at regular intervals.

60 MINUTES

Lab Exercise 14.01: Backing Up and Restoring in Windows 7

Depending on the Windows version, you have different tools available for backing up and restoring files. Windows 7 includes a backup utility that enables you to make compressed backups of your files and your system image to external media, and then restore from those backups using the same utility if the backups are later needed. This backup utility (also present in Windows 8.1, but not recommended) is awkward to use, and sometimes the backups it produces are unreliable. Windows 10 did away with the Windows 7 backup utility in 2018, although it provides a utility for restoring from Windows 7 backup sets. (Windows 8.1 and Windows 10 use a different type of backup utility called File History, covered in Lab Exercises 14.02 and 14.03.) People just aren't using this kind of backup much anymore on personal computers. For personal use, it's become easier to simply copy files off to safe locations as backup, without using a utility, because no complicated restore process is required to access the backups. For business use, data backup appliances and servers have automated the task of backing up important data. We still present it here, however, because it's still included in the 1002 exam objectives.

Learning Objectives

In this lab, you'll use the Backup and Restore utility in Windows 7.

At the end of this lab, you'll be able to

- Back up and restore files in Windows 7

Lab Materials and Setup

The materials you need for this lab are

- A PC running Windows 7
- A drive other than your primary hard disk drive with at least 2 GB of free space

Getting Down to Business

The PCs you support have a variety of operating systems on them. The ones that have Windows 7 can be backed up using the Backup and Restore utility.

Step 1   On a Windows 7 PC follow these steps to perform a backup of the files in the current user's personal Documents library. If there are a lot of files there (more than 1 GB or so), you might want to narrow the scope of the backup to one particular folder for this exercise; it doesn't really matter how much you back up, only that you back up something, for the practice.

    a.   Make sure you have a drive connected that you can use for the backup. Ideally it would be an external drive, but for this exercise you can use an additional hard drive (not your system drive) or even an optical disc. It should have at least 2 GB of free space on it (more or less—the actual required amount depends on the size of the files in the Documents library for the signed-in user).

    b.   Make sure there is at least one file in the Documents library on this PC. Create one there if you have to.

✔ **Tip**

If there are more than a couple of gigabytes of files in the Documents library, you might want to move some of them out of there temporarily so this exercise won't take a long time.

    c.   Open the Control Panel, click System and Security, and click Backup and Restore.

    d.   If Backup has not yet been set up, you'll need to do so. Click Set up backup. (You can click the Back up now button and skip to Step j if it's already set up.)

    e.   Select the drive on which to back up from the Save backup on list. Then click Next.

    f.   At the What do you want to back up? screen, click Let me choose. Then click Next.

    g.   Clear the Include a system image of drives checkbox. You don't want that now.

    h.   Under Data Files, expand the heading and clear all the checkboxes. Then mark the checkbox for the Documents Library only, as shown in Figure 14-1. Click Next.

    i.   Click Save Settings and Run Backup.

    j.   Wait for the backup to complete. A progress bar appears in the Control Panel window; you can click View Details to monitor it more closely if you like.

Step 2   Now you'll do a quick restore of the backup in Windows 7.

    a.   Open the Documents library in Windows Explorer and delete one file of your choice. (Don't delete an important one.) This is so you'll see a difference when you do a restore.

    b.   In the Backup and Restore section of the Control Panel, click Restore my files.

    c.   Click Browse for Folders.

    d.   Navigate to the backup location you chose in Step 1, select it, and click Add folder.

    e.   Click Next, and then click In the original location.

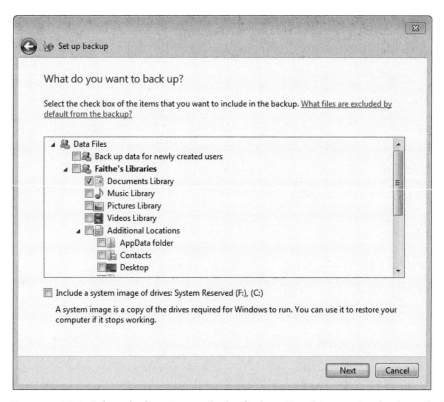

FIGURE 14-1 Select the locations to be backed up. For this exercise, back up the Documents library only.

f. Click Restore.

g. If you didn't delete *all* the files in the Documents library in Step a, you'll see a Copy File warning. Mark the Do this for all conflicts checkbox, and then click Don't copy.

h. Wait for the file that you renamed or deleted in Step a to be restored. All other files will be ignored. When the process is complete, click Finish.

i. View the Documents library in Windows Explorer to confirm that the file you deleted has been restored.

 **30 MINUTES**

Lab Exercise 14.02: Using File History in Windows 8.1

File History is a selective backup tool in Windows 8 and later that protects your data files by saving alternate versions of them to a different disk. That way if something happens to the original, you can get it back (or at least a recent version of it). This feature is disabled by default, but you can easily enable it. Then when you make changes to your files in the locations that it protects, backups of those files are automatically made.

Learning Objectives

In this lab, you'll use the File History feature in Windows 8.1.

At the end of this lab, you'll be able to

- Enable File History

- Restore a previous version of a file

Lab Materials and Setup

The materials you need for this lab are

- A PC running Windows 8.1 with at least one usable drive other than the primary hard drive

Getting Down to Business

File History doesn't start doing its thing until you enable it. The drawbacks of enabling it are that you need space on a drive other than your primary hard drive, and it may slow down system performance slightly. In the following steps, you'll turn on File History in Windows 8.1, create a file, make some changes to the file, delete the file, and then restore the original version from the File History archive.

Step 1   First up: enabling File History.

    a.   Open the Control Panel and navigate to System and Security | File History.

    b.   In the navigation pane at the left, click Select drive.

    c.   In the Select a File History drive list, click the drive on which to save the file history, and click OK.

    d.   If File History is off appears, click Turn on. It might already be on from Step c.

Step 2   Next you'll create a text file that you can use to experiment with the File History feature.

    a.   Open File Explorer, and open the Documents folder.

    b.   Right-click in the file area and click New | Text Document. Name the new text document **History Check**.

    c.   Double-click the file to open it in Notepad. Type **This is version 1**. Save the file and close Notepad.

Step 3   File History makes backups at regular intervals (every hour by default), but you can also tell it to Run Now at any time. Go back to the File History screen in the Control Panel, and click Run Now to make sure the archive is updated.

Step 4   Now you'll make a change to the History Check file, creating another version of it, and then use Run Now again to make sure that version is saved.

a.   Switch back to File Explorer. Double-click History Check to reopen it, and edit the text to read **This is version 2**. Save the file and close Notepad.

b.   Go back to the File History screen in the Control Panel, and click Run Now to make sure the archive is updated.

Step 5   Next, you'll delete the History Check file, and then restore it from File History.

a.   Switch back to File Explorer and delete the History Check file (select it and press DELETE).

b.   Return to the File History screen in the Control Panel and click Restore personal files.

c.   In the Home – File History window, double-click Documents.

d.   Click the History Check file and click the Restore to Original Location button (big green circle at the bottom; see Figure 14-2).

e.   Back in File Explorer, double-click History Check to open it in Notepad. Which version is it: 1 or 2? _____

Step 6   Finally, you'll restore the previous version of the file, and then turn File History off again.

a.   Switch back to Documents – File History and click the Previous Version button (left-pointing arrow button) to the left of the Restore to Original Location button.

b.   Click the History Check file and click the Restore to Original Location button. At the Replace or Skip Files dialog box, click Replace the file in the destination.

c.   Back in File Explorer, double-click History Check to open it in Notepad. Which version is it: 1 or 2? _____

d.   Switch back to the Documents – File History window and close it.

e.   In the File History window, click Turn off.

f.   Close the File History window.

FIGURE 14-2   Restoring a file from File History

→ **Note**

If you want to restore more than one version of a file, click Compare info for both files when the Replace or Skip Files dialog box appears. Click the checkbox for all versions listed and click Continue. Different versions of the file will be numbered when they are restored.

 **30 MINUTES**

Lab Exercise 14.03: Using File History in Windows 10

In our scenario, a few older systems have been replaced with systems running Windows 10. File History works differently in Windows 10 than in Windows 8.1, so we are covering how to use the Windows 10 version in this exercise.

Learning Objectives

In this lab, you'll use the File History feature in Windows 10.

At the end of this lab, you'll be able to

- Enable File History

- Restore a previous version of a file

Lab Materials and Setup

The materials you need for this lab are

- A PC running Windows 10 with at least one usable drive other than the primary hard drive

Getting Down to Business

File History doesn't start doing its thing until you enable it. The drawbacks of enabling it are that you need space on a disk other than your primary hard drive, and it may slow down system performance slightly. In the following steps, you'll turn on File History in Windows 10, create a file, make some changes to the file, delete the file, and then restore the original version from the File History archive.

Step 1   First up: enabling File History.

   a.   In Windows 10, open Settings | Update & Security | Backup.

   b.   Click Add a drive.

   c.   In the Select a drive list, click the drive on which to save the file history.

   d.   If Automatically back up my files is turned Off, click On. It might already be on from Step c.

Step 2 Next you'll create a text file that you can use to experiment with the File History feature.

a. Open File Explorer, and open the Documents folder.

b. Right-click in the file area and click New | Text Document. Name the new text document **History Check**.

c. Double-click the file to open it in Notepad. Type **This is version 1**. Save the file and close Notepad.

Step 3 File History makes backups at regular intervals (every hour by default), but you can also tell it to Back up now at any time. Go back to Update & Security | Backup in Settings, click More options, and click Back up now.

Step 4 Now you'll make a change to the History Check file, creating another version of it, and then use Back up now again to make sure that version is saved.

a. Switch back to File Explorer. Double-click History Check to reopen it, and edit the text to read **This is version 2**. Save the file and close Notepad.

b. Go back to the Backup page in Settings, click More options, and click Back up now to make sure the archive is updated.

Step 5 Next, you'll delete the History Check file, and then restore it from File History.

a. Switch back to File Explorer and delete the History Check file (select it and press DELETE).

b. Return to the Backup page in Settings, click More options, and click Restore files from a current backup.

c. In the Home – File History window, double-click Documents.

d. Click the History Check file and click the Restore to Original Location button.

e. Back in File Explorer, double-click History Check to open it in Notepad. Which version is it: 1 or 2? _____

Step 6 Finally, you'll restore the previous version of the file, and then turn File History off again.

a. Switch back to Documents – File History and click the Previous Version button (left-pointing arrow button) to the left of the Restore to Original Location button.

b. Click the History Check file and click the Restore to Original Location button. At the Replace or Skip Files dialog box, click Replace the file in the destination.

c. Back in File Explorer, double-click History Check to open it in Notepad. Which version is it: 1 or 2? _____

d. Switch back to the Documents – File History window and close it.

e. In the Backup window, click Off.

f. Close the Backup window.

→ Note

If you want to restore more than one version of a file, click Compare info for both files when the Replace or Skip Files dialog box appears. Click the checkbox for all versions listed and click Continue. Different versions of the file will be numbered when they are restored.

 20 MINUTES

Lab Exercise 14.04: Using System Restore

Recall from this chapter's scenario that you're gearing up to update some older PCs that haven't been updated in a while. When you do that, you run the risk that one of the updates is going to interact badly with some hardware or software and make the system run poorly (or not at all). At that point, you'll fervently wish you had the system back the way it was before you updated it. System Restore can grant your wish.

System Restore saves snapshots of your system files at regular intervals (and also when you manually ask it to do so), and then if system problems occur, you can use one of those snapshots to return to an earlier configuration. This is particularly useful if you install some questionable piece of software that makes changes to your system files that cause the system to run badly or some hardware to go all wonky. And speaking of wonky hardware, System Restore can also help if you install a bad driver.

In this lab exercise, you'll create a snapshot (restore point), make a change to system settings, and then restore that snapshot to get your old settings back. This lab exercise uses Windows 8.1, but System Restore is also available in other Windows versions too.

Learning Objectives

In this lab, you'll use the System Restore utility in Windows.

At the end of this lab, you'll be able to

- Save a System Restore snapshot

- Restore the system to an earlier time using a snapshot

Lab Materials and Setup

The materials you need for this lab are

- A PC running Windows 8.1 (preferably), Windows 7, or Windows 10

Getting Down to Business

In this lab exercise, you'll first create a restore point. Windows creates one every day automatically by default (unless one was created manually), but creating your own ensures that all the latest system changes are included.

Then you will install an app, and then restore back to a time before the app was installed. In real-life usage, you would use this feature to restore back to a point before the system failed, such as when the user installed a corrupted driver or some malware.

Step 1 First you'll create a restore point.

    a. Open the Control Panel and choose System and Security | System | System protection. The System Properties dialog box opens.

    b. On the System Protection tab, click Create.

    c. Type a description for the restore point, such as **Before Exercise 14.04**. See Figure 14-3.

    d. Click Create.

    e. At the confirmation message, click Close.

Step 2 Next, install an application from a source other than the Microsoft (Windows) Store (these apps cannot be removed with System Restore). Some useful and safe apps to consider include CPU-Z (https://www.cpuid.com), GPU-Z (https://www.techpowerup.com/gpuz/), or a Sysinternals utility (https://docs.microsoft.com/en-us/sysinternals/).

    a. Go to the Web site that contains the app you want to download.

    b. Download and install the app.

    c. Verify that the new app appears on the Start screen/menu.

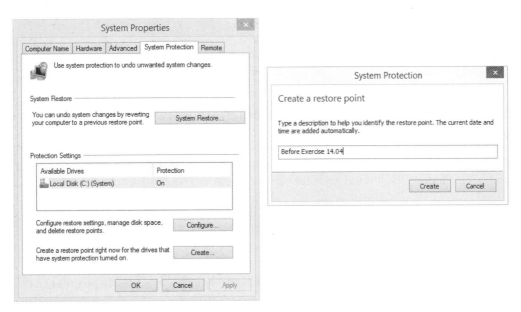

FIGURE 14-3 Create a restore point.

Step 3   Now restore the restore point you created in Step 1, as follows:

  a.   Switch back to the desktop, and to the System Properties window, which should still be open.

  b.   Click the System Restore button on the System Protection tab.

  c.   Do one of the following depending on your Windows version:

  - Windows 7: Click Next.

  - Windows 8.1 or 10: Click Choose a different restore point and click Next.

  d.   Click the restore point you created in Step 1. You will know it by its description.

  e.   Click Scan for affected programs. The program you installed in Step 2 should be listed.

  f.   Click Close.

  g.   Click Next.

  h.   Click Finish. At the warning, click Yes.

  i.   Wait for the restoration to complete. A confirmation dialog box appears; click Close.

  j.   Check the Start screen/menu to confirm that the app is no longer installed.

✔ **Tip**

If you wanted to undo the restore (going back to the time when that app was still installed), you could run System Restore again and choose Undo restore point.

 **30 MINUTES**

Lab Exercise 14.05: Managing Updates and Patches in Windows 7/8.1

Windows Update, a utility designed to download and install any available updates, patches, and service packs, has been around since Windows 95. It is the go-to tool for keeping your Windows system properly managed.

The CompTIA A+ 220-1002 exam uses several update-related terms that you should be familiar with. An *update* is a general maintenance update that fixes a problem, patches a security hole, or adds a minor feature. A *patch* is an update that's designed to fix one specific problem or patch a specific security hole. Microsoft doesn't call its updates "patches" anymore, even when they *are* patches, but you may see this terminology used by other software manufacturers. A *service pack* is a major update, usually involving a lengthy install process and one or more restarts, and resulting in one or more new features or capabilities. Microsoft no longer uses the term "service pack" in Windows 8 and later, but service packs were available for Windows 7, Windows Vista, and Windows XP. (For service packs, search www.catalog.update.microsoft.com.)

Learning Objectives

In this lab, you'll learn how to use Windows Update in Windows 7/8.1.

At the end of this lab, you'll be able to

- Check for updates

- Download available updates

- Adjust update settings

Lab Materials and Setup

The materials you need for this lab are

- A PC running Windows 7 or 8.1

Getting Down to Business

The PCs in our scenario for the chapter are a mixture of different operating systems, including Windows 7 and Windows 8.1. Windows Update works the same way in both versions, so you can use either one for these steps. (Windows 10's Windows Update works differently, and runs from the Settings app; see Lab Exercise 14.06.)

Step 1   First you'll check your Windows Update settings, and see if any updates are available. You'll install any updates you find.

 Tip

> **If a Windows Update causes a problem, you can use System Restore to revert to the earlier version of your system files. You can also remove some Windows updates, as you'll see in Step 3.**

---

a.   Open the Control Panel and choose System and Security | Windows Update.

b.   In the navigation pane, click Check for updates. If any updates are found, hyperlinks for them will appear, as shown in Figure 14-4.

c.   Click the hyperlink for the important update(s), or if there are none, click the hyperlink for the optional update(s).

d.   Review the available updates on both the Important and Optional tabs. See Figure 14-5. You can clear the checkboxes for any you don't want, but in most cases you will want to install the updates, because they solve problems, patch security holes, or add features.

e.   Click Install (Windows 8.1) or click OK and then click Install updates (Windows 7), and then wait for the updates to be installed. You can continue using the PC while the updates download and install.

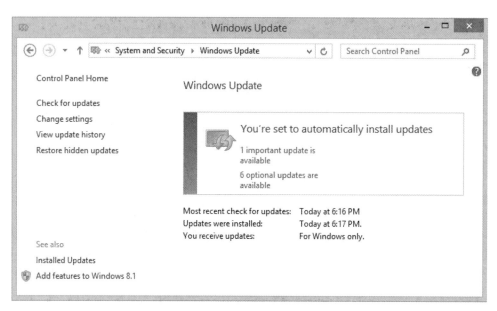

FIGURE 14-4 Windows Update found several updates.

✔ **Tip**

Certain updates may require you to accept a license agreement.

Step 2   While the updates are installing, do the following to further explore the feature:

a.   In the navigation bar, click Change settings.

b.   Open the Important updates drop-down list and peruse the options.

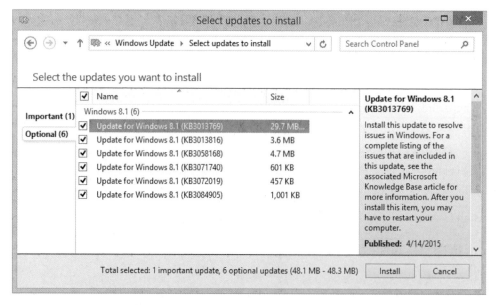

FIGURE 14-5 Review the available updates.

What are the four options you see on this list?

_____

_____

_____

_____

c. If you are using Windows 8.1, notice the checkbox under Microsoft Updates. This option lets you get updates for other Microsoft products automatically too, like Microsoft Office. Check this checkbox if it is not already checked. If you are using Windows 7, click the Back button from the Change settings page, then click the Find out more hyperlink. From the new web page that opens, click Allow to start the Microsoft Update installation process. From the new web page that opens, check the I agree to the terms of use checkbox for Microsoft Update, then click Install. Click Yes in the confirmation dialog box and click the User Account Control icon in the taskbar to install Microsoft Update.

d. Click OK to return to the Windows Update window.

e. Click View update history in the navigation pane. This screen lists the updates you have already installed.

f. Click the Installed Updates hyperlink above the update history list. This is where you would go to remove an update (for example, one that caused problems).

g. Click one of the updates on the list. Notice the Uninstall button that appears above the list. You could click it to uninstall the update. (Don't actually do it now.) If you don't see an Uninstall button, try another update; some updates cannot be uninstalled.

Step 3 Now return to Windows Update and finish up.

a. Click the Back button twice to return to the Windows Update window.

b. If the updates are still not finished, wait for them to finish. If prompted to restart, do so.

 **30 MINUTES**

Lab Exercise 14.06: Managing Updates and Patches in Windows 10

Windows Update in Windows 10, as in previous versions of Windows, is the go-to tool for keeping your Windows system properly managed.

Learning Objectives

In this lab, you'll learn how to use Windows Update in Windows 10.

At the end of this lab, you'll be able to

- Check for updates

- Download available updates

- Adjust update settings

Lab Materials and Setup

The materials you need for this lab are

- A PC running Windows 10

Getting Down to Business

For this exercise, let us assume that one of the Windows 7 or 8.1 computers in the office has failed and been replaced with a new system running Windows 10. The users of this computer need to understand how Windows Update works on this newer version of Windows.

Step 1   First you'll check your Windows Update settings, and see if any updates are available. You'll install any updates you find.

 Tip

If a Windows Update causes a problem, you can use System Restore to revert to the earlier version of your system files. You can also remove some Windows updates using Windows Update, as you'll see in Step 2.

a.   Open Settings | Update and Security | Windows Update.

b.   In the navigation pane, click Check for updates. If any updates are found, they are listed (see Figure 14-6). Updates may be installed right away or may be downloaded for installation after working hours. You can continue using the PC while the updates download and install.

 Tip

Certain updates may require you to accept a license agreement.

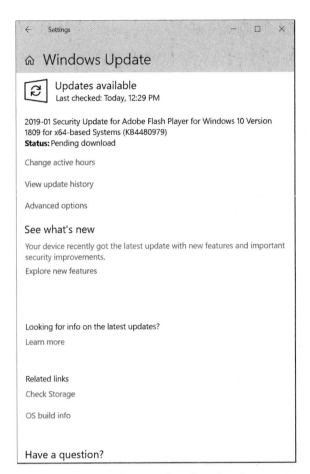

FIGURE 14-6 Windows Update found updates.

Step 2   While the updates are installing, do the following to further explore the feature:

   a.   In the Windows Update window, click Change active hours. Windows Update will install updates that require restarts outside of the active hours you specify.

   What are the active hours listed for your computer? _____ to _____.

   b.   If you typically use your computer at other times, change the settings as needed. Click Save to save your new times, or Cancel to return to the previous dialog box.

   c.   Click Advanced options.

   d.   Notice the slider for Give me options for other Microsoft products when I update Windows (see Figure 14-7). If this is set to Off, click it to turn it On to get updates for Microsoft Office.

   e.   Notice the slider for We'll show a reminder when we're going to restart. To be notified when an update requires a system restart, slide this to On.

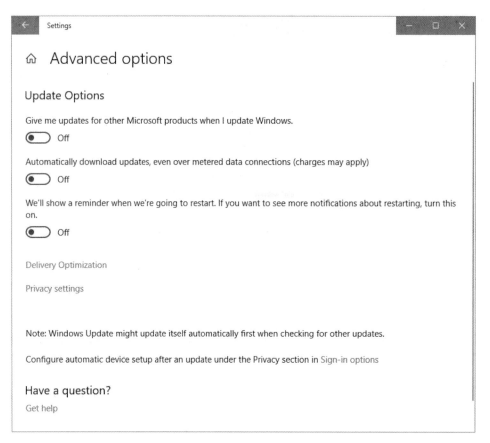

FIGURE 14-7 Advanced options for Windows Update in Windows 10. Windows 10 Pro offers additional settings.

f.　Click the Back button to return to the Windows Update window.

g.　Click View update history. This screen lists the updates you have already installed.

h.　Click the Uninstall updates hyperlink above the update history list. This is where you would go to remove an update (for example, one that caused problems).

i.　Click one of the updates on the list. Notice the Uninstall button that appears above the list. You could click it to uninstall the update. (Don't actually do it now.) If you don't see an Uninstall button, try another update; some updates cannot be uninstalled.

j.　Close the Installed Updates window.

Step 3　Now return to Windows Update and finish up.

a.　Click the Back button to return to the Windows Update window.

b.　If the updates are still not finished, wait for them to finish. If prompted to restart, do so.

 **30 MINUTES**

Lab Exercise 14.07: Scheduling Maintenance in Windows

Modern versions of Windows automatically schedule certain maintenance tasks, such as checking disks for errors and defragmenting them. You can adjust this schedule by changing the dates and times, changing the intervals, and even turning off automatic scheduling of the tasks altogether.

Learning Objectives

In this lab, you'll review a PC's scheduled tasks and create and delete a task.

At the end of this lab, you'll be able to

- View task scheduling
- Create a new scheduled task
- Delete a scheduled task

Lab Materials and Setup

The materials you need for this lab are

- A PC running Windows 7 or later

Getting Down to Business

Scheduling maintenance tasks is a great way of automating the routine upkeep on a PC, so that neither you nor its end user needs to worry about those chores. There are probably already scheduled tasks set up on your PC that you aren't even aware of. In the process of this lab exercise, you'll find out, and you'll learn how to modify those schedules.

Step 1 First you'll open the Task Scheduler and look at the Windows Defender schedule, which is probably already set.

- **a.** Open the Control Panel and navigate to System and Security | Administrative Tools.

- **b.** Double-click Task Scheduler to open that utility.

- **c.** In the navigation pane, browse down to Task Scheduler (Local) | Task Scheduler Library | Microsoft.

- **d.** If you see Windows Defender as a separate entry under Microsoft, click it. If you don't, click Windows and then choose Windows Defender under that.

- **e.** In the upper part of the center pane, click MP Scheduled Scan (Windows 7) or Windows Defender Scheduled Scan (Windows 8.1/10). The details of the schedule appear in the lower part of the center pane, as shown in Figure 14-8.

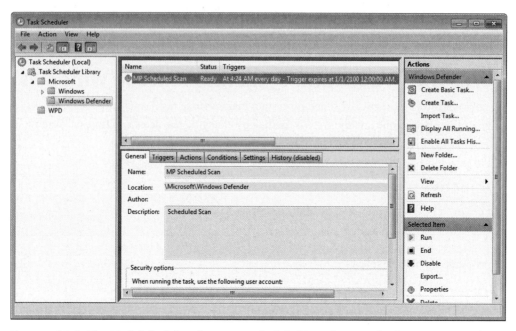

FIGURE 14-8 The Task Scheduler showing a scheduled Windows Defender scan in Windows 7

→ **Note**

If you don't see the MP/Windows Defender Scheduled Scan task, open the Windows Defender utility, click Tools, click Options, and mark the Automatically scan my computer checkbox. Click Save, then return to Task Scheduler and press F5 to refresh (or choose Action | Refresh).

Step 2   Next you'll look at a few other tasks that are already scheduled.

a.   In the navigation pane, expand the Windows category if needed, and then click the Defrag folder. Information about the defragmentation scheduled task appears.

b.   In the navigation pane, click DiskDiagnostic. Information about that scheduled task appears.

→ **Note**

If you don't see the DiskDiagnostic scheduled task, it's because no diagnostic has been scheduled yet.

---

c.   In the navigation pane, click SystemRestore. Information about that scheduled task appears.

Step 3 Let's look at the System Restore task a bit more closely, since you're familiar with the feature from Lab Exercise 14.04.

   a. Look in the Triggers column in the upper portion of the center pane. Note that multiple triggers are defined in Windows 7 (triggers might not be listed in Windows 8.1/10).

   b. In the lower portion of the center pane, click the Triggers tab. Note that this task is triggered at 12:00 A.M. every day, and also at system startup.

   c. Click the Actions tab; the action is for the program to start.

   d. Click the Conditions tab and browse the conditions under which the task will run.

Step 4 Now you'll create a new Windows Defender task that runs a full system scan weekly.

   a. In the navigation pane, click Windows Defender.

   b. In the right pane, click Create Basic Task.

   c. In the Create Basic Task Wizard, enter a name of **Weekly Defender Scan**. Leave the description blank. Click Next.

   d. Choose Weekly and click Next.

   e. Set the task to start on today's date at 2:00:00 AM and recur every week on Sundays.

   f. Choose Start a program and click Next.

   g. Click Browse. Browse to C:\Program Files\Windows Defender, select MpCmdRun, and click Open.

   h. In the Add arguments box, type **–Scan -2**. The –Scan argument runs a scan, and the -2 argument tells it to run a full system scan.

   i. Click Next.

   j. Check the checkbox to display the Properties for the task after creating it, and then click Finish.

   k. In the Properties box, on the General tab, set the Configure for setting to your current OS. For example, if you are running Windows 7, choose Windows 7, Windows Server 2008 R2.

   l. Click the Settings tab in the Properties box, and mark the *Run task as soon as possible after a scheduled start is missed* checkbox.

   m. Click OK.

Step 5 Finally, you'll delete the task you just created.

   a. Select the Windows Defender Weekly task in the upper part of the center pane in the Task Scheduler window.

   b. In the Actions pane on the right, under the Selected Item heading, click Delete.

   c. Click Yes to confirm. The task is deleted.

   d. Close the Task Scheduler.

 **30 MINUTES**

Lab Exercise 14.08: Installing and Removing Applications and Windows Components in Windows

Bringing the computers in our scenario up to date may also mean installing and/or removing applications on them. In Windows 8.1 and 10 there are two kinds of applications: desktop apps (originally made for Windows 7 and earlier versions) and Modern apps (aka Metro apps) made for Windows 8 and later. Desktop apps are managed from the Control Panel, and Modern apps from the Microsoft Store and the Start screen. In Windows 7 and earlier, there are only desktop apps. This exercise will use Windows 8.1 or 10, so you can get a look at both kinds.

In addition to working with applications, you sometimes also may be called upon to add or remove Windows components. Windows comes with certain optional components that are disabled or not installed by default; you can enable them at any time as needed.

Learning Objectives

In this lab, you'll install and remove a desktop app and a Modern app, and repair a desktop app.

At the end of this lab, you'll be able to

- Install and remove a desktop app

- Repair a desktop app

- Install and remove a Modern app

Lab Materials and Setup

The materials you need for this lab are

- A PC running Windows 8.1 or 10

- Microsoft Office (or some other desktop application with a Repair feature), either already installed or not

- A setup file or installation disc for a desktop application that is not yet installed

- An Internet connection

Getting Down to Business

Desktop applications are installed using their own Setup utility, which might come on an optical disc or via download. You run the Setup utility to copy files to the hard drive, add entries to the Registry, and create a shortcut for the application on the Start screen, and perhaps also on the desktop. In contrast, Modern apps are acquired only via download from the Microsoft Store. Downloading and installing them is a single step, usually with no installation choices. Uninstalling a Modern app occurs from the Start screen, and is equally simple.

Because desktop applications are rather large and complicated, they sometimes need repair. A repair operation checks all the application's files and refreshes any that aren't as they should be. Many large, robust applications come with a Repair feature, including Microsoft Office.

Step 1   Install a desktop application. To start the Setup program for the application, do one of the following:

- Double-click the Setup file for the application. (It might not be called Setup, although that is the most common name.)

- Insert the optical disc that contains the Setup program, and wait for Setup to start automatically. If it does not, browse the optical disc, locate the Setup file, and double-click it.

After starting the Setup program, follow the prompts to install the application. The steps vary depending on the application.

Which application did you install? _____

Step 2   Next, you'll examine the installed desktop applications, and repair one of the programs.

a.   In Windows 8.1, open the Control Panel and click Programs | Programs and Features. In Windows 10, click Start | Settings | Apps.

b.   A list of installed applications appears.

c.   Click one of the installed programs.

d.   In Windows 8.1, the commands available for that program appear in a bar above the list. You might see options such as Uninstall, Change, and/or Repair. See Figure 14-9.

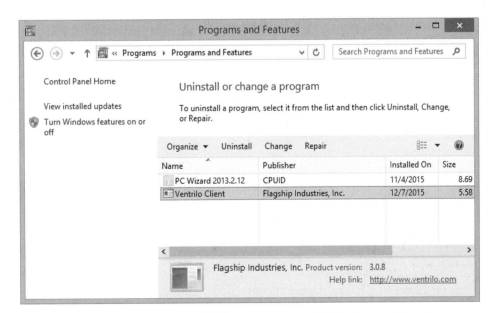

FIGURE 14-9   Windows 8.1 example showing two installed desktop applications

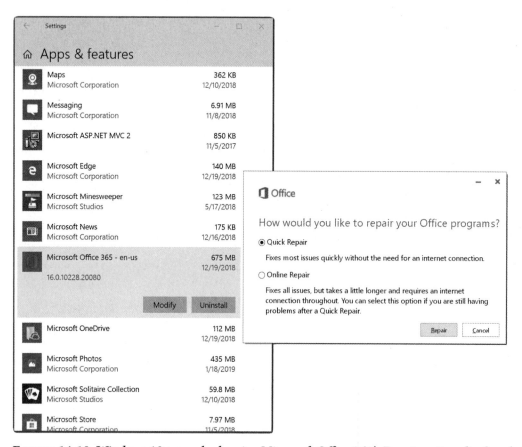

FIGURE 14-10 Windows 10 example showing Microsoft Office 365's Repair option displayed after clicking Modify

In Windows 10, the commands available for that program appear next to the selected program. You might see options such as Move, Modify, or Uninstall (see Figure 14-10). Depending on the app, the Repair option might be available when you click Modify, or you might need to click the Advanced options hyperlink first.

e. Click each of the installed programs until you find one that has a Repair option. Microsoft Office has this option, for example.

f. Click Repair, and follow the prompts to repair the application. The steps vary depending on the application. Which application did you repair? _____

Step 3 Next, you'll uninstall the application you installed in Step 1.

a. In the Programs and Features (Windows 8.1) or Apps & features (Windows 10) window, select the application you installed in Step 1.

b. Click Uninstall (or Uninstall/Change, if there are not separate buttons for those two actions).

c. Follow the prompts to uninstall the application. The steps vary depending on the application.

Tip

> **If you are asked whether you want to keep or remove any settings or configuration files, choose to remove them. You haven't done anything you need to keep in that application.**

Step 4 Next, you'll check out the interface where you can install and remove Windows components.

a. In the Windows 8.1 Programs and Features window, in the navigation bar, click Turn Windows features on or off. In the Windows 10 Apps & features window, click the Manage optional features hyperlink.

b. In Windows 8.1, a list of optional components appears. Items with a checkmark are installed. Items with a black square in the checkbox are partially installed; you can click the plus sign next to each (where applicable) to expand a list of components, and you'll see that some are marked and others aren't. Figure 14-11 shows an example. In Windows 10, only installed components are listed; to add a feature, click the Add a feature button (see Figure 14-12).

c. Install a feature you might want to try. For example, you might want to install Hyper-V, which is a virtual machine application. Chapter 22 covers virtualization. In Windows 8.1, check the checkbox for an item you want to install. In Windows 10, click the feature you want to add, then click Install.

Which component did you choose? _____

d. Click OK. The chosen item is installed.

e. In Windows 8.1, a confirmation dialog box appears; click Close. In Windows 10, click the Back button to return to the Apps & features window.

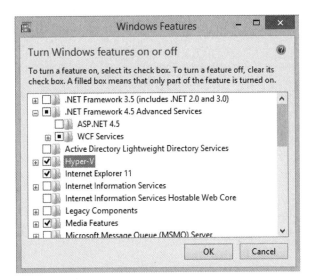

FIGURE 14-11 Browsing a list of optional Windows components (Windows 8.1)

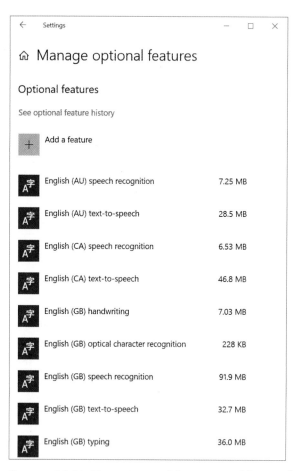

Figure 14-12 Preparing to add an optional feature (Windows 10)

Step 5   Now we'll shift attention to the Modern apps. These apps come only from the Microsoft Store online, so you must have an Internet connection to access them. Some are free; others require a credit card payment. In this exercise you'll install a free one. The steps are the same for Windows 8.1 and Windows 10.

    a.   Start the Store app.

    b.   Install any free app of your choice. To do so, click an app and then click Install.

    c.   Close the Store app, and verify that the new app appears on the Start screen. Which app did you install? _____

Step 6   Finally, you'll uninstall the app you installed in Step 5.

    a.   On the Start screen, right-click the app and click Uninstall.

    b.   A confirmation message appears; click Uninstall.

 **30 MINUTES**

Lab Exercise 14.09: Backing Up with Time Machine in macOS

Time Machine is the backup utility in macOS. It constantly keeps an up-to-date backup, from which the user can restore the entire system or individual files. It even interfaces with several Mac applications, such as Apple iWork (productivity apps) and iMovie, so users can restore individual files from within those programs.

> **→ Note**
>
> **Time Machine saves backups every hour. It retains hourly backups for the last 24 hours, daily backups for the last month, and weekly backups for previous months, until the backup volume runs out of space. It then starts deleting the oldest weekly backups.**

Learning Objectives

In this lab, you'll enable Time Machine on a Mac.

At the end of this lab, you'll be able to

- Enable Time Machine
- Restore a backed-up file

Lab Materials and Setup

The materials you need for this lab are

- A computer running macOS
- An external drive to be used for backups

Getting Down to Business

In this exercise, you'll create a data file to back up, and then back it up using Time Machine. Then you'll make changes to it, and then restore the earlier version.

Step 1 You'll start out this exercise by creating a new data file using the TextEdit app. You can actually use any data file from any application for this exercise, but the following steps walk through making a text file.

   a. Start the TextEdit application. To do so, click Launchpad on the Dock, and click Other; then click TextEdit.

   b. Click New Document.

   c.   In the new document window, type **This is my data**.

   d.   Click the Close button in the upper-left corner of the window.

   e.   At the prompt to save the file, type **My Data File**.

   f.   Open the Where drop-down list and choose Documents.

   g.   Click Save.

   h.   Quit the TextEdit application.

Step 2   Next, you'll set up Time Machine by specifying the drive to use. At the Mac desktop, do the following:

   a.   Make sure you have the external hard drive connected to the Mac.

   b.   On the Dock, click Launchpad.

   c.   Click Time Machine. Its location depends on the way the user may have customized Launchpad; you might find it in the Other group.

   d.   A message appears that you haven't selected a location for Time Machine backups. Click Set Up Time Machine.

   e.   If Time Machine is turned off, click the lock icon to change the setting.

   f.   Provide your password when prompted, then slide the Time Machine selector to On.

   g.   In the Time Machine dialog box, click Select Disk.

   h.   Select the external hard disk and click Use Disk. If there is anything on the disk already, you'll see a warning that it will be erased.

   i.   Click Erase. macOS repartitions and reformats the drive in the needed format.

Step 3   The Time Machine window now shows the Time Machine setting as On, as shown in Figure 14-13. A countdown appears, indicating that the next backup will start in a certain number of seconds. Let the backup run; you don't have to watch it. Leave the computer on. Now might be a good time to do the next lab exercise, which also uses the Mac. Come back when Time Machine has finished its initial backup, and then move on to Step 4.

Step 4   Proceed to this step only after Time Machine has completed its initial backup.

   a.   Open Finder, and click the Documents link in the navigation bar to browse to that folder.

   b.   Click My Data File.

   c.   Open the Perform tasks (gearbox) icon.

   d.   Choose Move to Trash.

Figure 14-13 Turning on the Time Machine app in macOS

Step 5 Now comes the payoff—where you restore the deleted file. All this work has led up to this moment.

    a. While Finder is still open to the Documents folder, reopen Time Machine. Rather than seeing the configuration screen, as you did initially, you now see a set of windows that represent the various snapshots taken of the Documents folder. The current version of the Documents folder appears on top.

    b. Click the up arrow on the right side of the screen to go back to the previous snapshot of that folder. Eureka, your file is there!

    c. Click the file.

    d. Click Restore. Time Machine closes, and the data file appears once again in the Documents folder in Finder.

Step 6 You probably don't want to dedicate that external drive for full-time use with this Mac, since it's just for practice, so now let's decommission Time Machine.

    a. Open System Preferences, and click Time Machine.

    b. If Time Machine settings are locked, click the lock icon. Provide your password when prompted.

    c. Drag the Time Machine slider to Off.

    d. Close the Time Machine window.

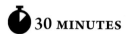 **30 MINUTES**

Lab Exercise 14.10: Managing Updates and Patches in macOS

In this chapter's scenario, there are several Mac computers to be updated, along with Windows PCs. Like Microsoft, Apple periodically makes updates available online. If a computer with macOS is connected to the Internet, it receives the updates automatically. Depending on the settings, these updates may install automatically or you may be prompted to install them.

As a technician, you should understand where to go in macOS to find any available updates and how to install them.

Learning Objectives

In this lab, you'll look for and install macOS updates for both the operating system and applications.

At the end of this lab, you'll be able to

- Update the operating system

- Update applications

Lab Materials and Setup

The materials you need for this lab are

- A computer running macOS

- An Internet connection

Getting Down to Business

In the following steps you'll make sure that the Mac is set to automatically check for, download, and install updates. You'll see available software updates, and install them.

Step 1 First you'll make sure the OS is configured to get system updates. These instructions assume that you have upgraded to macOS Mojave (macOS 10.14.x).

    a. Make sure the computer is connected to the Internet.

    b. Open the Apple menu and click System Preferences (or click the System Preferences icon on the Dock).

    c. Click Software Update.

FIGURE 14-14 Make sure updates are set to download and install automatically.

d. Make sure that Automatically keep my Mac up to date is checked.

e. Click Advanced to see specific settings. Make sure that the following checkboxes are all checked, as shown in Figure 14-14:

- Check for updates

- Download new updates when available

- Install macOS updates

- Install app updates from the App Store

- Install system data files and security updates

f. If any of these are not enabled, click the appropriate checkboxes. Click OK when done.

g. If an update is available for macOS, click Update Now to install it immediately (refer to Figure 14-14), or make sure your computer is running so it can update on the schedule listed.

Step 2 Next, you'll jump over to the actual App Store application to see available updates, and install any that have not already been installed.

a. Click App Store. The App Store opens, listing all available updates.

b. Click Updates to see specific updates you can install. In Figure 14-15, updates are available.

c. If there are applications listed for update, click the Update button next to each one to install its update.

d. To install all updates, click Update All.

e. Follow any prompts provided to complete the update process.

f. Close the App Store.

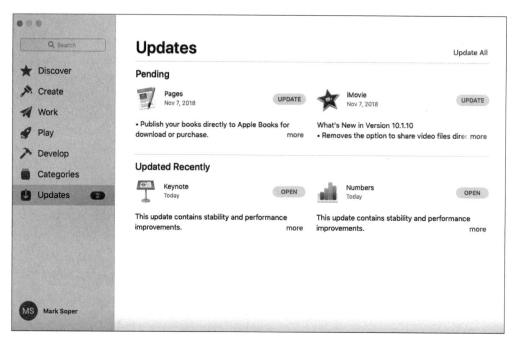

FIGURE 14-15 Update individual applications or click Update All.

Lab Analysis Test

1. Tommy wants to install an application in Windows 7 that requires Service Pack 1 to be installed. Explain how he can check to make sure it is installed, and how to install the service pack if it isn't already installed.

2. Jackie has a Windows 10 computer with thousands of pictures and music files. Naturally, she is very concerned about losing her data. Someone told her that she should create a complete system image every week and save it to network storage. Do you recommend this, or would she be better off using the File History feature? Explain your answer.

3. Judy has a Mac, and she has asked you whether she should buy a third-party backup utility to back up her important data files for work. What would you recommend?

4. John installed a new utility on his Windows system that promised to clean up his Registry, but apparently it wasn't a very good program, because now he is having severe performance issues on his Windows 10 system. How can he roll his system files back to before the utility made those changes?

5. Charles complains that his Windows computer is starting up and running more slowly than it used to. You suspect that there may be some unwanted software installed. How would you see what desktop applications are installed and potentially remove some of them?

Key Term Quiz

Use the following terms to complete the following sentences. Not all terms will be used.

App Store

Backup and Restore

File History

patch

service pack

snapshot

System Preferences

System Restore

Task Scheduler

Time Machine

1. _____ is the feature in Windows 8.1 and later that automatically saves backup versions of data files from your personal folders.

2. _____ is the feature in Windows 7 that performs a complete or partial backup of the entire system; it is not included in current versions of Windows 10.

3. _____ is the backup application in macOS.

4. To back up system files in Windows before installing something new that might potentially cause problems, use _____.

5. In macOS, you can make sure updates are set to be installed automatically by checking the settings in _____.

Chapter 15

Working with the Command-Line Interface

Lab Exercises

The CompTIA A+ 220-1002 exam objectives stipulate that PC technicians should know some of the basic commands and functions available at the command-line interface (CLI) in all versions of Windows, as well as macOS and Linux. There are several reasons a PC tech should know how to work with the CLI. For example, the CLI often provides a "back door" into a system when it won't boot normally into its graphical user interface (GUI). Also, a good technician can sometimes boot into a command-line environment and do some tweaking to get things going again—or at least pull off some important files before wiping the drive and starting over. The CLI can also be a time-saver. Sometimes it is easier to type in some commands directly than to click-click-click through multiple steps of the GUI. Finally, some commands (notably network management commands) are available only from the command line.

In the lab exercises in this chapter, you'll be switching back and forth between two test machines: one Windows and one Linux. That way you can compare and contrast the two command-line interfaces as you go, for a better understanding of their similarities and differences.

If you don't have a Linux machine to practice on, it is easy and free to get one. See Lab Exercise 11.07, "Installing Ubuntu Linux." If you don't have a separate computer to install Linux on, fire up a virtual machine. Skip ahead to Chapter 22 to learn about virtualization as needed. Using a virtual machine for the Linux portion of these exercises can help minimize the hassle of machine-switching, since you can do the Windows portion on the main desktop and the Linux portion in the virtual machine.

> ✖ **Cross-Reference**
>
> You get to practice using a CLI in other chapters too. In Chapter 13, for example, you set Linux file permissions at a command line, and you'll work with the command line in Chapter 19 when configuring networks.

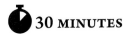

30 MINUTES

Lab Exercise 15.01: Exploring the Command-Line Interface in Windows

Before you can use the command line, you need to know the basics: ways to access it, manipulate and customize the look of it within the GUI, and close it down properly. This lab exercise covers those basics for a Windows system. The next lab exercise will cover the same skills in Linux.

Learning Objectives

In this lab, you'll practice opening, resizing, customizing, and closing a command-line window in Windows.

At the end of this lab, you'll be able to

- Open a command-line window from within Windows

- Identify the components of the command prompt

- Explore the customizable options of the command-line window

- Scroll the command display

- Exit the command-line window

Lab Materials and Setup

The materials you need for this lab are

- A PC with Windows 7 or later installed

Getting Down to Business

The first thing you'll need to do, obviously, is get to a command line. Spend the next several minutes becoming familiar with accessing the command-line window.

> **✖ Cross-Reference**
>
> **For details on how to access the command-line interface, refer to the "Accessing the Command-Line Interface in Windows" section in Chapter 15 of *Mike Meyers' CompTIA A+ Guide to Managing and Troubleshooting PCs.***

Step 1   While there are a number of ways to access the CLI, here is the easiest:

- Windows 7: Click Start, type **cmd**, and press ENTER.

- Windows 8.1 and some editions of Windows 10: Right-click the Start button and click Command Prompt.

- Windows 10: If you see Windows PowerShell instead of Command Prompt when you right-click the Start button, click the Cortana/Search box and type **cmd.** Click the Command Prompt icon that appears.

✔ Tip

The Command Prompt (Admin) option, available when you right-click the Start button in Windows 8.1 and some installations of 10, opens a CLI with elevated permissions; it allows you to execute certain commands that might normally be blocked for your own protection. You don't need that mode for this exercise. To access the Command Prompt (Admin) option on Windows 10 systems that use PowerShell instead of Command Prompt as the standard CLI, follow the instructions to find Command Prompt, right-click the matching icon, and select Run as administrator.

Step 2 Practice resizing the command-line window. Try out each of these ways:

- Drag the border of the window to resize it.

- Maximize and then restore the window using the window controls in the upper-right corner.

- Press ALT-ENTER to toggle between the full screen mode and a window.

Step 3 Locate the following landmarks on your own screen:

- The command prompt displays C:\Users*username*>. The > sign is the actual prompt; everything before it is the name of the active location (drive and folder path).

- A scroll bar appears on the right. Sometimes a command produces more output than will fit on one screen, so it scrolls quickly by. The scroll bar lets you scroll back to see what you missed.

- In the upper-left corner of the window is a control icon that looks like the C:\ prompt (see Figure 15-1). You can click it to open a menu. This is a normal window control menu in many respects, but it also has an Edit menu. You can use that menu to copy and paste text into and out of the command-line environment.

    a. Choose Defaults from the control menu. In the dialog box that appears, you set the default for new command windows. What can you control in this dialog box? Close the dialog box when finished.

    _____

    _____

    b. Choose Properties from the control menu. In the dialog box that appears, you set the properties for the current session only. Its options are identical to those in Step a. Close the dialog box when finished.

Click here to open the menu.

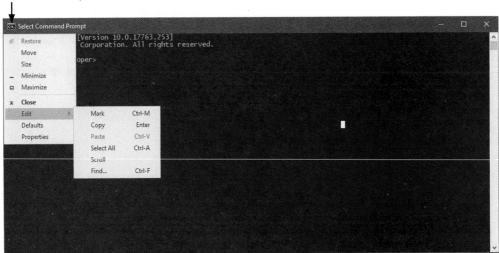

FIGURE 15-1 A command-line window in Windows 10

Step 4 Next, follow these steps to try out a couple of commands, and to learn about how to scroll the display.

a. Type **cd C:\Windows\System32** and press ENTER. The cd command (change directory) lets you change the focus of the working directory displayed in the command-line window.

b. Type **dir** and press ENTER. The dir command (directory) lists the filename, extension, file size (in bytes), and creation date/time of the files in the current folder.

c. Use the scroll bar to scroll upward as far as you can go back.

You won't be able to go back all the way to the beginning of the file listing, because System32 has over 15,000 files in it, and the scroll bar lets you go backward only a few full screens. To address this problem, there's a switch you can use that forces the information to be displayed one screenful at a time.

✔ **Tip**

A *switch* is a parameter you append to the end of a command that changes how it operates. In the Windows command-line environment, almost all switches begin with a forward slash (/). In Linux, it is more common for a switch to begin with a minus sign (–). You can find out about the syntax for a particular command by using the /? switch.

d. Type **dir /p** and then press ENTER. Adding the /p switch to the command tells it to pause after each screenful of text.

e. Press the SPACEBAR to display the next screenful. You can't go back if you're too quick with the SPACEBAR, so take a good look at each screen!

f. When you tire of paging through the screens, end the command by pressing CTRL-C.

g. Type **dir /?** and press ENTER. Information about this command's syntax appears, including all of its available switches.

h. Close the command-line window, either by clicking the Close (×) button on the window itself or by typing **exit** and pressing ENTER.

 15 MINUTES

Lab Exercise 15.02: Exploring the Command-Line Interface in Linux

Although most technicians don't spend as much time in Linux as they do in Windows, it's still important to have a basic familiarity with the Linux command-line interface. This lab covers the same basics as you learned in Lab Exercise 15.01, but this time for a Linux system.

Learning Objectives

In this lab, you'll practice opening, resizing, scrolling, and closing a command-line window in Ubuntu Linux.

At the end of this lab, you'll be able to

- Open a command-line window in Linux
- Resize the command-line window
- Understand the colors in a file listing
- Scroll the command-line interface
- Exit the command-line interface

Lab Materials and Setup

The materials you need for this lab are

- A PC with Ubuntu Linux (Desktop version) installed (or a virtual machine running it)

Getting Down to Business

In this lab, you'll open a terminal window in Linux and then familiarize yourself with the interface.

✖ Cross-Reference

For details on how to access the command-line interface, refer to the "Accessing the Command-Line Interface in macOS and Linux" section in Chapter 15 of *Mike Meyers' CompTIA A+ Guide to Managing and Troubleshooting PCs.*

Step 1 In your Ubuntu Linux desktop, press CTRL-ALT-T for a terminal window. (If that doesn't work, click the Activities icon in the upper left, type **terminal**, and select the Terminal application from the results that appear.) Resize the window if desired by dragging its border.

The command prompt might look something like this:

```
mike@Linux-Box:~$
```

Whereas in Windows the prompt is the > symbol, in Linux the prompt is a $ symbol. The text that appears before the prompt consists of the signed-in username, an @ symbol, and then the computer name. In the preceding prompt, the user mike is signed in and the computer's name is Linux-Box.

Step 2 As in Windows, the Linux prompt includes the current location, but it might not look that way. The current location is /home/*username*, where *username* is the signed-in user. This is also called the top level of the user's personal folders, and this location is referred to using a tilde (~) as shorthand.

To find out exactly where you are in the directory, without the shorthand, type **pwd** and press ENTER. That command is short for *print working directory*. That tells you the current location. It'll look something like this:

```
/home/mike
```

✔ Tip

Don't confuse the pwd command with passwd, the command that changes the password for a user account.

Step 3 Now, just like you did with Windows, follow these steps to try out a couple of commands, and to learn about how to scroll the display:

a. Type **ls** and press ENTER. That command is equivalent to dir at the Windows command prompt; it lists the content of the current location. Any results that appear in blue are folders; filenames appear in white.

→ **Note**

Recall that in Lab Exercise 13.07, "Setting File Permissions in Linux," in Step 2, we suggested that you open a GUI file management window alongside the CLI, to get a better sense of how the two represent different views of the same information. That's good advice here as well if you're new to command-line work.

b. Type **cd /bin** and press ENTER. The cd command (change directory) is the same in Linux as in Windows. Notice also that the command-prompt text reflects the location change, just like in Windows.

c. Notice that the prompt has changed to include the working directory. The current example looks like this now:

```
mike@Linux_Box:/bin$
```

d. Type **ls** and press ENTER. Because the bin directory contains so many items, the display will scroll.

e. The thin orange bar on the right side of the window is a scroll bar. Position the mouse pointer over it, and up and down arrows appear, as in Figure 15-2. Drag that arrow bar up to see what you missed.

f. Notice the rainbow of different colors for the item names in the command results. Table 15-1 provides a key to the defaults for Ubuntu Linux. These may vary depending on the Linux distribution (distro) and depending on the values set for the $LS_COLORS variable.

g. Type **exit** and press ENTER to leave the terminal window. (You could instead just close the terminal window.)

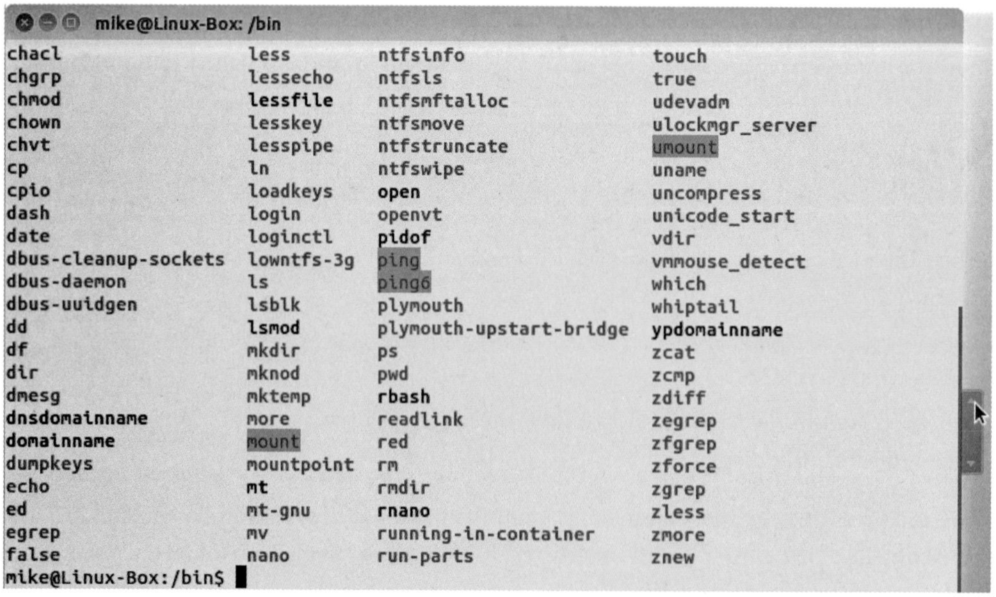

FIGURE 15-2 Scroll upward to review if a command's results fly by too quickly to see.

Color	Meaning
Blue	Directory
Sky blue	Symbolic link
Yellow	Device
Pink	Graphic image
Red	Archive
Green	Executable file

TABLE 15-1 Default Color Usage in the Ubuntu Linux Terminal

 **30 MINUTES**

Lab Exercise 15.03: Navigating Basic Commands in Windows

Before you can really use the command line, you must know the basic commands needed to navigate around a drive to locate and modify files. In this lab exercise, you'll learn more basic command-line commands that you would need to know when troubleshooting your computer or your client's computer. This lab exercise covers the command-line interface in Windows, and Lab Exercise 15.04 covers the same functions for Linux, so you can compare them.

→ **Note**

> For the most part, mistakes such as spelling a command or filename incorrectly won't be disastrous for you. But it is possible to misspell just incorrectly enough to delete the wrong file, or something similar, especially if you're using wildcards (we'll get to those in a bit). Typically, though, if you misspell a command or filename, the command line won't know what you're asking it to do and therefore won't do anything, or won't know what file you're asking to work with, and will return an error message.

Learning Objectives

In this lab, you'll learn or review commands for directory and file management while using the command line.

At the end of this lab, you'll be able to

- View, navigate, create, and delete directories using the command line
- Find, copy, rename, and delete files using the command line

Lab Materials and Setup

The materials you need for this lab are

- A PC with Windows 7 or later installed

✔ **Hint**

Any version of Windows will work just fine for this exercise, as long as you understand that the results may appear differently on your screen.

Getting Down to Business

The commands you learn about in this lab exercise will help you move around in the directory structure, view the contents of various locations, and create and delete directories.

Step 1   First, you'll practice moving around using the command line.

    a.   Open a command-line window in Windows, as you learned in Lab Exercise 15.01.

    b.   Type **cd ** and press ENTER. This changes to the root directory. The prompt now looks like this:

```
C:\>
```

To change to a particular directory, you type cd, then a space, then a slash (\), and then the directory name (including the path to it if needed). For example, to change to the Books directory, you would type **cd \books**.

✔ **Tip**

There are various little tricks to using the cd command. One of these is that you can go up one level in the directory hierarchy by typing cd .. and pressing ENTER. Another is that you can omit the slash if the directory to which you are changing is a subdirectory of the active location. For example, to go from C:\ to C:\Books, you could type cd books.

---

    c.   To change to a different drive (such as an optical drive or USB flash drive), type the drive letter and a colon and press ENTER. Pick an available drive and do this now. The prompt changes to the root directory of that drive, like this:

```
D:\>
```

→ **Note**

You can't change both the drive and the directory at once. You have to first change to the desired drive, and then change to the desired directory on that drive.

---

d.   Change back to the C: drive, and go back to the root directory if not already there.

e.   Type **cd Windows\System32\drivers** and press ENTER. That's an example of changing to a directory that is several levels deep with a single command.

f.   Type **cd ** and press ENTER. You jump back to the root directory.

Step 2   Next you'll gain some experience with the dir and cls commands.

a.   Type **dir** and press ENTER. A listing of the files and subdirectories (folders) in that location appears. Directories are marked with <DIR>. List three directories that appear:

_____

_____

_____

b.   Type **dir /w** and press ENTER. This time the contents appear with just the file and directory names, not all those other details. Directories appear in square brackets.

✔ **Hint**

Be careful not to confuse the backslash (\) and the forward slash (/). In a Windows command-line world, the path uses the backslash and command switches use the forward slash.

---

c.   Type **dir C:\Windows** and press ENTER. Even though the active directory is the root directory, this command shows the contents of the specified directory instead.

d.   Type **dir /ad** and press ENTER. Then type **dir /?** and press ENTER. Help information appears, explaining the syntax and switches for the command. What does the dir /ad command do, based on this help information?

_____

In the help information, everything in brackets ([ ]) is optional for the command. Notice that dir is the only mandatory part in that command even though there are several optional switches and parameters. This is the same for all the commands. The system will use defaults if you don't specify a switch or optional parameter. It's the defaults that can cause problems if you're not careful when using these commands.

✔ **Tip**

Instead of using the /? switch for a command, you can type help **and then the command name. For example,** help dir **is the same as** dir /?. **You can type** help **by itself to get a list of all available commands and what they do.**

---

    e.   Change to the Windows directory.

    f.   Type **dir *.exe** and press ENTER. The * symbol is a wildcard meaning any number of characters. The *.exe parameter means "show me every file of every name, as long as it has an .exe extension."

    g.   Type **cls** and press ENTER. That's short for *clear screen*, and that's what happens.

Step 3   Sometimes a technician needs to make a directory to store files on the system. This could be a temporary directory for testing purposes, or maybe a place to store something more permanently (diagnostic reports, for example). In any case, it's important that you know how to create and remove a directory. The CompTIA A+ 1002 exam will test you on this. Follow these steps:

    a.   Return to the top-level directory if not already there.

    b.   Use the help system to get information about the mkdir command. Type **mkdir /?** to see how the command is structured and view the available options.

➜ **Note**

In Windows, there are two commands that make directories: mkdir and md. They are interchangeable, and work exactly the same way. In Linux, the command to make directories is mkdir, so this chapter uses mkdir for Windows also so you have one less command to remember.

---

    c.   At the command prompt, type **mkdir Corvette** and press ENTER.

    d.   Type **dir** and press ENTER to confirm the existence of your new directory. Scroll back through the listing if necessary to view your new directory.

✖ **Warning**

Be careful—the new directory will always be created in the active directory when you issue the command, whether that's where you meant to put it or not. You must specify a path if you want it elsewhere. For example, to make a new directory called Text in C:\Books, regardless of the current location, you could type mkdir C:\Books\Text.

---

    e.   Type **rmdir Corvette** and press ENTER.

→ Note

Removing a directory is possible only if the directory is empty and is not the active directory.

    f.   Type **dir** to confirm that Corvette has been removed.

✖ Warning

Be *very* careful when you remove directories or delete files in the command line. There's no Recycle Bin for command-line deletions. When you delete a file or directory using the command line, it's gone, unless you use a third-party file undelete tool. Without one, if you make a mistake, there's nothing left to do but pout.

Step 4   In Step 5 you'll manipulate a file, but before that you need to create a file that isn't needed for any other purpose. Here's a quick-and-dirty way to do so:

    a.   Create a new directory in the root directory of the C: drive. Name it **practice**.

    b.   Change to the practice directory.

    c.   Type **copy nul > myfile.txt** and press ENTER.

Step 5   Now you'll copy and rename files.

    a.   Type **copy myfile.txt backup.txt** and press ENTER. You've just made a copy of the file. The copy command is useful for copying individual files, or groups of files using wildcards. Type **dir** and press ENTER to see the new file in the directory listing.

    b.   Type **ren myfile.txt yourfile.txt** and press ENTER. You've just renamed the original file. Type **dir** and press ENTER to see the new name in the directory listing.

    c.   Return to the top level of C: and type **xcopy practice practice2**. A prompt appears asking whether practice2 is a filename or a directory name. Type **D** to indicate it is a directory name. A copy of the practice folder is created, containing all the same files. The xcopy command is similar to copy, except it also lets you copy entire directories, including their contents.

d. Type **help robocopy** and press ENTER. Information appears about the robocopy command (which is short for robust copy). Read this over. This exercise doesn't use robocopy specifically, but you should know about it for the CompTIA A+ 1002 exam. In what ways is robocopy similar to and different from copy and xcopy?

_____

_____

_____

_____

Step 6 Finally, you'll delete files and remove a directory.

a. Change to the practice directory.

b. Type **del *.txt** and press ENTER. You've just deleted both of the text files (the original and the copy). The del command deletes files. (It doesn't delete directories.)

c. Type **cd ..** and press ENTER to move up one level. Then type **rmdir practice** and press ENTER. You've just removed (deleted) the directory.

d. Close the command-line window.

 **30 MINUTES**

Lab Exercise 15.04: Navigating Basic Commands in Linux

Now that you've seen how to get around in the Windows CLI, let's have a look at those same operations in Linux. In some ways the two CLIs are very similar, including some of the commands. However, they're different enough to trip up anyone who is familiar with only one or the other.

Learning Objectives

In this lab, you'll learn or review commands for directory and file management while using the command line in Linux.

At the end of this lab, you'll be able to

- View, navigate, create, and delete directories using the command line

- Find, copy, rename, and delete files using the command line

Lab Materials and Setup

The materials you need for this lab are

- A PC with Ubuntu Linux installed (or a virtual machine running it)

Getting Down to Business

The commands you learn about in this lab exercise will help you move around in the directory structure, view the contents of various locations, and create and delete directories.

Step 1 First, you'll practice moving around using the command line.

a. Open a terminal window in Ubuntu Linux, as you learned in Lab Exercise 15.02.

b. Type **ls** and press ENTER to find out which subdirectories are available in your current location.

 Tip

The prompt shows a tilde (~) before the $. The tilde character refers to the top level of your personal folder area.

---

c. Type **cd Documents** and press ENTER. Now the current user's Documents directory is the active directory.

d. Type **cd** and press ENTER to return to the top level of your personal folders.

e. Type **cd /** and press ENTER. Now you are at the top-level directory of the whole drive, not just your own folders. Use **ls** again to see for yourself.

f. Type **cd home/*username*** where *username* is your username (whatever appears before the @ symbol in the prompt). Now you're back where you started.

Step 2 Next you'll gain some experience with the ls and clear commands.

a. Type **ls** and press ENTER. A listing of the files and subdirectories (folders) in that location appears. Directories are blue. List three directories that appear:

_____

_____

_____

b. Type **ls –1** and press ENTER. This time the contents appear in a single column, one item per line. That's an example of a switch being used to modify how the command works.

✔ **Hint**

Linux command switches are preceded by a minus sign (–) rather than a slash as in Windows.

---

c. To find out which switches are available, consult the manual. Type **man ls** and press ENTER. A manual page appears explaining the syntax and switches for the command. Press the DOWN ARROW key to move downward through the information. What does the ls –r command do, based on this manual information?

_____

d. Press **q** to quit the manual page.

e. Type **clear** and press ENTER. That's the equivalent of the cls command in Windows.

Step 3 Now you'll create and remove a directory.

a. At the prompt, return to your Documents directory if you are not already there.

b. Type **mkdir Impala** and press ENTER. Then use **ls** to make sure the new directory is really there.

c. Type **rmdir Impala** and press ENTER.

d. Type **ls** to confirm that Corvette has been removed.

Step 4 You'll need a text file to play with in the upcoming steps, so here's how to create one:

a. Start in your Documents folder. Type **cat > sample** and press ENTER.

b. Type **This is my text** and then press ENTER.

c. Press CTRL-D to exit the file and return to the prompt.

Step 5 What you just did in Step 4 was a quick-and-dirty method, but you should also know how to use the vi editor to create a text file. Not only is vi mentioned in the CompTIA A+ 1002 objectives, but it's also a handy tool that a Linux admin works with a lot.

a. Start in your Documents folder. Type **vi another** and press ENTER.

You see blank lines, with a tilde (~) to their left, and a line at the bottom reporting the filename and status, like this:

```
"another" [New file]
```

The vi editor has two modes: command and insert. You're in command mode at the moment. In command mode, keyboard letters issue commands. You can get back to command mode at any time by pressing ESC. To type some text into the file, you have to switch to insert mode.

b. Type **i** to switch to insert mode.

c. Type **This is another text file**.

d. Press ESC to switch back to command mode.

e. Type **ZZ** to save and exit. (Make sure those are capital Zs.)

✔ **Tip**

There isn't room here to do it, but you should review all the basic commands in vi. Do a Google search for vi linux commands to find a reference. Here's one to start out with: **www.washington .edu/computing/unix/vi.html**.

Step 6 Now you'll manipulate sample.txt in several ways, and then delete the file and the directory.

a. Make sure you are in your Documents directory. Then type **cp sample myfile** and press ENTER. You've just made a copy of the file. The cp command in Linux is equivalent to the copy command in Windows.

✔ **Tip**

For the CompTIA A+ 1002 exam, be familiar with the dd command, which copies a file and converts the data at the same time, according to the parameters specified by the switches. For example, you could convert from EBCDIC to ASCII text encoding, which would be useful if you were copying files from an ancient IBM server to a modern UNIX or Linux server.

---

b. Type **ls** and press ENTER to see the new file in the directory listing.

c. Type **mv myfile yourfile** and press ENTER. You've just renamed the original file. Linux doesn't have a rename command, but what it does have is a move command (mv). By moving the file from one name to another, you are effectively renaming it.

d. Type **ls** and press ENTER to see the new name in the directory listing.

e. Type **rm -- *** and press ENTER. You've just deleted all of the files in the current directory. Linux uses rm (remove) instead of del (delete) but the action is the same.

f. Close the command-line window.

Lab Analysis Test

1. Gloria opens a terminal window in Ubuntu Linux and the prompt looks like this:

   ```
   thomas@manager-system:~$
   ```

   A. What is the active user's name? _____

   B. What is the device name? _____

   C. What is the current location? _____

   D. What should Gloria type to find out what directories are present in the current location?
   _____

2. Tina is curious about the available commands at the Windows command-line interface. How can she get a list of the available commands and brief descriptions of what they do?

3. In the current directory there are 1000 files, named File000.txt through File999.txt. Ruth needs to rename them all to Memo000.txt through Memo999.txt. What command can she use at the command line that will rename all the files with a single command?

4. Todd is trying to use the rd command at a Windows command prompt to remove a directory, but he gets a message that the directory is not empty. When he views the contents of the directory with dir, he sees no files there. How should he proceed?

5. Dawn needs to move a complicated set of directories and subdirectories from one volume to another using the command line on a Windows system. Is the copy command her best bet? Why or why not?

Key Term Quiz

Use the following terms to complete the following sentences. Not all terms will be used.

/?	ls
/p	man
/w	mkdir
copy	rd
cp	ren
dir	

1. The command used to create a new directory in both Linux and Windows is _____.

2. The command used to create a duplicate file in Linux is _____.

3. The _____ switch is used to get help about command syntax in Windows.

4. Get help in Linux using the _____ command.

5. For a listing of a directory's contents that displays only the filenames on a Windows system, use the _____ command with the _____ switch.

Chapter 16

Troubleshooting Operating Systems

Lab Exercises

In this chapter, assume that you have patched and updated all of the computers in a company that had a lot of problems with their systems. Unfortunately, those pesky users are still managing to find ways to render their PCs unusable. As a technician, you need to use Event Viewer to log what they do to their computers. A few of the computers have contracted malware, making the computers nonbootable. Let's take some time in this chapter to discover and use some of the available Windows troubleshooting tools.

 **30 MINUTES**

Lab Exercise 16.01: Examining and Configuring Log Files in Event Viewer

Windows Event Viewer is a valuable tool to anyone who maintains or troubleshoots systems. Event Viewer monitors various log files and reveals things about the health of the operating system. This utility reports real-time statistics, but normally, this data is only used with servers. Desktop computer users are less proactive and usually depend on the after-the-fact log files to help determine the cause of a problem.

Event Viewer displays important events from multiple log files. The log files you see depend on your system. The three most important log files are Application, Security, and System. (More log files are available in the server versions of Windows.) Figure 16-1 shows the contents of the System event log in Event Viewer.

Notice in Figure 16-1 that there are three levels of log entries: Information, Warning, and Error. The Security event log also shows two other types of entries: Success Audit and Failure Audit. These types of events are logged only when auditing is turned on; again, this is normally done only on servers.

Learning Objectives

You'll become familiar with using Event Viewer to analyze the different logs kept by the system.

At the end of this lab, you'll be able to

- Run the Event Viewer program
- Examine an event log entry
- Save the event log

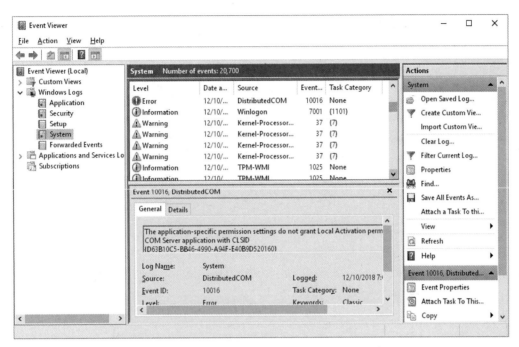

FIGURE 16-1 Viewing the System log in Event Viewer (Windows 10)

Lab Materials and Setup

The materials you need for this lab are

- A working PC with Windows 7 or later installed

Getting Down to Business

In Windows 7, go to the Start menu Search bar and type **Event Viewer**. Click the program that appears in the search results. In Windows 8.1/10, right-click the Start button and choose Event Viewer.

Step 1 When a log file becomes full, the oldest entries are deleted. By increasing the maximum size allowed for a log file, you are able to go back further in its history to investigate issues. Let's increase the maximum size of a single log file.

   a. In the left pane, expand the Windows Logs subfolder. Then right-click System and select Properties. Change the number in the Maximum log size box to **40960** KB and, if it isn't selected already, select Overwrite events as needed (see Figure 16-2).

   b. Click Apply, then OK to put these changes into effect.

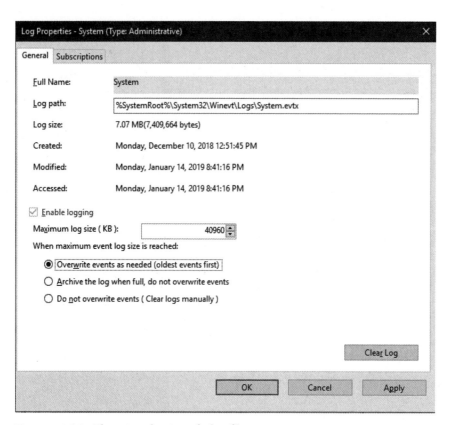

FIGURE 16-2 Changing the size of a log file

Step 2 Next you'll learn how to filter a log file, so you can more quickly find what you're looking for.

a. Select the System log from the left pane in the main Event Viewer screen, and then click Filter Current Log in the Actions list in the right pane. The Filter Current Log dialog box opens, as shown in Figure 16-3.

b. Choose the filter criteria. For example, check the Critical, Error, and Warning checkboxes.

➔ **Note**

You can filter events based on type/level, source, category, ID, user, computer, and more. This only controls what Event Viewer displays; all the events information will still be logged to the file, so you can change your mind about filter settings.

---

c. Click OK to close the Filter Current Log dialog box. The log is filtered to show only what you specified.

Step 3 Next, follow these steps to clear, archive, and open a log file:

a. Clear the System log by right-clicking System in the left pane and selecting Clear Log. See Figure 16-4.

b. When you're prompted to save the System log, click Save and Clear. A Save As dialog box opens.

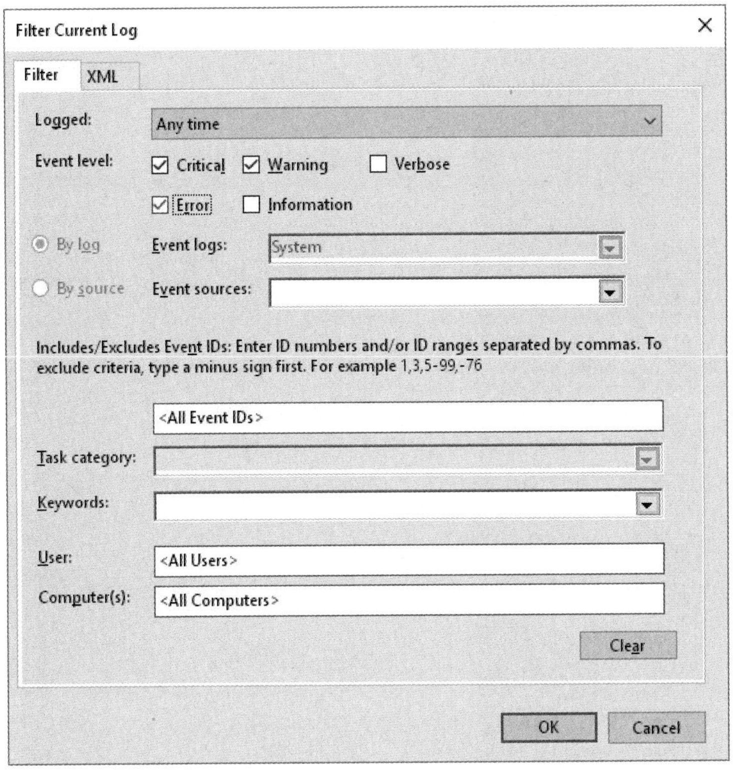

Figure 16-3 Set up a filter for the current log.

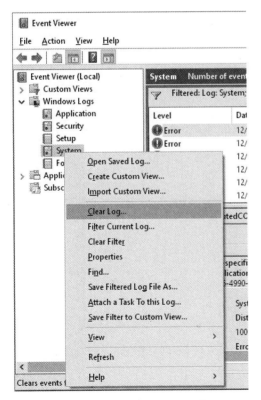

Figure 16-4 Clearing the System log

   c.   You can archive log files using different filenames each time (recommended) and select a location other than the default. Give your file a name you can remember and save it.

   d.   To open a saved file, choose Action | Open Saved Log. Select the file and click Open.

   e.   When prompted, click OK to open it in the Saved Logs branch of Event Viewer.

45 MINUTES

Lab Exercise 16.02: Troubleshooting in Safe Mode

An errant upgrade or a poorly written driver can cause the system to lock up. Some software problems, such as corrupt Registry files, will even prevent the system from booting normally. This means that you must be ready to use alternative methods to boot the system to make repairs or replace files.

One fairly simple way to get back into a system to make repairs is to boot into Safe Mode. Safe Mode is a special startup mode that bypasses all nonessential drivers and services, loading the most basic items only. In many cases you will be able to boot a system into Safe Mode when it won't boot normally. From there you can perform tasks that may solve the problem, such as updating or rolling back drivers, removing malware, uninstalling errant applications, and blocking certain applications from loading at startup.

Learning Objectives

You'll become familiar with Safe Mode as a method of gaining access to fix a system that will not boot normally.

At the end of this lab, you'll be able to

- Boot to Safe Mode

- Work in Safe Mode to restore system functionality

Lab Materials and Setup

The materials you need for this lab are

- A working PC with Windows 7 or later

Getting Down to Business

If your system won't boot normally because of some system problem, you need a way to gain access to the hard drive and your files to troubleshoot the problem. There are, happily enough, troubleshooting tools that give you access to these files if the normal boot process won't work. One of these ways is to use Safe Mode, as described in this lab exercise. (Another is to use the Windows Recovery Environment, covered in Lab Exercise 16.03.)

Step 1 First, you'll enter Safe Mode. If this were an actual won't-boot situation, you would probably not have to do the following, because after Windows fails to start normally, the next time it tries it displays a prompt letting you know, and offering to help you start in Safe Mode. So you just follow along with that prompt. But since we don't have a system that is really messed up at the moment, we'll use the following two methods instead.

ADVANCED BOOT OPTIONS METHOD FOR WINDOWS 7

First, we'll try to enter Safe Mode via the Advanced Boot Options menu in Windows 7.

    a. Power up the PC and, after the POST messages but before the Windows logo screen appears, press F8.

✔ **Tip**

Pressing F8 at the right time is tricky. Here's a tried-and-true method: when you first see text in the screen, start pressing and releasing F8 at one-second intervals over and over until you get to the Advanced Boot Options menu.

---

    b. If your timing is right, and if your system supports it, you will see an Advanced Boot Options menu. Record the various modes and provide a short description for each here:

_____

_____

_____

_____

    c. Choose Safe Mode and allow the system to boot into Safe Mode.

✖ **Cross-Reference**

For definitions of each of the boot modes, refer to the "Advanced Startup Options" section in Chapter 16 of *Mike Meyers' CompTIA A+ Guide to Managing and Troubleshooting PCs.*

ALTERNATIVE MSCONFIG METHOD FOR WINDOWS 7

If the F8 method didn't work for you, here's an alternative method for Windows 7:

    a.   Click Start, type **msconfig**, and press ENTER.

    b.   In the System Configuration dialog box, on the Boot tab, check the Safe boot checkbox and choose the Minimal option.

    c.   Click OK.

    d.   Click Restart. You'll have to come back here later and disable Safe boot in order to boot the system normally again.

ACCESSING ADVANCED BOOT OPTIONS FOR WINDOWS 8.1 FROM SETTINGS

Unfortunately, Windows 8.1 makes getting to the Safe Mode startup option a lot harder, with many additional steps compared to Windows 7. Follow these steps:

    a.   Move the mouse to the lower right-hand corner of the screen and click Settings.

    b.   Click Change PC settings.

    c.   Click Update & recovery.

    d.   Click Recovery.

    e.   Click Restart now.

    f.   On the Choose an option screen, list the options available:

    _____

    g.   Click Troubleshoot. What are the available options?

    _____

    h.   Click Advanced options. What are the options available on this screen?

    _____

    _____

    i.   Click Startup Settings.

    j.   Review the list of startup options, then click Restart.

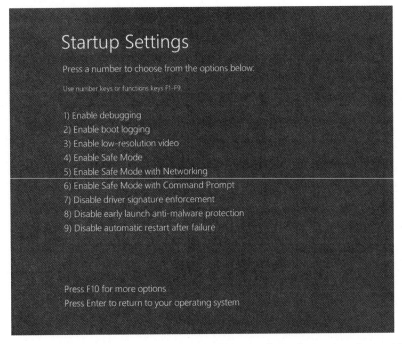

Startup Settings

Press a number to choose from the options below:

Use number keys or functions keys F1-F9.

1) Enable debugging
2) Enable boot logging
3) Enable low-resolution video
4) Enable Safe Mode
5) Enable Safe Mode with Networking
6) Enable Safe Mode with Command Prompt
7) Disable driver signature enforcement
8) Disable early launch anti-malware protection
9) Disable automatic restart after failure

Press F10 for more options
Press Enter to return to your operating system

FIGURE 16-5 Startup options for Windows 8.1 (Windows 10 is almost identical)

k. Choose a startup option (see Figure 16-5). For Safe Mode, press the #4 or F4 key on your keyboard. For Safe Mode with Networking (recommended if you need to download new drivers), press the #5 or F5 key on your keyboard. For Safe Mode with Command Prompt, press the #6 or F6 key on your keyboard.

ACCESSING ADVANCED BOOT OPTIONS FOR WINDOWS 10 FROM SETTINGS

Windows 10 uses a variation on the Windows 8.1 method to access Advanced Boot Options:

a. Click Start | Settings.

b. Click Update & Security.

c. Click Recovery.

d. Click Restart now.

e. On the Choose an option screen, list the options available:

f.   Click Troubleshoot. What are the available options?

_____

g.   Click Advanced options. What are the options available on this screen?

_____

_____

h.   If you don't see Startup settings, click See more recovery options.

i.   Click Startup Settings.

j.   Review the list of startup options, then click Restart.

k.   Choose a startup option (refer to Figure 16-5). For Safe Mode, press the #4 or F4 key on your keyboard. For Safe Mode with Networking (recommended if you need to download new drivers), press the #5 or F5 key on your keyboard. For Safe Mode with Command Prompt, press the #6 or F6 key on your keyboard.

ACCESSING ADVANCED BOOT OPTIONS IN WINDOWS 8.1/10 FROM THE SIGN-IN SCREEN

You can also get to the Startup options this way:

a.   From the sign-in (Lock) screen, hold down the SHIFT key.

b.   Click the Power button, then select Restart while holding down the SHIFT key.

c.   On the Choose an option screen, click Troubleshoot.

d.   Click Advanced options.

e.   Click Startup Settings.

f.   Review the list of startup options, then click Restart.

g.   Choose a startup option. For Safe Mode, press the #4 or F4 key on your keyboard. For Safe Mode with Networking (recommended if you need to download new drivers), press the #5 of F5 key on your keyboard. For Safe Mode with Command Prompt, press the #6 or F6 key on your keyboard.

A Windows Help and Support window appears onscreen explaining Safe Mode, and after you close that, you see the Safe Mode desktop, shown in Figure 16-6.

There's no value, of course, in simply booting into Safe Mode. The value comes in what you _do_ once you get into the system in Safe Mode. The following steps tour you through some of the places you might go to make repairs.

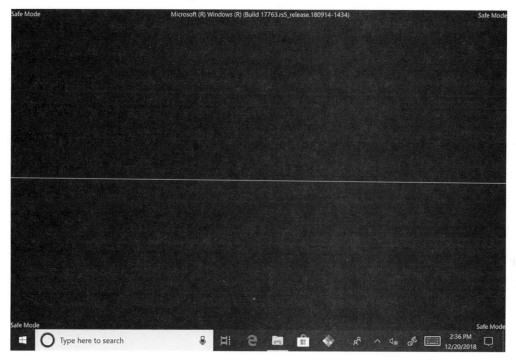

FIGURE 16-6 Windows 10 running in Safe Mode

Step 2: All Windows Versions System Restore is your first stop on the "what's wrong with my system?" tour. You learned about this utility in Chapter 14, but here's how to access it from Safe Mode:

a. Do one of the following depending on your Windows version:

- Windows 7: Click Start | Control Panel | Recovery (note that Control Panel in Safe Mode in Windows 7/8.1 uses the Large icons view by default)

- Windows 8.1: Mouse over the lower-right corner and click Settings | Control Panel | Recovery

- Windows 10: Click Start | Settings, and type **Recovery** into the Settings search box

b. Click Open System Restore.

c. If this were a real problem system, you would work through System Restore to try to go back to a restore point dated before the problem first occurred. Because we're just touring at this point, and you've already practiced System Restore in Chapter 14, close the System Restore window without going through all that now.

Step 3 If System Restore didn't work, the next step is to make sure there aren't any driver problems in Device Manager.

a. Open Device Manager:

- Windows 7: Choose Start | Control Panel | System and Security | System | Device Manager
- Windows 8.1/10: Right-click the Start button and click Device Manager

b. Look for any symbols on devices that indicate problems, such as question marks (Windows 7 only), exclamation points, or downward-pointing arrows (Windows 7, 8.1, and 10). Note that some devices won't work in Safe Mode. However, if a device wasn't working before you booted into Safe Mode, it actually has a problem. See Figure 16-7.

c. Note the following:

Which devices have exclamation marks, if any? _____

Which have downward-pointing arrows, if any? _____

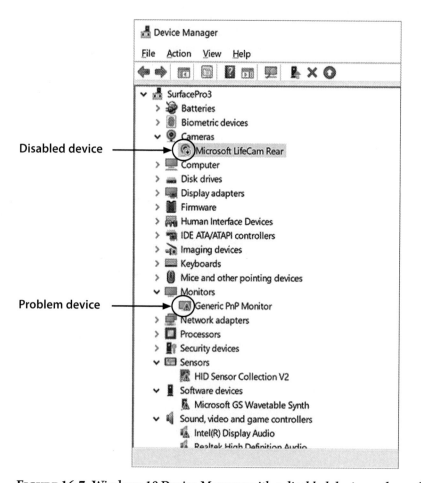

FIGURE 16-7 Windows 10 Device Manager with a disabled device and a problem device

If you see other indications of problems, what are they?

_____

d. If you find a device with a problem, double-click it to open its Properties dialog box.

e. If you recently installed a new driver for the device and you suspect it's the cause of the problems with booting, click Roll Back Driver and work through the wizard to go back.

f. If you can't make the device right, and it's causing the boot problems, click Disable to disable the device, so at least it won't cause you any more problems in the short term. (You can then troubleshoot the device at your leisure later.)

g. Click OK to close the Properties dialog box for the device, and then close the Device Manager window and the Control Panel (Windows 7 only).

Step 4 Another common cause of startup problems is an errant program trying to load automatically at Windows startup and failing to do so—or doing so at the expense of something else. Some malware loads itself at startup, for example, and to remove it, you have to boot into Safe Mode, prevent it from loading at startup, and then remove it.

WINDOWS 7

In Windows 7, you can use the System Configuration utility to control what loads at startup, as follows:

a. Click Start, type **msconfig**, and press ENTER. The System Configuration utility opens.

b. Click the Startup tab. A list of applications set to load automatically at startup appears. (There might not be any, although that's uncommon.)

c. If this were an actual troubleshooting situation, you would clear the checkbox for the item that you think might be causing the startup problem and click Apply. But for now just look.

d. If you used the alternative method in Step 1 for entering Safe Mode (by turning on Safe boot in the System Configuration utility), turn that back off now on the Boot tab of the dialog box. Otherwise you won't be able to boot normally at the next startup.

e. Click OK to close the dialog box.

f. Restart the computer.

WINDOWS 8 AND LATER

In Windows 8 and later, you use Task Manager to control what loads at startup. The msconfig utility still exists, but its Startup tab redirects you to Task Manager. You can open Task Manager by pressing CTRL-ALT-DELETE and then clicking Task Manager, or by right-clicking the taskbar and choosing Task Manager. In Task Manager, a Startup tab appears, listing the items that start automatically. To disable an item, click it and then click Disable.

30 MINUTES

Lab Exercise 16.03: Repairing from Windows Installation Media

Safe Mode is great if it works, but sometimes a system is too badly fouled up for even Safe Mode to save the day. In cases like that, you'll need to boot into the Windows Recovery Environment (Windows RE or WinRE). There are multiple ways of getting there, but the most foolproof is to boot from the Windows installation DVD (or other media that it came on). In this lab you'll do just that, and explore the recovery possibilities therein.

Learning Objectives

You'll become familiar with alternative methods of booting a faulty system.

At the end of this lab, you'll be able to

- Boot to Windows RE

- Use utilities and command-line commands in Windows RE

Lab Materials and Setup

The materials you need for this lab are

- A working PC with Windows 7 or later

Getting Down to Business

As a technician, you should keep working copies of operating system installation media close at hand. You're going to need them. When a system won't boot normally, you can then use installation media to access the Windows Recovery Environment, as you'll learn in the following steps.

Step 1 is so different for Windows 7 versus Windows 8.1/10 that we've included two separate versions of it. Follow only the version of Step 1 applicable to the OS you are using. The remainder of the steps are identical for both operating systems.

Step 1: Windows 7   Suppose that you were unable to get into Safe Mode because the system is too badly damaged. The next step is to boot from the installation media and try doing a repair.

a.   Boot from the Windows 7 installation DVD (or other media). At the Install Windows initial screen, click Next.

b.   Click Repair your computer. The System Recovery Options dialog box opens (see Figure 16-8).

At this point the path diverges. If you happen to have a system image stored (which you might have created with the Windows 7 Backup tool), you can choose to use it. (That takes awhile and we don't recommend doing it just for practice.) Alternatively, you can go with the default option, *Use recovery tools that can help fix problems starting Windows.*

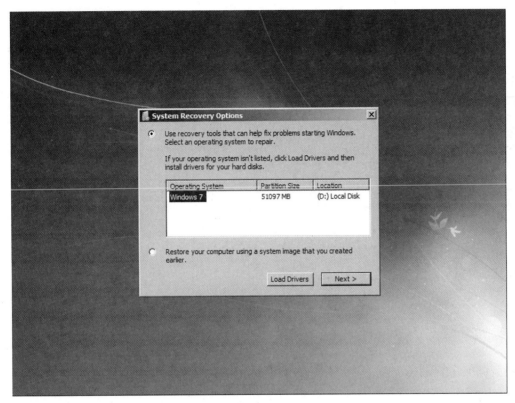

FIGURE 16-8 After booting from the Windows 7 DVD, you can choose to use recovery tools or restore from a system image.

c. Make sure Windows 7 is selected (it's probably the only choice) and click Next. A menu of recovery options appears, as shown in Figure 16-9.

d. At this point your best bet on an actual system would probably be Startup Repair, which attempts an automatic repair of the system files. However, because this is a practice environment right now, click Command Prompt. A command-line window opens, similar to the one you worked with in Chapter 15.

Step 1: Windows 8.1/10 Suppose that you were unable to get into Safe Mode because the system is too badly damaged. The next step is to boot from the installation media and try doing a repair.

a. Boot from the Windows 8.1/10 installation DVD (or other media). At the Install Windows initial screen, click Next.

→ **Note**

You might need to change the boot order to boot from a DVD or USB flash drive. To do this, you must change your system BIOS or UEFI firmware settings. On a system using a traditional BIOS, restart the system and enter BIOS setup using the key(s) displayed onscreen. Most systems using Windows 8.1 or later have UEFI firmware. Use the UEFI Firmware Settings option on the Advanced Options screen (see Figure 16-10) to make this change.

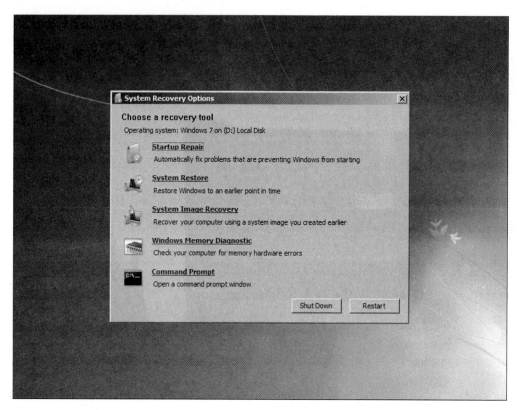

FIGURE 16-9 These system recovery tools are available from the Windows 7 installation media.

b.   Click Repair your computer.

c.   Click Troubleshoot. What are the options that appear?

_____

_____

_____

In a real-life troubleshooting situation, Refresh your PC (Windows 8.1) is the option to try first on a nonbootable system. This option does an automatic refresh and repair of system files without disturbing any programs or data. However, it takes some time and is not available on Windows 10, so we're going to bypass that right now. (You can try it on your own if you have time later.)

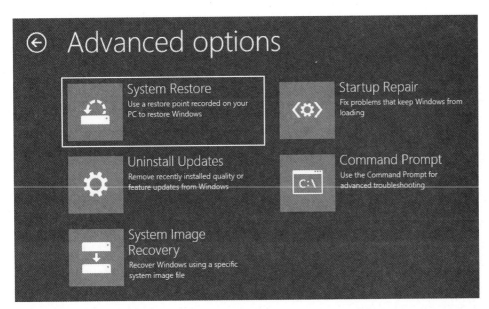

FIGURE 16-10 The Advanced options menu for Windows 10 (Windows 8.1 is similar, but lacks the Uninstall Updates option).

d. Click Advanced options to display the Advanced options menu (see Figure 16-10). If you worked through the similar set of steps for Windows 7, you'll notice that the options available are similar to those for Windows 7 (shown in Figure 16-9); they are just presented in a different format.

e. At this point your best bet on an actual system would be Startup Repair, which attempts an automatic repair of the system files. However, because this is a practice environment right now, click Command Prompt. A command-line window opens, similar to the one you worked with in Chapter 15.

Step 2 Next, you'll have a look at some of the commands you can execute at the command line. You can type a command followed by /? to get an explanation of the command's use. (You probably remember that from Chapter 15, right?) Some of the commands available in Windows RE are not available when you open a command prompt in Windows normally.

Several commands are worth reviewing; for the CompTIA A+ 1002 exam, you should know what the following commands do:

- **chkdsk**   Checks the clusters and sectors of a disk (fixed or removable) and, if possible, repairs bad clusters or sectors

- **diskpart**   Opens a partitioning tool

- **sfc**   Checks system files

Step 3   Try out a few of the commands by doing the following:

a.   Type **chkdsk C:** and press ENTER. The utility runs a quick check on the C: drive. But wait…it's not the same C: drive that you use in Windows. It's not your main volume where your files are stored. That's because in Windows RE, the hidden system partition is the C: drive. (The letters get swapped when Windows loads.)

b.   Type **chkdsk D:** and press ENTER. This time the utility checks your main hard drive. No errors are corrected because you didn't use the /f switch.

→ Note

On a few systems, the hidden system partition is not identified as C: On those systems, chkdsk C: checks the main hard drive as in a normal Windows startup.

---

c.   Type **sfc /verifyonly** and press ENTER. In an actual troubleshooting situation, you would want to use the /scannow switch instead, which does repairs; in this test situation we're just checking them. If you see a message that there is a system repair pending that requires reboot to complete, restart Windows and try this step again. If you continue to get that same message, skip this step; it's not essential.

Step 4   Now we'll take a look at diskpart, the disk partitioning utility. Be careful with this one, as it doesn't have any of the safety precautions of Disk Management in Windows.

a.   Type **diskpart** and press ENTER. A few lines of text appear, and then a command prompt returns. But wait…this isn't an ordinary command prompt. The prompt appears as DISKPART>. You are in the diskpart utility now.

b.   Type **help** and press ENTER. You see a list of all the commands you can execute within the diskpart utility.

c.   Type **list disk** and press ENTER. You see a list of all the disks and their status.

d.   Type **list volume** and press ENTER. You see a list of all the volumes and their status.

e.   Read over the commands, and answer the following questions:

What command would you use to format a volume or partition? _____

What command would you use to change the partition type? _____

What command would you use to assign a drive letter? _____

f.   Type **exit** and press ENTER to leave the diskpart utility.

g.   Type **exit** and press ENTER again to close the command-line window.

Step 5   It's been fun in the Windows Recovery Environment, but now it's time to go. Click Restart (Windows 7) or Continue (Windows 8.1/10). Windows restarts normally.

Lab Analysis Test

1. John is trying to start his Windows 7 computer in Safe Mode. Explain two different ways he could do this.

2. After installing a new sound card, Nicole's Windows 7 PC won't start up normally. She sees a prompt offering to start in Safe Mode, and she chooses to do that. What should she do next?

3. Tim has made a bad change to the Registry in Windows 10, and now the system won't boot at all, even in Safe Mode. How can he repair the Registry and restore functionality?

4. Laurie suspects that someone is trying to log on to her computer and is failing over and over again. She wants to know when this intrusion attempt is happening, so she has set up auditing for login events on her Windows 10 computer. Where will she go to see the record of intrusion attempts?

5. After completing Lab Exercise 16.02, William's computer keeps restarting in Safe Mode, no matter how many times he reboots. What has he forgotten to do?

Key Term Quiz

Use the following terms to complete the following sentences. Not all terms will be used.

Advanced Boot Options	msconfig
Advanced options	Safe Mode
Application log file	security log file
bootrec	system log file
chkdsk	System Recovery Options
diskpart	Troubleshoot
Event Viewer	Windows Recovery Environment

F8

1. You can repair the master boot record on a Windows 7 computer using the _____ command.

2. The _____ command can be issued at a command prompt in the Windows Recovery Environment to reformat a hard disk.

3. The _____ menu in Windows 10 includes System Restore, System Image Recovery, Startup Repair, Command Prompt, and Startup Settings.

4. Booting from Windows installation media places you into the _____, where you can troubleshoot startup problems.

5. _____ provides log files to assist with the troubleshooting of a Windows operating system.

Chapter **17**

Display Technologies

Lab Exercises

Few components affect the PC user like the video system, the primary output for the PC. As you know from Chapter 17 of *Mike Meyers' CompTIA A+ Guide to Managing and Troubleshooting PCs*, the video system has two main hardware components—monitor (or video display) and display adapter (or video card)—that work together to produce the image on your screen. Both components must be installed and configured properly in Windows, or your viewing pleasure will be seriously compromised. Good techs know how to do video right!

In this set of labs, you'll install a display adapter, hook up a monitor, load video drivers, and configure Windows for optimal viewing. You'll then practice using multiple monitors (for example, a projector and a laptop screen) to expand your desktop viewing area. The last lab exercise will run you through some of the typical troubleshooting issues that techs face when dealing with video.

> ✖ **Warning**
>
> If you happen to encounter a CRT monitor, don't open it up and snoop around inside. CRTs contain powerful capacitors that can store up to 50,000 volts or more, and can kill you. You won't be working with CRTs in this chapter anyway; they're obsolete, and getting rarer every day in the field.

 **45 MINUTES**

Lab Exercise 17.01: Installing Video

Your office staff's computers need a serious video upgrade. Some of the PCs have old 17-inch monitors that simply have to go, while others have decent 19-inch and 20-inch LCDs that have a year or two of life left in them. Your boss has bought new PCIe video cards and some 24-inch-widescreen LCD monitors. You're tasked with installing the cards, loading drivers, and setting up everything in Windows.

Learning Objectives

In this lab exercise, you will determine if the system has a display adapter installed, if it has a slot for a display adapter, identify the display adapter (if any), and make adjustments to both monitor and display adapter settings.

At the end of this lab, you'll be able to

- Identify the make and model of a video card

- Install a video card

- Adjust the monitor for the proper display

- Optimize the video settings in Windows

Lab Materials and Setup

The materials you need for this lab are

- A working PC with Windows 7, 8.1, or 10 installed and Internet access

- A working LCD monitor

Getting Down to Business

To begin this lab, you'll become familiar with the video components in your system. You'll then step through the proper installation and configuration of a video card. Look for a system that has a video card for this exercise.

> ✖ **Warning**
>
> **Make certain you have current drivers available for your video card, or a source to get drivers if necessary. You shouldn't need them, because they're already installed in Windows, but better safe than sorry.**

Step 1 Shut down your system properly and unplug the power cable from the system unit and the wall.

a. Examine the rear of the computer. Where is the cable from the monitor connected to the computer?

   _____

   If it is connected to the port cluster, the computer is using a built-in display adapter port. Many of these systems can also accept a video card. If it is connected to an expansion card, the computer is using a video card that can be replaced.

b. Next, remove the cover from the PC to expose the expansion buses.

   If the system is using a video card, locate it in the system. In what type of slot is the display adapter installed? _____

✔ **Hint**

Many systems include display adapters integrated right into the electronics of the motherboard. On desktop systems with this configuration, the connector will appear in line with the built-in ports (port cluster) on the rear of the motherboard. If your system uses this type of display adapter, the overall performance of the system may suffer unless you have a lot of RAM installed, because the display typically "steals" some of the system RAM to serve as video RAM. Laptops are usually designed around this limitation, but if your desktop system is of this type, you can increase the performance (and usually the video quality) by installing a video card and disabling the onboard video in the BIOS.

---

c. Detach the monitor's cable from the video card. Take a picture of the video card inside the case before you remove it. Using good ESD avoidance procedures, remove the screw that holds the card in place, put it in a secure location, and then remove your video card. Disconnect any power leads to the video card.

Figure 17-1 shows a card that includes three large cooling fans for the graphics processing unit (GPU) and the onboard RAM chips; some cards have a very large fan shroud that blocks the next expansion slot. Be careful not to touch the expansion slot contacts on the card to avoid ESD damage to the card!

FIGURE 17-1 A typical video card

d. Look for a name or model number on the adapter's circuit board or chipset (check both sides of the card for this information). Who is the card manufacturer, who is the GPU manufacturer, and/ or what is the model number? Write down as much information as you can collect from the display adapter for a later assignment.

_____

_____

e. Reinsert the video card into the same slot, and make sure it is properly seated. Reattach any power lead used by the video card. Reattach the monitor cable and test your system with the case still open to see if it works. This could save you the frustration that results when you close the case, fire up the system, and get a video error.

✔ **Hint**

Video card slots can be a little tricky. The card must be seated perfectly or it will not work. Some video card slots have locking levers to ensure good seating. If you were observant when you removed the card initially, you'll know what you have to do now for proper physical installation.

f. Boot your system. To learn more about your display adapter, download TechPowerUp GPU-Z from www.techpowerup.com/gpuz/ and run it. Record this information:

GPU type: _____

DirectX support: _____

Memory type: _____

Memory size: _____

GPU clock speed: _____

Memory speed: _____

g. Open your favorite browser to search the Web. Conduct your search using the information you've gathered about the manufacturer and model number of your card. If you can find the specifications for your display adapter, note the following:

What is the highest resolution you can achieve with your video card according to these specifications? _____

How much memory is available? _____

What type of memory is used? _____

Does the adapter support SLI or CrossFire? _____

Note any other features, such as an HDMI connector, the adapter has: _____

Step 2   Enter the UEFI/BIOS setup utility, as you learned to do in Lab Exercise 5.02, "Accessing BIOS Settings via the CMOS Setup Program." Search around a bit and you'll find video options. Some system setups have a number of video-related settings; others have just a few. (You're more likely to find lots of video settings on a desktop's motherboard than on a laptop's.) Complete each of these questions based on your specific UEFI/BIOS, skipping any that you don't have. Some of the names of the sections will undoubtedly differ from the ones presented here.

   a.   On the Standard System Setup or similar screen, how many choices are there for video, and how is your video set?

   _____

   b.   Note if there are there any PCIe-specific settings:

   _____

   c.   If there's an onboard display adapter, what are the settings, if any, for the amount of RAM the onboard adapter will use?

   _____

   d.   On the Power Management Setup or similar screen, if you have settings to control how the monitor and video card will react when not in use for a period of time, what are your settings?

   _____

   e.   On the Integrated Peripherals or similar screen, if you have an Initialize Display First setting (or similar), what are the choices?

   _____

   f.   What setting is enabled? When this setting is wrong, the display might not work.

   _____

   g.   Exit from UEFI/BIOS setup. Do not save your changes.

Step 3 You'll now examine a monitor and see what external controls it has. If you're not in a computer lab, you can go to your local computer store and examine a wide variety of monitors.

Figure 17-2 shows the control buttons for adjusting the display attributes for an LCD monitor. Some monitors have additional controls on the back too. One of the buttons typically opens a menu system onscreen, and the other buttons move forward and backward through the menu system.

A monitor can have quite a few adjustable features. How many of the following can you adjust on your LCD monitor? Enter Yes in the second column for each feature you can adjust.

Brightness	
Contrast	
Clock	
Onscreen display	
Color temperature	
Auto balance	
Sharpness	
Gamma	
Source	
Language	

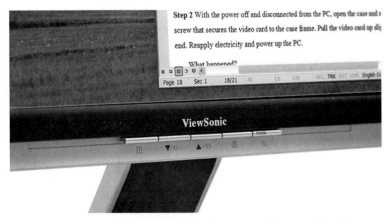

FIGURE 17-2 An LCD monitor with front-panel buttons for adjustments

Play with the controls of your monitor or a test monitor. If the current settings use percentages, write down the settings before doing any adjustments:

_____

_____

Then follow these steps:

    a.   Change the settings such as color and sizing. Don't be shy!

    b.   Put the settings back as close as possible to their original positions.

    c.   Optimize the screen for clarity and position.

Step 4   The hardware is set up properly and the BIOS/UEFI firmware settings should be correct, so now you need to configure and optimize the Windows settings that determine your video display characteristics. To do this, you need to use the Display applet in the Control Panel (Windows 7/8.1) or Display Settings (Windows 10).

One adjustment you can make is to change the screen resolution—that is, the number of pixels that comprise the display. The higher the resolution, the finer grained the display image will be, and the smaller the icons, text, and windows will appear onscreen. On older systems with CRT monitors, changing the resolution was the primary way people adjusted the text and icon size onscreen. This was possible because CRTs looked good at a variety of resolutions; they didn't suffer from the fuzziness that LCDs do when running at less than their maximum resolution (also known as recommended resolution).

Now that almost all systems use LCD monitors, adjusting the resolution is much less common, because nobody wants a fuzzy display. When users on modern systems want to make the text and icons larger onscreen, they change a Windows display setting instead.

In the following steps you will see how to adjust both resolution and display settings.

Windows 7/8.1

    a.   Open the Control Panel and click Hardware and Sound.

    b.   Under the Display heading, click Adjust screen resolution.

    c.   If you have multiple monitors, choose the one you are referring to from the Display drop-down list.

    d.   Open the Resolution drop-down list and drag the slider to choose a different resolution. See Figure 17-3.

    e.   Click Apply to apply the setting.

    f.   If asked whether you want to keep the new resolution, click Keep changes.

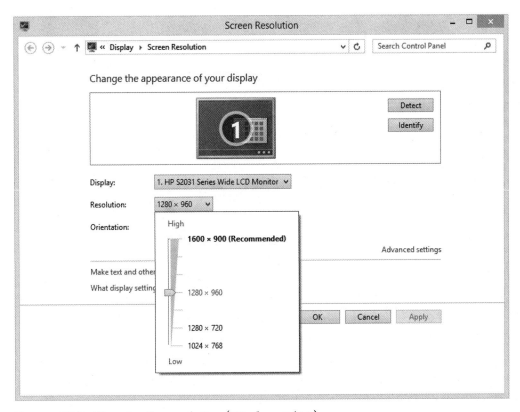

FIGURE 17-3 Changing the resolution (Windows 7/8.1)

g. Click Make text and other items larger or smaller.

h. Choose a setting:

- Windows 7: As shown in Figure 17-4, the three choices are Smaller – 100% (default), Medium – 125%, and Larger – 150%. Click an option button to make your choice.

- Windows 8.1: Drag the slider in the *Change the size of all items* section to adjust the size. You can also optionally set the size for individual types of text, as shown in Figure 17-5.

✖ **Warning**

Some applications are written with the assumption that text size will be set to 100% (the smallest setting), and if you make text larger than that, there may be visual glitches. For example, if the application specifies a fixed size for a message box and the text is larger than expected, some of the text in the message may be truncated. If this turns out to be a problem, you can always adjust the text size back down again.

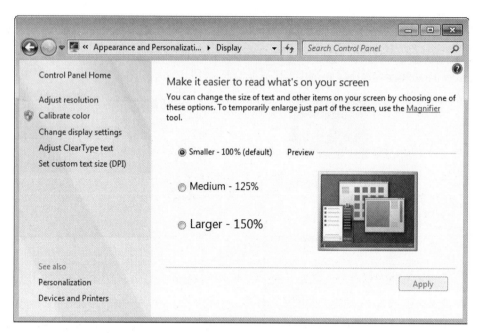

FIGURE 17-4 In Windows 7 you can choose from among three settings for text and icon size.

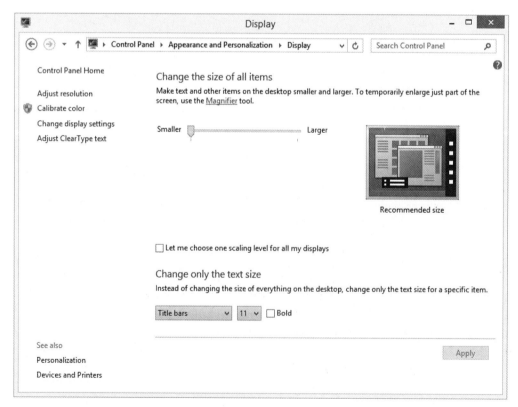

FIGURE 17-5 Display options in Windows 8.1 enable you to set an overall size for text and icons and also individual sizes for certain kinds of text.

WINDOWS 10

a. Open Settings | System | Display.

b. If you have multiple monitors, choose the one you want to change.

c. Click the Resolution drop-down menu to choose a different resolution. See Figure 17-6.

d. If asked whether you want to keep the new resolution, click Keep changes.

e. Windows 10 automatically adjusts the size of text, apps, and other items as resolution changes. However, you can choose from settings ranging from 100% up to 225%. For additional choices, such as custom scaling or fixing blurred text, click the Advanced scaling settings hyperlink shown in Figure 17-6.

Step 5 Next you'll explore a few less-common display settings that you might occasionally need to access.

a. In the navigation bar in the Control Panel Display applet (Windows 7/8.1) click Change display settings to return to the screen where you set the resolution earlier. In Windows 10, scroll down past the Multiple displays section of Display settings.

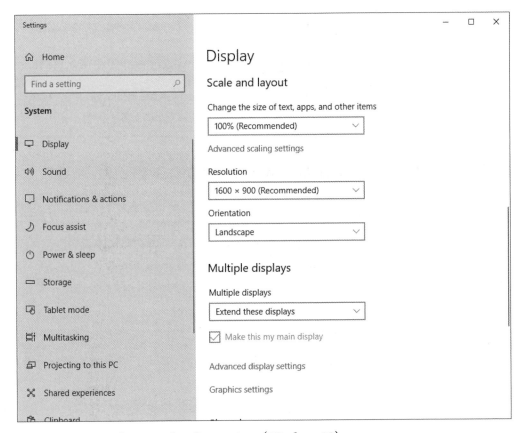

FIGURE 17-6 Resolution and scaling options (Windows 10)

b.   Click Advanced settings (Windows 7/8.1) or Advanced display settings | Display adapter properties (Windows 10). A Properties dialog box opens. On the Adapter tab, you'll see information about your display adapter, as shown in the example on the left in Figure 17-7.

c.   Click the Monitor tab. Here you'll see information about the monitor hardware, as shown in the example on the right in Figure 17-7.

d.   Open the Screen refresh rate drop-down list and examine the choices available there. Depending on your monitor, there might only be one choice. Write the available choices:

→ **Note**

Screen refresh rate used to be a big deal on CRT monitors. At lower refresh rates, a monitor flickered, causing eyestrain problems, so it was usually a good idea to set the refresh rate to a fairly high setting, like 100 Hertz or so, to make the monitor easier to look at for long periods of time. On today's LCD monitors, refresh rate is not as much of an issue, and you usually don't need to change this setting.

---

e.   In Windows 7, open the Colors drop-down list on the Monitor tab and write the available choices. This option is not available in Windows 8.1/10.

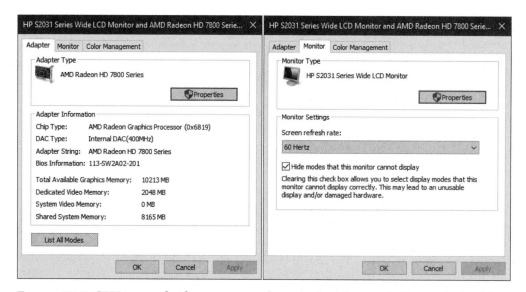

FIGURE 17-7   GPU type and video memory is shown in the Adapter tab. You might be able to adjust refresh rates on the Monitor tab.

f. In Windows 7, click the Troubleshoot tab and click the Change settings button (if available; if it is grayed out, this option is not available on your system). This option is not available in Windows 8.1/10. A dialog box appears with a Hardware acceleration slider in it. Normally you want full hardware acceleration for best video performance. However, some applications that have wonky video problems sometimes can be fixed by decreasing the Hardware acceleration setting. Just keep this setting in the back of your mind as something to try when troubleshooting video problems in the future. Click Cancel to close the Display Adapter Troubleshooter dialog box.

g. Click the Color Management tab, and then click Color Management. In the Color Management dialog box, you can set up profiles associated with various printing devices so that the colors seen onscreen match the colors in the printer's output more closely. This setting is mostly used in professional desktop publishing and printing facilities; the average user will never need it.

h. Click Close to close the Color Management dialog box; then click Cancel to close the Properties dialog box.

i. Close the Control Panel (Windows 7/8.1) or Settings app (Windows 10).

Step 6   Next, you'll check the version number and date on your display adapter driver, and install an update if one is available.

a. Open Device Manager, locate your display adapter, and then double-click it to display its Properties dialog box.

b. Click the Driver tab and note the Driver Date and Driver Version here:

---

c. Click Update Driver, and then click Search automatically for updated driver software. Wait for Windows to look for a driver. If one is found, follow the prompts to install it. If the best driver is already installed, click Close.

d. Close the Properties dialog box and close Device Manager.

e. Go online and find the manufacturer's Web site. If you bought the display adapter as part of a whole system, go to the PC manufacturer's Web site and look up the drivers for your system according to your model number, serial number, or service tag. If the display adapter was purchased separately from the PC, go to the manufacturer's site for the display adapter.

f. If a newer driver is available, download and install it. (Do this on a test machine first. Get comfortable with the whole process before you do this on your personal computer.)

✔ **Hint**

New drivers will sometimes fail to work properly, thereby crippling your PC. Remember that the Roll Back Driver feature is available in the adapter's Properties dialog box in Device Manager. It enables you to go back to a driver that worked correctly in case you encounter problems.

---

    g.   Did you notice any performance change as a result of updating the display adapter driver? If so, what?

_____

Step 7   To finish up, adjust the amount of idle time on the system before the display turns off.

    a.   Open the Control Panel and choose Hardware and Sound | Power Options.

    b.   In the navigation bar, click Choose when to turn off the display.

    c.   Set the Turn off the display drop-down list to the desired amount of time, such as 10 minutes.

    d.   Click Save changes.

    e.   Close the Control Panel.

 **30 MINUTES**

Lab Exercise 17.02: Configuring Multiple Displays

Almost every PC today supports the capability to install multiple display adapters and use multiple monitors. Even most laptops and many tablets have a secondary video output that lets you plug in a second monitor. Having several monitors allows the user to keep many windows open at once and monitor them at a glance, without having to switch back and forth (or make each window tiny). For example, a security guard with 12 video cameras to watch might have three monitors, each one showing the output from four of the cameras.

To connect multiple monitors, the system needs multiple monitor ports, of course. Many video cards have at least two ports on them (such as an HDMI and a DVI, and one or two DisplayPorts—some still have support for the old VGA port), so the system can have two monitors without adding more hardware. You can also add another video card if there is an available motherboard slot (this is typically used to boost 3D performance using technologies such as NVIDIA's SLI or AMD's CrossFire). The best display adapters are all PCIe ×16, and many motherboards have only one ×16 slot (some motherboards with two or more PCIe ×16 slots run the second or third slots at slower speeds). However, PCIe ×1 cards are also available. You can also buy adapters that will enable an ×16 card to connect to an ×1 slot (with some loss of performance, of course).

✖ **Cross-Reference**

For additional information on configuring your multiple displays, refer to the "Installing and Configuring Video" section in Chapter 17 of *Mike Meyers' CompTIA A+ Guide to Managing and Troubleshooting PCs.*

Learning Objectives

In this lab exercise, you will learn how to install and configure additional displays, and to extend the Windows Desktop across displays.

At the end of this lab, you'll be able to

- Configure a system to use multiple displays

- Expand the desktop across two or more displays

Lab Materials and Setup

The materials you need for this lab are

- A working PC with Windows 7, 8.1, or 10 installed

- A display adapter that supports multiple monitors

- At least one additional working monitor

Getting Down to Business

In this lab exercise you will start with a working PC with a single monitor. You will then add another monitor, and configure Windows to extend the desktop across both monitors so that each monitor can display different content.

Step 1   First, you'll connect the second monitor and make sure Windows sees it.

   a.   Examine the video card or port cluster the monitor is currently connected to. If there is an unused VGA, DVI, HDMI, or DisplayPort port, you can use it to connect an additional display (Step g). If not, follow Steps b–f to install an additional display adapter or replace the current video card with one that has provision for two displays.

➔ **Note**

It might be necessary to use adapters on some ports to enable a particular display to connect to the available video display connectors on a card or port cluster.

b.   Shut down your system properly and unplug the power cable from the system unit and the wall.

c.   Remove the cover from the PC to expose the expansion bus slots.

d.   Verify the type and location of the current video display adapter. If the system has an additional PCIe ×16 slot, you can install a second PCIe ×16 display adapter (preferably using the same chipset as the first card). If a PCIe ×1 slot is available, you can install a PCIe ×1 card (preferably using the same chipset as the first card). To avoid using additional slots, you might prefer to replace the current video display adapter with a PCIe ×16 card that supports at least two displays.

e.   Using proper ESD avoidance procedures, install an additional card or remove the current card and replace it. Be sure to provide power as needed to the card.

f.   Connect the original monitor to the appropriate connector on the display adapter.

g.   Attach the second monitor cable to the display adapter, and test your system with the case still open to see if it works.

To verify that the second monitor has been installed correctly, is recognized by the system, and has drivers available, open Device Manager and expand the display adapter's icon. View the properties of the newly installed card and select the Drivers tab. Does everything appear to be in order? If not, what problems do you see?

_____

h.   If the new display adapter is not working properly, you may need to install specific drivers or updated drivers. Access the Internet to download and install the appropriate drivers for your monitor or display adapter.

Step 2   Now that the hardware is set up and functioning properly, you will configure Windows to expand your desktop across two monitors.

WINDOWS 7/8.1

a.   Open the Control Panel and navigate to Appearance and Personalization | Display | Screen Resolution. This shows the monitor settings. Now there is an additional drop-down list that you didn't have back in Figure 17-3: Multiple displays (see Figure 17-8).

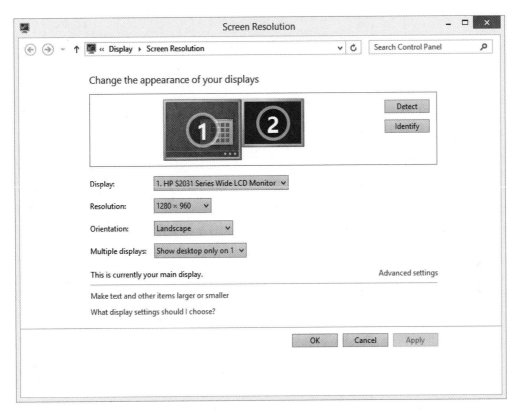

FIGURE 17-8 The Screen Resolution dialog box of the Control Panel Display applet, showing two monitors available (Windows 7/8.1). The second monitor is not yet enabled.

b. To use the second display to show the same information as the first display, open the Multiple displays drop-down menu and select Duplicate these displays (see Figure 17-9). Click Apply to use this setting, then click Keep changes.

c. To use the second display to show additional programs, select Extend these displays (see Figure 17-10). Click Apply to use this setting, then click Keep changes.

d. Drag the Screen Resolution dialog box from monitor 1 to monitor 2, and then back to monitor 1.

WINDOWS 10

a. Open Settings and navigate to System | Display. This shows the monitor settings (see Figure 17-11).

b. To use the second display to show the same information as the first display, open the Multiple displays drop-down menu and select Duplicate these displays (see Figure 17-12). Click Apply to use this setting, then click Keep changes.

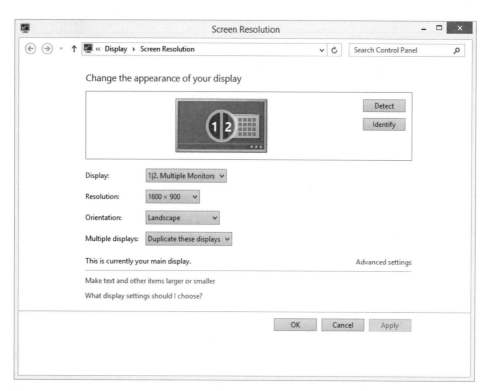

FIGURE 17-9 Using two monitors to show the same information (mirrored or duplicate mode) in Windows 7/8.1

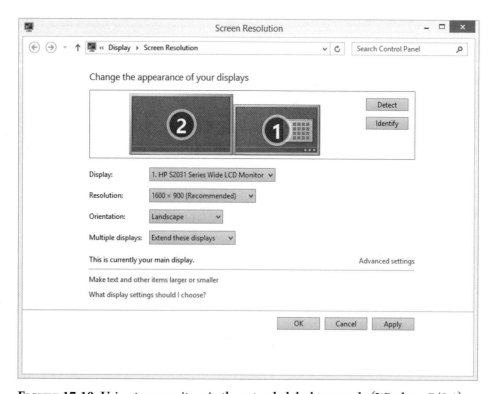

FIGURE 17-10 Using two monitors in the extended desktop mode (Windows 7/8.1)

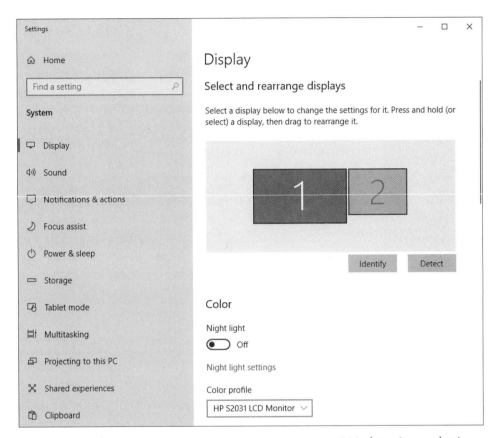

FIGURE 17-11 Display Settings, showing two monitors available (Windows 10). The second monitor is not yet enabled.

c. To use the second display to show additional programs, select Extend these displays (refer to Figure 17-12). Click Apply to use this setting, then click Keep changes.

d. Drag the Display settings window from monitor 1 to monitor 2, and then back to monitor 1.

Step 3 Now let's continue by experimenting with some of the other settings in the Screen Resolution or Display settings dialog box.

a. Click the Identify button. What happens?

_____

b. If the monitor graphics in the dialog box are not arranged to match the actual positioning of the monitors in relation to one another, drag one of them to move it.

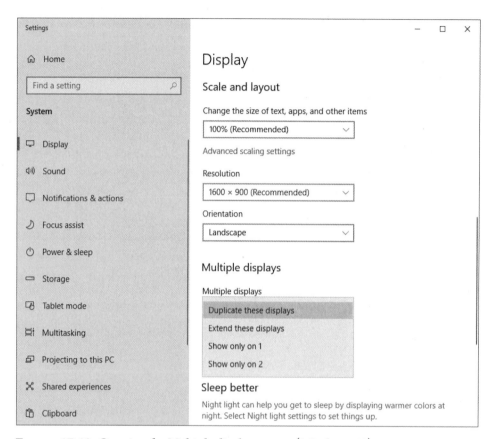

FIGURE 17-12 Opening the Multiple displays menu (Windows 10)

c.   Click the monitor 1 graphic in the dialog box. The Display, Resolution, and Orientation settings all apply to that monitor.

d.   Click the monitor 2 graphic. Notice the change to the Display, Resolution, and Orientation settings.

e.   Change the Orientation setting to Portrait and then click Apply. When the confirmation message appears, click Revert. What just happened?

_____

f.   Change the Orientation setting to Landscape (Flipped) and click Apply. When the confirmation message appears, click Revert. What just happened?

_____

    g. With monitor 2 selected in the dialog box, check the Make this my main display checkbox. Then click Apply. What just happened?

_____

    h. Repeat Step g to return monitor 1 to being the main display.

Step 4 To finish up, you'll return to the normal display settings and remove the second monitor.

    a. Open the Multiple displays drop-down list and choose Duplicate these displays; then click Apply.

    b. At the confirmation box, click Keep changes.

    c. Close the Control Panel or Settings app.

    d. Shut down the computer and disconnect the second monitor.

    e. Restart the computer and confirm that the display is configured as it should be.

 **30 MINUTES**

Lab Exercise 17.03: Troubleshooting Video

Video troubleshooting really boils down to two distinct questions. First, are the physical video components installed and configured properly, as discussed in Lab Exercise 17.01? Second, do the current video display adapter and CPU support the software technologies you're trying to use? (Or have you loaded that killer game and completely overwhelmed your video subsystem?) In this lab exercise, you'll create connectivity problems to simulate real-world installation problems, and use the DirectX Diagnostic Tool to analyze your system.

Learning Objectives

In this lab exercise, you will learn how to troubleshoot display problems in Windows.

At the end of this lab, you'll be able to

- Recognize and fix typical video installation and connectivity problems
- Use the Microsoft DirectX Diagnostic Tool to analyze and test the graphic display attributes of a PC system

Lab Materials and Setup

The materials you need for this lab are

- A working PC with Windows 7, 8.1, or 10 installed
- Any version of the Microsoft DirectX Diagnostic Tool installed

Getting Down to Business

If you went through Lab Exercise 17.01 and had typical results—video card not seated properly, forgetting to plug things in all the way, and so on—you can probably skip Steps 1 and 2 of this lab. If you had a perfect reinstall, on the other hand, then definitely do all of the steps!

Step 1   If your display uses a VGA or DVI cable, loosen the screws that hold the monitor data cable securely to the video card. With the system fully powered up and in Windows—and being gentle with your hardware—turn off the display, then partially disconnect the monitor cable.

What happened to the screen?

With analog monitor connections (VGA connector), a loose cable sometimes results in a degraded display. Colors fade out or a single color disappears, or the display may appear grainy or snowy, for example. If you run into these symptoms in the field, check your connectivity!

Connect the monitor cable, tighten the restraining screws (on a VGA or DVI cable), and turn the display back on to resume normal operation.

Step 2   With the power off and disconnected from the PC, open the case and remove the screw that secures the video card to the case frame. Pull the video card up slightly on one end. Reapply electricity and power up the PC.

What happened?

You might have to run through this a couple of times to get the desired effect, which is a seemingly dead PC and some beeping from the system speaker. That long-short-short beep code is pretty universally recognizable as the PC's cry for help: "Hey! My video card isn't seated properly!"

With the power off and disconnected, reseat your video card, reinstall the restraining screw, and power up your PC to resume normal operation.

Step 3   Access the Microsoft DirectX Diagnostic Tool. To do so:

a.   Windows 7: Click the Start button, type **dxdiag** into the Start menu Search bar, and press ENTER.

b.   Windows 8.1 and Windows 10: Click the Start button, click Search, type **dxdiag** into the Search box, and then click dxdiag in the search results.

Step 4 Select the Display tab (see Figure 17-13). Record the information that appears about your display adapter. If you have multiple monitors, each monitor shows up as its own tab (Display 1, Display 2, and so on). If that's the case, record information only for Display 1.

What is the name of your display adapter? _____

How much total memory is on the adapter? _____

What is the current display mode? _____

What is the driver name and version? _____

Does it display a driver version date? If so, record it here: _____

→ **Note**

Use the information about display driver version and date to determine if you need a more current driver. You can find out by comparing this information to the display driver information available at your video card or GPU vendor's Web site.

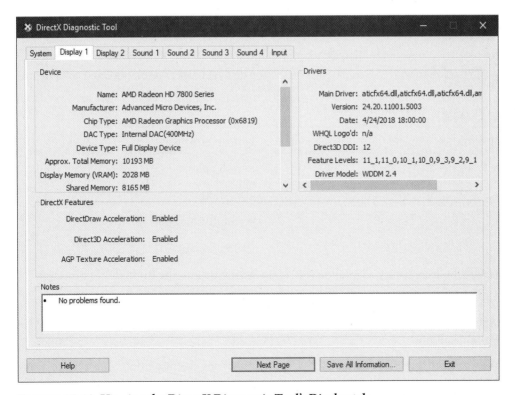

FIGURE 17-13 Viewing the DirectX Diagnostic Tool's Display tab

Step 5   Check out the Notes box at the bottom of the Display tab, and read the information provided. This is where you can find out about any conflicts or problem areas.

Do you see any information about conflicts or problems? If so, what's the conflict or problem?

_____

Click Exit to close the utility when you are finished with it.

Lab Analysis Test

1.   Troy wants to add another monitor to his desktop system, but his current display adapter has only one monitor port on it. His current display adapter is in the motherboard's only PCIe ×16 slot. What are his options?

2.   Your nephew Brian visited and used your computer last night, and this morning your monitor is dead. What should you do first, second, and third?

3.   Ben is setting up a security system and he wants to have six monitors on a single PC, for monitoring security cameras. What hardware will he need, and what open slots must the motherboard have? What concerns should he have regarding cooling and power requirements?

4.   Teresa installed a new game, but she is frustrated because it responds too slowly. What might she check?

5.   Taylor installed a new video display adapter, but the best setting she can adjust it to is 800 × 600 resolution with 256 colors. What must she do to get higher resolutions and color depth?

Key Term Quiz

Use the following terms to complete the following sentences. Not all terms will be used.

color depth	refresh rate
Control Panel	resolution
Direct3D	Screen Resolution
DirectX Diagnostic Tool	setup program

1.   To disable a built-in display adapter on the motherboard, go into the BIOS/UEFI firmware
_____ .

2.   If an LCD monitor's display looks fuzzy, it may be set to a lower _____ than the monitor's maximum.

3.   To make icon size larger in Windows 7/8.1 without lowering the resolution, adjust the text and icon size in the _____ .

4.   _____ was an important setting on CRTs to prevent eyestrain due to flickering, but on LCD monitors it is not necessary to adjust it.

5.   To configure the Windows Desktop to extend across multiple monitors in Windows 10, go to the _____ section of Settings.

Chapter 18

Essentials of Networking

Lab Exercises

A PC technician is sometimes called upon to be a network guru, answering connectivity questions and making recommendations on the best price/performance considerations for homes and businesses. This happens frequently, especially in smaller companies that can't afford to hire multiple people to support both the network *and* the PCs. The CompTIA A+ certification exams reflect these changing roles of the PC technician and include many questions related to computer networking.

This chapter, the first of several on networking, focuses on hardware. Here you'll become familiar with common networking hardware, and you'll learn how to evaluate a network cable to determine its wire arrangement. The next several chapters will take you even deeper into networking, focusing on Windows network configuration and troubleshooting.

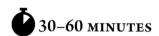 30–60 MINUTES

Lab Exercise 18.01: Identifying Local Area Network Hardware

Your boss has decided to upgrade the office network, which is about five years old. With the changes in networking technology, she wants your ideas about purchasing the right equipment for the upgrade. Your company is a small one, so the task is quite doable, but you need to make sure you know what you're talking about before you give your report.

Learning Objectives

In this lab, you'll familiarize yourself with networking hardware.

At the end of this lab, you'll be able to

- Identify different kinds of network cabling

- Identify different network interface cards (NICs)

- Identify different types of network connection boxes

Lab Materials and Setup

The materials you need for this lab are

- Access to a PC running Windows

- Access to a working LAN and the Internet (you may have demonstration devices provided by your instructor)

✖ **Cross-Reference**

Be sure to check out Chapter 18 of *Mike Meyers' CompTIA A+ Guide to Managing and Troubleshooting PCs* for help identifying network cables and connectors. It's a good idea to have the textbook handy while you progress through this lab.

Getting Down to Business

One of the best ways to find out what a network is made of is to physically look at all of its pieces. In this lab exercise, you'll examine the physical components that make up a local area network (LAN).

Step 1 If you have access to a LAN (the classroom computer lab network, a home network, or your company's network), spend some time exploring the physical hardware connections and devices. If possible, acquire the diagram of the physical layout of the network, or create a simple diagram of the layout to familiarize yourself with the various devices and connections associated with the network you're analyzing.

✖ **Warning**

Don't disconnect anything, and be careful while probing around. One small mistake, like removing a cable or turning off the wrong device, can disrupt the entire network. If you're using the classroom network, ask the instructor what you can and can't remove while you make closer inspections of the cables and devices.

What sort of cabling does the network use, or is it wireless? If wired, note any writing on the cable that indicates its category (such as Cat 5e or Cat 6):

What sort of NICs do the machines have? Are the NICs cards (see Figure 18-1) or built into the system (see Figure 18-2)? If cards, describe the back of the card. Does it have a single connector, as in Figure 18-1,

FIGURE 18-1 A wired network interface card (NIC)

or a combination of connectors? Does it have an antenna? Is there a link and/or activity LED? Which of the LEDs is on steadily? Which is flashing? Describe the NIC here:

_____

_____

_____

Many computers use USB wireless network adapters (see Figure 18-3). If your computer uses a USB wireless network adapter, what standards does it support? What is the brand and model number? Record that information here:

_____

_____

FIGURE 18-2 A built-in network adapter

FIGURE 18-3 A USB wireless network adapter

Some ultrathin laptops and tablets, such as the Microsoft Surface Pro, don't have a built-in Ethernet port. Instead, a USB-Ethernet network adapter can be used (see Figure 18-4). If your computer uses a USB-Ethernet network adapter, what speeds of Ethernet does it support? What brand and model number? Record that information here:

_____

_____

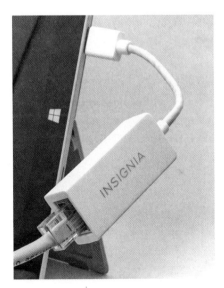

FIGURE 18-4 A USB-Ethernet network adapter

✔ **Hint**

If you are having trouble connecting to a wired network or communicating to other machines on the network, the link and activity lights are a good place to start your troubleshooting. The LEDs on a NIC serve two purposes. The link light illuminates when there is a valid electrical connection between the PC and the network device, usually a switch. This does not guarantee network connectivity—it just means that the electrical connection is intact. The activity light blinks to indicate that data is being transferred between the networking devices. It does not guarantee that the data is usable—it just means that data is moving.

Step 2   In almost all networks there is a central physical gathering box to which the PCs connect, either with cables or wirelessly.

    a.   On a separate piece of paper, draw a diagram of the physical connections of your LAN to that central box.

    b.   Compare and contrast each type of device. How do they achieve their functionality? In what situations would you use one versus another?

Hub:

_____

_____

_____

Switch:

_____

_____

_____

Router:

_____

_____

_____

FIGURE 18-5 A LAN switch with multiple cables/devices attached

c. Now take a look at the hub, switch, or router on your network. Figure 18-5 shows an example. What is the brand name and model number? How many devices can be attached? Is wireless connectivity an option? At what speed(s) can it send and receive data? Record your findings here:

_____

_____

_____

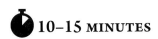 **10–15 MINUTES**

Lab Exercise 18.02: Evaluating a UTP Cable

Unshielded twisted pair (UTP) cables are the staple of most LANs, with their RJ-45 connectors on each end. There are two variants of these, however: straight-through (patch) and crossover. Straight-through cables are used to connect PCs and other network-capable devices to hubs, switches, and routers. Crossover cables are used in specialized situations where two devices of the same type need to communicate, such as to connect one PC to another.

Learning Objectives

In this lab, you'll evaluate a UTP cable to determine whether it is straight-through or crossover based on the order of the colored wires in the connector.

At the end of this lab, you will be able to

- Differentiate between a straight-through cable and a crossover cable

Lab Materials and Setup

The materials you need for this lab are

- A Cat 5, Cat 5e, or Cat 6 cable (either crossover or straight-through)

Getting Down to Business

The RJ-45 connector on each end of a cable arranges the wires in a very specific order. The wires can be arranged in one of two patterns: T568A and T568B. On a straight-through cable, both ends use the T568B arrangement. On a crossover cable, one end uses T568A and the other uses T568B. Tables 18-1 and 18-2 detail these arrangements. Pin numbers are from left (1) to right (8).

Step 1   Examine one end of the cable you are working with, and record the wire colors, from left to right, as you are holding the cable with the clip (the part you press to release the cable) at the top.

What are the wire colors, from left to right?

_____

Based on Tables 18-1 and 18-2, which type is this end of the cable: T568A or T568B? _____

Pin #	Wire
1	Green stripe
2	Green solid
3	Orange stripe
4	Blue solid
5	Blue stripe
6	Orange solid
7	Brown stripe
8	Brown solid

TABLE 18-1 T568A

Pin #	Wire
1	Orange stripe
2	Orange solid
3	Green stripe
4	Blue solid
5	Blue stripe
6	Green solid
7	Brown stripe
8	Brown solid

TABLE 18-2 T568B

Step 2 Examine the other end of the cable you are working with, and record the wire colors, from left to right, as you are holding the cable with the clip (the part you press to release the cable) at the top.

What are the wire colors, from left to right?

_____

Based on Tables 18-1 and 18-2, which type is this end of the cable: T568A or T568B? _____

Which type of cable is this: straight-through or crossover? _____

Step 3 Examine the cable, looking for any writing on it that might indicate the cable type, which might be 5e, 6, 6a, or (less likely) something else. See Figure 18-6 for a typical example. What writing appears on the cable, and which type of cable do you think it is?

_____

FIGURE 18-6 A typical Cat 6 (CAT6) network cable

 **20–30 MINUTES**

Lab Exercise 18.03: Determining a MAC Address

Every NIC has a built-in hardware address known as a media access control (MAC) address. The MAC address is used by the physical (hardware) layer of networking communications to make sure that data gets delivered to the right NIC. When troubleshooting device issues, you may be called upon to look up a MAC address. It's not difficult, but you have to know where to look.

Learning Objectives

In this lab, you'll learn five ways of looking up MAC addresses.

At the end of this lab, you will be able to

- Look up a MAC address in Windows

- Look up a MAC address at a command prompt

- Look up a MAC address on a macOS computer

- Look up a MAC address on a Linux computer connected to a wired network

- Look up a MAC address on a Linux computer connected to a wireless network

Lab Materials and Setup

The materials you need for this lab are

- A working computer with Windows and at least one NIC installed

- A working computer with macOS and at least one NIC installed (optional)

- A working computer with Linux and at least one NIC installed (optional)

Getting Down to Business

A NIC's MAC address is a string of six two-digit hexadecimal numbers, like this: C6-50-01-15-D4-EA. It's unimportant to end users, but depending on the problem you are troubleshooting, it may be significant to the technician. In the following steps you'll learn how to retrieve a NIC's MAC address from the operating system.

Step 1   First, we'll use the Windows GUI to get a MAC address.

   a.   Open the Control Panel and choose Network and Internet | Network and Sharing Center.

   b.   The Connections field identifies the current network connection listed. It might be Local Area Connection or Wireless Network Connection. Either way, click it.

   c.   In the Status box that appears, click Details. The Network Connection Details dialog box opens.

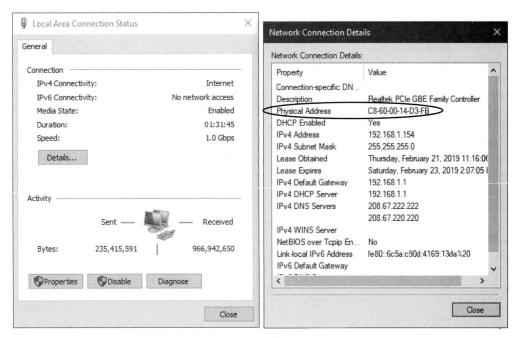

Figure 18-7 Viewing Network Connection Details to find an adapter's MAC (physical) address

d. Find the Physical Address line (see Figure 18-7). That's your MAC address. Write it here:

_____

e. Close all open windows.

Step 2 The method you learned in Step 1 enables you to get the MAC address for the NIC that is currently in use for your network connection, but sometimes you might want to get the MAC addresses for *all* your networking devices. The easiest way to do that is at a command line.

a. Open a command-line window, as you learned to do in Lab Exercise 15.01, "Exploring the Command-Line Interface in Windows."

b. Type **ipconfig /all** and press ENTER. Detailed information appears for each network device. You will need to scroll up to see the beginning of it.

c. Find the information for the adapter you are interested in. (Find one that's in use if possible. It'll have "Lease" information included for it.) It might look something like Figure 18-8.

d. Write the Physical Address:

_____

```
Microsoft Windows [Version 10.0.17763.316]
(c) 2018 Microsoft Corporation. All rights reserved.

C:\Users\Mark E. Soper>ipconfig /all

Windows IP Configuration

    Host Name . . . . . . . . . . . . : Tiger-Athlon
    Primary Dns Suffix  . . . . . . . :
    Node Type . . . . . . . . . . . . : Hybrid
    IP Routing Enabled. . . . . . . . : No
    WINS Proxy Enabled. . . . . . . . : No

Ethernet adapter Local Area Connection:

    Connection-specific DNS Suffix  . :
    Description . . . . . . . . . . . : Realtek PCIe GBE Family Controller
    Physical Address. . . . . . . . . : C8-60-00-14-D3-FB
    DHCP Enabled. . . . . . . . . . . : Yes
    Autoconfiguration Enabled . . . . : Yes
    Link-local IPv6 Address . . . . . : fe80::6c5a:c90d:4169:13da%20(Preferred)
    IPv4 Address. . . . . . . . . . . : 192.168.1.154(Preferred)
    Subnet Mask . . . . . . . . . . . : 255.255.255.0
    Lease Obtained. . . . . . . . . . : Thursday, February 21, 2019 11:16:06 AM
    Lease Expires . . . . . . . . . . : Saturday, February 23, 2019 2:07:05 PM
    Default Gateway . . . . . . . . . : 192.168.1.1
    DHCP Server . . . . . . . . . . . : 192.168.1.1
    DHCPv6 IAID . . . . . . . . . . . : 231235584
    DHCPv6 Client DUID. . . . . . . . : 00-01-00-01-1A-6C-94-27-C8-60-00-14-D3-FB
    DNS Servers . . . . . . . . . . . : 208.67.222.222
                                        208.67.220.220
    NetBIOS over Tcpip. . . . . . . . : Disabled
```

FIGURE 18-8 The ipconfig /all command reports detailed information about each network adapter.

e. If any other devices are listed that have Physical Address settings listed, write their names and their addresses here:

_____

_____

f. Close the command-line window.

Step 3   In this step, we will use the macOS System Preferences app to find the MAC (hardware) address for the installed network adapter.

a. Start your macOS computer.

b. Click the Apple icon in the top-left corner and select System Preferences from the Apple menu.

c. Click Network.

d. Click the Advanced button.

e. Click the Hardware tab (see Figure 18-9). Record the MAC address: _____

f. Click Cancel to close the Network dialog box.

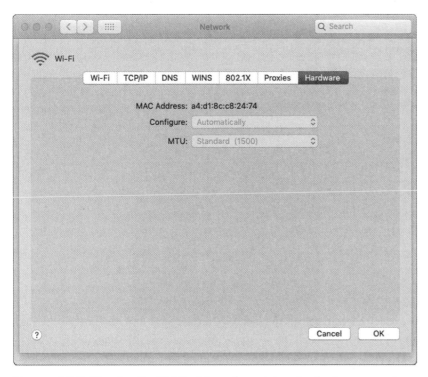

FIGURE 18-9 Viewing the MAC address for a network adapter on a system running macOS

Step 4 In this step, we will use the Linux nmcli utility (part of NetworkManager) to view the hardware (MAC) address on a system running Linux with a wired network.

a. Start Linux.

b. Open a terminal window, as you learned to do in Lab Exercise 15.02, "Exploring the Command-Line Interface in Linux."

c. Type **nmcli** and press ENTER.

→ **Note**

If this command isn't found, install NetworkManager. On a Debian-based system such as Ubuntu, enter this command:

sudo apt install network-manager

Enter the following commands to start and enable NetworkManager:

sudo systemctl start network-manager
sudo systemctl enable network-manager

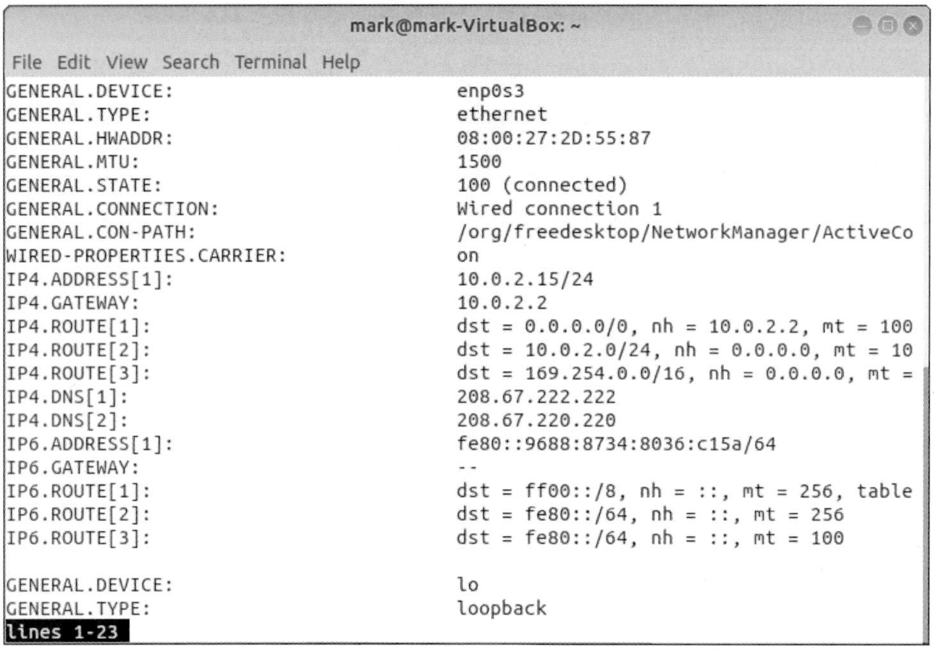

FIGURE 18-10 Using the nmcli device show command on a system running Ubuntu Linux 18.04

    d.   Type **nmcli device show** and press ENTER.

    e.   Record the HWADDR (MAC address) for the device enp0s3 (see Figure 18-10, third line):

        _____

    f.   Type **exit** to close the terminal window.

Step 5   In this step, we will use the Linux ifconfig utility to view the hardware (MAC) address on a system running Linux with a wireless (Wi-Fi) network.

    a.   Start Linux.

    b.   Open a terminal window.

    c.   Type **ifconfig wlan0** and press ENTER.

    d.   Record the Link encap:Ethernet Hardware address (MAC address): _____

    e.   Type **exit** to close the terminal window.

Lab Analysis Test

    1.   Tom needs to create a small network for his family at home, for sharing files and accessing the Internet. He found an old hub in an equipment closet at his workplace, and his boss says he can have it. Should he use it for his home network? Why or why not?

2. Joan wants to buy a NIC for an older computer that doesn't have built-in Ethernet, so it can join her LAN. What does she need to check inside the PC before making the purchase?

3. Jerry is trying to use an old cable he has found in the supply cabinet to connect a laptop to a router, but it isn't working. You suspect it might be a crossover cable. Explain to Jerry how to tell whether it is a crossover cable, and why that won't work to connect the laptop to the router.

4. Sylvia needs to get the MAC address of a network adapter that is installed in her Windows PC but not currently in use. How can she get this information?

5. Bill is trying to get a MAC address using the Windows ipconfig command but he doesn't see Physical Address listed as one of the properties for the connection. What has he forgotten?

Key Term Quiz

Use the following terms to complete the following sentences. Not all terms will be used.

cables	RJ-45
hardware	router
ipconfig	static
MAC	subnet mask
Network and Sharing Center	switch
NIC	tracert
nslookup	twisted pair

1. At a minimum, an Ethernet LAN requires a(n) _____ for each PC, a central gathering point such as a(n) _____ or a(n) _____, and _____ to connect them.

2. A UTP cable requires a length of _____ cable and _____ connectors for each end.

3. You can check a NIC's _____ address from the _____.

4. At a command prompt, the _____ command provides information about the installed network adapters.

5. The MAC address is also known as the _____ address.

Chapter 19
Local Area Networking

Lab Exercises

Even if networks aren't your specialty, as a PC technician you will end up working with them. Whether you're troubleshooting your Uncle Ray's home network at Christmas or assisting with the configuration of a thousand-seat client/server network at your company, you'll likely be asked to configure and fix networks at least now and then. You'll also be expected to know networking fundamentals for the CompTIA A+ 220-1002 exam.

In this chapter, you'll learn the software side of local area networking. You'll explore the network configuration and TCP/IP settings in Windows, macOS, and Linux, and learn how to test a LAN connection in all three operating systems. You'll also practice sharing resources on a Windows network.

 **30 MINUTES**

Lab Exercise 19.01: Exploring Local Area Network Configuration Options

To prepare for the CompTIA A+ exams and to build your toolbox of skills as a PC technician, you need to be able to set up, configure, and troubleshoot networks that use Windows clients. From a network configuration standpoint, each version of Windows is very similar. The CompTIA A+ exams will test your configuration knowledge for Windows 7, Windows 8.1, and Windows 10, including the paths you use to locate configuration settings.

→ **Note**

> This lab exercise assumes that the networking hardware is already installed and connected, and that you're familiar with it. Revisit Lab Exercise 18.01, "Identifying Local Area Network Hardware," if you need to review.

Learning Objectives

In this lab, you'll explore the network configuration options in a Windows environment.

At the end of this lab, you'll be able to

- Configure network access using the networking applets

Lab Materials and Setup

The materials you need for this lab are

- A network-ready PC with Windows 7, 8.1, or 10 installed (preferably multiple PCs with different versions, for practice)

- Access to the hub, switch, or router for the LAN

Getting Down to Business

When Windows detects that a PC is connected to a network, it automatically configures the connection using default settings. That means that a network connection almost always just starts working automatically when you plug in the cables. That's great for a small home network to give folks Internet access, because the user doesn't have to know anything about networking. However, the default settings are rarely ideal in any other situation, and certainly not good for most business environments.

Each computer that will be connected to the LAN must have the following:

- A NIC with correct drivers installed

- The appropriate client software, protocols, and services installed for the network type

- A computer name

- A workgroup name

In the following steps, you'll confirm these items, and learn how to make configuration changes to them if needed.

Step 1 Open Device Manager and verify that the network adapter is working properly. (Double-click it to open its Properties dialog box, and check its status on the General tab.) Troubleshoot as needed if it's not working. Refer to Lab Exercise 11.06, "Post-Installation Tasks: Drivers and Updates," if you need help using Device Manager and updating drivers.

Step 2 Next, you'll verify that the required network services are installed.

a. Open the Control Panel and choose Network and Internet | Network and Sharing Center.

b. Click Change adapter settings.

c. Right-click the network connection you want to work with (which may be labeled Local Area Connection, Ethernet, or some other name) and choose Properties.

You should find the following components listed in a selection window. Your system may have others as well.

> ✔ **Hint**
>
> **Nothing is necessarily wrong if you don't see any or all of the following components listed or if you see more than the ones listed previously.**

- **Client**   Client for Microsoft Networks (default)
- **Protocol**   There should be two here: Internet Protocol version 6 (TCP/IPv6) and Internet Protocol version 4 (TCP/IPv4)
- **Service**   File and Printer Sharing for Microsoft Networks

Write down what client(s), protocols, and services, other than the preceding ones, are listed in your system:

_____

_____

_____

Step 3   Now that you've found the network configuration screen, take a look at the various options:

- **Install**   The Install button enables you to add network components. Clicking the Install button gives you three choices:
  - **Client**   Adds a client to the configuration (must have at least one).
  - **Protocol**   TCP/IP is the default (must have a protocol to communicate).
  - **Service**   File and Printer Sharing must be enabled for other computers on the network to access the one on which you're working.
- **Remove/Uninstall**   The Remove or Uninstall button enables you to remove network components.
- **Properties**   The Properties button displays a variety of dialog boxes based on the network component selected.

You might at some point need to install new clients, protocols, or services or adjust the properties of one, so keep this dialog box in mind for later use. For now, however, we won't be making any changes.

Step 4   A computer's name specifies how other computers and users will see it when browsing the network. For example, in a home network in which multiple people use each machine, you might name each of the PCs with its hardware make/model. In an environment where there is a one-to-one relationship between people and PCs, you might name each computer with the primary user's name. You can change a computer's name at any time.

PCs in a peer-to-peer network must be in the same workgroup in order to communicate. The default name is WORKGROUP. (In earlier versions of Windows, the default name was MSHOME, and you might see that out there in the field occasionally.)

To determine the computer's name and workgroup, follow these steps:

a.   Open the Control Panel and choose System and Security | System.

b.   Record the computer name and workgroup.

Computer name: _____

Workgroup name: _____

c.   Click Change settings. The System Properties dialog box appears.

d.   On the Computer Name tab, if desired, type a description in the Computer description box.

e.   Click the Change button. The Computer Name/Domain Changes dialog box opens. See Figure 19-1.

f.   If you wanted to change the workgroup or computer name, you would do so here. For this exercise, though, we're just looking, so click Cancel.

g.   Click Cancel again to close the System Properties dialog box, and then close the Control Panel.

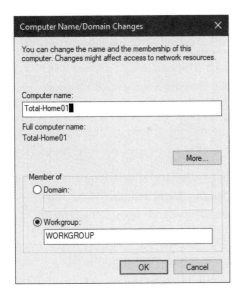

FIGURE 19-1 Set the computer's name and workgroup here.

 **30 MINUTES**

Lab Exercise 19.02: Verifying TCP/IP Settings in Windows

As you are probably aware, TCP/IP has emerged as the standard transport protocol for network communication. Microsoft operating systems normally use the Dynamic Host Configuration Protocol (DHCP), which automatically retrieves and assigns client TCP/IP settings from a DHCP server. This makes it easy to set up a small home or business network of PCs. All systems in the network will communicate with each other using these settings. The problem is that many businesses have their own set of TCP/IP settings (either automatically configured through DHCP or manually configured) that must be used for all new or repaired systems introduced into the network. Your responsibility as a PC technician is to verify the TCP/IP settings.

✖ Cross-Reference

> **To review additional details of TCP/IP, re-read the "Configuring TCP/IP" section in Chapter 19 of**
> **Mike Meyers' CompTIA A+ Guide to Managing and Troubleshooting PCs.**

Learning Objectives

In this exercise, you'll access and verify the TCP/IP settings for a given PC system.

At the end of this lab, you'll be able to

- Define Automatic Private IP Addressing (APIPA)

- Use the ipconfig command-line utility

- Manually configure the TCP/IP settings on a PC

Lab Materials and Setup

The materials you need for this lab are

- A PC system that's properly configured for LAN access using Windows

- A list of TCP/IP settings provided by the instructor

Getting Down to Business

Typically, in corporate environments, the network protocol configuration scheme has been defined by the senior systems administrators. Unless you've had some experience with the configuration, you would not automatically know all of the TCP/IP settings for a network. For instance, even when you're setting up a small network (one that connects to the Internet), you'll need to contact your Internet service provider (or at least read the user's manual) to set up your router's TCP/IP settings. So don't worry if you have no idea what settings to use. The trick is to learn how to get to them so that you know what they are.

TCP/IP requires each system to have two basic settings for accessing a LAN and two additional settings for accessing other LANs or the Internet. You can either configure your system to automatically obtain the following settings when you log on (Microsoft's default settings) or you can specify them manually, depending on the requirements of your network:

- IP address (unique to the PC)
- Subnet mask (identifies network information)
- Default gateway (address of the router to the external realm)
- Domain Name System (DNS) server

Step 1 First, check the IPv4 assignment method by doing the following:

a. Open the Control Panel and choose Network and Internet | Network and Sharing Center.

b. Click Change adapter settings.

c. Right-click the network adapter and choose Properties.

d. Select Internet Protocol Version 4 (TCP/IPv4) from the list of items.

e. Click the Properties button. On the General tab, you will see either that the system obtains an IP address automatically (see Figure 19-2) or that it uses a static address.

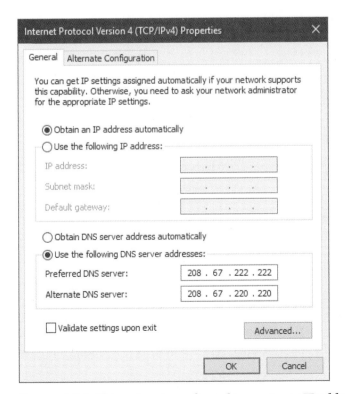

FIGURE 19-2 This system is configured to receive an IP address automatically.

    f.   If the settings are manually configured, note them here, and verify them with the settings given to you by the instructor.

        IP address: _____

        Subnet mask: _____

        Default gateway: _____

        Preferred DNS server: _____

        Alternate DNS server: _____

        If the system is configured to obtain an address automatically, you will not be able to verify the values of the TCP/IP settings from this window.

    g.   Close this window by clicking OK.

Step 2   Next you'll use an alternate method of determining the IPv4 address; this works regardless of the address assignment method.

    a.   Launch a Command Prompt window (as described in Chapter 15) and, at the prompt, type the following command:

        `ipconfig /all`

    b.   This produces a listing similar to the one shown in Figure 19-3. Use these values to fill in the following settings for your primary network adapter and then verify them with your instructor.

        IPv4 Address: _____

        Subnet Mask: _____

        Default Gateway: _____

        DNS Servers: _____

➜ **Note**

If you are having trouble determining which is your primary network adapter (that is, the adapter that's in use), look for the one with a "Lease Obtained" line.

Step 3   If you are on a network that has its own DHCP server, your network adapter will have an assigned IP address. In a home network where a router shares an Internet connection, the router serves as the local DHCP server, and typically assigns local IPv4 addresses in the 192.168.x.x range. If Windows is configured to obtain an IP address automatically and no DHCP server is available, Windows automatically

```
Command Prompt                                              —  □  ✕

C:\Users\Mark E. Soper>ipconfig /all

Windows IP Configuration

    Host Name . . . . . . . . . . . . : Tiger-Athlon
    Primary Dns Suffix  . . . . . . . :
    Node Type . . . . . . . . . . . . : Hybrid
    IP Routing Enabled. . . . . . . . : No
    WINS Proxy Enabled. . . . . . . . : No

Ethernet adapter Local Area Connection:

    Connection-specific DNS Suffix  . :
    Description . . . . . . . . . . . : Realtek PCIe GBE Family Controller
    Physical Address. . . . . . . . . : C8-60-00-14-D3-FB
    DHCP Enabled. . . . . . . . . . . : Yes
    Autoconfiguration Enabled . . . . : Yes
    Link-local IPv6 Address . . . . . : fe80::6c5a:c90d:4169:13da%19(Preferred)
    IPv4 Address. . . . . . . . . . . : 192.168.1.154(Preferred)
    Subnet Mask . . . . . . . . . . . : 255.255.255.0
    Lease Obtained. . . . . . . . . . : Monday, January 28, 2019 11:45:26 AM
    Lease Expires . . . . . . . . . . : Tuesday, January 29, 2019 11:45:16 AM
    Default Gateway . . . . . . . . . : 192.168.1.1
    DHCP Server . . . . . . . . . . . : 192.168.1.1
    DHCPv6 IAID . . . . . . . . . . . : 231235584
    DHCPv6 Client DUID. . . . . . . . : 00-01-00-01-1A-6C-94-27-C8-60-00-14-D3-FB
    DNS Servers . . . . . . . . . . . : 208.67.222.222
                                        208.67.220.220
```

FIGURE 19-3 Windows ipconfig /all command results on a system configured to use DHCP

assigns an address in the 169.254.x.x range. That is called Automatic Private IP Addressing (APIPA). Follow these steps to explore APIPA:

a. In a classroom lab environment, have the instructor disable the DHCP server if applicable. Alternatively, you can disconnect the DHCP server's UTP cable from the hub or switch, or modify the router settings to not provide DHCP service.

b. Verify that your TCP/IP Properties settings are set to *Obtain an IP address automatically* and *Obtain DNS server address automatically*. Close all windows and reboot the system.

c. Launch a Command Prompt window and, at the prompt, type the following command:

ipconfig /all

d. Use the values that appear to fill in the following settings and then verify them with your instructor.

IPv4 Address: _____

Subnet Mask: _____

Default Gateway: _____

DNS Servers: _____ and _____

e. Exit the Command Prompt window and launch the TCP/IP Properties dialog box again. Return all settings to the normal classroom configuration. Click OK to finish, and close all the windows. Reboot the system, and verify that it's working properly and that you have reestablished network communication to its prior state.

 15 MINUTES

Lab Exercise 19.03: Verifying TCP/IP Settings in Linux

TCP/IP is the standard transport protocol for both local area networks and the Internet. Thus, any computers or devices on a LAN will use TCP/IP. If you work with networks that include Linux devices, you need to verify the TCP/IP settings they use.

Learning Objectives

In this exercise, you'll access and verify the TCP/IP settings for a given Linux system.

At the end of this lab, you'll be able to

- Install (if necessary) and use the NetworkManager and nmcli utilities

- Run nmcli to find the information needed

Lab Materials and Setup

The materials you need for this lab are

- A Linux system that's properly configured for LAN access

- A list of TCP/IP settings provided by the instructor

Getting Down to Business

Typically, in corporate environments, the network protocol configuration scheme has been defined by the senior systems administrators. Unless you've had some experience with the configuration, you would not automatically know all of the TCP/IP settings for a network. For instance, even when you're setting up a small network (one that connects to the Internet), you'll need to contact your Internet service provider (or at least read the user's manual) to set up your router's TCP/IP settings. So don't worry if you have no idea what settings to use. The trick is to learn how to get to them so that you know what they are.

TCP/IP requires each system to have two basic settings for accessing a LAN and two additional settings for accessing other LANs or the Internet. You can either configure your system to automatically obtain the following settings when you log on or you can specify them manually, depending on the requirements of your network:

- IP address (unique to the PC)

- Subnet mask (identifies network information)

- Default gateway (address of the router to the external realm)

- Domain Name System (DNS) server

Step 1   First, determine if your system has NetworkManager and nmcli installed.

   a.   Open a terminal window, as you learned to do in Lab Exercise 15.02, "Exploring the Command-Line Interface in Linux."

   b.   Type **nmcli** and press ENTER.

➔ **Note**

If this command isn't found, install NetworkManager. On a Debian-based system such as Ubuntu Linux, enter this command:

   sudo apt install network-manager

Enter the following commands to start and enable NetworkManager:

   sudo systemctl start network-manager
   sudo systemctl enable network-manager

Step 2   Type **nmcli device show** and press ENTER.

   a.   Refer to Figure 19-4 and record the following information:

      Name of active network adapter and type (General Device and General Type):

```
                          mark@mark-VirtualBox: ~                    ⊖⊡⊗
 File  Edit  View  Search  Terminal  Help
GENERAL.DEVICE:                   enp0s3
GENERAL.TYPE:                     ethernet
GENERAL.HWADDR:                   08:00:27:2D:55:87
GENERAL.MTU:                      1500
GENERAL.STATE:                    100 (connected)
GENERAL.CONNECTION:               Wired connection 1
GENERAL.CON-PATH:                 /org/freedesktop/NetworkManager/ActiveCo
WIRED-PROPERTIES.CARRIER:         on
IP4.ADDRESS[1]:                   10.0.2.15/24
IP4.GATEWAY:                      10.0.2.2
IP4.ROUTE[1]:                     dst = 0.0.0.0/0, nh = 10.0.2.2, mt = 100
IP4.ROUTE[2]:                     dst = 10.0.2.0/24, nh = 0.0.0.0, mt = 10
IP4.ROUTE[3]:                     dst = 169.254.0.0/16, nh = 0.0.0.0, mt =
IP4.DNS[1]:                       208.67.222.222
IP4.DNS[2]:                       208.67.220.220
IP6.ADDRESS[1]:                   fe80::9688:8734:8036:c15a/64
IP6.GATEWAY:                      --
IP6.ROUTE[1]:                     dst = ff00::/8, nh = ::, mt = 256, table
IP6.ROUTE[2]:                     dst = fe80::/64, nh = ::, mt = 256
IP6.ROUTE[3]:                     dst = fe80::/64, nh = ::, mt = 100

GENERAL.DEVICE:                   lo
GENERAL.TYPE:                     loopback
lines 1-23
```

FIGURE 19-4   Using the nmcli device show command on a system running Ubuntu Linux 18.04

IPv4 Address: _____   Default Gateway: _____

DNS Servers: _____ and _____

IPv6 Address: _____

b. If you see an address starting with 169. listed, that means the computer did not receive an IP address from a DHCP server. Note the address here: _____

 **15 MINUTES**

Lab Exercise 19.04: Verifying TCP/IP Settings in macOS

TCP/IP is the standard transport protocol for both local area networks and the Internet. Thus, any computers or devices on a LAN will use TCP/IP. If you work with networks that include macOS devices, you need to verify the TCP/IP settings they use.

Learning Objectives

In this exercise, you'll access and verify the TCP/IP settings for a given macOS system.

At the end of this lab, you'll be able to

- Find and view macOS TCP/IP settings from the macOS GUI

Lab Materials and Setup

The materials you need for this lab are

- A macOS system that's properly configured for LAN access

- A list of TCP/IP settings provided by the instructor

Getting Down to Business

Typically, in corporate environments, the network protocol configuration scheme has been defined by the senior systems administrators. Unless you've had some experience with the configuration, you would not automatically know all of the TCP/IP settings for a network. For instance, even when you're setting up a small network (one that connects to the Internet), you'll need to contact your Internet service provider (or at least read the user's manual) to set up your router's TCP/IP settings. So don't worry if you have no idea what settings to use. The trick is to learn how to get to them so that you know what they are.

TCP/IP requires each system to have two basic settings for accessing a LAN and two additional settings for accessing other LANs or the Internet. You can either configure your system to automatically obtain the following settings when you log on or you can specify them manually, depending on the requirements of your network:

- IP address (unique to the PC)

- Subnet mask (identifies network information)

- Default gateway (address of the router to the external realm)

- Domain Name System (DNS) server

Step 1 Start your macOS system and log into it. Then follow these instructions:

a. Click the Apple icon in the top-left corner and select System Preferences from the menu.

b. Click Network.

c. Click the Advanced button.

d. Click the TCP/IP tab (see Figure 19-5) and note the following:

IPv4 Address: _____

Subnet Mask: _____

Router: _____

IPv6 Address (if applicable): _____

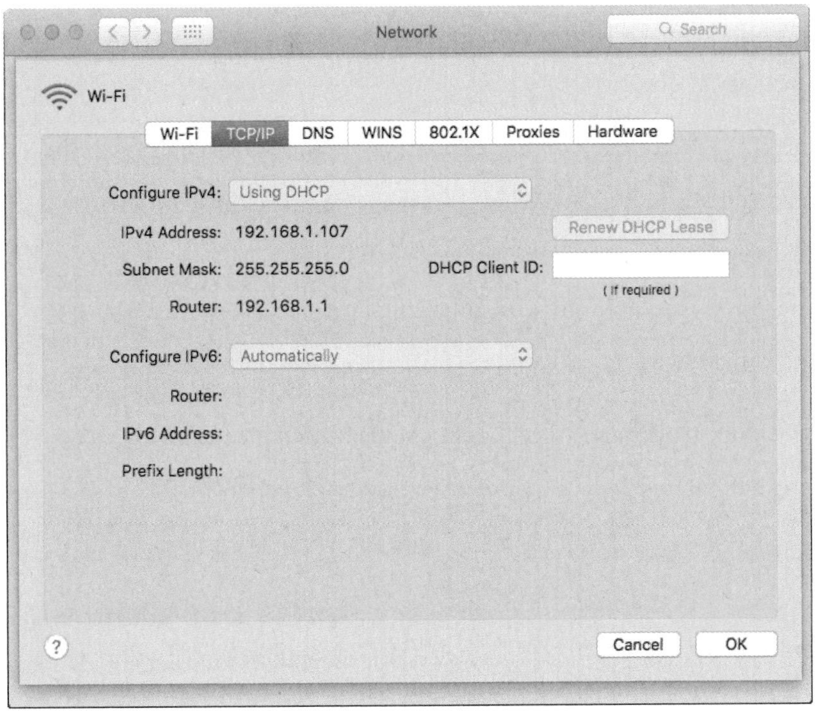

FIGURE 19-5 Viewing TCP/IP information on a system running macOS

    e.   Click the DNS tab and note the following:

       DNS Server: _____

       Record additional servers listed: _____

    f.   Click Cancel to close the Network dialog box.

 **30 MINUTES**

Lab Exercise 19.05: Testing Your LAN Connections in Windows, Linux, and macOS

Various tools are available that will help you test and troubleshoot your network. Chapter 19 of *Mike Meyers' CompTIA A+ Guide to Managing and Troubleshooting PCs* covers using these tools in detail. Some of these tools will be beneficial to you as a CompTIA A+ certified technician and are covered on the CompTIA A+ exams. This lab exercise lets you practice using several key network troubleshooting tools.

Learning Objectives

In this exercise, you'll be introduced to troubleshooting tools for determining proper installation of the network components. These tools are covered in order of importance. First, you'll verify the local settings. Next, you'll try to access other systems on the same LAN. Finally, you'll test the Internet connectivity.

At the end of this lab, you'll be able to

- Use the ipconfig command to determine local network settings
- Use the net config command to check the local system name and who is logged on as a user
- Use the ping command to test the local TCP/IP software and adapter
- Use the net view command to check for other computers on the network
- Use the ping command with switches to test connectivity to other computers
- Use the tracert command to check the path to other computers
- Use Linux/macOS equivalents for ping and tracert

Lab Materials and Setup

The materials you need for this lab are

- A PC system that's properly configured for network access using Windows
- A Linux or macOS system properly configured for network access
- Access to the Internet

✔ **Hint**

If you are not sure if the LAN is operational, test it by accessing another computer on the network using Windows Explorer/File Explorer, as described in Lab Exercise 19.06.

Getting Down to Business

As a PC technician, you should be familiar with several networking tools, both for your own good and because they're covered on the CompTIA A+ exams. You'll begin by using Windows commands, starting with ipconfig. Commands for Linux and macOS are covered later in this lab.

✔ **Hint**

Since you have already used the ipconfig /all command, run through the steps again, either on your own system or on a different lab machine. Ask the instructor if any different networks or system configurations are available to explore.

Step 1   You have already examined ipconfig for Windows in Lab Exercise 19.02. You'll now use the ipconfig command again to determine local network settings. As you have already learned, checking the TCP/IP settings is easy: just open a Command Prompt window, type **ipconfig /all**, and press ENTER. The details of your local network connection appear on the screen. If there are multiple network connections, focus on your primary network adapter (that is, the one that's currently providing your network connection).

➔ **Note**

If you are having trouble determining which is your primary network adapter, look for the one with a "Lease Obtained" line.

Record your settings here:

IPv4 Address: _____

Subnet Mask: _____

Default Gateway: _____

DNS Servers: _____

Leave the Command Prompt window open; you'll use it throughout the rest of this exercise.

Step 2   You'll now use the net config command to check the local system name and to see who is logged on as a user. To confirm the computer name and discover who is currently logged on, you'll again use the command line.

Type **net config workstation** at the command prompt and press ENTER. You'll see how the identification is set up for your local PC. There's a lot of information listed, but you're only interested in a couple of items (see Figure 19-6).

Note how these are listed:

Computer name: _____

User name: _____

Workstation domain (workgroup): _____

Software version: _____

Step 3   You'll now use the ping command to test the local TCP/IP software and adapter.

At the command prompt, type **ping 127.0.0.1** (including the periods) and press ENTER. This is known as the IPv4 loopback or localhost address and will test the TCP/IP software and the internal part of the local network card. Look at Figure 19-7 to see a successful test. If you don't see the test results, there are serious problems with the software. Reinstall your network drivers, and reconfigure the TCP/IP settings.

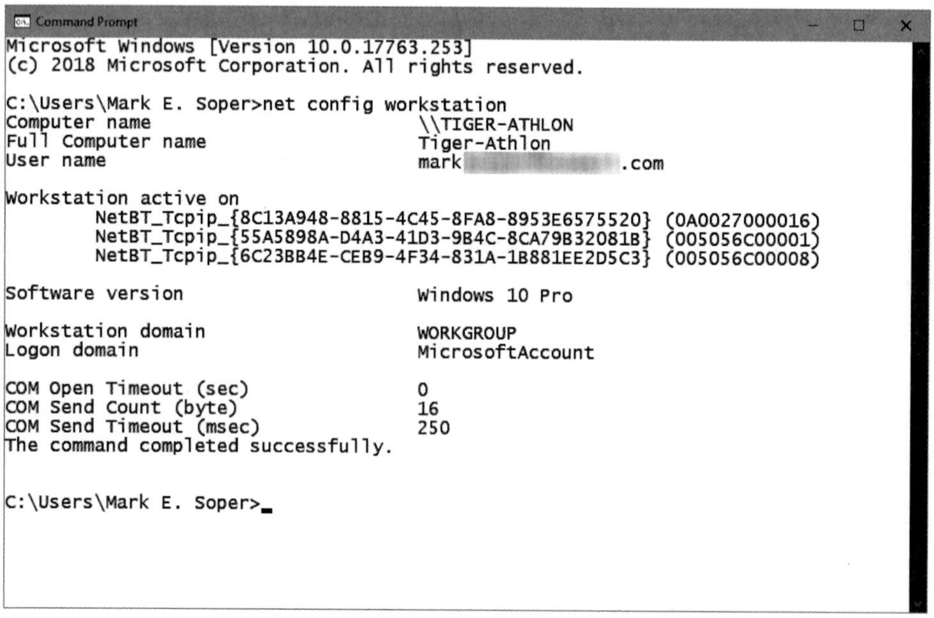

```
Command Prompt                                              —   □   ×
Microsoft Windows [Version 10.0.17763.253]
(c) 2018 Microsoft Corporation. All rights reserved.

C:\Users\Mark E. Soper>net config workstation
Computer name                    \\TIGER-ATHLON
Full Computer name               Tiger-Athlon
User name                        mark            .com

Workstation active on
        NetBT_Tcpip_{8C13A948-8815-4C45-8FA8-8953E6575520} (0A0027000016)
        NetBT_Tcpip_{55A5898A-D4A3-41D3-9B4C-8CA79B32081B} (005056C00001)
        NetBT_Tcpip_{6C23BB4E-CEB9-4F34-831A-1B881EE2D5C3} (005056C00008)

Software version                 Windows 10 Pro

Workstation domain               WORKGROUP
Logon domain                     MicrosoftAccount

COM Open Timeout (sec)           0
COM Send Count (byte)            16
COM Send Timeout (msec)          250
The command completed successfully.


C:\Users\Mark E. Soper>_
```

FIGURE 19-6 Using the net config workstation command in Windows 10

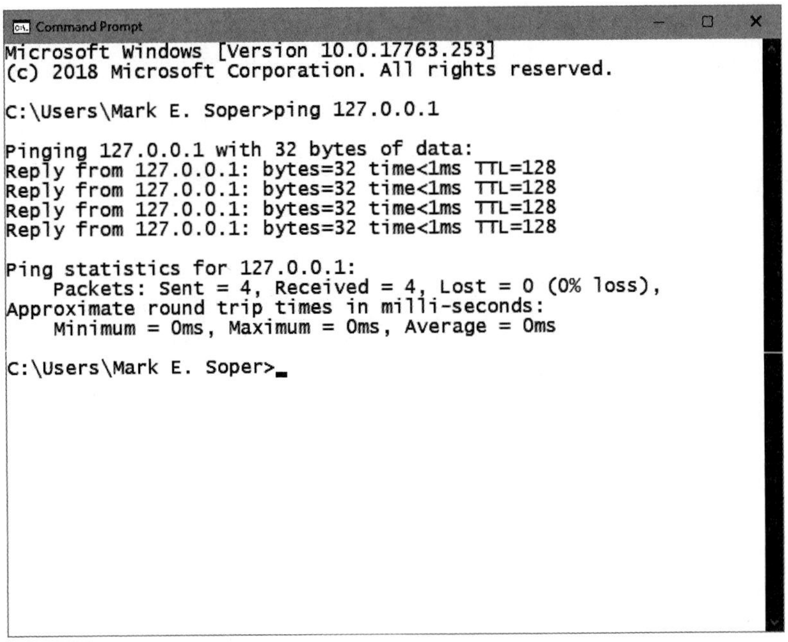

```
Command Prompt                                          —   □   ×
Microsoft Windows [Version 10.0.17763.253]
(c) 2018 Microsoft Corporation. All rights reserved.

C:\Users\Mark E. Soper>ping 127.0.0.1

Pinging 127.0.0.1 with 32 bytes of data:
Reply from 127.0.0.1: bytes=32 time<1ms TTL=128
Reply from 127.0.0.1: bytes=32 time<1ms TTL=128
Reply from 127.0.0.1: bytes=32 time<1ms TTL=128
Reply from 127.0.0.1: bytes=32 time<1ms TTL=128

Ping statistics for 127.0.0.1:
    Packets: Sent = 4, Received = 4, Lost = 0 (0% loss),
Approximate round trip times in milli-seconds:
    Minimum = 0ms, Maximum = 0ms, Average = 0ms

C:\Users\Mark E. Soper>_
```

FIGURE 19-7 A successful ping test in Windows

➜ **Note**

> **Want to see some IPv6 action? At the command prompt, type** ping ::1**. The IPv6 loopback address is ::1. When you ping it, it's just like running ping using 127.0.0.1, but it uses IPv6 instead.**

Step 4 You'll now use the net view command to check for other computers on the network.

You want to establish that other computers are available on the network so that you can test that your network card can transmit and receive data in Step 5.

At the command prompt, type **net view** and press ENTER. You'll see which other computers are on the network by a listing of their computer names (see Figure 19-8).

Step 5 Now you'll use the ping command to test your ability to connect to other computers on the network.

In Step 4 you obtained the names of other systems on the LAN, so now you want to check whether you can actually communicate with them.

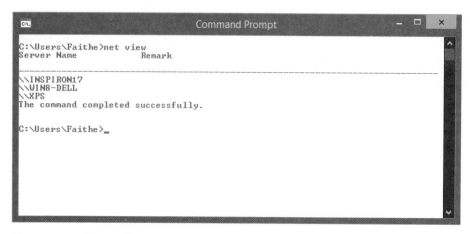

FIGURE 19-8 Using the net view command

At the command prompt, type **ping *computer name* –4**, where *computer name* is another PC's host name on the network you found in Step 4, and press ENTER. Be sure to put a space between the ping command and the computer name. The –4 switch forces IPv4 addressing. The results will look similar to when you used ping to see your own computer, but with the other computer's IP address (see Figure 19-9). If you get errors, use the net view command again to be certain of the computer name's spelling. If the DNS is down, you can adjust by pinging the other computer's IP address instead of its name.

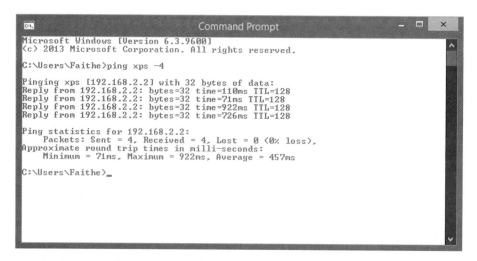

FIGURE 19-9 Pinging a computer by its name

✔ Try This: Ping Switches

The humble ping command is one of the most frequently used troubleshooting tools for TCP/IP. As you saw in Step 5, you can actually use ping to test whether DNS is working. If you do not receive a response from the computer using its host name, but you do receive a response when using the IP address, this points to a problem with DNS.

Ping also has a number of switches that add to the functionality of the command. If you need to explore the switches, type the following at the command prompt:

```
C:\>ping /?
```

This will list all of the available switches and their functions. The following combination is typically used for a connection that seems to drop packets intermittently. You would run the command indefinitely and increase the packet size to overload the connection. Type the following command:

```
C:\>ping -t -l 65000 computername
```

To stop the continuous ping, press CTRL-c to break the program.

Step 6 You'll now use the tracert command to check the path to other computers or Web sites on the Internet.

This command will show you where the bottlenecks are in the Internet. The tracert command will list the time it takes to get from your PC to the Web site or other system you're accessing. Follow these steps:

a. Type **tracert google.com**, and then press ENTER. If it was successful, note the following:

How many hops did it take? _____

What's the IP address of the first hop beyond your network? _____

b. Use the nslookup command with the IP address of the first hop to see where your first server is located.

Step 7 You'll now use the Linux and macOS ping and traceroute commands to check network and Internet connectivity.

Follow these steps:

a. Start Linux or macOS and open a terminal window.

b. Type **ping google.com** and then press ENTER.

If google.com responded, did the ping command stop after four pings? _____

c. Press CTRL-c to stop ping.

d. Type **traceroute –I google.com**, and then press ENTER. If it was successful, note the following:

How many hops did it take? _____

What's the IP address of the first hop beyond your network? _____

→ **Note**

You must use the –I option or traceroute will not provide a complete list of IP addresses. For additional options, use traceroute –help.

→ **Note**

You might need to install traceroute. In a Debian-based distro such as Ubuntu, install it with this command: sudo apt install inetutils-traceroute.

 **30 MINUTES**

Lab Exercise 19.06: Sharing Folders in Windows

With the network all set up properly, the next thing to do is decide how you want to share resources. You can share any folder or other resource. Optical drives, hard drives, and printers can all be shared.

Learning Objectives

In this lab, you'll set up file sharing for others to access information from their system.

At the end of this lab, you'll be able to

• Enable and configure shared directories and other resources

Lab Materials and Setup

The materials you need for this lab are

• Two Windows PCs on the same LAN or in the same Windows workgroup

Getting Down to Business

In a home network, it is common to share files among the PCs, such as music, documents, and videos. You can share any folders you like.

Step 1   First, verify that File and Printer Sharing is enabled on both PCs.

a.   Open the Network and Sharing Center.

- Windows 7/8.1: Right-click the network icon in the notification area and choose Open Network and Sharing Center. (That's a shortcut for the usual Control Panel method of accessing it.)

- Windows 10: Open Network & Internet Settings, scroll down, and click Network and Sharing Center.

b.   Click Change advanced sharing settings.

c.   Under Private (current profile), make sure that the following settings are enabled, as shown in Figure 19-10.

- Turn on network discovery

- Turn on file and printer sharing

- Allow Windows to manage homegroup connections (recommended)

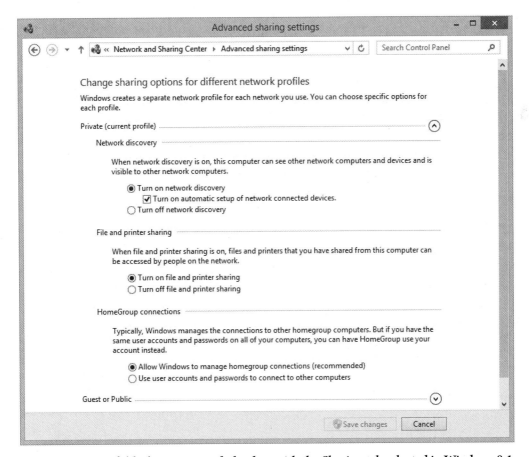

FIGURE 19-10   A folder's Properties dialog box with the Sharing tab selected in Windows 8.1

→ **Note**

Homegroup support was removed in Windows 10.

    d.   If you made any changes in Step c, click Save changes.

    e.   Close the Advanced sharing settings window.

Step 2   For this step, we'll arbitrarily designate one computer PC1 and the other PC2. Follow these steps to create and share a folder on PC1:

    a.   Open Windows Explorer/File Explorer and view the top level of the C: drive.

    b.   Create a new folder on the C: drive. Name it **Shared**.

    c.   Right-click the Shared folder icon and choose Properties. This will open the folder's Properties dialog box.

    d.   Click the Sharing tab.

    e.   Click the Share button. The *Choose people to share with* dialog box opens.

✔ **Tip**

Instead of Steps 2c through 2e, you can right-click the folder and choose Share with | Specific people.

    f.   Open the drop-down list and choose Everyone.

    g.   Click Add. The Everyone user represents global permissions that apply to all users.

    h.   In the Everyone row, open the drop-down list in the Permission Level column and choose Read/Write. See Figure 19-11.

    i.   Click the Share button.

    j.   Click Done.

    k.   Click Close.

    l.   Double-click the Shared folder to enter it.

    m.   Now create a file, just to have something to share. Right-click in the folder and choose New | Text Document. Type **ShareMe** and press ENTER.

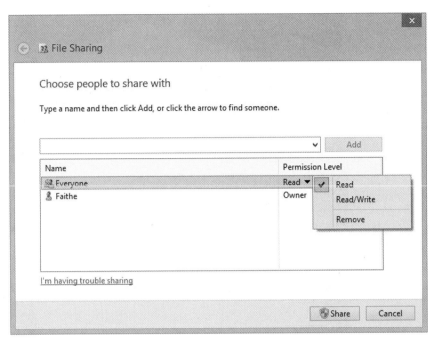

FIGURE 19-11 Change the Permission Level setting to Read/Write for the Everyone group.

Step 3   Now go to PC2 and open up Windows Explorer/File Explorer. Then do the following:

a.   In the navigation bar, click Network.

b.   In the Computer section, double-click the icon for PC1 to browse its files.

c.   Double-click the Shared folder. You should be able to browse its contents. It is empty at the moment.

d.   Double-click the ShareMe.txt file. Type a few words of text in it, save your work, and close it.

e.   Go back to PC1 and open up ShareMe.txt. Confirm that the text entered on PC2 appears in it; then close it.

f.   Right-click the Shared folder again and choose Share with | Stop sharing. That's an easy way to turn off the sharing for a folder.

g.   Right-click the Shared folder again and choose Properties. Check on the Sharing tab to confirm that the file is no longer shared. Then click Cancel to close the Properties box.

Lab Analysis Test

1. Joyce is trying to browse another Windows computer on her LAN via File Explorer. When she clicks Network, several other computers appear, but not the one she wants. What should she check?

2. Tom has just added to his home network a notebook computer that used to be part of a workgroup at his office. None of the existing computers can see or share files with the new computer, even though File and Printer Sharing is enabled for all of them. What should he do?

3. Larry has a home network that uses a router to share an Internet connection. When Larry uses ipconfig /all to get his computer's IP address, it comes back as 169.254.0.3. What does that tell you about Larry's router settings?

4. Rick is troubleshooting a problem with his network adapter, and a friend has told him to ping the loopback address. What command should Rick type at a command prompt?

5. Beth has several Windows computers and would like all of them to be able to share files. What feature must be enabled to enable computers to locate each other on the network?

Key Term Quiz

Use the following terms to complete the following sentences. Not all terms will be used.

APIPA	Network and Sharing Center
IPv4	ping
IPv6	TCP/IP
net config	tracert
net view	

1. The _____ is the area of the Control Panel in which you can access your network's properties and configuration.

2. _____ is the suite of protocols used both on the Internet and on most LANs.

3. 192.168.0.1 is an example of a(n) _____ address.

4. The _____ command can show other computers on the network from a command prompt.

5. The _____ command can test connectivity to other computers from a command prompt or terminal window.

Chapter 20
Wireless Networking

Lab Exercises

Wireless networks are very common today, so it's important for CompTIA A+ certified technicians to know as much about wireless networks as possible to provide quality service in any situation to the users they support. You need to know not only how to set up a wireless network, but also how to configure, troubleshoot, and secure that network. In the lab exercises in this chapter, you'll set up, configure, troubleshoot, and secure a couple of wireless networks so that you are prepared to do the same in a real-world setting.

 30 MINUTES

Lab Exercise 20.01: Setting Up a Wireless Network

Your friend is interested in starting a home business and has asked you to help him set up a wireless network. The only equipment he currently has is a desktop computer, a laptop computer, a mobile phone, and a USB printer, all of which he is considering using with his business. He wants to be able to communicate with his clients wirelessly from any room in his house. He's asked you to help him decide what additional equipment he needs to purchase.

Learning Objectives

This lab tests basic wireless network setup skills and helps you to think about scenarios you might encounter.

At the end of this lab, you'll be able to

- Recommend proper wireless equipment (for example, wireless cards and routers)

- Identify solutions for proper placement of equipment

- Set up and configure a wireless router

Lab Materials and Setup

The materials you need for this lab are

- A working desktop computer running Windows, with some form of broadband Internet connection

- A laptop with Wi-Fi capability

- Two Ethernet cables

- A wireless router

- A macOS computer with Wi-Fi capability (optional)

Getting Down to Business

First, you will help your friend identify his current hardware, and select a wireless router if he doesn't already have one. He'll also need a Wi-Fi adapter for his computer (if he doesn't have one already). Once he's purchased the necessary equipment, he needs to connect it.

Step 1 First, your friend will need to determine whether he already has a wireless router. The question is not as facile as it sounds, because many broadband modems have wireless router capabilities built into them. If he has such a unit, he doesn't need to buy a separate wireless router.

Here are some ways to tell whether the modem includes a wireless router:

- Look on the back of the modem. Are there multiple Ethernet ports? If so, that's a clue that the unit doubles as a router. If there's only one Ethernet port, it's probably a stand-alone modem, and that one port is for connecting to a separate wireless router.

- Use a wireless-capable device, such as a phone or laptop, to check for a wireless network. The device may already be broadcasting a wireless signal, unbeknownst to you.

- Have your friend call his Internet provider and ask them.

If your friend already has wireless router capability, you can skip Step 2. (For the purposes of learning, though, you may want to do Step 2 anyway, even if the equipment you are working with for this lab contains wireless capability.)

Step 2 If your friend doesn't have a wireless router, he will need to shop for one. It doesn't need to be an expensive one, but at a minimum it should support IEEE 802.11ac if he is buying a new one. (802.11n support is okay too if you already have a router with that capability on-hand, but 802.11ac is the newer standard.) IEEE 802.11 standards are mostly backward compatible, so an 802.11ac router will support devices that use 802.11a, b, g, or n.

➔ **Note**

The newest Wi-Fi standard, IEEE 802.11ax, is now available. It supports more efficient use of wireless spectra and data modulation for better throughput. 802.11ax also offers more channels and supports more simultaneous transmit-receive connections (MU-MIMO) than 802.11ac.

Go online and find three routers that would serve the purpose, and write information about them here:

	Router 1	Router 2	Router 3
Brand and model			
802.11 standard supported			
Price			
Special features, if any			

Step 3   Next, figure out how your friend's desktop computer is physically connected to the Internet. If you are at his home, chances are that he has a broadband modem that connects to his computer via an Ethernet cable.

If you're working with equipment where the router and the broadband modem are separate boxes, you'll need to insert the wireless router into the system. (Skip this step if your router and broadband modem are a single unit.)

a.   Disconnect the Ethernet cable from the computer, and plug it into the router instead. There is often a specific jack labeled "Internet" or "Uplink" or an Internet symbol indicating the jack to use (Figure 20-1).

b.   Plug in the router and turn it on, if it doesn't turn on automatically. The router is ready when all the lights remain on and steady. There may be one or two blinking lights—it's okay. If most of the lights are green, an amber or red light can signal a problem.

c.   Get a second Ethernet cable (Cat 5e or faster) and use it to connect the computer to one of the Ethernet jacks on the wireless router.

You may be thinking that this wireless network isn't looking very wireless so far, but think of it this way: how often do you pick up your entire desktop setup and move it into another room? Not very often, I'd wager. Wired connectivity is faster and more reliable than wireless, so if you have a computer sitting right next to the wireless router, it's best to connect them with a cable.

Step 4   Now that all the cables are in place, go to the Windows laptop and see if you can find the wireless network.

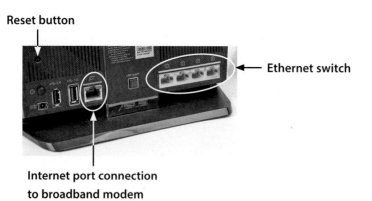

FIGURE 20-1 The rear of a typical wireless router with a built-in Ethernet switch

FIGURE 20-2 Connecting to a wireless network in Windows 7

You should see a wireless network icon in the notification area with a starburst on it; this indicates wireless networks are available. Click that icon to see the available networks. Then click the desired network (its name probably includes the brand name of the router in some form), and click Connect. Figure 20-2 shows a network available in Windows 7. In Windows 8.1, clicking the network icon in the notification area opens the Settings panel. From there, you can click an available network and click Connect, as shown in Figure 20-3. In Windows 10, clicking the network icon opens network-related settings in Quick Actions as well as available wireless networks, as shown in Figure 20-4.

FIGURE 20-3 Connecting to a wireless network in Windows 8.1

FIGURE 20-4   Connecting to a wireless network in Windows 10

→ **Note**

A new router usually doesn't have any security set up on it right out of the box, so you connect
to it immediately when you select it. If the router already has security enabled, you will need to
type a password or key code to connect to it. You'll learn more about security settings in Lab
Exercise 20.02.

Step 5 (optional)   Go to the macOS computer and see if you can find the wireless network.

You should see a wireless network icon at the top of the screen (see Figure 20-5). Click that icon to see the
available networks. Then click the desired network to connect to it (its name probably includes the brand name
of the router in some form).

FIGURE 20-5   Connecting to a wireless network in macOS

30 MINUTES

Lab Exercise 20.02: Configuring and Securing a Wireless Network

Now that you've installed a wireless router for your friend, you must configure it properly so that it is secure from pesky invaders. Be sure to follow these step-by-step instructions so you can reduce the chances of your friend's data being exposed, stolen, or attacked by hackers.

Learning Objectives

This lab enables you to configure and secure your friend's network.

At the end of this lab, you'll be able to

- Properly configure a wireless router

- Set up security options to keep intruders out

Lab Materials and Setup

The materials you need for this lab are

- A computer with a wireless network adapter running Windows 7 or later, already set up to connect to the wireless router

- A computer with a wired Ethernet connection to the router (optional but desirable; can be the same computer as in previous bullet)

- A wireless router
- An Ethernet cable

Getting Down to Business

Many people will simply hook up a wireless router, turn it on, and go about their business, not realizing what they've opened themselves up to. Without configuring security on a wireless router, you leave the network open to anyone who happens to come into range with a Wi-Fi-capable device. They not only can use the shared Internet connection, but can browse the shared files on the network, and potentially steal or even vandalize or delete private data. They might even change the router's password so that your friend is locked out of it. For this reason, it's important to password-protect access to the router, so that only authorized devices can use it.

The exact steps involved in configuring a router depend heavily on the router's built-in configuration software. The following steps lead you through the basics, but for more details, check the manual that came with the device.

Step 1   To secure your friend's wireless network, you will use the configuration tool included with his router/wireless access point.

If possible, it is best to access the configuration tool using a wired Ethernet connection to the router rather than a wireless one. The reason is that when you change the security settings, you may get bumped off of a wireless connection, but you won't have that problem with a wired connection. If the PC you are using has both wired and wireless network adapters, you can use the same PC for the whole exercise; if not, use two different PCs. A single PC with only a wireless connection may also work (some routers are configured to use only a wired connection for configuration), but you will need to log in again to the configuration utility at some point during the process.

To access the configuration utility, open a Web browser and type **http://192.168.1.1** (or sometimes **192.168.0.1** or **192.168.2.1**) into the address bar. Those are the most common addresses used for the setup utility.

What is the IP address of your router? _____

✔ **Hint**

Here's a way to determine the router's IP address if the addresses suggested don't work. Open a Command Prompt window and type ipconfig /all. **Look at the Default Gateway address; that's probably the router's address. You can also look in the router's documentation, either in the materials that came with the router or on the manufacturer's support Web site.**

You may get a pop-up dialog box or other screen asking for a user name and password. The defaults for these are often **admin** and **password**. This is true across multiple brands, which is all the more reason to change them as soon as possible!

Write down the router's default user name and password:

User name: _____

Password: _____

✔ **Tip**

If you can't get access to the router's configuration utility but you know you're using the correct address, first make sure you are including http:// at the beginning of the address. Some browsers require that. You might also try connecting to the router with an Ethernet cable rather than wirelessly. Sometimes this makes a difference.

Step 2 You should now be in the setup utility. Different devices use different names, but look for the Wireless Settings page. Figure 20-6 shows an example, but yours may look very different. Consult the router's documentation if you need help.

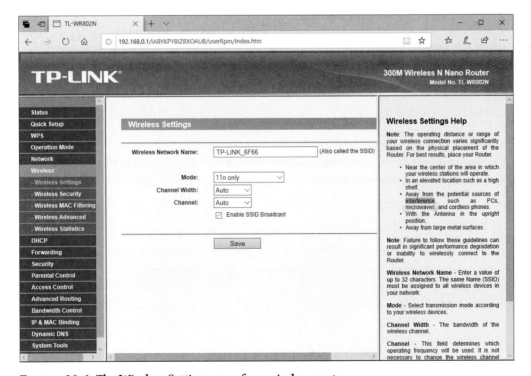

FIGURE 20-6 The Wireless Settings page for a wireless router

Look for a screen with network name options, security options, or MAC address options. Once you've found it, find the box used to enter a network name, or SSID. The default name is probably the brand name of the router. Delete the existing name and create a new one that is unique but memorable.

Step 3   Usually on the same page as the network name are Security Mode and Authentication options (although they may be on a separate page). These include choices such as WEP, WPA, WPA2, and None. If it's available, select WPA2-PSK or WPA-PSK+WPA2-PSK; otherwise, select WPA-PSK. WEP is an older encryption technology that is far less secure; use it only if the others aren't available (and on modern routers, they will be). Where prompted for Encryption Technique, choose TKIP+AES.

Where did you find these settings in the configuration utility? _____

There should also be an empty box labeled Pre-Shared Key (PSK), Password, or Passphrase. Enter a unique and memorable password of between 8 and 63 characters. It can include spaces and symbols. Save these settings.

What password did you set? _____

Step 4   Now that you've secured the wireless connection by enabling WPA2 or another encryption option, you need to secure the router itself. The default user name and password for every make and model of router is documented everywhere. Failing to change the defaults is an invitation to intruders. Find the setup utility's administration options, or something similar, and change the user name and password to something unique and memorable.

Write down the router's new user name and password:

User name: _____

Password: _____

→ **Note**

> You may hear suggestions that turning off the SSID broadcast will help secure your wireless Internet. This is actually a bit of a mixed bag. Users will still need to learn the SSID of your network to join it, but modern versions of Windows display available wireless networks even if the SSID isn't broadcast. Disabling the SSID broadcast makes it more difficult to join a wireless network, but it doesn't entirely hide your network.

Step 5   Now that the router has been secured, you'll need to connect to the router wirelessly using the new password. If you are connected to the router with an Ethernet cable on the PC you want to use to connect wirelessly, disconnect the Ethernet cable. (If you're using two separate PCs for this exercise, move to the PC with the wireless connection.)

Click the Network icon in the notification area to see the available networks, and choose the desired router (keeping in mind that you changed its SSID earlier in the exercise). You'll be prompted for the password; enter it and press ENTER. Windows will remember the password on this PC, so you don't have to re-enter it each time you connect.

→ **Note**

Some routers have an alternate method of allowing devices to connect called Wi-Fi Protected Setup (WPS). On some models it is referred to by other names, like push-button configuration. A WPS-capable router has an extra button (usually on the top), which may or may not be labeled. Check the documentation. When you push the button, the router becomes temporarily open to accepting new connections without a password. Then on the device, try connecting to the router. The router and the device will automatically negotiate a connection. You have to do it fast, though, because the router's openness expires within a couple of minutes, and you have to push the button again if you miss that window of opportunity. WPS is less secure than other setup methods.

 **20 MINUTES**

Lab Exercise 20.03: Troubleshooting Wireless Connectivity in Windows

There are many points of possible failure for a wireless network connection, and even more when you throw in Internet connectivity through the router. Fortunately, Windows provides a pretty good troubleshooting utility that can help you figure out what is wrong. In this lab exercise, you'll practice using this utility to identify and solve wireless problems.

Learning Objectives

This lab shows how to troubleshoot a wireless network connection.

At the end of this lab, you'll be able to

- Use the Windows Network Diagnostics utility to troubleshoot a problem

Lab Materials and Setup

The materials you need for this lab are

- A Windows 7 or later PC with a wireless connection to a router that provides Internet access

Getting Down to Business

It's not much good to troubleshoot a system where there's no problem, right? So in the following steps, you'll simulate some common problems, and then solve them.

Step 1   First we'll simulate a situation where the network adapter isn't working at all. This can happen for a variety of reasons. If it's an external adapter (USB, for instance), it might be unplugged. If it's a built-in wireless adapter, like on a laptop, the switch to enable/disable it might have gotten flipped.

    a.   Disable the wireless network adapter. If there's a button or switch on the device that does it, use that. (Most laptops have that.) If not, disable it in Device Manager, or put the PC in Airplane Mode (Windows 8 and higher).

    b.   In the notification area, how does the network icon appear now?

    _____

    c.   Right-click the network adapter and choose Troubleshoot problems.

    d.   The Windows Network Diagnostics wizard runs. What does it recommend you do?

    _____

    e.   Re-enable the network adapter.

    f.   Click Check to see if the problem is fixed. Windows should detect that the problem is fixed.

    g.   Click Close.

Step 2   Next, you'll see what happens when the network is working fine but there's no Internet.

    a.   Disconnect the Ethernet cable between the cable/DSL modem and the router. How does the network icon appear in the notification area now?

    _____

→ **Note**

> You can't do Step 2a if you have a combination modem and router, as provided by some cable and DSL providers. If that's the case, go to Step 3.

    b.   Right-click the network adapter and choose Troubleshoot problems.

   c.   The Windows Network Diagnostics wizard runs. What does it report?

_____

   d.   Reconnect the Ethernet cable between the modem and the router.

   e.   Click Next.

   f.   Click Close.

   g.   Display a Web site in your browser, just to make sure the Internet is working again.

Step 3   Next you'll simulate a situation where the adapter has lost its IP address, perhaps because the DHCP server is unavailable.

   a.   Open a command prompt with elevated privileges and run the command **ipconfig /release**.

✖ Cross-Reference

For details on opening a command prompt with elevated privileges, refer to the "Accessing the Command-Line Interface in Windows" section in Chapter 15 of Mike Meyers' CompTIA A+ Guide to Managing and Troubleshooting PCs.

   b.   Right-click the network icon in the notification area and choose Troubleshoot problems. What problem does it report?

_____

   c.   Click Try these repairs as an administrator.

   d.   Click Close.

   e.   Display a Web site in your browser, just to make sure the Internet is working again.

 **20 MINUTES**

Lab Exercise 20.04: Resetting a Wireless Router

Your friend failed to follow your advice about setting up a password for his router, and now he's in a pickle: some kid in his neighborhood hacked into his router and changed the wireless password, so none of his wireless devices can connect to it anymore. In this lab exercise you'll reset his router to the default factory configuration.

Learning Objectives

This lab shows how to reset a router to default factory settings.

At the end of this lab, you'll be able to

- Locate and use the Reset button on a router
- Locate and use the Restore Factory Defaults command in the configuration utility

Lab Materials and Setup

The materials you need for this lab are

- A wireless router
- A PC with a wired Ethernet connection to the router

Getting Down to Business

There are two ways to reset a router. If you can get into the configuration utility using a wired Ethernet connection, you can use the Restore Factory Defaults command in the utility. However, this method may require you to type an administrator password, and if you don't know it, you won't be able to reset it that way, and you'll need to use the hard Reset button on the router itself.

✖ Warning

If the wireless router is from the Internet service provider, or if it's a combined unit with a broadband modem, it might be configured in some non-default ways to work with your friend's Internet connection. If that's the case, don't go through with the resets in the following steps; follow the steps up to the point where you would do the actual reset, and then turn back.

Step 1 First let's look at the reset capabilities inside the configuration utility, assuming optimistically that you can get into it.

On a PC that is connected via wired Ethernet to the router, open a Web browser and connect to the router's configuration utility, as you did in Lab Exercise 20.02. Browse through the available options, looking for a Restore Factory Defaults setting. When you find that command, run it. You might be prompted to enter the router's administrator password, and there will probably be several "Are you sure?" confirmations and warnings.

Where did you find the reset command in the configuration utility? _____

FIGURE 20-7 Press the router's Reset button to wipe out all user-configured settings.

Step 2   Next, we'll go the route you must take if you can't get into the router setup, or you don't know the password required to do a factory reset there.

Scout around on the outside of the router for a button labeled Reset or Factory Reset. Figure 20-7 shows an example (a different example is shown in Figure 20-1). You might be able to press it with a finger, or you might need a bent paperclip or some other pointed object to press it. Press and hold the button for 10 seconds, and then release it. Then try accessing the configuration utility again. This time it should be in a pristine, factory-fresh state, with no passwords.

Where did you find the Reset button, and how was it labeled?

_____

✔ **Tip**

> If pressing the Reset button doesn't seem to do anything, check the router's documentation; it
> is possible you might have to hold down some other button at the same time, or press the Reset
> button as you power-on the router. Each model has its own quirks.

Step 3   Finally, put things back the way they need to be on the router for the next student who will be using it. Ask your instructor what that entails. Resetting the router wipes out all user-configured settings, including security settings and passwords, so if your friend in our scenario were going to continue to use this router, you would have to repeat Lab Exercise 20.02 at this point to re-enable security. Ask your instructor if you should do this, or leave the router in its present state.

Lab Analysis Test

1. Suppose you have a laptop with a built-in 802.11n adapter. Will it work with an 802.11ac router? Why or why not?

2. What are the primary differences between WEP, WPA, and WPA2?

3. What does it mean when the network icon in the notification area has a yellow triangle with an exclamation point on it?

4. Why is it important to enable security on a wireless router?

5. How do you start the Windows Network Diagnostics troubleshooter?

Key Term Quiz

Use the following terms to complete the following sentences. Not all terms will be used.

802.11ac	Start menu
802.11b	WEP
desktop	WPA
notification area	WPA2
PSK	wireless router

1. A wireless network adapter connects a computer to a(n) _____.

2. When shopping for a wireless router, look for one that supports the _____ standard.

3. A(n) _____ is a password needed to connect a device to a wireless router.

4. To troubleshoot a network connection in Windows, right-click the Network icon in the _____ and choose Troubleshoot problems.

5. When securing your wireless network, use _____ encryption because it is the most secure.

Chapter 21

The Internet

Lab Exercises

The Internet is a complex system of communication that enables computers, in-business networks, mobile computers, and home PCs to share information worldwide. With smartphones, tablets, and other personal devices, we can connect to the Internet from almost anywhere and access applications, download music, and do many other tasks.

Because nearly everyone wants access to the Internet, implementing and troubleshooting Internet connectivity is a PC technician's bread and butter. The CompTIA A+ certification exams recognize this and test you on the details of installing and configuring a connection to the Internet.

This heightened usage brings with it a new task for the PC technician: Internet security! Since most computers are now communicating with the world through the Internet, the exposure to malicious intruders and programs has greatly increased. Two components that go hand-in-hand with the Internet are firewalls and wireless network security. You just finished setting up and configuring the hardware portion of a wireless network in the last chapter, so now you'll look at the software side of network security. This chapter's first lab exercise guides you through the properties of current Internet connection technologies. The next lab takes you through the steps needed to evaluate the Internet connection technologies available in your neighborhood. Finally, you'll explore the configuration of Windows Firewall.

✖ Cross-Reference

Computer security is such an important component of a PC technician's training that the topic receives its own chapter in both the textbook and the lab manual. Refer to Chapter 27 in *Mike Meyers' CompTIA A+ Guide to Managing and Troubleshooting PCs*. Chapter 27 of this lab manual also includes additional lab exercises to build your security awareness.

 30 MINUTES

Lab Exercise 21.01: Assessing Current Internet Connectivity

A new client has signed up with your firm, requesting that you evaluate their current Internet connectivity and recommend the best upgrade path for their six-person office, which consists of four desktop PCs and two laptops. Your first job is to assess what method each machine is currently using to connect to the Internet and what speeds it is achieving, and to make a recommendation for upgrades if necessary.

Learning Objectives

In this lab exercise, you will evaluate an existing Internet connection to determine its method, properties, and performance.

At the end of this lab, you'll be able to

- Verify the current Internet connectivity method

- Check the properties of a connection

- Benchmark the current connection speed

Lab Materials and Setup

The materials you need for this lab are

- A working computer running Windows with some form of Internet connection

- Internet connectivity to perform your research

Getting Down to Business

First, you will visually inspect each computer and its surroundings for the method used to connect to the Internet. Then you will run an Internet utility to determine the speed of the connection and appropriate upgrade paths.

Step 1   Look at the back of the computer:

- Are there any USB or network (RJ-45) cables plugged into the system? Trace the wires. Do they connect to a broadband modem? This could be your connectivity method. The modem is probably associated with cable or DSL service. To distinguish between them, note how the modem connects to a wall outlet. If it uses a telephone cable, it's DSL; if it uses coaxial cable, it's cable.

- Is there a network patch cable plugged into the NIC that connects it directly into a router or to an Ethernet jack in the wall? You may be connecting to the Internet through a LAN.

- Are you on a system with wireless connectivity? You could have access to the Internet through a wireless access point (WAP) or wireless router connected to a broadband modem.

- Is there a satellite dish outside the building provided by Viasat or HughesNet? You could have satellite service. There will be a broadband modem that works with that satellite dish inside the building, similar to the broadband modem provided for cable or DSL.

These are the possibilities a technician is faced with today, so the more you can explore the various methods of connectivity, the more knowledgeable you will be.

Examine the physical components that constitute the method your system uses to connect to the Internet, and then record the details of the hardware/connectivity type here:

_____

_____

Step 2   Now you'll test the current Internet connection speed using two different utilities.

    a.   Open a browser window on one of the PCs you want to assess (any browser will do).

    b.   Navigate to www.dslreports.com/speedtest. This is DSL Reports' Speed Test.

    c.   Follow the onscreen instructions to test the speed of your connection. Record the test results:

        Download speed: _____

        Upload speed: _____

    d.   Navigate to www.speedtest.net.

    e.   Follow the onscreen instructions to test the speed of your connection. Record the test results:

        Download speed: _____

        Upload speed: _____

Step 3   Do a Web search to find out the difference in technology and performance between ADSL, ADSL2, and ADSL2+ and explain your findings.

_____

_____

Step 4 Based on the results of the analysis of your client's Internet connection method and performance, what recommendations would you make to improve the performance of the Internet connections?

_____

_____

_____

 **30 MINUTES**

Lab Exercise 21.02: Evaluating Internet Connection Choices

You determine that the client's office is currently sharing a single standard ADSL (ADSL1) line among all the PCs in the network, using a simple six-port router that supports both wired and wireless connections. Standard ADSL has a theoretical maximum of 8 Mbps, but in practice the client's machines are actually achieving about 2 Mbps. You decide to recommend either a higher-speed ADSL service or cable or fiber, depending on availability in the office location. You'll research the options available at your current address (or another address of your choosing, or as assigned by your instructor) and evaluate which is the fastest and the best value.

Learning Objectives

In this lab exercise, you will research the Internet connection possibilities at a certain location, and estimate the performance to be had if a certain technology is selected.

At the end of this lab, you'll be able to

- Determine the available Internet connection technologies at a specific address
- Estimate the expected speed of service using a specific technology at a specific address

Lab Materials and Setup

The materials you need for this lab are

- A computer with Internet access

Getting Down to Business

Fiber, where available, provides the highest-speed service for a small business, followed by cable. Newer DSL technologies are also appealing, and may be less expensive, but for DSL service speed over traditional copper wires, the farther away you are from the central office (the phone company's DSL hub), the slower the speed.

If any part of the path is over fiber optic cable, that distance is not a factor on the fiber optic portion, however, and since more and more DSL providers are using fiber optics these days, including running fiber optics all the way to the individual house, distance has become less of an issue in recent years.

In our scenario company, we already know that standard ADSL is available because that's what the company is using now. It remains to be determined, however, whether other DSL technologies are available, and whether cable is available.

Step 1   First, find the central office closest to you, and determine how many feet it is between it and the desired service address.

a.   Open a web browser and go to www.sandman.com/colookup.asp.

b.   Enter the area code or ZIP code of the location for which you want to look up the nearest central office and click Search. A list of locations matching that area code or ZIP code appears. Locate the one that's closest to the actual address, and see who owns it. For example, in Figure 21-1, there are two central offices in the ZIP code 46060: one owned by Ameritech and the other by Verizon. (One of them has four different listings, but the same address for each listing.)

The company or companies listed are the ones you will want to shop for DSL service. Write the company name(s) here: _____

Central Office (CO) Search Results   (Click **HERE** to Search Again)

Search by Address

Area/Ex	CLLI	Address	CO Type/Owner/Company Type
Central Offices with matching Address			
317770	NBVLIN01DS0 Map It! Test Numbers	212 S 9TH ST NOBLESVILLE, IN 46060 Show All COs at this address -or- Show All Exchanges at this CO	Siemens EWSD Switching System AMERITECH INDIANA RBOC
317773	NBVLIN01DS0 Map It! Test Numbers	212 S 9TH ST NOBLESVILLE, IN 46060 Show All COs at this address -or- Show All Exchanges at this CO	Siemens EWSD Switching System AMERITECH INDIANA RBOC
317774	NBVLIN01DS0 Map It! Test Numbers	212 S 9TH ST NOBLESVILLE, IN 46060 Show All COs at this address -or- Show All Exchanges at this CO	Siemens EWSD Switching System AMERITECH INDIANA RBOC
317776	NBVLIN01DS0 Map It! Test Numbers	212 S 9TH ST NOBLESVILLE, IN 46060 Show All COs at this address -or- Show All Exchanges at this CO	Siemens EWSD Switching System AMERITECH INDIANA RBOC
317877	WSFDINXBRS0 Map It! Test Numbers	6299 E 211 ST WESTFIELD, IN 46060 Show All COs at this address -or- Show All Exchanges at this CO	Auto/Elec GTD5-EAX Digital Remote VERIZON NORTH INC.-IN ICO

FIGURE 21-1   **Example search results for the nearest central office**

    c. Click Map It! to see the location in MapQuest. If the link doesn't work, manually open a mapping program, like MapQuest or Google Maps. Get directions from this address to the desired service address to find out the distance in miles.

    d. Convert the distance from miles to feet. There are 5280 feet in 1 mile. How many feet is the location from the central office? _____

Step 2 Now you'll estimate ADSL performance at the service address. Here's a way to roughly estimate standard ADSL service:

- 6-Mbps service:

  - On fiber optics for all or most of the distance (less than 6000 feet between you and where the fiber optics ends), or

  - Within 6000 feet of the central office with copper cable only

- 3-Mbps service:

  - On fiber optics but more than 6000 feet from where the fiber optics ends, or

  - Within 12,000 feet of the central office with copper cable only

- 1.5-Mbps service:

  - On fiber optics but more than 12,000 feet from where the fiber optics ends, or

  - Within 18,000 feet of the central office with copper cable only

Not assuming any help from fiber optics (because there's no easy, reliable way of finding out where the fiber optic cables are in your area), what is the highest speed of ADSL service you can expect to get at this location?

_____

Step 3 For the company or companies you identified in Step 1b, visit their Web site and go through the process of inquiring about ADSL service. Find out the maximum speed available to the service location and the cost per month. Write your findings here:

_____

_____

_____

_____

Step 4   Visit the Web site of AT&T (www.att.com) and go through the process of inquiring about AT&T Internet (formerly U-verse) service. AT&T Internet is a high-speed type of DSL service (VDSL2+ or ADSL2+) that uses fiber optic cable to achieve higher speeds than are normally possible with ADSL. Find out the maximum speed available to the service location and the cost per month. Write your findings here:

_____

_____

_____

_____

Step 5   Visit the Web site of your local cable TV provider and go through the process of inquiring about broadband Internet service. Find out the maximum speed available to the service location and the cost per month. Write your findings here:

_____

_____

_____

_____

Step 6   Based on the research you did in the preceding steps, what is the best balance of performance and value for this client? Explain your answer:

_____

_____

_____

_____

 **60 MINUTES**

Lab Exercise 21.03: Working with Firewalls and Ports

Assuming that the new Internet connection is up and running for your client, you'll now want to have a look at the firewall situation. You'll need to make sure that each PC is protected by a firewall of some kind. In this lab exercise, you will check each PC to make sure Windows Firewall is enabled, and you'll poke around in the router's configuration utility to see if there is a firewall there that could potentially be enabled. Then you'll use a free utility called CurrPorts to check out what ports are in use during normal PC operations. Finally, you'll review the commonly used port numbers for various activities, which you may need to know when you take the CompTIA A+ 220-1001 exam, and take a look at an e-mail application in which you can choose specific ports to use for mail.

Learning Objectives

Completing the following steps, you will make sure Windows Firewall is enabled, and configure it to allow a certain application through the firewall. You'll check the router's configuration utility for a firewall feature, and you'll check port usage on one of the PCs.

At the end of this lab, you'll be able to

- Access Windows Firewall settings
- Allow an application to pass through Windows Firewall
- Assess a router's firewall capabilities
- Assess port usage
- Configure Outlook to use specific ports with a particular mail server

Lab Materials and Setup

The materials you need for this lab are

- A working computer running Windows 7 or later
- An Internet connection through a router
- Microsoft Outlook 2013 or later (other e-mail applications may also work, but steps will be different)

Getting Down to Business

As a technician, you'll need a good basic understanding of firewalls and ports: what they are and what they do. You'll need to understand the difference between software and hardware firewalls, and how each one protects individual computers and LANs. You'll also need to understand the role of ports in network and Internet operation, and be able to identify which ports are traditionally used for certain activities.

Step 1   First, you'll check to see whether Windows Firewall (also known as Windows Defender Firewall in Windows 10) is already enabled, and enable it if not.

Windows 7/8.1

a.   Open the Control Panel and choose System and Security | Windows Firewall.

b.   From this screen you can determine whether or not the firewall is currently enabled. If there are green bars and checkmarks, it's enabled. If there are red bars and Xs, it's disabled. In Figure 21-2, Windows Firewall is disabled for private networks and enabled for public ones.

c.   If the firewall is not turned on for both Private networks and Guest or public networks, click Use recommended settings to turn it on.

Windows 10

a.   Click Start | Settings | Update & Security | Windows Security | Firewall & network protection to see Windows Firewall settings (or open the Windows Defender Firewall applet in the Control Panel).

b.   From this screen you can determine whether or not the firewall is currently enabled. If there are green checkmarks, it's enabled. If there are red Xs, it's disabled. In Figure 21-3, Windows Firewall is enabled for all networks.

c.   If the firewall is not turned on for all networks, click each network and turn it on.

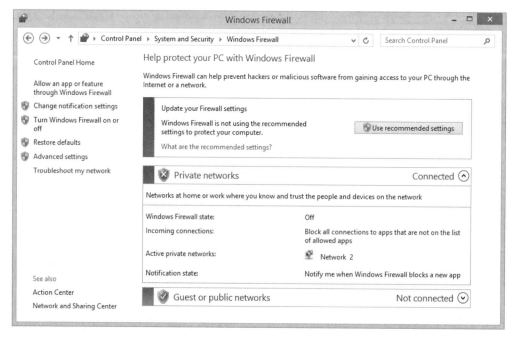

FIGURE 21-2 Windows Firewall is enabled for public networks.

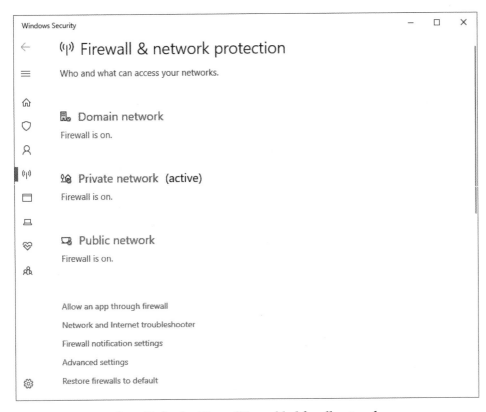

FIGURE 21-3 Windows Defender Firewall is enabled for all networks.

Step 2 Windows Firewall sometimes makes mistakes. If it thinks a particular program's activity is suspicious, it blocks it, and that means the program can't work as intended. Here's how to allow a program through the firewall:

a. From the Windows Firewall applet (see Figures 21-2) or Firewall Settings (see Figure 21-3), click Allow an app or feature through Windows Firewall or Allow an app through firewall.

b. By default, the list is read-only. Click Change settings to make it editable.

c. Scroll down to Remote Event Log Management and check the Private check box. See Figure 21-4.

d. Click Details to see information about the item you just enabled. Click OK to close the dialog box.

e. Click OK to close the Allowed apps window.

f. Back in the Windows Firewall applet, click the Restore defaults hyperlink at the left (in Windows 10 Firewall Settings, click the Restore firewalls to default hyperlink).

g. Click the Restore defaults button.

h. Click Yes to confirm.

i. Close the Control Panel or Settings app (Windows 10).

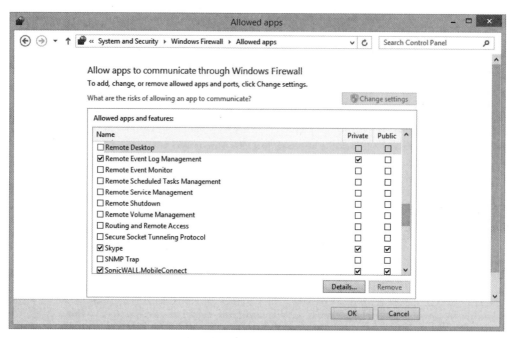

FIGURE 21-4 You can allow or disallow individual applications and services here.

Step 3   Most routers have their own firewall functionality, but it may be disabled by default. Check your router to see the available options.

a.   Using a Web browser, access your router's configuration utility, as you did in Lab Exercise 20.02.

b.   If you find a firewall, enable it, and write the steps you took here:

_____

_____

_____

c.   In Windows, do the following to simulate what an average user would need on the Internet: send and receive mail, visit secure and unsecure Web sites, and connect to an FTP site. Make sure that none of them are blocked by the router firewall. In the following space, record the applications you checked and whether or not each one worked normally.

_____

_____

_____

✔ **Tip**

If you have a hardware firewall in your router, do you need Windows Firewall? The short answer is yes. The two overlap in functionality, but they are not the same. A router protects against threats from the Internet (that is, traffic from outside your LAN), but it doesn't protect against infection from within your LAN. If one of the computers gets infected (perhaps while it's connected to some other network) and you bring it home to your LAN, it could infect the other computers on the LAN. A software firewall such as Windows Firewall protects against this type of internal network infection.

Step 4 In some earlier versions of Windows (such as Windows XP), Windows Firewall enabled you to browse and configure specific ports easily. Modern versions of Windows don't allow that, but you can still browse ports using a third-party utility. Follow these steps to experiment with CurrPorts, a simple utility that can tell you which port(s) particular applications and processes are using.

➜ **Note**

Ports can use either TCP or UDP to send and receive data. The application decides which to use, based on the data. TCP includes error correction, and is used in situations where you need to receive all the packets, such as when transferring data via FTP. UDP is faster because it includes no error correction; it's used when a few lost packets aren't important, such as in video streaming and online gaming.

a. Open a Web browser, navigate to www.nirsoft.net/utils/cports.html, and download CurrPorts. (The download link is near the bottom of the page.) It comes in a .ZIP file.

b. Copy the executable out of the .ZIP file and place it in any folder you like. Then double-click it to run cports.exe.

c. Note what ports your Web browser uses. Are they TCP or UDP?

_____

d. Click the Local Port Name column heading to sort by that field, and then scroll down to the bottom of the list to see all the port numbers that also list local port names. Note which port number is associated with the local port name *netbios-ns*. Is it TCP or UDP?

_____

e. Open Task Manager. To do so, press CTRL-ALT-DELETE and then click Task Manager.

f. If you don't see the tabbed view, click More Details.

g. Click the Details tab.

h. Find the explorer.exe line, and note the process ID (PID): _____

i. Switch back to the CurrPorts utility and click the Process ID column to sort by that field. Then locate the corresponding line for the PID you noted in Step h. What local port number is this process using? _____

j. Close Task Manager. Leave CurrPorts open for the next step.

Step 5 Certain ports are commonly assigned to certain application and utility protocols. You need to know these for the CompTIA A+ 220-1001 exam.

a. Fill in the port numbers in Table 21-1, entering any that you already know from memory and then using Tables 21.1 and 21.2 in *Mike Meyers' CompTIA A+ Guide to Managing and Troubleshooting PCs* or an online reference to fill in the gaps.

Application/Utility Protocol	Function	Port Number(s)
AFP	macOS file services	
DHCP	Automatic IP addressing	
DNS	Allows the use of DNS naming	
FTP	File transfer	
HTTP	Web pages	
HTTPS	Secure Web pages	
IMAP	Incoming e-mail	
LDAP	Querying directories	
POP3	Incoming e-mail	
RDP	Remote Desktop	
SFTP	Secure file transfer	
SIP	Voice over IP	
SMB	Windows naming/folder sharing; also CIFS	
SMTP	Outgoing e-mail	
SNMP	Remote management of network devices	
SSH	Encrypted terminal emulation	
Telnet	Terminal emulation	

TABLE 21-1 Common TDP and UDP Protocols

b. Using the port numbers from Table 21-1, sort the list in CurrPorts by the Local Port column, and then see which of these common port assignments are in use. Note them here:

_____

_____

_____

_____

➔ **Note**

Don't worry if you don't find many match-ups in Step 5b. CurrPorts lists only ports that are actively in use. So, for example, if you weren't sending e-mail the moment that CurrPorts generated its listing, you won't see SMTP using port 25.

c. Close the CurrPorts application.

Step 6 An e-mail application will tend to use the default port assignments for an e-mail account unless told otherwise. In other words, for a POP3 account, it'll use port 110 for incoming mail and 25 (SMTP) for outgoing mail. Some e-mail providers require you to use different ports, though, mainly to achieve greater security.

In most e-mail client applications, you can configure an account to use whatever ports the provider specifies. Here's how to make a change to an account's ports in Microsoft Outlook. (If you don't have Outlook available, feel free to follow along to review the steps.)

a. Open Outlook, and choose File | Account Settings | Account Settings.

b. Click the account you want to work with (any POP3/SMTP account will do) and click Change.

c. Click More Settings.

d. Click the Advanced tab. The port numbers in use appear, as shown in Figure 21-5.

What is the port listed for the incoming server? _____

What is the port listed for the outgoing server? _____

Is the port for the incoming server the same as the one listed in Table 21-1 in Step 5?

_____

Is the port for the outgoing server the same as the one listed in Table 21-1 in Step 5?

_____

e.   Mark or clear the This server requires an encrypted connection (SSL) checkbox. How did the Incoming server change? Click it again to return it to its previous setting.

_____

f.   Click Use Defaults. Did any values change to the values listed in Table 21-1 in Step 5? Which ones?

_____

_____

_____

_____

g.   Click Cancel to close the dialog box without saving the changes.

h.   Close all remaining dialog boxes without saving changes and exit Outlook.

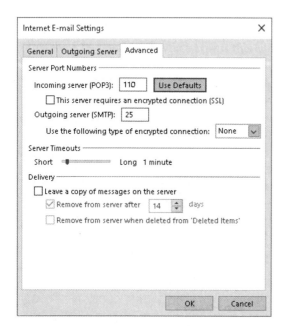

Figure 21-5 You can use specific ports for an e-mail account in some mail applications (Outlook 2016 shown here).

Lab Analysis Test

1. Tanner has paid extra to his cable company for the highest speed of Internet connectivity, but browsing speeds seem slow. How can he determine what speed he is actually getting?

2. Brandon lives out in the country, where no cable or DSL is available. He is currently on dial-up; what type of service might he consider instead?

3. Andrew is considering a fiber optic ADSL2+ Internet service, but he lives more than 18,000 feet from the central office. Will he be limited to 1.5 Mbps service? Why or why not?

4. Cindy wants to use an FTP program that she has just installed, but it doesn't find an Internet connection. All her other applications find the Internet just fine. What should she check?

5. Mary recently enabled the firewall feature on her home router. When her son Tom comes home from school and tries to play his favorite online game, it tells him that it can't get an Internet connection. Can Tom solve this problem by adjusting the Windows Firewall settings? Why or why not?

Key Term Quiz

Use the following terms to complete the following sentences. Not all terms will be used.

80	copper
110	dial-up
443	digital
Administrative Tools	fiber optic
analog	firewall
cables	packets
central office	ports
Control Panel	Services app

1. Port number _____ is used for Web sites that begin with https://.

2. To access Windows Firewall, go through the _____.

3. ADSL using _____ line is not subject to the same distance restrictions as regular DSL over _____ line.

4. A(n) _____ can be either hardware-based or software-based.

5. Firewalls secure a network by blocking unauthorized access to _____.

Chapter 22
Virtualization

Lab Exercises

Virtualization has taken over the computing world, especially when it comes to nearly every server on the Internet. Using virtual machines, you can run an entire virtual operating system on top of your existing OS. If you have Windows 10 installed, for example, you can download a virtualization application like Oracle VM VirtualBox, install Ubuntu Linux on it, and run Ubuntu inside Windows! The difference between software and hardware gets confusing when you realize that the virtual OS uses virtual hardware to re-create almost everything in the system case beneath your desk.

Virtualization promotes efficient use of hardware and energy resources, and also enables you to easily create images of the virtual machine, providing excellent fault tolerance and disaster recovery options.

In this chapter, you'll explore some of the features of common virtual machine technologies, install a couple of different virtual machine manager (VMM) programs (*hypervisors*), and install an operating system on each one. Although VMware is the most popular virtual machine software, the two hypervisors we'll be using in this chapter, VirtualBox and Hyper-V, have the advantage of being free.

In Lab Exercises 22.02 and 22.03, you will be using virtualization software to create virtual machines. Virtual machines are exactly like physical computers in that they need operating systems to work. Prior to beginning the lab exercises, you will want to prepare the operating system installation media. Lab Exercise 22.02 requires a copy of Ubuntu Linux, which you can download from www.ubuntu.com. Create an installation disc or copy the installation disc image (ISO) to a flash drive for use in the lab exercises. You can find instructions for this procedure on the Ubuntu Web site. Lab Exercise 22.03 requires any version of Windows on a bootable CD or DVD, or an equivalent ISO file.

 **20 MINUTES**

Lab Exercise 22.01: Identifying Virtualization Technologies

As discussed in the introduction to this chapter, virtualization takes on many aspects of the physical devices used every day in the computing environment. Organizations may choose to install multiple virtual servers on one physical machine to handle Web services, e-mail services, file sharing, and print services, to name a few. Before you work with the actual virtualization programs and before you take the CompTIA A+ certification exams, you will want to explore all of the technologies associated with virtualization.

Time to explore!

Learning Objectives

In this lab exercise, you will research virtualization technologies.

At the end of this lab, you'll be able to

- Define virtual desktop technologies
- Define virtual server technologies

Lab Materials and Setup

The materials you need for this lab are

- A PC with Internet access

Getting Down to Business

You will actually install and configure a number of virtualization technologies and operating systems in upcoming lab exercises. Before you do, it is important that you understand the underlying solutions that virtualization technology provides. In this lab, you will use the Internet to develop a brief description and summary of the characteristics of the virtualization technologies. Refer to Chapter 22 of *Mike Meyers' CompTIA A+ Guide to Managing and Troubleshooting PCs* to supplement your research.

Step 1   Start by researching virtual desktop technology. There's plenty of information to be found using Google. Use keywords like "virtualization" or "VMware" (a popular brand) to locate good information. What are the key features of most virtual desktops?

_____

_____

_____

Step 2   Virtual servers are similar to virtual desktops but provide some advanced features and support for applications not found in the virtual desktop offerings. Describe the differences between a virtual desktop and a virtual server.

_____

_____

_____

_____

 **60 MINUTES**

Lab Exercise 22.02: Installing and Using VirtualBox

To introduce you to virtualization, you will download Oracle VM VirtualBox, install it on a Windows 7 or later machine, and then run Ubuntu Linux in the virtual machine. You'll see what it's like running a second OS inside your native OS.

VirtualBox is not going to be your first choice for a heavy-duty production environment where you are managing lots of virtual servers. It's a fairly simple utility, although it's very good at what it does. Most businesses use one of the commercial versions of VMware, which has the largest market share and is the most powerful and flexible hypervisor. However, for our purposes in this lab exercise, VirtualBox is perfect, because it's simple, it's free, and it doesn't take long to download and install. It works under most versions of Windows, and there are also versions available for macOS, Oracle Solaris, and Linux. (Contrast this to Hyper-V, covered in Lab Exercise 22.03, which works only in Windows 8 and later.)

→ **Note**

> If Hyper-V is already installed on your computer, it will prevent VirtualBox from working properly. Turn off Hyper-V before installing VirtualBox and creating a VM for Ubuntu Linux. For details, see Lab Exercise 22.03.

Learning Objectives

In this lab exercise, you will use VirtualBox virtualization software to install a virtual Ubuntu machine on a Windows PC. You will then navigate a few of the Ubuntu programs and commands.

At the end of this lab, you'll be able to

- Install and configure VirtualBox on a Windows host system

- Install and run Ubuntu Linux as a virtual operating system in VirtualBox

Lab Materials and Setup

The materials you need for this lab are

- A system connected to the Internet

- Ubuntu 64-bit installation media (bootable CD/DVD or USB flash drive)

- A Windows 7 or later system

Getting Down to Business

You will be working with the VirtualBox application to install a virtual operating system. Before proceeding, make sure you have a Linux installation optical disc, Linux installation thumb drive, or a Linux ISO file. Turn to Lab Exercise 11.07, "Installing Ubuntu Linux," and complete Steps 1 and 2 to get one if needed.

Step 1 Do the following to download and install VirtualBox:

a. In a Web browser, navigate to www.virtualbox.org/wiki/Downloads. Figure 22-1 shows which version of VirtualBox the Web site offered on the day the screenshot was captured, but by the time you get there, a later version may be available.

b. Click the link to download the latest VirtualBox version for Windows hosts.

c. When the file has finished downloading, run it and work through the prompts to install VirtualBox. Accept all the defaults.

FIGURE 22-1 Download and install VirtualBox.

Step 2   Now you will launch VirtualBox, create a new virtual machine, and install Ubuntu on it.

    a.   Start VirtualBox. A shortcut for it should be on your Start menu/screen.

    b.   On the toolbar at the top of the VirtualBox window, click New. The Create Virtual Machine dialog box opens.

    c.   In the Name box, type **Ubuntu Linux**.

    d.   Open the Type drop-down list and choose Linux.

    e.   Open the Version drop-down list and choose Ubuntu (64-bit). Figure 22-2 shows the dialog box at this point.

    f.   Click Next.

    g.   Set the memory size to be allocated. You can accept the recommended memory size if you like, or increase the memory. In a VM you would actually be using, you might have strategic reasons for increasing the memory, but since this is just an experiment, leaving the recommended size is fine. Then click Next.

    h.   Choose Create a virtual hard disk now, and then click Create.

    i.   When prompted for the hard disk file type, choose VMDK and click Next.

→ **Note**

If VirtualBox were the only hypervisor you were going to use, you would go with VDI, the default format for VirtualBox. However, in case you want to experiment with importing an existing VM into Hyper-V, VMDK is a better choice for this particular situation.

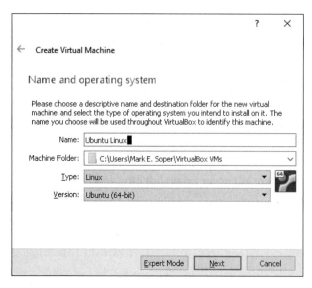

FIGURE 22-2 Create a new virtual machine for Linux.

j. When prompted whether you want dynamically allocated or fixed size, choose Dynamically allocated. In an actual production environment, you might weigh this decision of disk space usage versus speed, but for this exercise, dynamic allocation is better because it doesn't eat up your hard disk space unnecessarily. Then click Next.

k. When prompted for the location for the virtual hard disk file, leave it set to the default. The default used by VirtualBox VM is a location in your user folder, such as C:\Users*username*\VirtualBox VMs\ Ubuntu Linux.

l. When prompted to select the size of the virtual hard disk in megabytes, leave the default set. Again, in an actual production environment, this decision is more important than it is for our experiment. If you chose a dynamic size in Step j, the amount you are choosing here is a maximum, not the initial size.

m. Click Create.

Step 3 At this point, you see the new VM you created, with all its information displayed, as shown in Figure 22-3. Even though this VM has "Ubuntu Linux" splashed all over it, it doesn't actually contain that operating system yet. We'll take care of that next.

a. Click Start. The Select start-up disk dialog box appears.

b. Open the drop-down list and select the drive containing the Ubuntu Linux installation files, and then click Start.

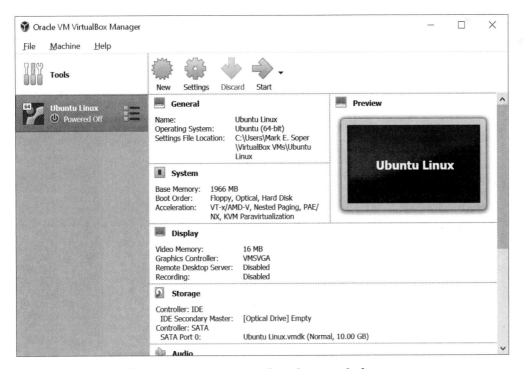

Figure 22-3 VirtualBox now contains a virtual machine, ready for use.

→ **Note**

As Linux boots, you may see information bars across the top of the window; you can close these by clicking the Close (×) button on each bar.

c. Wait for Linux to boot up. It may take a few minutes, but eventually you'll come to a Welcome screen that prompts you to either Try Ubuntu or Install Ubuntu.

✔ **Tip**

Ask your instructor how to proceed at this point. If you are going to use your VirtualBox copy of Ubuntu Linux for other labs, proceed with the rest of these steps to install Ubuntu Linux. If you aren't going to do any more with Linux in VirtualBox, click Try Ubuntu and follow the prompts.

d. Click Install Ubuntu.

e. Accept the default settings and click Continue. A message appears that the computer currently has no detected operating systems. The Erase disk and install Ubuntu option is selected. Leave it so.

f. Click Install Now. A dialog box appears warning you that changes will be written to disks. Click Continue.

g. Select or type your location and click Continue.

h. Select your language and click Continue.

i. Enter your personal information (your name, computer name, username, and password) and click Continue.

j. Wait for Linux to be installed on the virtual machine. When it's finished, click Restart Now.

When Linux restarts, it does so in a VirtualBox window, like the one shown in Figure 22-4. Continue to the next step to experiment with it.

Step 4 Some of the settings in VirtualBox you can adjust while the VM is running; other settings require the VM to be off. Do the following to explore some of the settings you can adjust:

a. In the Ubuntu Linux VirtualBox window, choose File | Preferences. A Preferences dialog box opens, as shown in Figure 22-5.

b. Click each of the categories on the left side of the Preferences dialog box to see what settings are available. When you are finished looking, click Cancel.

c. Choose Machine | Settings. A Settings dialog box opens. Settings apply only to the current VM.

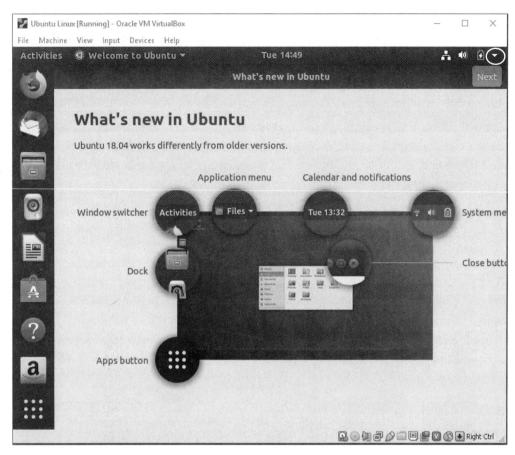

FIGURE 22-4 Ubuntu Linux in a VirtualBox window

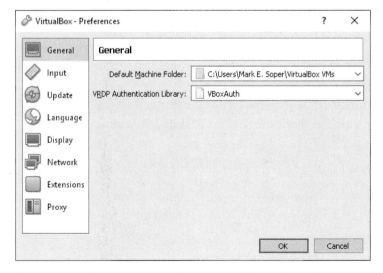

FIGURE 22-5 Preferences for the running VM in VirtualBox

d. Click through the categories to see what's available. Notice that most of the settings are grayed out because you can't change them while the VM is running. Click Cancel when you're finished looking.

e. Open the Machine menu again, and note the other commands. Take Snapshot captures the current state of the OS, for later restoration; Pause freezes the OS temporarily; Reset restarts it; ACPI Shutdown shuts it down.

f. Open the View menu and note the commands available. One feature on this menu is that it offers different viewing modes. You can choose between Full Screen Mode, Seamless Mode, and Scaled Mode. Play around with these modes, and briefly describe how they work and what shortcut keys move between modes.

_____

_____

_____

g. Open the Devices menu and then point to each item on the list to see its submenu. How could you mount a disk image?

_____

Step 5   There's a minor issue with Ubuntu Linux under VirtualBox in that the default screen resolution is tiny and truncates part of the screen, and you can't change it. Here's how to fix that problem:

a. Choose View | Virtual Screen 1. Notice that all the display modes are grayed out. To enable them, you'll need to install some guest additions.

b. Choose Devices | Insert Guest Additions CD Image. When a confirmation box appears, click OK. Then wait a few minutes for the guest additions to install. When they're finished, you're prompted to press ENTER to close the installation window.

c. At the top-right corner of the Linux screen, click the Menu icon (the down arrow, circled in Figure 22-4). A menu appears; click the Shut Down button. At the confirmation, click Restart. The VM restarts itself.

d. After Linux restarts, choose View | Virtual Screen 1 | Resize to 1024×768 (or whatever resolution you want). Problem solved!

e. Click the Menu icon again, and click Shut Down. This time at the confirmation, click Power Off. The VM window closes.

Step 6   We'll finish up by exploring the Settings window for the VM in greater detail.

In the Virtual Box Manager window, click Settings, and the Settings dialog box reopens, but this time more of the settings are available. Then Browse through the settings and describe how you would do the following tasks:

A.   Change the boot order so that the hard disk is preferred over the optical disc:

_____

B.   Add another network adapter:

_____

C.   Enable the shared clipboard and drag-and-drop from the host OS to the guest VM:

_____

D.   Add another virtual hard drive:

_____

Close the Oracle VM VirtualBox Manager window when you are finished.

60 MINUTES

Lab Exercise 22.03: Installing and Using Hyper-V

Hyper-V is the free hypervisor program that comes with Windows 8 and later. Hyper-V is the replacement for an earlier hypervisor that came with Windows 7 and earlier, called Windows Virtual PC.

Hyper-V is a decent choice for someone who wants to install a couple of client OSs to play around with on a desktop or notebook PC without spending any money or downloading any extra software. It has its quirks and limitations, such as not allowing access to USB flash drives from within the VM, so it's not that popular with IT professionals. You may find that you prefer the simplicity of VirtualBox, or the powerhouse features of VMware. But for exploration purposes in this lab exercise, Hyper-V works fine.

Learning Objectives

In this lab exercise, you will install Hyper-V and then install Windows 7 on a VM within it.

At the end of this lab, you'll be able to

- Install Hyper-V

- Install and configure a Windows 7 virtual machine in Hyper-V

Lab Materials and Setup

The materials you need for this lab are

- A PC running 64-bit Windows 8/8.1 Pro or Windows 10 Pro with Internet connectivity and at least 20 GB free hard disk space

- An installation DVD or ISO file for Windows 7 (any edition)

✖ Warning

To create a new virtual machine, as you'll do in this lab exercise, Hyper-V must be run on a 64-bit version of Windows. However, the Hyper-V client software is available on 32-bit versions as well, so you can run existing VMs on that platform.

Getting Down to Business

Hyper-V may not be set up on your Windows 8/8.1 or 10 PC by default, but it's easy enough to set up; it comes with Windows, but some versions don't make it available unless you enable it. In the following steps you'll find Hyper-V, and create a new VM in which you'll install Windows 7.

Step 1   Click the Start button, and then type **Hyper-V**. If the Hyper-V Manager application appears in the search results, click it to start Hyper-V Manager. You're done here; move on to Step 2.

If the Hyper-V Manager application doesn't show up in your search, do the following to set it up:

  a.   Open the Control Panel and choose Programs.

  b.   Click Turn Windows features on or off.

  c.   Mark the Hyper-V checkbox (see Figure 22-6) and click OK.

  d.   Wait for Hyper-V to be set up; then click Restart now.

Step 2   One of the annoying ways that Hyper-V is more work than VirtualBox is that Hyper-V VMs don't detect the host's network connection and start using it automatically (VirtualBox does all this easily—yay VirtualBox!). Instead, you have to set up a virtual switch. (Well, some might consider

FIGURE 22-6   Enable Hyper-V.

this a "feature," in that you can configure multiple network connections and decide which ones are assigned to which VMs, but for our simple purposes here in this lab exercise, it's just one more thing to worry about.)

So let's get the setup of the virtual switch out of the way:

a.   Open the Hyper-V Manager application (search for it), and in the Actions list on the right side of the Hyper-V Manager window, click Virtual Switch Manager.

b.   In the left pane of the Virtual Switch Manager window, click New virtual network switch.

c.   In the right pane, click External, and then click Create Virtual Switch.

d.   In the Name box, assign a name to the virtual switch (for example, Host System Network Connection, as shown in Figure 22-7).

e.   Under Connection type, choose External network. Then choose your host PC's network adapter from the list. If the host system has multiple adapters (for example, both wired and wireless), make sure you choose the one that will provide an Internet connection.

f.   Click OK. If a warning appears that pending changes may disrupt network connectivity, click Yes.

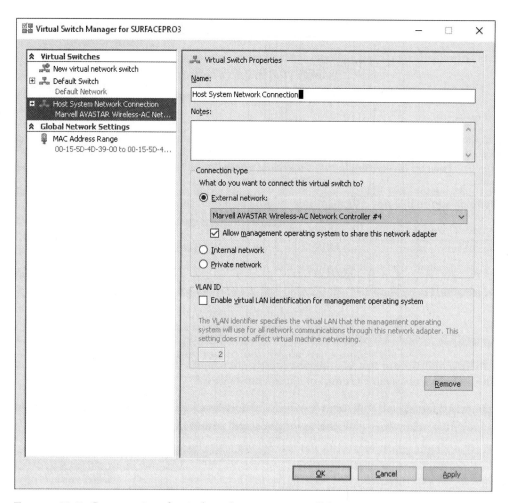

Figure 22-7 Create a virtual switch so that your VMs will have Internet access.

Step 3   Now you'll create the VM on which Windows 7 will be installed.

    a.   In the Hyper-V Manager window, in the Actions pane, click New, and then click Virtual Machine.

> **→ Note**
>
> **If you don't see the New command in the Actions list, check to make sure the host OS is 64-bit.
> If you have a 32-bit host system, you can only read existing VMs, not create new ones.**

    b.   The New Virtual Machine Wizard runs. Click Next to begin.

    c.   In the Name box, type the name for the virtual machine (for example, Windows 7). Then click Next.

d. When prompted to choose Generation 1 or Generation 2, read the descriptions. You have to use Generation 1 if you are installing a 32-bit OS. Generation 2 requires a 64-bit OS, and supports more virtualization features. For this exercise, choose Generation 1, and then click Next.

e. When prompted for the amount of startup memory, leave the default set of 1024 MB. Windows 7 runs okay with 1 GB of RAM, and we're not going to be doing anything too taxing with this VM, so you won't need more than that. Then click Next.

f. When prompted to configure networking, open the Connection drop-down list and choose the virtual switch you created in Step 2. Then click Next.

g. When prompted to create a virtual hard disk, type a name in the Name box. Leave the location set at the default. Set a size in the Size box. (For this exercise, you don't need a large virtual drive; 100 GB is plenty.) Then click Next.

h. When prompted for installation options, click Install an operating system from a bootable CD/DVD-ROM. Choose the host system's DVD drive from the Physical CD/DVD drive list, or choose Image file and then select the ISO file for Windows 7 from one of the host system's local hard drives, if you happen to have that. Click Next to continue.

➜ Note

If you need to create an installation DVD or ISO file for Windows 7, 8.1, or 10, visit www.microsoft.com/software-download and click the appropriate icon, then follow the prompts.

i. Click Next.

j. Click Finish. The new VM is now created.

Step 4   Now you'll install Windows 7 on the VM.

a. Insert the Windows 7 installation DVD in the host system's optical drive. Skip this step if you selected an ISO file in Step 3h.

b. In the Hyper-V Manager window, in the Virtual Machines list (center pane), double-click the Windows 7 VM. A small window appears, letting you know the VM is turned off.

c. In that window, choose Action | Start, or click the Start button (green circle) on the window's toolbar.

d. Install Windows 7. When the installation is complete, Windows 7 will be running in the Hyper-V window.

➜ **Note**

If you need help with the installation process for Windows 7, see https://www.petri.com/ultimate-guide-to-installing-windows-7 .

---

    e.   In the Windows 7 window, choose Start | Shut Down.

    f.   When a message appears that the virtual machine is turned off, close its window.

Step 5   Next, have a look at some of Hyper-V's settings for the VM.

    a.   In the Hyper-V window, right-click the Windows 7 VM and choose Settings. A Settings dialog box opens, with categories down the left side.

    b.   Click each of the categories to see what settings are available. Write down how you would do the following tasks:

        A.   Change the boot order so that the hard disk is preferred over the optical disc:

        _____

        B.   Increase the amount of memory allocated:

        _____

        C.   Remove the SCSI Controller from the VM's hardware list:

        _____

        D.   Add another virtual hard drive on the IDE bus:

        _____

    c.   Close the Settings dialog box when finished.

Lab Analysis Test

    1.   Matthew has worked through the lab exercises in this chapter, but he is still unclear about the exact differences between a virtual desktop and a virtual server. Detail some of the characteristics of each to help Matthew with his studies.

    2.   Create three short examples that help to explain why someone might use virtualization in the workplace.

3. While downloading VirtualBox, Jonathan notices that there is an extension pack available. Read the section of the VirtualBox installation manual that pertains to the extension pack (found here: www.virtualbox.org/manual/ch01.html#intro-installing) and explain why it might be useful.

4. Maria tries to set up Hyper-V in Windows 8.1, but it doesn't appear in the list of optional components she can install. Why not?

5. Tonya sets up Hyper-V in Windows 10, and it seems to install okay, but she can't create a virtual machine; there's no Add command. Why not?

Key Term Quiz

Use the following terms to complete the following sentences. Not all terms will be used.

bare-metal	virtual desktop
guest additions	virtual machine manager (VMM)
hosted virtual machine	virtual server
hypervisor	virtual switch
snapshot	VirtualBox

1. The two terms typically used to describe virtualization software are _____ and _____.

2. When working with virtual machines, one of the convenience features is to be able to take a _____ to capture the current configuration of the machine.

3. Typically, when building a virtual server, the virtualization software is going to be of the _____ variety. This is also known as a "native" virtual machine.

4. In order to change the display resolution of a VM in VirtualBox, you must install _____.

5. In order to get network connectivity for a VM in Hyper-V, you must create a _____.

Chapter 23
Portable Computing

Lab Exercises

Many laptops have easily replaceable parts. You can swap out a fading battery for a newer one, for example. Lurking beneath access panels on the underside or below the keyboard on some models are hardware components such as RAM, a hard drive, a network card, and a modem—just like laptop batteries, these units can be easily accessed and replaced by a technician. Some laptops even have panels for replacing the video card and CPU.

In this series of lab exercises, you'll do five things. First, you'll use the Internet to research the upgrades available for portable computing devices so you can provide proper recommendations to employers and clients. Second, you'll open a laptop and gut it like a rainbow trout—removing and replacing RAM, the most common of all hardware upgrades. Next, you'll remove and replace mass storage (hard disk or SSD), another common upgrade. Fourth, you'll perform the traditional task of a portable PC technician, tweaking the power management options to optimize battery life on particular models. Finally, you'll familiarize yourself with the latest and greatest portable offerings.

 30 MINUTES

Lab Exercise 23.01: Researching Laptop Upgrade Paths

Your boss just sent word that one of your most important clients wants to extend the life of their sales force's laptop computers by upgrading rather than replacing. You've been asked to provide an upgrade track for your client. This requires you to research the laptops used by the company to determine which upgrades you can make, and to verify that the laptops themselves are not so old that the cost to upgrade them outweighs the cost of new laptops with new technology. You have to determine whether you can add RAM, replace the hard drives, or replace the aging batteries. Get to work!

Learning Objectives

Given the manufacturer and model number of a laptop computer, you'll figure out how to upgrade your client's computers.

At the end of this lab exercise, you'll be able to

- Determine the replacement price of a battery

- Determine memory upgrades, including the quantity and type of RAM

- Determine hard drive upgrades, including the capacity and price of a hard drive

Lab Materials and Setup

The materials you need for this lab exercise are

- A working PC with Internet access

Getting Down to Business

Limber up your surfing fingers because you're about to spend some time on the Web. Researching information about hardware and software is something technicians do all the time. The better you are at it, the better you are at your job!

When you're searching for replacement and upgrade parts and information, always take a look at the device manufacturer's Web site. Most major PC manufacturers, such as Dell, HP, and Lenovo, have comprehensive product specification sheets available to the public on their sites. You can even order replacement parts directly from them, assuming you don't mind paying full retail price. A popular tactic for purchasing upgrades is to grab the upgrade specs from the manufacturer's site and then search the Internet for the best prices. Not only are you doing your job well, but you'll be saving your company money too!

In the following steps, you'll navigate the tumultuous seas of the Internet in a quest to find the Golden Fleece of laptop battery, memory, and hard drive upgrades.

Step 1   Fire up your Web browser, and surf over to the device manufacturer's Web site or do a Google search for **laptop battery**. Many sites sell every type of laptop battery imaginable. The goal of this exercise is to become familiar with using the Internet to identify parts, confirm the specifications, and purchase replacement batteries. Once you reach a suitable Web site, answer the following questions.

You need replacement batteries for several Dell Latitude E7440 laptops. These laptops were manufactured back in 2014, and their batteries are reaching the end of their lives and starting to fail, although they are still good machines other than that.

What's the vendor's part number and price for this battery?

_____

What's the voltage and power capacity of the battery?

_____

✔ **Tip**

Just like any other electrical power source, batteries are rated according to voltage (9.6 V, for instance), current capacity (2600 milliamps per hour, or mAh), and sometimes power capacity (72 watts per hour, or Wh or WHr). When purchasing laptop batteries from third-party vendors (that is, vendors other than the laptop manufacturer), make sure to buy a battery that matches the voltage recommended by the manufacturer. However, it's not uncommon to find a battery with a higher capacity than the original battery. This is not a problem—increased current/power capacity means longer run times for your portable PC.

Step 2   Search the manufacturer's Web site for information on memory. If that isn't available, flip your browser over to www.kahlon.com to check RAM prices and availability. If the site isn't available, perform a Google search to find other Web sites that sell **laptop memory**. Then answer the following questions, based on your client having a Dell Latitude E7440 with 2 GB of RAM.

What is the maximum amount of RAM this system can have, and how many slots are there?

_____

What type of RAM sticks does it require?

_____

Step 3   The machines have some overheating problems, and your client thinks that replacing the hard disk drives (HDDs) with solid-state drives (SSDs) might help. Does the vendor have SSD replacement drives available? If not, try www.crucial.com.

How much would it cost to replace the current HDDs with 500-GB SSDs? _____

Do you think this replacement is a smart purchase for the company? Why or why not?

_____

Step 4   One of your client's Dell Latitude E7440 machines needs a new keyboard. Find two different Web sites where you can buy a replacement keyboard for this model and record them here, along with the price at each site:

_____

_____

 30 MINUTES

Lab Exercise 23.02: Replacing and Upgrading RAM

Your client settled on the RAM upgrades as the first step for making their laptops more usable, and you've been tagged as the person to remove the old RAM and install the new. Upgrading RAM is the most common technician-performed upgrade on portable PCs and something you're likely to be asked to do in the real world.

Learning Objectives

In this lab exercise, you'll learn essential skills for upgrading portable PCs.

At the end of this lab exercise, you'll be able to

- Access the RAM panel in a laptop
- Remove RAM in a laptop
- Install RAM properly in a laptop

Lab Materials and Setup

The materials you need for this lab exercise are

- A working laptop computer
- A very tiny Phillips-head screwdriver
- An antistatic mat

> ✖ **Warning**
>
> **Opening a portable computer can result in a nonfunctional portable computer. Don't use the instructor's primary work laptop for this exercise!**

Getting Down to Business

You're about to open the sensitive inner portions of a portable computer, but before you do, it's a great idea to refresh your memory about avoiding electrostatic discharge (ESD), covered in Chapter 1. The inside of a laptop looks different from the inside of a desktop or tower case, but the contents are just as sensitive to static electricity. Use your antistatic mat and wrist strap, and try not to touch anything that you don't have to touch. Handle the RAM circuit boards only by their edges.

Step 1   Using your handy screwdriver or other handy tool, open the access panel for the RAM. Every portable PC offers a different way to access the RAM, so we can't give you explicit directions here. Most often, you'll find a removable plate on the bottom of the laptop secured with one or two tiny Phillips-head screws.

FIGURE 23-1 Opening the access panel to find RAM

Some laptops require you to remove the keyboard, unscrew a heat spreader, and then access the RAM. Figure 23-1 shows a typical panel, accessible from the underside of the laptop.

Step 2   Once you have the panel open, push outward on the restraining clips on the RAM stick(s) (see Figure 23-2). This will cause the RAM to pop up partially.

Step 3   Remove the RAM gently, gripping only at the noncontact edges. Place the stick(s) on an antistatic pad or in an antistatic bag.

Step 4   Install the replacement RAM into the laptop, reversing the process of removal. Place the stick(s) at an angle into the RAM slots and push firmly (Figure 23-3). Once the contacts have disappeared, press the body of the RAM into the restraining clips.

✔ **Hint**

If you don't have new RAM to install, simply install the RAM you removed in Step 3. This gives you the opportunity to practice!

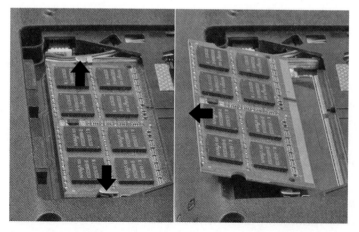

FIGURE 23-2 Releasing the RAM

FIGURE 23-3 Installing an SODIMM RAM module

Step 5 Replace the access panel.

Step 6 Power on the laptop to confirm that the new RAM is recognized and functioning properly.

 **30 MINUTES**

Lab Exercise 23.03: Replacing and Upgrading Mass Storage

Your client agreed with your assessment that the onboard mass storage in the old laptops was too small and too slow and needed to be replaced. Once again, you're in charge of backing up the old SATA hard disk or SSD, transferring data to the new drives, and installing them. Upgrading a SATA hard disk or SSD to a newer, larger, faster model can be very simple or extremely complex, based on the design of the laptop.

→ **Note**

Many newer laptops use the M.2 form factor for SSD mass storage. To learn more about M.2 drives, see Lab Exercise 8.04, "Choosing an M.2 SSD," in Chapter 8.

Learning Objectives

In this lab exercise, you'll learn essential skills for upgrading portable PCs.

At the end of this lab exercise, you'll be able to

- Access the hard disk panel in a laptop

- Remove a hard disk or SSD in a laptop

- Install a hard disk or SSD properly in a laptop

✔ **Tip**

If you decide to replace the existing hard drive or SSD with a different one, be sure to use a drive-cloning app to copy the contents of the old drive to the new drive. You can attach the new drive to the computer with a USB connection such as a drive dock, enclosure, or USB/SATA conversion cable. Use the USB 3.0 or 3.1 connection (USB 2.0 is at least ten times slower!). We recommend performing the cloning process overnight before starting this lesson.

Lab Materials and Setup

The materials you need for this lab exercise are

- A working laptop computer with a hard disk accessible from the bottom panel

✖ **Warning**

Opening a portable computer can result in a nonfunctional portable computer. Don't use a primary laptop for this exercise!

- A Phillips-head screwdriver

- An antistatic mat

✔ **Tip**

Before starting this exercise, review the service manual for each laptop model you have available (search online for any manuals you don't have them). If you find that the laptops available to you don't have user-removable hard drives or SSDs, such as models that require a complete disassembly to get to these components, try to obtain nonfunctioning models with removable hard drives or SSDs from a local electronics retailer, computer store, or thrift shop. If you can't obtain any, then search online for service manuals for laptop models that have removable hard drives or SSDs and review the following process in the manuals.

FIGURE 23-4 Opening the access panel to find a SATA hard disk or SSD

Getting Down to Business

As noted in Lab Exercise 23.02, make sure to review your ESD avoidance procedures before you open the sensitive inner portions of a portable computer. The inside of a laptop looks different from the inside of a desktop or tower case, but the contents are just as sensitive to static electricity. Use your antistatic mat and wrist strap, and try not to touch anything that you don't have to touch. Handle the hard disk or SSD by its edge, and don't touch its power or data connectors.

Step 1 Using your handy screwdriver, open the access cover over the hard disk or SSD. Every portable PC offers a different way to access mass storage, so we can't give you explicit directions here. Sometimes, you'll find a removable plate on the bottom of the laptop secured with two tiny Phillips-head screws. Some laptops require you to remove the entire bottom panel to gain access to the hard drive or SSD (you might need to remove as many as a dozen screws), and others require you to remove the keyboard. Figure 23-4 shows a typical panel, accessible from the underside of the laptop.

Step 2 Once you have the panel open, unscrew the retaining bolt(s) holding the SATA hard disk or SSD in place (see Figure 23-5).

FIGURE 23-5 Removing the SATA hard disk/SSD retaining bolts

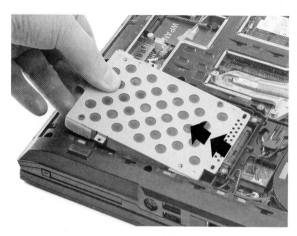

FIGURE 23-6 Removing the SATA hard disk/SSD from the laptop

Step 3   Pull (or push) the hard disk or SSD away from the SATA interface (see Figure 23-6), and lift it out of the laptop.

Step 4   Unscrew the mounting frame or bracket from the drive (see Figure 23-7). Retain the mounting frame or bracket and screws for reuse.

Step 5   Remove the drive from the mounting bracket or frame (see Figure 23-8).

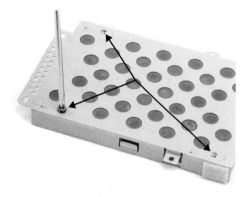

FIGURE 23-7   Removing the SATA hard disk/SSD mounting frame

FIGURE 23-8 Removing the SATA hard disk/SSD from the mounting bracket or frame

Step 6 Reverse the preceding steps to install a new drive into the laptop. If a new drive is not available, reinstall the existing drive.

Step 7 Power on the laptop to confirm that the new hard disk or SSD is recognized and functioning properly.

 **30 MINUTES**

Lab Exercise 23.04: Adjusting Power Management to Optimize Battery Life

Several of your sales staff members have to attend a conference on the other side of the country. The conference came up on short notice, so everyone needs time to prepare, even while on the flight to the conference. You've been tasked with configuring power management on their laptops to optimize battery life so they can work as long as possible while on the plane.

Learning Objectives

In this lab exercise, you'll adjust the power management features for a laptop PC, a task that's vital to keeping portables running as long as possible on battery power.

At the end of this lab exercise, you'll be able to

- Enable and disable power management in the system setup
- Change power management settings in Windows

Lab Materials and Setup

The materials you need for this lab exercise are

- A working computer with Windows 7 or later installed, preferably a laptop rather than a desktop
- A BIOS that supports power management (and almost all do these days)

✔ **Hint**

Having a laptop computer available is a plus. Performing these steps on a laptop computer will allow you to configure the settings for a battery-oriented power scheme and then remove the power cord, running on battery power to experience the actual results. If you're practicing on a regular desktop PC, keep in mind that a laptop will have two options for each adjustment: one for when the laptop is using battery power, and one for when it's connected to the alternating current (AC) source, whereas a desktop PC has only one option for each adjustment.

Getting Down to Business

Some laptops have power management settings in the system setup. This seemed like a good idea over a decade or so ago, but as Windows' power management features developed, the BIOS power management settings often conflicted with the Windows ones, causing odd power-related problems. Therefore, most of the systems built today have no BIOS power management. In this lab you will check the system setup program to see if there are any power management settings there, and disable them if you find any. Then you will configure Windows power management settings to handle things.

✖ **Cross-Reference**

Refer to the "Power Management" section in Chapter 23 of *Mike Meyers' CompTIA A+ Guide to Managing and Troubleshooting PCs* **for more information on power management on portable PCs.**

Step 1   Enter the system setup program. (Refer to Lab Exercise 5.02, "Accessing BIOS Settings via the CMOS Setup Program," if you need help with that.) Look for power management settings that allow the BIOS to put the PC in a low-power state after a certain period of inactivity—Sleep, Suspend, that sort of thing. If there are any such settings, and they are enabled, disable them. (Don't disable ACPI, though.) Then exit and save your changes, rebooting the PC to Windows.

Record what settings you found and what settings you changed:

_____

_____

_____

✔ **Hint**

ACPI is short for Advanced Configuration and Power Interface, a power management specification developed by Intel, Microsoft, and Toshiba. ACPI enables the operating system to control the amount of power given to each device attached to the computer. With ACPI, the operating system can turn off peripheral devices, such as optical drives, when they're not in use.

Step 2   Follow these steps to configure power management in Windows:

    a.   Windows 7/8.1: Open the Control Panel and navigate to System and Security | Power Options.

         Windows 10: Open Settings | System | Power & Sleep | Additional power settings.

    b.   Click the Show additional plans arrow button if needed. You see a list of several preset combinations of settings, such as High performance, Balanced, and Power saver.

    c.   Choose Power saver, and then click the Change plan settings hyperlink next to it.

    d.   In the Edit Plan Settings window, you'll see drop-down lists for two basic settings: Turn off the display and Put the computer to sleep. If you're working on a PC with a battery, there are two separate settings for On battery and Plugged in, as shown in Figure 23-9. If you're working with a desktop, only one setting is available.

➜ **Note**

Sleep is a low-power mode that shuts down most components but keeps RAM powered, so the computer can spring back into action quickly when you resume your work. It takes only a few seconds to resume from sleep mode. _Hibernate_ is a mode that copies the contents of RAM to the hard drive and then completely shuts down the computer. When you resume from it, the RAM content is copied back into RAM as it wakes up. It can take 5 to 10 seconds or more to resume from hibernate mode, but a machine can remain in hibernate mode indefinitely because no power is required to sustain it.

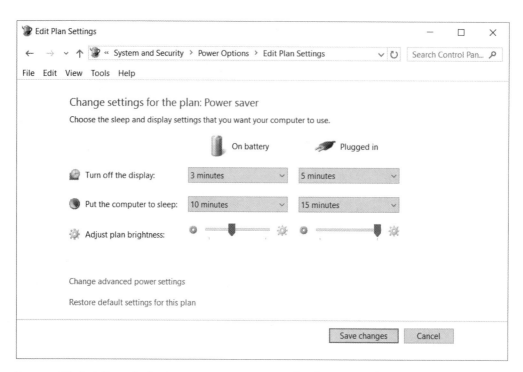

FIGURE 23-9 Adjust the basic power saving settings for the power plan.

e. Under On battery, set the Turn off the display setting to 3 minutes, and adjust the Put the computer to sleep setting to 10 minutes.

f. Drag the Adjust plan brightness slider for On battery to about 25 percent of the maximum.

g. Click Change advanced power settings. A Power Options dialog box opens (see Figure 23-10).

h. Set the Turn off hard disk after setting to 5 minutes when on battery power.

i. In the Sleep section, set the Hibernate after setting when on battery to 60 minutes.

j. In the Battery section, make sure the Critical battery action setting when on battery power is Hibernate.

✖ Warning

Some PCs and some components don't like hibernate mode. Using it can cause your computer to lock up. Be aware of that, and if your computer locks up, don't allow Power Management to place the computer into hibernate mode for any reason.

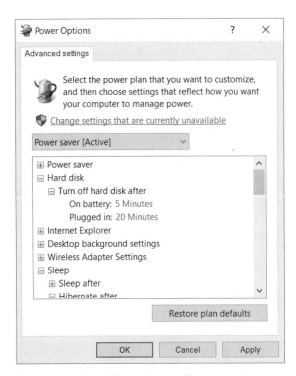

FIGURE 23-10 Adjust advanced power options.

k. Click OK to close the dialog box.

l. Click Save changes in the Edit Plan Settings window.

m. Make sure the Power saver plan is selected, and then close the Control Panel.

Step 3 Now you'll test the settings you just adjusted. (This step assumes you have a PC that has a battery.)

a. Unplug the computer from AC power, so it is running on battery. Let the computer sit idle for 3 minutes. What happens at 3 minutes?

_____

b. Continue to let the computer sit idle for 2 more minutes. What happens at 5 minutes?

_____

c.   Continue to let the computer sit idle for 5 more minutes. What happens at 10 minutes?

_____

d.   Wake up the computer. What did you need to do?

_____

e.   Let the computer sit idle for at least 60 minutes. Then wake it up. What did you need to do?

_____

Step 4   Once you've finished experimenting, enable or disable power management as you prefer.

 OPEN

Lab Exercise 23.05: Browsing the Latest Portable PCs

The best way to understand portable PCs (laptops, tablet PCs, convertible laptops, and 2-in-1 PCs) is to play with one. If there isn't one available in the classroom, then this exercise is for you.

Learning Objectives

This lab exercise will take you into the field for a little computer browsing—for educational purposes, of course!

At the end of this lab exercise, you'll be able to

- Recognize the variations in key features among different portable PCs

Lab Materials and Setup

The materials you need for this lab exercise are

- A local computer store or other retailer with a good selection of portable PCs you can examine

✔ **Hint**

If you don't have a store nearby, use the Web to browse a computer store such as Newegg (www.newegg.com), or go to a manufacturer's Web site such as Dell's (www.dell.com) and customize a laptop to your heart's content. Be sure to explore all the options and customizations you can add to it. Just make sure you don't click Buy!

Getting Down to Business

Portable PCs are manufactured by a wide variety of companies, and no two are created equal. For example, some laptops feature a slim and lightweight profile and are designed for the busy traveler; others feature a full complement of ports and rival desktop PCs in their power and features. Convertible models can switch between notebook and tablet modes and feature support for Windows Ink. 2-in-1 models have a display that incorporates laptop-style hardware and a separate keyboard. Most, but not all, use a touchscreen display. Take a look at all the available models and compare their features.

Step 1   Go to your local computer store or office supply store and check out the portable PCs on display. Try to find a store with a variety of brands. Bring this lab manual (or a copy of the following chart) with you to record the different specs you find.

Step 2   Pick out three portables, preferably from different manufacturers. For each portable, record the following information:

Feature	Portable 1	Portable 2	Portable 3
Operating system			
Size/weight			
Screen type/size			
CPU			
RAM installed/maximum			
Pointing device(s)			
I/O ports			
SATA HDD or SSD			
Optical drive(s)			
M.2 SSD			

Lab Analysis Test

1. Bill wants to upgrade his memory from 4 GB to the maximum amount of RAM his laptop can take. He has a Dell Latitude E7440 laptop. How much RAM does he need to buy?

2. Teresa complains that her Windows laptop turns itself off without any warning. What should she adjust?

3. Maanit will be traveling from the United States to India. He'll use his laptop to watch DVDs on the way, usually on battery power. Lately, the battery seems to run out of juice well before the battery specifications indicate. What could possibly cause this recent development? Are there any recommendations you would make to Maanit to improve his laptop's performance?

4. Tomika's computer won't go into sleep mode, even if the power management settings tell it to do so, and even if she uses the Sleep command in Windows. What should she check?

5. David's computer goes into hibernate mode okay, but won't come back out again; he ends up having to do a hard reset by holding down the power button for 5 seconds to wake the computer back up again. Then he sees an error message that Windows did not shut down properly. What do you recommend?

Key Term Quiz

Use the following terms to complete the following sentences. Not all terms will be used.

ACPI	memory
battery	Power Meter
hard drive	Power Options
hibernate	Power Plan
laptop	sleep

1. _____ is a Windows power mode that copies the contents of RAM to the hard drive and then shuts down the PC completely.

2. _____ is a Windows power mode that shuts down most components but leaves RAM powered.

3. You can use the _____ applet in the Control Panel to set the power conservation options for the notebook computer.

4. The battery, _____, and _____ are all upgradeable laptop components.

5. The amount of power remaining in a battery can be determined by looking at the _____ in the notification area.

Chapter 24
Understanding Mobile Devices

Lab Exercises

The Internet-connected experience has jumped off of our desks and into our hands. Smartphones and tablets, grouped into a category called "mobile devices," enable you to consume, communicate, and create all sorts of digital goodies on the go. You don't even need to sync them with your desktop if you don't want to; they can function independently of any other device. In fact, many of today's smartphones and tablets are more powerful than the PC you had five years ago.

Wearables provide a further expansion of mobile information by bringing information from your smartphone to your wrist or by providing on-the-go monitoring of personal health. These devices are everywhere, so you need to know something about them. As a PC tech, people will assume you know how to fix anything technical, including smartphones, tablets, and wearables. The following lab exercises are meant to familiarize you with the most basic features of Apple iOS and Google Android smartphones and tablets and popular categories of wearables.

 30 MINUTES

Lab Exercise 24.01: Comparing Mobile Device Platforms

Several companies compete for mobile device dominance. The two most popular platforms (and most important for the CompTIA A+ 220-1002 exam) are Apple iOS and Google Android.

→ **Note**

Windows 10 Mobile was a distant third-place contender in the battle for smartphone OS dominance. Windows 10 Mobile will reach end-of-support status by December 10, 2019. Chrome OS is a browser-based OS used primarily on low-cost laptops. This chapter focuses on Apple iOS and Google Android.

Learning Objectives

In this exercise, you'll research the differences between Apple iOS and Google Android.

At the end of this lab, you'll be able to

- Differentiate between smartphone and tablet platforms
- Identify wearables that work with specific smartphone and tablet platforms

Lab Materials and Setup

The materials you need for this lab are

- An Internet-capable PC for research
- Optional: Mobile phones or tablets using iOS and Android operating systems

Getting Down to Business

At first glance, all smartphones have a lot in common: big touchscreens, icons you can tap, Web pages you can swipe, and so on. Peek under the surface, however, and you'll see how different the mobile operating systems really are. You need to understand how they operate, what they have in common, and how they differ.

Step 1 First take a look at Apple's mobile operating system, iOS. A mobile operating system is a lot different from a desktop OS, so make sure you know all the details. Open your Web browser and search for the following topics.

What is the latest version of Apple iOS? _____

List at least three devices that use iOS:

_____

List five features of the latest version of iOS:

_____

_____

Approximately how many apps are available for iOS? _____

Identify three wearable devices that work with iOS:

_____

Step 2   Next, take a look at Google's mobile operating system, Android. Android devices don't all use the latest OS, and most device manufacturers customize the OS with a special user interface. Keep this in mind when searching for information about Google Android.

What is the latest version of Google Android? _____

List a few smartphone and/or tablet manufacturers that use Android:

_____

List five features of the latest version of Android:

_____

_____

Approximately how many apps are available for Android from Google Play? _____

Identify three wearable devices that work with Android:

_____

Step 3   Complete the following table to the extent possible with the phones or tablets you have access to. (You might not have access to a phone or tablet of every type, and that's okay. Try to compare at least two.)

	iOS	Android
Describe your overall impression of the main screen. Is it easy to see? Easy to navigate?		
How customizable is the interface, and how easy is it to customize?		
What is your impression of the default Web browser app? Would you enjoy using it frequently?		
Of the businesses you deal with most often in your daily life (banks, stores, etc.), how many of them have apps available for this platform?		
Of the wearables you have or want to get, will they connect with this platform?		

45 MINUTES

Lab Exercise 24.02: Installing Mobile Applications

Installing an app (the most commonly used term for "application") is probably one of the more important skills to have when using any mobile device. In this exercise, you'll connect to a wireless access point and download an app using an Apple iOS device like the iPad or iPhone.

A second component in this lab is to install a new app on an Android phone or tablet and document the process for doing so. If you have multiple phones or tablets available, we highly encourage you to complete this optional portion of the lab, because it will give you some extra perspective.

Learning Objectives

In this lab, you'll connect to a wireless access point, then download and install an app.

At the end of this lab, you'll be able to

- Configure an iOS device for wireless access and install a new app

- Compare the app installation process of iOS with that of Android

Lab Materials and Setup

The materials you need for this lab are

- An iOS-compatible device with access to the Internet

- An Apple ID

- An Android device with access to the Internet

Getting Down to Business

You've likely heard the line, "There's an app for that," but you're about to test that theory. Finding and installing the right app is what makes a modern smartphone or tablet smart.

iOS

Step 1 First, you will connect your iOS device to a Wi-Fi network so that you can get on the Internet. If you don't have an available Wi-Fi connection, or if you get unlimited data on your data plan, read through the steps anyway so that you're familiar with the procedure when someone in the workplace asks you to connect their device to a Wi-Fi network.

   a. On your iOS device, go to the home screen by pressing the Home button on your device (the big physical button beneath the screen on iPads and all iPhone models before the iPhone X series) or by swiping up from the gesture bar (iPhone X series).

   b. Tap the Settings icon (see Figure 24-1); you might need to swipe to another screen if you've moved the Settings icon.

FIGURE 24-1 iOS Settings icon

c. Tap Wi-Fi, and set Wi-Fi to On if it is not already so. If the device does not automatically connect to a network, click a network in the Choose a Network section. You might have to type a password to connect to it. After you've connected, your screen should resemble Figure 24-2.

d. Return to the home screen. When connected to a wireless network, you should see your Wi-Fi signal strength in the status bar at the top of the screen, near the time.

Step 2 Now that you are connected to the Internet, you will download an app from the App Store.

a. Tap the App Store icon, then tap Top Charts. Tap Free to see only the free apps. What are the current Top 5 Free apps?

_____

_____

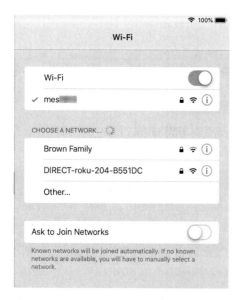

FIGURE 24-2 Wi-Fi network settings screen

b. Tap Search, then tap in the Search box at the top of the screen. Type **mactracker** in the search box.

c. Tap Mactracker. (It should be the top search result.)

d. From the screenshot(s) and/or description provided, what do you think this application does?

_____

e. Tap Get and then tap Install. Enter your Apple ID password and click OK when prompted.

f. The Mactracker app will download and install onto your device. Depending on your Internet connection speed, this might take a while. When it is finished, an Open button appears. Tap it to open the app.

Step 3 Now you'll explore the Mactracker app.

a. The Mactracker app is a catalog of all Mac computers ever made. What is the current version of this app? (Hint: tap About.) _____

b. Use the app to find information about the iPhone X. Tap iPhone X. Fill in the following specifications:

Initial price for the 64-GB model: _____

Display resolution: _____

Capacities: _____

Processor: _____

Processor speed: _____

Number of cores on processor: _____

What version of iOS was released with this device? _____

How long will the battery last while talking over a cellular network? _____

c. Exit the app by pressing the Home button (iPhone 8 and earlier) or swiping upward (iPhone X series). Once you are at the home screen, you might think the app has been closed because you can't see it anymore. But guess what? That app is still loaded in your device's RAM.

d. Do the following to close all open apps:

- iPhone 8 and earlier: Double-press the Home button quickly. Thumbnail pages of each open app appear. Swipe up on each thumbnail to close that app. Close all open apps this way.

- iPhone X series: Swipe up from the bottom of the screen and pause momentarily to see app cards. Press and hold an app card until you see an icon of a red circle with a white minus symbol (−). Tap that icon to close the app.

Step 4   Now that you've used the Mactracker app, you will uninstall it from your iOS device.

    a.   To uninstall the Mactracker app, find it on one of the home screens. If you don't see it after pressing the Home button (iPhone 8 and earlier) or swiping up from the gesture bar (iPhone X series), swipe to the left to find it. Tap and hold the Mactracker icon. The entire screen will enter jiggle mode. Tap the icon showing a black × on the gray circle. When asked for a confirmation, tap Delete.

    b.   Press the Home button (iPhone 8 and earlier) or swipe up from the gesture bar (iPhone X series) to exit jiggle mode.

ANDROID

Step 1   Now, it's time to connect your Android device to a Wi-Fi network so that you can get on the Internet. If you don't have an available Wi-Fi connection, or if you get unlimited data on your data plan, read through the steps anyway so that you're familiar with the procedure when someone in the workplace asks you to connect their device to a Wi-Fi network. The following instructions are based on Samsung Galaxy tablets and smartphones.

    a.   On your Android device, go to the home screen by pressing the Home button on your device, which is usually located below the screen, or on some recent models, is a so-called "soft button" on the screen surface near the bottom of the phone.

    b.   Tap the Settings icon (see Figure 24-3); you might need to swipe to another screen if you've moved the Settings icon.

    c.   Tap Connections, then Wi-Fi, and set Wi-Fi to On if it is not already so. If the device does not automatically connect to a network, click a network in the Choose a Network section. You might have to type a password to connect to it. After you've connected, your screen should resemble Figure 24-4.

    d.   Return to the home screen. When connected to a wireless network, you should see your Wi-Fi signal strength in the status bar at the top of the screen, near the time.

Step 2   Now that you are connected to the Internet, you will download an app from the Android app store, Play Store (also known as Google Play).

    a.   Tap the Play Store icon, then tap Top Charts. Tap Top Free Apps to see only the free apps. What are the current Top 5 Free apps?

_____

_____

FIGURE 24-3 Android Settings icon

FIGURE 24-4 Wi-Fi network settings screen

b.   Tap in the Search box at the top of the screen. Type **Translate** in the search box.

c.   Tap Google Translate. (It should be near the top of the search results.)

d.   From the screenshot(s) and/or description provided, what do you think this application does?

_____

e.   Tap Install. If prompted, enter your Google ID and password (you might need this information only for paid apps, depending upon your system's settings).

f.   The Google Translate app will download and install onto your device. Depending on your Internet connection speed, this might take a while. When it is finished, an Open button appears. Tap it to open the app.

Step 3   Now you'll explore the Google Translate app.

a.   The Google Translate app is designed to translate text you enter, signs (via your digital camera), handwriting, and voice to and from other languages.

What is the default language to translate from? _____

What is the language to translate to? _____

b.   If you select a different language to translate from, what is it? _____

If you select a different language to translate to, what is it? _____

c.   Enter text via typing or handwriting to translate.

d.   Exit the app by tapping the Overview button, which might be to the left of the Home button or on the bottom of the screen. All running apps are listed. Tap the × in the upper right corner of the app window (Samsung) or drag the app off-screen (most other brands).

Step 4   Now that you've used the Google Translate app, you will uninstall it from your Android device.

    a.   To uninstall the Google Translate app, tap Settings, then Apps.

    b.   Scroll down the list to Translate and tap the icon. Tap Uninstall. Tap OK on the confirming dialog. The app is removed from your device and the device returns to the Home screen.

 **30 MINUTES**

Lab Exercise 24.03: Setting Up E-mail on a Mobile Device

Most mobile device users employ their devices not only for phone calls and texts, but for e-mail and Web browsing. Setting up an e-mail account on a mobile device is an important basic skill to have, as you're likely to be asked to help set up mobile devices for others.

Learning Objectives

In this lab, you'll configure an e-mail account on an iPhone or iPad. If you have a phone or tablet available that runs the Android OS, you will also configure an e-mail account on it and document the process.

At the end of this lab, you'll be able to

- Set up an e-mail account in iOS

- Set up an e-mail account in Android

Lab Materials and Setup

The materials you need for this lab are

- An iOS-compatible device with access to the Internet

- The user name, password, and mail server information for an e-mail account

- An Android device with access to the Internet

Getting Down to Business

Setting up an e-mail account on a mobile device allows the user to send and receive e-mail on-the-go, even when Wi-Fi is not available. Mail can be sent and received using the 3G, 4G, or 5G service that the device itself uses.

iOS

Step 1   Setting up e-mail in iOS starts not with the Mail app, as you might expect, but with the Settings app.

  a.   On the home screen, tap the Settings icon. Then scroll down and tap Passwords & Accounts (or Mail, Contacts, Calendars before iOS 12).

  b.   Under the Accounts heading, tap Add Account. A list of popular mail services appears.

  c.   If your service appears on the list, tap it. Then fill out the form to connect your iOS device with the service. You may be asked for differing information depending on which service it is. Work through the screens that appear to complete the setup, tapping Save at the end, and you're done.

If your service does *not* appear, you've got some more steps to complete:

  d.   Tap Other and then tap Add Mail Account. Then fill out the form that appears, asking for Name, Email, Password, and Description.

  e.   Tap Next. Depending on the account server, more information may be required, or you may be done at this point.

  f.   If you see Save, tap it to finish up. If other prompts appear, complete them by filling in the requested information. For example, you might be prompted for server names, ports, or other settings.

Step 2   Now test the account to make sure it can send and receive mail.

  a.   Return to the home screen and tap the Mail app.

  b.   Tap All Inboxes to see the incoming mail for all accounts, or tap an individual account to see only the mail in that account.

  c.   Create a message addressed to your own account, and send it.

ANDROID

Step 1   If you have an Android device with Internet access, follow these steps to set up e-mail on it. However, be aware that Android is customizable. The steps provided here are for a basic, generic Android environment, but certain Android devices may have slightly different steps.

  a.   From the home screen, tap Settings.

  b.   Tap the link for Accounts, such as Accounts & sync or Cloud and accounts.

  c.   If necessary, tap Accounts. Scroll down.

  d.   Tap Add account.

  e.   Tap the type of account you want to set up. For example, there are separate items on the list for Microsoft Exchange, IMAP, and POP3 accounts. If you don't know what type of account it is, tap Email for generic settings.

   f.   The steps after this point depend on the type of account you chose. Set up your e-mail account, and
            document the steps here:

   _____

   _____

   _____

   _____

 **30 MINUTES**

Lab Exercise 24.04: Using Wi-Fi and Bluetooth on a Mobile Device

Nearly all mobile devices have two different network connection methods: Bluetooth and Wi-Fi. They have
different uses, of course; Bluetooth is used to connect with other devices nearby, such as wireless headsets and
speakers. For example, you could have a Bluetooth device in your car that connects to your iPhone, allowing
you to play music from your iPhone over your car's speakers. Wi-Fi is used to connect to LANs, to get Internet
access without having to use bandwidth from the device's data plan. Wi-Fi connectivity can also be used to
enable the device to function as a hotspot, so that nearby computing devices can use its 3G, 4G, or 5G service
to connect to the Internet when no Internet service is otherwise available.

Learning Objectives

In this lab, you'll learn several useful skills for interacting with wireless networking on an iPhone or iPad. You'll
also try out these skills on an Android device.

   At the end of this lab, you'll be able to

   • Enable and disable Wi-Fi and Bluetooth connectivity

   • Pair a Bluetooth device to the phone or tablet

   • Set a phone or tablet to serve as a Wi-Fi hotspot

Lab Materials and Setup

The materials you need for this lab are

   • An iOS-compatible device with Bluetooth and Wi-Fi capabilities

   • A Bluetooth device, such as a microphone, headset, or speaker

- Another device with Wi-Fi capability (a PC, tablet, or another phone) to test the Wi-Fi hotspot

- An Android device with Bluetooth and Wi-Fi capabilities

Getting Down to Business

Smartphones are best known for their connection to 3G/4G/5G cellular networks, but most of them support other network technologies as well, such as Bluetooth and Wi-Fi. When a phone is configured to use Bluetooth, it can be used with a wireless headset or speaker. When a phone is within range of a Wi-Fi access point, it can connect to it to get Internet service without using any of its monthly data plan bandwidth. And when no Internet service is directly available via a Wi-Fi access point, a cell phone can serve as an access point by allowing other devices to get Internet service through its 3G/4G/5G connection (a feature known as a hot spot).

Cellular-enabled tablets can be used with the same types of networks as smartphones and can act as Wi-Fi access points, but even tablets without cellular support can be used with Wi-Fi and Bluetooth networks.

Step 1   Our first task is to turn on Bluetooth on the device.

iOS

a.   From the home screen, tap Settings.

b.   Find the Bluetooth setting. It will be set to either Off or On.

c.   If Bluetooth is Off, tap Bluetooth and then drag the Bluetooth slider to On.

Android

a.   From the home screen, tap Settings.

b.   Tap Connections.

c.   Drag the Bluetooth slider to the On position if it is not already on.

Step 2   Next, pair the Bluetooth device with the phone or tablet. Most Bluetooth devices are either input (such as a microphone) or output (such as a speaker), or sometimes both (such as a headset).

iOS

a.   Do whatever is needed to place the Bluetooth device in Pair mode. There may be a button you need to press on it, for example.

b.   From the home screen on the iOS device, tap Settings.

c.   Tap Bluetooth. A list of available devices appears.

d.   Tap the desired device to pair with.

e.   Click Pair or OK when prompted.

ANDROID

    a.   Do whatever is needed to place the Bluetooth device in Pair mode. There may be a button you need to press on it, for example.

    b.   From the home screen on the Android device, tap Settings, and then tap Bluetooth.

    c.   Tap Scan. When the new device appears on the list, tap it to connect.

Step 3   Next, enable Wi-Fi on the phone, and connect to a wireless network. (You did this in Lab Exercise 24.02, so you can skip this if you're already familiar with the process.)

iOS

    a.   From the home screen, tap Settings, tap Wi-Fi, and drag the Wi-Fi slider to On.

    b.   In the Choose a Network list, tap the network to which you want to connect.

    c.   If prompted, type the password for the network and click Join.

ANDROID

These instructions are for generic Android devices. Since Android can be customized for various devices, some brands and models might use slightly different steps.

    a.   From the home screen, tap Settings, tap Connections, and drag the Wi-Fi slider to On.

    b.   Tap Wi-Fi, and tap the desired network.

    c.   Enter the password if prompted, and click Connect.

Step 4   Finally, we'll turn the phone or cellular-equipped tablet into a wireless access point, and allow another device (like a PC or tablet) to connect to it.

> **→ Note**
>
> **This step requires that the phone or tablet has cell service; if it doesn't, the option will not be available. Normally having cell service would be a given for a smartphone, but if you're working with test phones for lab purposes, some of them might not have active cell service.**

iOS

    a.   From the home screen, tap Settings.

    b.   Tap Cellular.

    c.   Tap Personal Hotspot.

d. Drag the slider to On. The hotspot's name will be the same as your device name (such as Mike's iPhone).

e. Tap Wi-Fi Password. Enter (or change) the password. Then tap Done.

f. Read the instructions below the Wi-Fi Password section about connecting via Wi-Fi, Bluetooth, or USB. Pick one of these methods, and connect another device to the phone to share its Internet connection. (Disable that device's normal Internet connection temporarily so it will be forced to use the phone.) Document which method you used and the steps that were required:

_____

_____

_____

_____

g. Test the Internet connection on the device to which you just connected.

h. Go back to the phone and disable the personal hotspot by repeating Steps a, b, and c and dragging the Personal Hotspot slider to Off.

i. If you disabled the Internet connection on the other device in Step f, re-enable it if needed.

ANDROID

a. From the home screen or Apps, tap Settings and then tap Connections.

b. In the Wireless Networks section, tap More.

c. Tap Tethering & portable hotspot.

d. Mark the box next to Portable Wi-Fi hotspot.

e. Then tap Portable Wi-Fi hotspot settings.

f. Edit the network name and choose a password.

→ **Note**

On some Android devices, tap Mobile Hotspot and Tethering in step b. Slide the Mobile Hotspot setting to On. Then tap the On link, edit the network name, and choose a password.

 **30 MINUTES**

Lab Exercise 24.05: Researching Chargers and Charging Ports

Over time, the charging ports used by different smartphones and tablets have changed several times. Apple, for example, has used proprietary 30-pin cables on older devices and uses proprietary, unkeyed Lightning cables on recent and most current devices. Apple is using the USB Type-C connector on its newest iPad Pro. Old Android smartphones used mini-USB cables, while more recent models use micro-USB (also known as USB On-The-Go) and, most recently, USB Type-C cables. Some older Android devices have a proprietary connector (usually still based on USB technology) for this purpose, but almost all of these are tablets.

While device charging cables have varied a great deal, chargers have had fewer variations. The requirement for full-speed smartphone charging is 1 amp (1000 mA; 500 mA is supported for slow charging). The minimum requirement for tablet charging is 2.1 A (2100 mA). Making sure you have the correct charging cables and chargers is important, especially if you have a mixture of devices.

Learning Objectives

In this lab, you'll learn which cables and chargers work with your devices, and whether you can use a computer's USB ports to charge your devices.

At the end of this lab, you'll be able to

- Select the correct charging/sync cable for use with your device
- Select chargers with compatible amperage for use with your device
- Evaluate the computers available to determine their capability to charge a smartphone or a tablet

Lab Materials and Setup

The materials you need for this lab are

- An iOS smartphone
- An iOS tablet
- An Android smartphone
- An Android tablet
- A PC with USB 2.0 and USB 3.0 ports; preferably one that also has high-amperage charging ports
- Chargers rated at 1 A and 2.1 A or higher

Getting Down to Business

Smartphones and tablets have endless uses when they are charged, but are simply expensive paperweights when their batteries are exhausted. Keeping them charged is second nature when you're at home or the office, but in an unfamiliar location where you might need to borrow a charger and cable, choosing the wrong combination could leave you without any power.

Step 1   Your first task is to determine which power/sync connector(s) your device uses. Compare the photos in the following table and record which cable(s) your device(s) use.

Apple 30-pin cable	
Apple Lightning cable	
micro-USB (USB On-The-Go [OTG]) cable	
USB Type-C cable	

Step 2   Next, look at the amperage of the charger(s) you use for each device and record the charger information (name, model #, amperage) and device(s) you use it with:

_____

_____

_____

_____

_____

Do you notice a pattern? The chargers with higher amperage (2.1 A or higher) are used with tablets, while the chargers with lower amperage (rated 1 A) are used with smartphones.

Step 3

a. Take a look at the USB ports on computers in your lab. Connect the appropriate charging cable for your smartphone to a standard USB 2.0, USB 3.0, or USB Type-C port on your computer. Is the phone charging? _____

b. Disconnect the smartphone (and cable if necessary) and connect a tablet to the same port. Is the tablet charging? _____

c. Do you see any USB ports marked in yellow or red? _____ These are usually sleep and charge ports that stay on when the computer is sleeping to enable devices to be charged.

d. Connect your smartphone and tablet to the yellow or red ports, and perform the same tests that you did in Steps a and b. Can you charge a tablet? _____ If your tablet can now charge, the port also supplies a higher amperage than normal.

e. (Optional) If you have a system that has red or yellow USB ports, check the system documentation or CMOS settings to determine if the charging amperage can be increased beyond the standard 500 mA for USB 2.0 or micro-USB devices. What did you find out?

_____

_____

Lab Analysis Test

1. Rosalind has a Windows 10 Mobile phone. She wants to use her local credit union's app to deposit checks, and she wants to use her local grocery store's coupon app. Neither business's app supports her phone. What would you advise?

2. Maria's friends have been talking about a certain restaurant review app, and she would like to try it for herself. How can Maria get this app for her iPhone?

3. Todd uses his mobile phone to listen to music all day at work, but he often has data overages on his data plan because he loses track of the amount of time he listens. How can he decrease his data usage?

4. Matilda has just bought a Bluetooth headset for her phone, so she can talk while driving. Explain how to pair a headset to a phone.

5. Rodney has just found out his flight has been delayed and is sitting at the airport waiting. He tries to connect his laptop to the airport's Wi-Fi but the service wants him to pay $10 a day to connect. How can Rodney connect his laptop to the Internet using his cell phone's data plan?

Key Term Quiz

Use the following terms to complete the following sentences. Not all terms will be used.

3G	iPad
Android	pairing
apps	smartphone
Bluetooth	swipe
Ethernet	sync
iOS	Wi-Fi

1. A(n) _____ is an example of a device that uses the iOS operating system.

2. Because _____ is open source, smartphones that use it tend to be less expensive than others.

3. Connecting two devices via Bluetooth is known as _____.

4. You can allow a 4G or 5G phone to use a(n) _____ connection to cut down on the amount of data used in the phone's data plan.

5. Use the Store app on a mobile phone to download _____.

Chapter 25

Care and Feeding of Mobile Devices

Lab Exercises

For a tech who is used to working with desktops and laptops, mobile devices are surprisingly self-maintaining. They are designed to be popular with the average nontechnical person, and to hide any core functionality that the person might inadvertently foul up. Consequently, the OS ecosystem is mostly closed on a mobile device, and there isn't a lot of opportunity for creative tinkering (unless you get into writing your own apps, which is a whole other book). There are three basic maintenance activities: securing, updating, and resetting.

In this chapter's scenario, you've just been assigned to do IT support for 50 users, all of whom have smartphones or tablets. Most are iOS devices, but there are a few Android units too. The main issue you have been tasked with is beefing up device security. Some users don't have passwords set on their devices, so you'll show them how to do that. You'll also show users how to install updates both for the OS and for individual apps. Finally, you'll respond to a few troubleshooting requests where the units are locked up entirely and need to be reset.

 30 MINUTES

Lab Exercise 25.01: Configuring Mobile Device Security

Just like your computer, a smartphone or tablet can contain a lot of private information. In addition to all the standard embarrassing stuff (romantic texts to your spouse, compromising photos, and the like), a mobile device can also contain sensitive financial information, like credit card and bank account numbers. It's smart to enable a lock screen for the device and set a password for access. While this is not a perfect solution, it will slow down most casual snoops and thieves.

→ **Note**

> Most devices have two levels of security. For basic access to the device, a passcode is used. For more ambitious activities, such as purchasing applications through a Store app, a full password may be required. (Apple devices use your Apple ID account's password for this.)

Learning Objectives

In this exercise, you'll change the PIN for access to an iOS device, and record fingerprints for touch ID.

At the end of this lab, you'll be able to

- Change the passcode for an iOS device

- Record fingerprints for secure access

Lab Materials and Setup

The materials you need for this lab are

- An iOS-capable device such as an iPhone or iPad, preferably an iPhone 5S through iPhone 8, iPad Pro, iPad Air 2, or iPad Mini 3 or later (for fingerprint recognition capability)

- An Android phone or tablet

→ **Note**

The iPhone X series of phones do not include fingerprint sensors. These phones use Face ID facial recognition instead.

Getting Down to Business

Whenever an iOS device falls asleep (usually after a few minutes of inactivity), or when you turn it off, it displays a lock screen and prompts for a password when it wakes up. In this lab exercise you will learn how to configure that setting.

iOS

Step 1 First, you will check out the current state of the passcode feature.

   a. Turn on your iOS device and go to the home screen.

   b. Tap the Settings icon, then tap Touch ID & Passcode (or Passcode Lock on some older models).

   c. If prompted, type your current passcode (see Figure 25-1).

   d. Scroll down and find the Turn Passcode Off or Turn Passcode On command. Is the passcode on or off at this point? _____

Step 2 Next you will enable a passcode if there isn't already one, or change the passcode if there is.

   a. If the passcode is currently off, tap Turn Passcode On. Or, if the passcode is currently on, tap Change Passcode.

   b. If you see a prompt about saved fingerprints, tap Keep.

FIGURE 25-1 Entering a passcode on an iPhone

c.   If you are changing the passcode, you are prompted to type your old passcode. Do so.

For the new passcode, you'll be prompted for either a four- or six-digit entry by default (depending on your OS version). For this exercise we'll use the older, four-digit passcode.

d.   If presented with a six-digit prompt, as in Figure 25-2, tap Passcode Options. Then tap 4-Digit Numeric Code.

e.   Type the four-digit numeric code you want to use.

f.   Type the same code again.

g.   If prompted to use the new passcode as your iCloud security code, tap Use Same Code or Don't Change Security Code, whichever is appropriate for your situation.

h.   If you chose Use Same Code in Step g, type your Apple ID password and tap OK.

i.   Press the Home button or, on iPhone X series, swipe up, to return to the home screen.

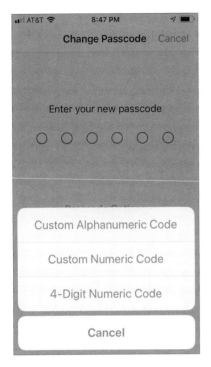

FIGURE 25-2 Tap 4-Digit Numeric Code.

Step 3 Next you'll record your fingerprints for secure access without a passcode. If your device doesn't support it, read through the steps to see how the process works.

a. From the home screen, tap Settings, and then tap Touch ID & Passcode.

b. Type your passcode.

c. In the Use Touch ID For section, make sure the iPhone Unlock or iPad Unlock option is enabled.

d. In the Fingerprints section, tap Add a Fingerprint.

➜ **Note**

You can have up to five fingerprints recorded. If you don't have any open slots, tap an existing fingerprint and tap Delete Fingerprint.

FIGURE 25-3 Adding a fingerprint on an iPhone

e. Follow the prompts to record your fingerprint. You will press and lift your finger on the Home button repeatedly during the process. Figure 25-3 shows the completed print capture.

f. If desired, record additional fingerprints. For example, you might record both your thumb and your index finger, for maximum flexibility.

g. Press the Home button to return to the home screen.

Step 4   Now that you've enabled the passcode (and maybe fingerprint recognition too, depending on your model), test that it works.

a. Tap the power button (lock button) to make your screen go dark. Tap it again to wake up your device.

b. If you set up fingerprint recognition, rest your finger on the Home button (but don't press the button) until your fingerprint is recognized (1 or 2 seconds is usually enough). If a touchpad appears instead, your fingerprint was not recognized. If you don't have fingerprint recognition, swipe to bring up the touchpad.

c. Enter your passcode.

✔ **Tip**

If you forget a device's passcode, see this article to learn about the options for restoring it: https://support.apple.com/en-us/HT204306.

ANDROID

Step 1   If you have an Android device, follow these steps to find out where you would set and change a passcode:

a.   From the home screen, tap Settings.

b.   Tap Lock Screen (or Lock screen and security on some Android versions).

c.   Tap Select screen lock (or Screen lock type on some versions).

d.   Tap one of the screen lock options. You'll see different screen lock options such as Swipe, Knock Code, Pattern, PIN, Fingerprints, or Password (these vary by Android version and any updates). For this exercise, choose PIN (see Figure 25-4).

e.   Type the desired PIN, and then tap Next.

f.   Type the same PIN again and tap OK.

To remove the PIN:

a.   Tap Select screen lock.

b.   Enter the current PIN and tap Next.

c.   Tap None.

FIGURE 25-4 Android screen lock choices

**20 MINUTES**

Lab Exercise 25.02: Installing Updates

Computer operating systems get updated periodically, as you've learned in earlier chapters. For example, Windows Update delivers the latest Windows patches and improvements automatically over the Internet. Similarly, mobile OSs also get periodic updates. Installing the updates as they become available helps make the device more secure, because some of those updates pertain to security. Applications also periodically have available updates that add new features and increase stability.

Learning Objectives

In this lab exercise, you'll check for OS updates on a mobile device, and also check for application updates. This will prepare you to help out the users you support on mobile devices.

At the end of this lab, you'll be able to

- Check for OS updates, and install any that are found
- Check for application updates, and install any that are found

Lab Materials and Setup

The materials you need for this lab are

- An iOS or Android smartphone or tablet

Getting Down to Business

OS updates are important because they may contain security patches, bug fixes, and feature enhancements. On nearly all mobile platforms, OS updates are free. You might need to restart the device after the update has installed, but other than that, the install should be relatively painless.

The following sections include step-by-step instructions for both of the major mobile OSs. However, be aware that Android is customizable. The steps provided here are for a basic, generic Android environment, but certain Android devices may have slightly different steps.

Step 1 First up, you'll check for OS updates. The process is different on each OS.

iOS

    a. From the home screen, tap Settings, and then tap General.

    b. Tap Software Update to expand that category.

    c. If an update is available, tap Install Now. Then follow the prompts. The device might restart after the update, or it might not, depending on the scope of the update.

ANDROID

a. From the home screen, tap Settings. Then scroll all the way to the bottom of the list and tap About (or About Phone).

b. Tap Update Center, and then tap Software Update (see Figure 25-5). You might find Software Update on the main Settings screen on some Android devices.

c. Tap OK (or equivalent command, such as Update now, depending on version). The device connects to a server and lets you know if updates are available. If there are any, follow the prompt to install them.

FIGURE 25-5 AT&T customized software update screen

Describe which device(s) you were able to use for this step, and what happened on each device:

_____

_____

_____

_____

Step 2 Now you'll check for application updates. Again, the process is different depending on the OS.

iOS

    a.   From the home screen, tap App Store.

    b.   If the Updates screen doesn't appear automatically, tap Updates at the bottom of the screen. The Updates icon has a number on it, indicating the number of available updates.

    c.   Under the Available Updates heading, all the available updates appear. Tap the Update button for each app you want to update.

ANDROID

    a.   From the home screen, tap Play Store. Tap the three-line menu icon in the upper-left corner.

    b.   Tap My apps and games.

    c.   Apps that need updating are listed on the Updates tab.

    d.   Tap Update All to update all listed apps.

    e.   To update a specific app, scroll to it and tap its Update button.

Describe which device(s) you were able to use for this step, and what happened on each device:

_____

_____

_____

_____

 **20 MINUTES**

Lab Exercise 25.03: Backing Up and Resetting a Mobile Device

Occasionally something goes wrong with a mobile device, such that it no longer functions normally. It might be completely bricked (that is, dead like a brick), or it might spin endlessly at startup or fail in some way after it boots up.

When this happens, you need to reset the device. There are two kinds of reset: soft and hard. A soft reset restarts the operating system but doesn't touch any settings or saved content. A hard reset wipes everything out and goes back to the bare walls. You lose all content and customization (unless you have backed it up ahead of time, such as to a cloud service).

Most users don't know how to reset their phone or tablet without looking up the procedure, because it's not needed very often. You can look it up online easily enough with a simple Web search, or you can refer to the steps provided in this lab exercise.

Learning Objectives

In this lab exercise, you'll back up your mobile device's settings online, and then perform a hard reset on the device. Finally, you'll restore the device's settings from your backup.

At the end of this lab, you'll be able to

- Back up a mobile device's settings online

- Perform a hard reset on a mobile device

- Restore a mobile device's settings from a backup

Lab Materials and Setup

The materials you need for this lab are

- An iOS or Android smartphone or tablet, preferably one that contains no essential data you need to keep (although you'll back up the data, no backup/restore process is perfect)

- Access to an online account for your mobile device's backup method

Getting Down to Business

Sometimes, wiping out all the data on a mobile device and starting over is the only way to cure a pernicious problem, such as a corrupted system file or an update gone bad. It's nobody's first choice, of course, because who wants to deal with recovering all that data? But planning ahead by doing regular backups of your device's data can help make the experience just a bit less agonizing.

✔ **Tip**

If the device is completely unresponsive, check the obvious: is it charged up? Plug it in for an hour or so and try again before you get all draconian and start resetting.

Step 1   This step is performed *before* you have a problem. By backing up your device's data to cloud storage, you make it possible to get that data back if you have to do a hard reset later.

iOS

    a.   Make sure you have an iCloud account and that you can access it. You probably created one when you set up the iOS device.

    b.   From the home screen, tap Settings, tap your name, tap iCloud, and then tap iCloud Backup.

    c.   If iCloud Backup is not on, drag its slider to turn it on (see Figure 25-6).

    d.   Tap Back Up Now. Then wait for the backup to occur.

FIGURE 25-6 Turning on iCloud Backup on an iPhone

ANDROID

a. Make sure you know your Gmail account user name and password. You will need them later to retrieve your backup.

b. From the home screen, tap Settings, and then tap Backup & reset.

c. Check the Back up my data checkbox in the Backup & Restore section.

d. Make sure that your Gmail account appears in the Backup Account box. If it doesn't (or if you don't have a Gmail account), tap Backup Account and configure that.

Step 2 Next, you'll learn how to do a soft reset—in other words, a restart or reboot. Sometimes when a mobile device locks up, a soft reset will do the trick. And if possible, this is the kind of reset you want to do, because you don't lose data this way.

- **iOS device other than iPhone X series** If the device will respond at a basic level, press and hold the Sleep/Wake button until the red slider appears. Then drag the slider to turn the device completely off. After the device turns off, press and hold Sleep/Wake until you see the Apple logo.

  If the device will not respond at a basic level, you can force a restart. Press and hold both the Sleep/Wake and Home buttons until you see the Apple logo (10 seconds or longer).

- **iOS iPhone X series** If the phone will respond at a basic level, press and hold the Power/Sleep (right side) button and either volume button until the red slider appears. Then drag the slider to turn the device completely off. After the device turns off, press and hold Sleep/Wake until you see the Apple logo.

  If the phone will not respond at a basic level, you can force a restart. Press and quickly release Volume Up, then press and quickly release Volume Down. Then press and hold down the Sleep/Wake button until you see the Apple logo (10 seconds or longer).

- **Android device** Press and hold the Power button until a message appears offering to turn the device off. Select Power off, or select Restart (see Figure 25-7).

  To force restart an Android device, take out the battery for a few seconds if it is removable. If it's not, try holding down the Power button and the Volume button at the same time until the screen goes black. Then hold down the Power button until the device restarts.

→ **Note**

There is a wide variety of methods for force-restarting Android devices, depending on the brand and model; if the method presented here doesn't work, research online to find the procedure for your model.

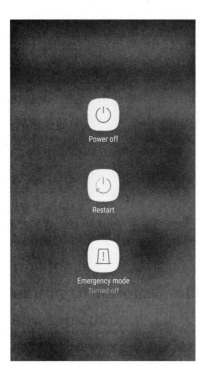

FIGURE 25-7 Powering off an Android phone

Step 3 Now you'll learn how to reset the device the hard, ugly way, the way you have to do it when you run out of other options.

- **iOS device** You'll need a computer with iTunes installed for this fix. Connect the device to the computer and open iTunes. Press and quickly release Volume Up, then press and quickly release Volume Down. Then press and hold down the Sleep/Wake button until you see the Apple logo (10 seconds or longer). Keep holding them until you see the Recovery mode screen. A message appears in iTunes letting you know that there's a problem with the device that requires it to be updated or restored. Click Update, and wait for iTunes to fix the device. If it takes more than 15 minutes, your device will exit recovery mode and you'll need to try again.

  If the preceding method doesn't work, try it again, but this time choose Restore rather than Update in iTunes.

- **Android device** On an Android device, you will want to access the Factory data reset screen. It has a single question on it: *Erase all user data & restore default settings?* Your choices are No and Yes, and you select them with the volume buttons and execute the chosen command with the Power button.

The tricky part is that different Android device brands and models access this screen differently. For example, one Android vendor uses this procedure: with the device powered off, hold down Volume Down and Power. When the brand logo appears, release the Power button only and then immediately press it again. Then release both buttons when the Factory reset data screen appears. Your model may be very different, though, so do some Internet research, and record the method here that worked for you.

_____

Step 4   After a hard reset, if you're savvy (or lucky) enough to have backed up the phone's settings beforehand, you can restore them as follows:

- **iOS device**   When the device comes back up after a hard reset, the Setup Assistant will run. Go to Set up your device, tap Restore from a Backup, and sign in to iCloud. Tap Choose backup, and then select the backup you want to use. Then just follow the prompts to wrap up the process.

- **Android device**   After the hard reset, you are prompted to walk through a setup process. As part of it, you're prompted to sign in to Google. When you do so with the Gmail account you used for backup in Step 1, your data is automatically restored to that device.

Lab Analysis Test

1.   Joe just got a new iPhone X and he is concerned about security. Describe two features of the iPhone X series that will help keep his data private.

2.   Kelly is having problems with a particular mobile app on her Android phone, and she wonders if an update for that application is available. Where should she look for an update?

3.   Brenda has just heard about a major security update for her Android phone on AT&T. Where should she look to install the update?

4.   Mark wants to change the passcode for his iPhone 8 from a six-digit code to a four-digit code. Describe the steps he must take to do so.

5.   In order for Sheila to restore data to her Android device after it has been reset, what kind of account must she have backed up the data to?

Key Term Quiz

Use the following terms to complete the following sentences. Not all terms will be used.

About	Microsoft ID
App Store	My apps & games
Apple ID	passcode
back up	Play Store
fingerprint	restore
Gmail account	Settings
hard reset	soft reset
home screen	Touch ID

1. An iOS device requires you to have a(n) _____ to make app purchases and to back up and restore device data.

2. When a device will not operate normally and will not restart, it may be necessary to do a(n) _____, which wipes out all its data.

3. A lock screen protects the device against unauthorized use by prompting the user for a(n) _____.

4. On an Android device, you get application updates by choosing _____ from the _____; on an iPhone, you get them from the _____.

5. Most system configuration changes begin by selecting _____ from the _____.

Chapter 26

Printers and Multifunction Devices

Lab Exercises

Printers continue to be a major part of the day-to-day working environment, both at home and in the office, despite attempts to create a "paperless office." What this means is that the PC technician will have to understand the operation of several types of printers and be able to keep them in good working order. Many companies have service contracts for their more expensive printers (they're usually leased property), but there will always be printers that need a good technician's love and care.

This chapter's lab exercises will take you through a scenario in which your boss walks into your office and tells you three printers are being delivered to you—two USB inkjet printers, and a multifunction laser printer using a network interface. You need to install them and make sure they work properly so that they're accessible by anyone in the company who needs them. You'll learn about some of the key differences between laser, inkjet, and 3-D printers, and you'll load printer drivers. You'll look at some of the maintenance issues that are required to keep the printers up and running and some of the techniques to follow when they stop functioning properly. You will also learn how to use virtual printers such as PDF creators.

 30 MINUTES

Lab Exercise 26.01: Examining Types of Printers

There's an enormous amount of information on the Internet about printers. All of the top printer manufacturers—HP, Epson, Brother, Lexmark, Canon, and so forth—have Web sites that can provide insight into modern printers. As a PC technician, you'll need to visit these sites for information about your new printers, and to download the most current drivers for those printers.

In addition to physical printers, several software vendors, most notably Adobe and Microsoft, have created virtual printers, which are printer drivers that create documents on disk. Applications that have Adobe PDF support in the Printer or Save As menu enable you to create a PDF file. Microsoft Office applications include both Adobe PDF and Microsoft XPS Document support. See the Adobe and Microsoft Web sites to learn more about PDF and XPS support, and also see Lab Exercise 26.05.

You should also be familiar with the basic principles of 3-D printing, which uses plastic filaments in place of ink or toner to create 3-D objects.

→ **Note**

You must have access to the Internet for this exercise. If you don't have access, refer to the section "Printer and Multifunction Device Components and Technologies" in Chapter 26 of *Mike Meyers' CompTIA A+ Guide to Managing and Troubleshooting PCs* for a review.

Learning Objectives

In this lab, you'll compare the features of impact, inkjet, laser, and 3-D printers using the Internet.

At the end of this lab, you'll be able to

- Recognize the key differences between inkjet, laser, and 3-D printers
- Identify and visit Web sites dedicated to printers and printer troubleshooting

Lab Materials and Setup

The materials you need for this lab are

- A working computer
- A connection to the Internet
- Access to either an inkjet printer or a laser printer

✔ **Hint**

A trip to your local computer store or other retailer with a good selection of printers would be beneficial for a general knowledge of printers.

Getting Down to Business

Fire up your favorite Web browser and head out on the Information Superhighway. The Internet is just brimming with helpful information about printers.

✔ **Hint**

Web sites have the annoying tendency to either disappear or drop the information that was once relevant to a particular subject. If any of the links in this exercise are no longer active or don't seem to contain the relevant information, you may need to do a little Web research of your own. As always, practice safe surfing! There are thousands of online forums available, and they can contain questionable hyperlinks, poor-quality information, and in some cases, outright wrong information. Try to stick with legitimate manufacturer and technical Web sites, examine where that hyperlink is going to reroute your computer, and visit multiple sites to verify information you discover in the forums. Consider it excellent practice for real-world tech work!

Step 1   To find information about inkjet printers, access the following Web site to complete this step: https://computer.howstuffworks.com/inkjet-printer.htm/printable. If this link doesn't work, you can also do a Google search and look for information about how inkjet printers work (and consult Chapter 26 of the textbook).

A.   Is an inkjet considered an impact printer, or non-impact? _____

B.   What part of an inkjet printer moves the printhead back and forth across the page?

_____

C.   List the two ways in which the droplets of ink are formed in inkjet printers.

_____

D.   The type of paper used in an inkjet printer greatly influences the quality of the image produced. What are the two main characteristics of inkjet printer paper that affect the image the most?

_____

Step 2   For information about laser printers, access this site to complete this step: https://computer.howstuffworks.com/laser-printer.htm. Do a Google search or refer to the textbook if this site isn't available.

A.   What's the primary principle at work in a laser printer? _____

B.   What moves the image from the drum to the paper? _____

C.   Printer Command Language (PCL) and PostScript are both examples of what? _____

D.   What's toner? Is it an ink, wax, or something else? _____

Step 3   Using the numbers 1–7, put these steps in the printing process of a laser printer in the correct order (don't forget to reference the textbook as well):

Charge: _____

Clean: _____

Develop: _____

Fuse: _____

Transfer: _____

Expose: _____

Process: _____

Step 4   If you have access to a laser printer, open it and carefully examine the insides. Also read the printer manual for details on the specifications. Access the manufacturer's Web site for additional information.

If you don't have access to a laser printer, go to your local office supply or computer store and ask a salesperson to show you the differences between various impact, inkjet (black and white as well as color), and laser printers.

Look inside your laser printer.

What parts are easily removable and replaceable?

_____

Practice removing and reinserting the toner (see Figure 26-1) and paper.

✖   Warning

**Remember to turn off and unplug the printer before removing anything but the toner or paper.
Also, be careful not to spill any toner inside the printer.**

Figure 26-1   A toner cartridge with its photosensitive drum exposed

Look at the manual or the manufacturer's Web site for these specifications. Some of these questions apply to only laser or only inkjet printers, while others apply to both types.

How much RAM can it hold? _____

Can you upgrade the RAM? _____

What type of RAM does it use? _____

How does the amount of RAM affect the cost of a new printer?

_____

Are the drum and toner separate, or are they one replaceable part? _____

Can you install a module to change the printer language? _____ If yes, what choices are available? _____

Does the printer support duplex (double-sided) printing? _____

What is the speed of the printer (pages per minute)? _____

What is the quality of the output (resolution)? _____

What are the number and types of ink cartridges?

_____

Does the printer use refillable ink reservoirs or ink cartridges? _____

What is the price if you were going to buy this printer new? _____

What is the cost per page? _____

✔ **Hint**

Most inkjet (and even laser) printers are priced very low, so they're affordable to buy initially. Using them is another question. Research the cost of the ink or toner cartridge(s) included with a printer and how many pages it'll print. Printers are often bundled with low-capacity "starter" ink or toner cartridges. So, after you perform the same steps with a standard-capacity and high-capacity cartridge, these calculations will amaze you. They're not so cheap after all.

What can you conclude from your research about the true total cost of printing, including consumables (such as ink)?

_____

Step 5   For information about 3-D printers, access this site to complete this step: https://computer .howstuffworks.com/3-d-printing.htm. Do a Google search or refer to the textbook if this site isn't available.

A.   What's the primary principle at work in a 3-D printer? _____

B.   What is the most common material used by a 3-D printer? _____

C.   What technology does Direct 3-D printing use? _____

D.   Binder 3-D printing combines which two materials? _____ and _____

E.   Which types of 3-D printing use a laser? _____ and _____

F.   Sintering is a type of 3-D printing that works with _____ as well as plastic.

G.   A 3-D CAD file must be converted to which type of file before it can be used as a guide for 3-D printing? _____

Step 6   Go to www.newegg.com, search for 3-D printer, and list three of the models you find there. Then, complete this comparison table. Some of the information may need to be obtained from the manufacturer's Web site or from review sources.

Feature	Printer 1	Printer 2	Printer 3
Price			
Maximum size of finished product			
Materials supported			
Cost of ABS material			
Metal printing support			
Software programs supported			
Print speed			
How controlled (USB, SD card, etc.)			

Which of these printers would be suitable for making figurines? _____

Which of these printers would be suitable for making objects with moving parts? _____

30 MINUTES

Lab Exercise 26.02: Installing a Printer in Windows

The key to a successful printer installation is having the correct software drivers and understanding how the printer will interface with the computer. You'll most likely need the drivers when you install those three printers your boss is having delivered to you, and you'll also have to configure the printers you are installing to use USB or network interfaces. A common practice in multiple-user environments—companies considered to be small office/home office (SOHO)—is to use a printer with its own wired or wireless network interface card (NIC), so that computers from anywhere in the network can print directly to the printer through the network interface.

Learning Objectives

In this lab, you'll install a printer, first as a directly connected device, and then as a network device. You will then explore and change its settings.

At the end of this lab, you'll be able to

- Install a local printer in Windows

- Install a network printer in Windows

- Change printer settings in Windows

Lab Materials and Setup

The materials you need for this lab are

- A working computer with Windows installed

- An inkjet or laser printer, preferably with its own NIC interface

Getting Down to Business

These days, installing a printer is a fairly straightforward task. This is good news, because you'll probably do your fair share of it as a computer technician. Windows can usually detect the printer and install a basic driver for it automatically. However, you might want to use the driver that came with the printer on optical media, or download the latest driver from the Internet.

Step 1   Install the printer as a local printer on an individual PC, as follows:

    a.   Check the printer documentation, and see whether a setup utility should be run before connecting the printer. If so, run it.

> ✖ **Warning**
>
> In some cases you run into trouble if you allow Windows to autodetect a printer and install a driver for it rather than letting the printer's setup utility do its thing. (That's more common with older printers and older Windows versions than it is today, fortunately.) Make sure you read the printer manual and do what is recommended.

b.   Connect the printer to your system via a USB port. Allow Windows to detect it and set it up. If prompted for a driver, follow the prompts to search for one online, or to use the driver on the optical disc that came with the printer.

c.   (Optional) If the setup disc that came with the printer has any extra utilities on it that you want, install them from the disc. For a regular printer, there is nothing you need there. For a multifunction device, however, you might need to run that setup utility to enable features like copying, scanning, and faxing.

Step 2   Now you'll install a printer (it could be the same printer or a different one) as a network-enabled printer. When you connect a printer directly to the network via its own network adapter, any computer on the network can use it.

> ➔ **Note**
>
> When Windows references a printer, it doesn't mean the printer hardware; it means an instance of the driver set up to be addressable in Windows. So you can have multiple "printers" in Windows that all talk to the same physical printer. This can be useful when you want different default settings for different kinds of print jobs, for example.

Follow these steps to connect to a network-enabled printer over the network:

a.   Connect the printer to the network via its RJ-45 jack, or via its wireless interface if it has one. Make sure the printer is powered on.

b.   Open the Control Panel and choose Hardware and Sound | Devices and Printers | Add a printer. In Windows 10, you can also use this method: Settings | Devices | Printers & scanners | Add a printer or scanner.

c.   Select the printer from the list of network printers. You can tell it's a network printer because it has an IP address. See Figure 26-2. Then click Next.

d.   If there is already a driver for the printer installed in Windows (for example, if you installed one in Step 1), a message appears; click *Use the driver that is currently installed.* Then click Next.

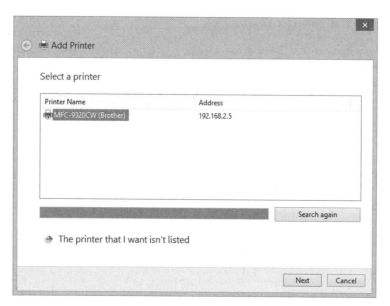

Figure 26-2 The Add Printer Wizard finds the available printers.

e.   In the Printer Name box, change the name if desired. Then click Next.

f.   Clear the Set as the default printer checkbox if you don't want this to be the default.

g.   (Optional) Click Print a test page if you want one. (Ask your instructor if you should print one.)

h.   Click Finish.

Step 3   Once a printer has been installed in Windows (either local or network), you can adjust its settings. The thing is, there are *three* different places you can adjust printer settings, and each one has different options. In the following steps you'll take a tour.

a.   Open the Devices and Printers applet of the Control Panel (Hardware and Sound | Devices and Printers).

b.   Right-click the printer's icon and choose Properties. A dialog box appears that describes the printer (manufacturer, model, that sort of thing). See Figure 26-3.

c.   There's not much you can do in this dialog box; click OK to close it.

d.   Right-click the printer's icon again and choose Printer properties. An entirely different dialog box opens. This one has a lot more going on, as you can see in Figure 26-4.

FIGURE 26-3 Right-click a printer's icon and choose Properties to see a dialog box like this.

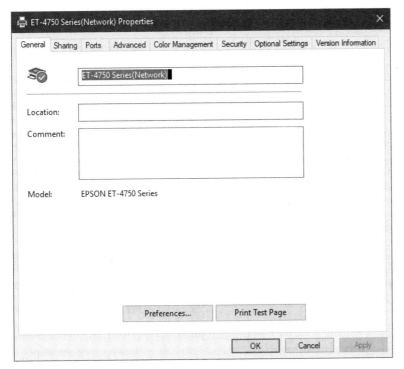

FIGURE 26-4 For a full array of settings you can adjust for a printer, right-click its icon and choose Printer properties.

e.   Click through the tabs and list in the following grid eight useful things you can do in this dialog box. The exact options available will depend on your printer.

Tab	Feature	Useful Thing

f.   Close the dialog box.

g.   Right-click the printer again and choose Printing preferences. In the following grid, list four useful things you can do in this dialog box.

Tab	Feature	Useful Thing

h.   On the Layout tab, click Advanced (on some printers, this might be listed as More Options). A dialog box appears with additional printing preference options. The choices available depend heavily on the printer type and model. List four settings you can change in this dialog box for your printer:

_____

_____

_____

_____

i.   Close all open dialog boxes and close the Devices and Printers applet and the Control Panel.

 30 MINUTES

Lab Exercise 26.03: Supporting a Multifunction Device

Among the printers you have been tasked to work with is a multifunction laser printer with a network interface. It didn't come with any documentation or drivers, so you're on your own. It's time to get creative as you research this device, locate drivers for it, and figure out how to set it up to function on the LAN.

Learning Objectives

In this lab, you'll research a multifunction device online. You'll find out its capabilities and download the software needed to make it work. Then you'll figure out how to access its network capabilities and get it connected to the local network.

At the end of this lab, you'll be able to

- Download and install printer drivers and other support software

- Find printer documentation online

- Connect a printer to a LAN

Lab Materials and Setup

The materials you need for this lab are

- A working computer with Windows installed and an Internet connection

- A multifunction printer, preferably with wired or wireless network capability

Getting Down to Business

Pre-Internet, technicians zealously safeguarded the driver discs that came with multifunction devices (MFDs), because they provided the only reliable means of installing the devices' drivers. Windows came with a short list of printer drivers, and could sometimes provide a driver that would make the unit print, but that only made the *printer* part work; the rest of the device's capabilities were severely crippled (or completely unusable) without the corresponding software. Nowadays, of course, the situation is much different because anyone can download a multifunction device's software quickly and painlessly, and it'll probably be a more up-to-date version than the one that came on the disc with the device, too.

In the following steps, you'll walk through the process of getting a bare MFD (no drivers, no docs) up and running on your network.

> **→ Note**
>
> **If you have an actual MFD in your possession, use it for this lab exercise. If not, use any MFD model you like for the Internet research portion of things (Steps 1 and 2). If you don't know what make and model to use, go with Brother MFC-L3710CW. You won't be able to complete Steps 3 and later if you don't have an actual MFD to work with.**

Step 1   First you'll identify the MFD make and model, and find its support site online.

What is the make and model of the device you are using?

_____

Find the manufacturer's Web site, and find the Support section of the site. What is that URL?

_____

Step 2   At the support Web site:

a.   Find the support information for your specific model, and download the complete driver package for it. Make sure you get the complete package for the MFD, not just a driver for the printer portion.

b.   Download a user manual for the device, which may be in PDF format.

The rest of the steps you can do only if you have an actual MFD to work with.

Step 3   If you have the actual MFD (and aren't just using a dummy model for the exercise), do the following to set it up:

a.   Run the setup program you downloaded in Step 2. Start off with the MFD *not* connected to the computer. Connect the MFD to the computer with a USB cable and power it up only when prompted to do so in the setup utility.

b.   Print a test page to confirm that the printer portion works.

c.   If you are using an inkjet MFD, check the ink levels.

Step 4   Test the scanner portion of the unit by using Windows Fax and Scan to scan a picture or a page of text. To start Windows Fax and Scan, search for it (you can type **wfs** into the Search window to find it) and click the matching program. Describe here the steps you took, and whether the process worked:

_____

_____

Step 5   Test the copier portion of the unit by making a copy of the picture or page you scanned in Step 4. Describe here the steps you took, and whether the process worked:

_____

_____

Step 6   Consult the user manual that you downloaded in Step 2 to determine how to set up the MFD for network use. Then do so, and describe here the steps you took:

_____

_____

_____

Step 7   Disconnect the printer from its local USB connection to the computer, and remove its driver from Devices and Printers in the Control Panel. (If prompted to delete the drivers for the unit, do not do so.)

Step 8   Connect the computer to the printer via your LAN. Describe here the steps you took. Refer as needed to Lab Exercise 26.02.

_____

_____

_____

 30 MINUTES

Lab Exercise 26.04: Maintaining and Troubleshooting Printers

It is estimated that technicians, especially those working for the help desk or desktop support group for a small-to medium-sized organization, spend approximately 30 percent of their time on printer issues. If you think about it, of all the components used in computing technology, printers have the highest percentage of moving parts. Moving parts are more likely to need maintenance than are static components.

Printers also like to be finicky and stop printing, usually resulting in a phone call from the client to the help desk for quick resolution. The following exercises will help you develop some understanding of laser printer and inkjet printer maintenance, and what steps to take when they stop printing.

Learning Objectives

In this lab, you'll research laser printer maintenance kits, clean dirty inkjet nozzles, and troubleshoot a failed print job.

At the end of this lab, you'll be able to

- Select a proper maintenance kit for various laser printers
- Clean and verify operation of inkjet nozzles
- Manage print jobs in Windows
- Restart a stalled print spooler

Lab Materials and Setup

The materials you need for this lab are

- A working computer with Windows installed
- A connection to the Internet
- Access to an inkjet printer

Getting Down to Business

The following exercises will round out your activities as you finish with the rollout of the new printers in your office. You will want to get your Internet connection fired up again and research the supplies and replacement parts for your laser printer. Then you'll check the printhead nozzles of the inkjet printers and run the cleaning routine if necessary. Finally, you should prepare for any print errors so that you can correct them quickly and efficiently.

Step 1   All printers require some kind of ink or toner, of course, so it's a no-brainer that you'll need to buy ink or toner periodically. What many people don't realize, though, is that it doesn't stop there. Many printers include replaceable parts that have a certain expected duty life, and they have to be replaced after a certain number of pages have been printed in order to ensure continued high-quality printouts. For a laser printer, the most commonly replaced of these components is the drum (or multiple drums, if it's a color printer). You might also need to replace some of the rollers or belts inside the printer, or replace the waste toner reservoir.

✔ **Hint**

For some laser printer models, you can buy "maintenance kits" containing several parts needed to refurbish an aging printer. The exact content varies depending on the printer model, but usually includes a fuser assembly, a transfer roller, and various feed rollers. A maintenance kit will come with instructions as to how to use it. Maintenance kits are most common for HP and Lexmark printers.

On an inkjet printer, the printheads also have to be replaced periodically. On some printer models, the printheads are built into the ink cartridges, so every time you replace the ink cartridge, you automatically get new printheads. On other models, they are separate, and the printheads are replaced much less frequently than the ink cartridges. (By the way, that's one reason why some inkjet cartridges are so expensive—and why the manufacturers don't recommend that you have them refilled.)

a. Select a laser printer make and model, and perform an Internet search to identify the parts available, the part numbers, and their cost.

✔ **Tip**

Try www.precisionroller.com and www.printertechs.com for printer parts and maintenance kits.

b. Gather the following information:

Printer model: _____

Item	Part Number	Cost
Toner cartridge (black)		
Toner cartridge (each color)		
Drum(s)		
Fuser		
Transfer roller or belt assembly		
Maintenance kit		
Waste toner container		

c. If a maintenance kit is available, what does it contain?

_____

_____

    d.   Look up the price for a new printer of this model, or the equivalent modern model from the same manufacturer with similar capabilities if this one is no longer made.

        Price: _____

    e.   Suppose the printer needs a new fuser and a new transfer roller, a new transfer roller/belt, and new drums. Given the costs you researched earlier, would it be a good value to refurbish this printer, or would it be better to recycle it and buy a new one? _____

Step 2   If an inkjet printer sits idle for an extended period of time (a few weeks or months), the ink tends to dry up in it, causing the nozzles to become clogged. You might need to run the printer's head-cleaning utility to fix that. Cleaning utilities work by forcing new ink through the nozzles vigorously, blowing out any clogs. As you can imagine, this wastes ink, so you wouldn't want to do this unless there was a problem. A "problem" looks like one or more ink colors not printing, or a printout having stripes or blotches where a solid color should be.

    To check the status of the inkjets, print a test page and see how well each color performs. Follow these steps:

    a.   Open the Devices and Printers applet of the Control Panel (Hardware and Sound | Devices and Printers).

    b.   Right-click the printer and choose Printer properties.

    c.   On the General tab, click Print Test Page. If the test page looks good, you don't need to clean the heads. If one or more colors are spotty, striped, or missing, you do.

    The procedure for cleaning the printhead varies between models. There is probably a command you can access through the printer's own LCD control panel, independent of any PC, and there is probably also a command you can issue in the printer's properties in the operating system to trigger that same process. Consult the printer's documentation for specific instructions.

Record here the steps you took to access the cleaning utility:

_____

_____

Step 3   When you are called upon to troubleshoot a failed print job, you should follow a logical step-by-step process to make sure that no obvious, possibly simple failure has occurred. If the power cord or data cable has been kicked out or the paper tray is open, troubleshooting the network connectivity or the printer driver would waste valuable time. Once you know the print device is online and ready and there are no paper jams or mechanical errors, it might be time to open the print spooler (also known as Print Manager in Windows) and attempt to restart the document.

The following steps are meant to be a rough guideline to troubleshoot and diagnose a failed print job:

a. First, check the physical print device:

- Is the printer plugged in, and is the power turned on?
- Is the printer out of paper or is there a paper jam?
- Is the toner low or in need of replacement?
- Are there any error messages on the printer's LCD readout or any error indicator lights flashing?
- Is the printer online and ready to print?

If you examine all of these areas and find everything appears to be in working condition, then you may have a problem with the connectivity between the computer and the printer, or there may be problems with the document or drivers.

b. Make sure that the connections between the computer and the printer are in good condition and securely fastened.

✔ Hint

To create a failed print job, disconnect the printer cable, shut off the power on the printer, or open the printer paper tray. Send a print job to the printer; the printer icon should appear in the notification area indicating that the print job has failed. Then continue with Step 3.

c. After checking all of the physical components, try to resend the document. Open the print queue for the printer (see Figure 26-5) by clicking the printer icon in the notification area. Or, if you don't see one there, open the Control Panel and navigate to Devices and Printers. Double-click the printer. If its queue doesn't immediately appear, click See what's printing.

d. In the print queue, select the failed print job by highlighting the job with Error in the Status column (see Figure 26-5).

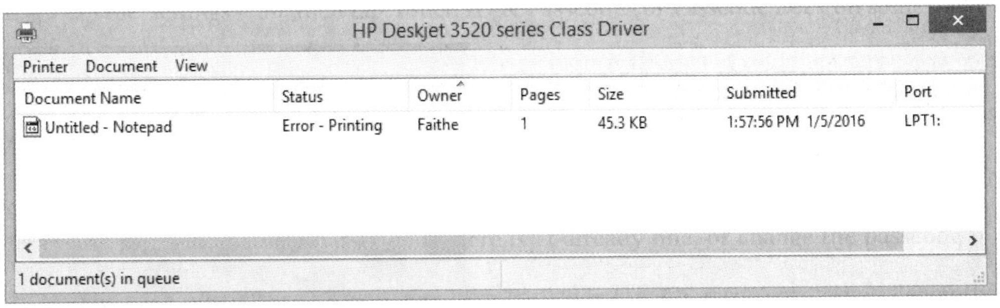
HP Deskjet 3520 series Class Driver
Printer Document View
Document Name
Status
Owner
Pages
Size
Submitted
Port
Untitled - Notepad
Error - Printing
Faithe
1
45.3 KB
1:57:56 PM 1/5/2016
LPT1:
1 document(s) in queue

FIGURE 26-5 The Windows print spooler, Print Manager, showing error status on a Word Notepad file

e.   Select Document | Restart. You might see another error in the notification area, or the print job might simply continue to report an error in the print queue.

f.   Select Document | Cancel to delete the print job from the queue.

If this were a real scenario, you would verify that the print drivers were installed and are the correct drivers for the operating system. You would then go on to Step 4 to see if the problem is related to the print spooler.

Step 4   If the print device is online and ready, there are no paper jams or mechanical errors, and restarting the document is of no help, you can check to see if the print spooler is stalled. The print spooler is a holding area for print jobs and is especially important for network printers. If the print device runs out of paper while printing a document, you may have to stop and start the print spooler before the print device will receive jobs again.

To do this, you will use the Services snap-in for the Microsoft Management Console (MMC).

a.   Open the Control Panel and navigate to System and Security | Administrative Tools, and then double-click the Services icon.

b.   In the Services window, scroll down and select Print Spooler. Choose Action | Properties. You should see that the print spooler is started and running (see Figure 26-6).

c.   Click the Stop button. The print spooler indicates that it has stopped.

d.   Click the Start button. The print spooler indicates that it has started.

FIGURE 26-6 Print Spooler Properties dialog box

e.   Alternatively, you can select Print Spooler in the Services console and choose Action | Restart. You'll see a message stating that the print spooler is stopping, and then another message indicating that the print spooler is starting.

In the real-world scenario, your print spooler service would be restarted, and you should have a healthy, functioning print server once again.

 30 MINUTES

Lab Exercise 26.05: Using a Virtual Printer

As an alternative to sending a document to a physical printer, you can use a so-called "virtual printer," a software program that creates formatted documents including fonts and images that can be viewed on-screen or sent to physical printers later. The most common of these is support for the Adobe Portable Document Format (PDF), but Microsoft Windows also includes support for its own XPS document format.

Virtual printers can be used in two ways: through the Print dialog, or by using Save As, depending upon the specific way that virtual printer support was provided and the app in use.

Learning Objectives

In this lab, you'll use the virtual printer features built into Windows.

At the end of this lab, you'll be able to

- Create a PDF or XPS file from within Windows

- View these files

- Learn how to access virtual printers in Windows

- Discover how to add virtual printer support in Windows 7 and Windows 8.1

Lab Materials and Setup

The materials you need for this lab are

- A working computer with Windows 7, 8.1, or 10 installed

- A connection to the Internet

Getting Down to Business

The following steps will help you learn how to locate and use virtual printers in Windows. Along the way, you will learn where to find virtual printer support if it is not already installed.

Step 1   In this step, you will create a document and turn it into an XPS file.

a.   Start Windows.

b.   Open WordPad.

c.   Create a short (under one page) document that includes various fonts, font sizes, and colors.

d.   Open the File menu, select Save As, and choose Other formats.

e.   Open the Save as Type menu. Do you see a reference to PDF or XPS file types? _____ If yes, you can use File | Save As to create a PDF or XPS file. If no, you must use the Print menu to create these files.

f.   Save the document as Virtual using the Rich Text Format (RTF) file format.

g.   Open the File menu and select Print | Print.

h.   Click Microsoft XPS Document Writer.

i.   Click Print.

j.   Enter a name for the file: VirtualXPS and click Save. The XPS file is saved to the current user's Documents folder.

k.   Did you see a PDF writer printer, such as Microsoft Print to PDF, in Step g (see Figure 26-7)? _____

Step 2   In this step, you will view the XPS file you created in Step 1.

a.   Open Windows Explorer (Windows 7) or File Explorer (Windows 8.1/10).

b.   Open the Documents folder.

c.   Double-click the VirtualXPS file.

d.   Scroll through the file to view it, then close the app.

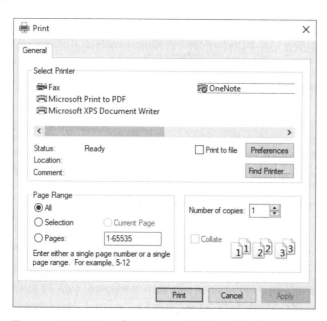

FIGURE 26-7   Virtual printers available in Windows 10

→ **Note**

> If the file did not open, you need to install the Windows XPS Viewer. In Windows 10, it is available from Settings | Apps | Apps & features | Manage optional features | Add a feature. Click XPS Viewer, Install. In Windows 7/8.1, it is available from Control Panel | Programs and Features | Turn Windows features on or off | check box for XPS Viewer | OK. After the app is installed, try Step 2c again.

Step 3   In this step, you will turn the document you created in Step 1 into a PDF file.

   a.   Switch back to WordPad. If the document you created in Step 1 has been closed, reopen it.

   b.   Open the File menu and select Print | Print.

   c.   Click Microsoft Print to PDF.

   d.   Click Print.

   e.   Enter a name for the PDF file: VirtualPDF and click Save. The PDF file is saved to the current user's Documents folder.

   f.   If another PDF printer is also available, repeat Steps b–d with another PDF printer.

   g.   Name the PDF file VirtualPDF2 and click Save.

Step 4   In this step, you will view the PDF file(s) you created in Step 3.

   a.   Open Windows Explorer (Windows 7) or File Explorer (Windows 8.1/10).

   b.   Open the Documents folder.

   c.   Double-click the VirtualPDF file.

   d.   Which app was used to open the file? _____

   e.   Close the app.

   f.   Double-click the VirtualPDF2 file in Windows Explorer/File Explorer.

   g.   Was the same app used to open this file as in Step d? _____

   h.   Close the app.

✔ **Try This: Install a PDF Writer**

> If you are using Windows 7 or 8.1, these versions of Windows don't include a PDF writer. If your system doesn't already have one installed, open your preferred web browser and search for PDF maker for Windows 7 or PDF maker for Windows 8.1 to locate third-party apps. Install one and use it to make PDF files.

Lab Analysis Test

1. Patrick's laser printer ejects pages with loose toner on them. What component has failed inside the printer?

2. Theresa just bought a secondhand multifunction device that didn't come with any documentation or drivers. She connects it to her Windows PC and a basic printer driver is installed automatically, but the computer doesn't see the scanner. How can she enable the scanner?

3. Danyelle has been called in to evaluate a laser printer that has frequent paper jams and poor print quality. The office manager doesn't want to replace the printer. What can she do to help it perform better?

4. Brandon has sent a document to the printer, but the document never actually prints. Where can Brandon check to see the status of the document?

5. When Sally prints in color on her inkjet printer, the only color that appears is yellow. What should she do?

Key Term Quiz

Use the following terms to complete the following sentences. Not all terms will be used.

dpi

inkjet

IP address

laser

primary charge roller

primary corona

toner

transfer corona

transfer roller

USB

1. The part of the laser printer that actually causes the toner image to be created on the paper is the _____ or _____ .

2. A network-enabled printer has its own _____ on the network.

3. The resolution of a printer is measured in _____ .

4. The printer that spits ink onto the paper is a(n) _____ printer.

5. A laser printer's _____ is responsible for writing the image onto the drum.

Chapter 27
Securing Computers

Lab Exercises

Obviously, keeping your computer secure is important. Several chapters have already been devoted to securing your systems and networks. But there are still a few more helpful tools you should know about to keep things running smoothly. Local Security Policy in Windows enables you to set a variety of rules about using the system; Event Viewer shows you information about events you didn't even know were happening; and Windows Defender is a free tool that enables you to clean your system of, and protect your system against, viruses and other malicious software (malware). Each of these tools increases the power you have over your own security and the security of your computer. You'll also learn how to handle a computer that has illegal materials on it or is part of a criminal investigation.

 15 MINUTES

Lab Exercise 27.01: Configuring Local Policies

NTFS permissions are powerful tools to control with great detail what users and groups can do to folders and files. However, NTFS does not cover a number of important security issues that don't directly involve the file system. For example, what if you don't want a particular user group to shut down the computer? What if you want to make sure all accounts use a password of at least eight characters? What if you want to prevent certain users from reformatting the hard drive? These types of security settings are all controlled under the umbrella term of *local policies*.

✔ **Hint**

> There are hundreds of different policies that you may configure for a system. This lab only covers a few of the most basic policies!

Learning Objectives

At the end of this lab, you'll be able to

- Locate and open the Local Security Policy utility

- Create, modify, and delete local policies with Windows

Lab Materials and Setup

The materials you need for this lab are

- A Windows PC running on a workgroup (this lab will not work on a system configured for a Windows domain)

- Administrator privileges on that system

- Internet access

Getting Down to Business

Local Security Policy is a very powerful applet that enables you to adjust all sorts of settings for and details about your system. Simply put, it is a series of rules you define, ranging from how many attempts to log on a user is allowed, to who can change the time on the clock!

Step 1   Follow these steps to require user passwords to meet complexity requirements. This is a simple policy change, but it gives you the basic idea of how the Local Security Policy applet works.

a.   Sign into Windows using an account with administrator rights.

b.   From the Control Panel, navigate to System and Security | Administrative Tools.

c.   Double-click Local Security Policy. When opened, it should look something like Figure 27-1.

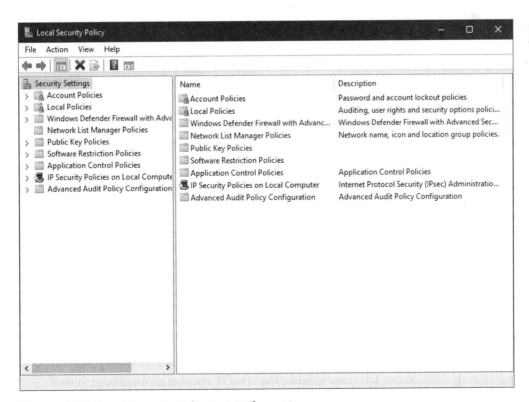

FIGURE 27-1   Local Security Policy in Windows 10

d.   Double-click Account Policies to expand its contents: Password Policy and Account Lockout Policy.

e.   Click Password Policy in the left column, and double-click *Password must meet complexity requirements* in the right column to open this policy's Properties dialog box.

f.   Click Enabled to enable this policy, and click OK.

Step 2   Now let's test that restriction to see if it's really in effect, and what it looks like to a user.

a.   Using the procedure for your Windows version for creating a new Windows user account (it varies, as you learned in Lab Exercise 13.01, "Managing Users in Windows"), create a standard local user account and call it **Janet**. Try assigning a simple password like **janet** and see what happens.

Read these articles to find out what the password complexity requirements are:

- Windows 7, 8/8.1: https://technet.microsoft.com/en-us/library/hh994562.aspx

- Windows 10: https://docs.microsoft.com/en-us/windows/security/threat-protection/ security-policy-settings/password-must-meet-complexity-requirements

If these articles are not available for some reason, research Windows password complexity requirements by doing your own search.

What do you need to include to make an acceptable password in Windows 7/8/8.1? (Summarize as best you can.)

_____

_____

What do you need to include to make an acceptable password in Windows 10?

_____

_____

b.   Switch back to the user account creation screen and try a new password that meets the requirements for your Windows version. Finish creating the account.

Step 3   Next, we'll check out the password history policy. This policy prevents users from cycling through the same old passwords (which can be a security risk) when they change passwords.

a.   Switch back to the Local Security Policy window.

b.   With Password Policy selected in the left column, double-click Enforce password history to open its Properties dialog box.

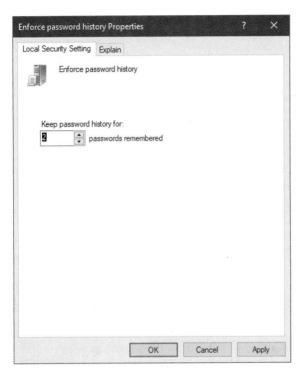

FIGURE 27-2 Windows can remember previous passwords to prevent their reuse.

c. Change the number of passwords remembered to 2 (as in Figure 27-2) and click OK.

d. Open to the User Accounts section of the Control Panel (or Settings app, if in Windows 8.1/10) and try to change a password to the same password you already have. What happens?

_____

e. Go back to the Enforce password history Properties dialog box and set the Keep password history for setting to 0 (or whatever it was before you changed it in Step c).

Step 4 Next we'll take a look at the account lockout policy. An account lockout occurs when the operating system no longer allows a certain account the right even to *try* to log on. This is a precaution you can take to prevent someone from trying to guess your password, because it cuts them off after a certain number of wrong guesses.

a. In the Local Security Policy window, in the left pane, select Account Lockout Policy under Account Policies.

b. In the right pane, double-click Account lockout threshold to open its dialog box, and set the *Account will not lock out* counter to 3. Then click OK.

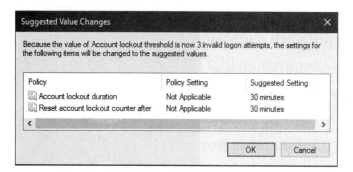

FIGURE 27-3 Windows suggests other policies that should be changed to work as a team with the lockout policy threshold.

c. In the Suggested Value Changes dialog box that appears (see Figure 27-3), click OK to accept the changes to other policies.

d. Sign out of Windows and then try to log on to the Janet account you created earlier. Intentionally attempt to log on using incorrect passwords. What happens after the third try?

_____

e. Sign back in with the administrator account, reopen Local Security Policy, and under Account Policies | Account Lockout Policy, check the value shown for Reset account lockout counter after. How long will Janet have to wait before she can try again to access her account? _____

f. Close the Local Security Policy window.

→ **Note**

You can delete the Janet account at this point if you like; you're done with it.

**20 MINUTES**

Lab Exercise 27.02: Reviewing Security Events

A lot goes on in the background as Windows operates, and most of it you can ignore completely. Applications run, processes execute, informational messages are saved to logs, and so on. All trivia, from an end-user perspective. However, if you're the PC tech who is charged with checking for security vulnerabilities or breaches on a PC, having access to all that backchannel chatter becomes useful.

As you learned in Chapter 16, the utility for viewing those logs is called Event Viewer. You saw in Chapter 16 how to use Event Viewer as a troubleshooting tool; now we'll use it as a security-awareness tool.

Learning Objectives

In this lab, you'll practice using Event Viewer to check for security issues.

At the end of this lab, you'll be able to

- Work with Event Viewer to track events on your system

Lab Materials and Setup

The materials you will need for this lab are

- A PC with Windows

Getting Down to Business

Think about your actions on a computer as a series of events: you log on, you open an application, you close it, you log off, and so forth. This is how Event Viewer sees things, but in a lot more detail. If something goes wrong, Event Viewer usually records it. It also records a lot of things that are perfectly normal—the trick is being able to sort through all the information.

Step 1 Open Event Viewer and browse around the logs by doing the following:

   a. Open the Control Panel and navigate to System and Security | Administrative Tools.

   b. Double-click Event Viewer.

   c. In the left pane, double-click Windows Logs to see a list of logs.

   d. In the left pane, click Application, as shown in Figure 27-4. The events in this log all concern the operation of applications on your system.

   e. Click a few different events in the top of the center pane to view information about them. Information appears in the bottom of the center pane.

Step 2 Next, let's have a look at the System log.

   a. In the left pane, click the System log to display it.

   b. Scroll down through the log events to find some logs other than Information. For example, you might see Warning, Error, and/or Critical.

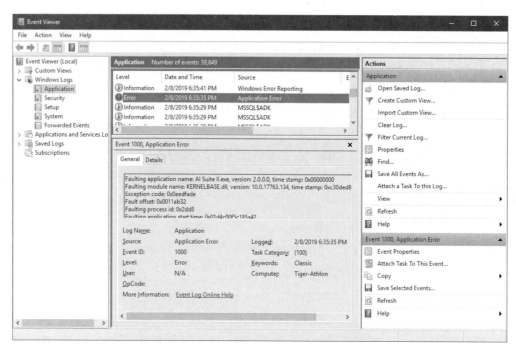

FIGURE 27-4 Event Viewer

→ **Note**

Warnings do not indicate that something bad *is* happening but rather that something bad *will* happen. An example of a Warning event is when Windows is low on resources, such as disk space. Errors are more serious. These events occur when there is a failure or loss of functionality, such as when an application crashes.

---

   c.   Click the Level column to sort by level. Then look for any critical errors (at the very top or very bottom of the list, depending on sort order).

   d.   Double-click one of the more serious-looking errors you find to display a dialog box of information about it.

✔ **Tip**

A lot of Event Viewer's reports can be very cryptic, which is why Windows has a handy Event Log Online Help hyperlink built into Event Viewer.

---

   e.   While viewing the details of an event, click the Event Log Online Help hyperlink.

f. A dialog box appears asking for permission to send information about the event over the Internet. Click Yes.

g. A browser window opens with information about the error, if available. There isn't information available on every single event, but it can be very useful in tracking down problems.

You can also record the Event ID number that is listed with the event and search for it on the Internet. For example, if it is Event ID 1002, simply search for **"Event Viewer ID 1002"** (use the quotes as part of the search) and see what comes up. You're likely to find out at least a little more than you knew before.

Step 3 Search through the Security log to see what sort of events it records. Write down three Task Categories recorded by the Security log:

_____

_____

_____

Step 4 Sometimes it can be difficult to discern which event log item goes with what actual event. To make this simpler, clear the log by doing the following:

a. In the right pane, under Actions, click Clear Log.

b. Click Clear.

Now that the logs are clear, it'll be easier to identify an event that pertains to a specific activity.

Step 5 Minimize the Event Viewer window and go back to the Local Security Policy applet, which you worked with in Lab Exercise 27.01. Disable the *Password must meet complexity requirements* policy if you left it enabled before (or enable it and then disable it if you didn't do that lab).

Step 6 Switch back to Event Viewer and look in the Security log. (Refresh it by clicking some other log and then clicking back to it.) Find the item where you changed the security policy, and record information about it here:

_____

_____

✔ **Hint**

Look in the Task Category column to see which event has something to do with a policy change.

When you're finished, close the Event Viewer and Local Security Policy windows.

 **30 MINUTES**

Lab Exercise 27.03: Removing Malware from a Computer

What kinds of computer threats are out there? Here are a couple of data points: a recent survey conducted by Cofense PhishMe showed that 97.25 percent of phishing e-mails collected contained ransomware. Two studies presented at a recent Black Hat USA conference indicated that up to 45 percent of users who understood the dangers of clicking unknown links clicked them anyway. With more sophisticated attacks combined with careless computer use, it's no wonder that Best Buy's Geek Squad has reported that over 75 percent of their service calls involve cleaning malware off of a computer and then showing customers how to protect their PCs from malware and other attacks.

➜ **Note**

Learn more about current and recent security threats at the AlertLogic Security Blog (https://blog.alertlogic.com/).

Windows comes with many programs and features to protect your computer, but these tools are useless if they are not used properly. In this lab exercise, you will check the computer for malware, clean the malware from the computer, and then go through the steps to reduce the likelihood of another attack.

Learning Objectives

In this lab exercise you'll learn how to remove malware and how to configure a PC to minimize the likelihood of future malware infections.

At the end of this lab, you'll be able to

- Remove malware from a Windows system

- Configure Internet security software (antivirus/anti-malware)

Lab Materials and Setup

The materials you need for this lab are

- Windows 7 PC with an Internet connection, or a Windows 8.1 or 10 PC

 Hint

> This is a great lab for students who want to bring a PC from home—or one that belongs to a friend—for testing and cleaning.

Getting Down to Business

A new system brings with it new problems. You've set up user accounts with passwords and activated firewalls, but there is still one more important piece of protection required. Antivirus and anti-malware software can actively and passively protect you from unwanted malicious activity. Actively, you can usually scan entire computers for any issues. Passively, many tools are available that will constantly monitor your PC as you use it and watch out for viruses and other problems you may encounter on the Internet.

Microsoft offers the free Microsoft Security Essentials software for users of Windows 7, available for download. Starting in Windows 8, Microsoft rolled its features into Windows Defender, which comes with Windows itself, so Microsoft Security Essentials is no longer required for (and doesn't work with) Windows 8 and later.

Step 1   If you are running Windows 7, the first step is to download the software (if you haven't already done so): https://support.microsoft.com/en-us/help/14210/security-essentials-download.

When you open the executable, it will extract itself and begin the installation. Follow the instructions. Then it will run itself, update itself, and scan itself—it's all quite impressive to watch (see Figure 27-5).

There's no download needed for Windows 8 and later systems. Run the Windows Defender applet from the Start screen/Start menu. Then on the Home tab in the application, choose Quick or Full, and then click Scan Now. The scan runs, and reports its findings.

Whichever utility you use, it will finish the scan and report its findings. It will give you the option to clean your computer or perform another action, but the defaults are usually correct. If a malicious file is found, the file can be quarantined or destroyed, and the utility will alert you when it has finished.

Step 2   Now that you've completed your initial scan, there are other options available to you. You can pick between running a Quick scan or a Full scan. A Full scan performs the same actions as the Quick scan, but also goes through the Registry. You can also set up a Custom scan to scan only certain directories.

The Update tab allows you to update virus and spyware definitions, although Microsoft Security Essentials and Windows Defender also do this automatically. The History tab keeps track of all the potentially harmful

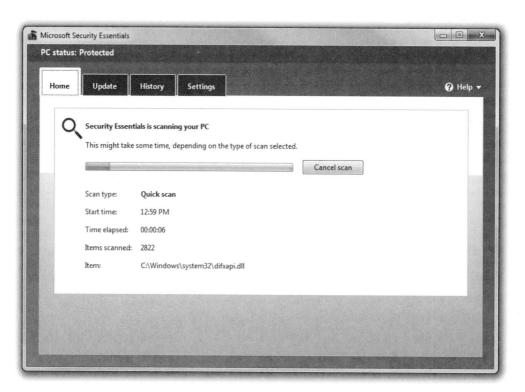

FIGURE 27-5 Microsoft Security Essentials performing a scan

items the software finds and what actions it performed. The Settings tab allows you to set up the program as you wish, including scheduling regular scans, setting what files and locations to exclude from scans, and adding removable drives to the scan.

To add removable drives to the scan, under the Settings tab, click Advanced in the left column. Check the box for Scan removable drives. Microsoft Security Essentials or Windows Defender will now scan the contents of each removable drive, such as USB thumb drives.

✔ Try This: The EICAR Virus Test File

If your scans didn't find any malware to remove, you can download a free harmless test file called EICAR from http://2016.eicar.org/86-0-Intended-use.html; click the Download link. The EICAR test file is used to test antivirus and anti-malware apps. To download it, temporarily turn off real-time protection in Microsoft Security Essentials/Windows Defender. After you download it, select a custom scan of the Downloads folder (or the folder you use for downloads) to locate and remove the file.

Step 3 Minor malware is easy to remove, as you just saw. But what if it's a thornier infection, and the default Windows utilities can't touch it? One workaround is to try a third-party virus detection and removal utility such as TrendMicro's free HouseCall.

a. Disable System Restore from creating any more restore points. Reason: restore points will save the infection, and you don't want that. To do this, open the Control Panel and navigate to System and Security | System | System Protection | Configure. Choose Disable system protection and click OK.

✔ **Tip**

If you were troubleshooting an actual infection, your next step would be to try restoring from an existing restore point that was saved before the symptoms of the infection occurred. To do this, open the Control Panel and navigate to System and Security | System | System Protection | System Restore. Then work through the wizard. Because you don't actually have an infection at the moment, we're not going to take the 10+ minutes required to do that right now.

---

b. Open a browser and navigate to www.trendmicro.com/en_us/forHome/products/housecall.html. Download the appropriate version of HouseCall for your system, and run it. Let it install, and then click Scan Now. Then wait for it to complete. If it finds anything, follow the steps it recommends. It takes awhile to scan your system, so go get a snack, or work on something else.

c. If HouseCall found anything, what did it find, and how did you proceed?

_____

_____

 15 MINUTES

Lab Exercise 27.04: Researching Missing Security Fixes with Belarc Advisor

Windows is designed to prevent many security issues, but its ability to do so depends on timely updates, many of which relate specifically to security issues. The free (for home use) Belarc Advisor identifies missing security fixes for Windows and third-party apps and many other details about your system.

> **✖ Warning**
>
> Belarc Advisor is free for use at home, but is not licensed for classroom or corporate use (Belarc offers commercial programs for these environments). This lab must be performed at home, and the students can bring a printout or PDF of the results to the classroom.

Learning Objectives

In this lab exercise you'll learn how to use the Belarc Advisor to see if your Windows home computer has all relevant security updates.

At the end of this lab, you'll be able to

- View security updates needed by your system
- Download needed security updates

Lab Materials and Setup

The materials you need for this lab are

- Windows PC with Internet access at home

> **✔ Tip**
>
> If it is not possible to have students share the results of using Belarc Advisor, go to www.belarc. com/en/products_belmanage#screenshots, scroll down, and look at sample screenshots from the BelManage enterprise management app (it has many similar features to Belarc Advisor). You can also refer to the screenshots later in this lab.

Getting Down to Business

A Windows system, if not properly updated, becomes more vulnerable to security threats over time. Belarc Advisor provides a great deal of information about your system, including a detailed analysis of missing security updates.

Step 1   On your home computer, download Belarc Advisor from www.belarc.com/products_belarc_advisor.

Step 2   When you open the executable, it will extract itself and begin the installation. Follow the instructions. Click Yes when prompted to check for new Advisor security definitions. Click OK to continue. It may take a couple of minutes to complete the system scan. Figure 27-6 shows the top of a typical scan from the author's home computer. Note that this computer is missing some security updates.

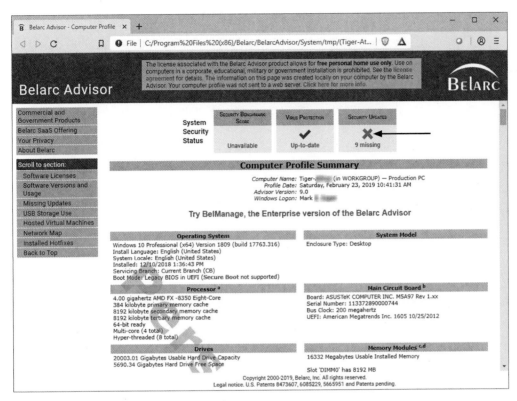

FIGURE 27-6 Belarc Advisor scan results

Step 3

a. If your computer has missing security updates, click the Security Updates box to go directly to that portion of the report (see Figure 27-7).

b. Right-click each link and select Open link in new tab. Click any links provided to get updates.

c. Download and install the updates recommended.

Step 4

a. Scroll down to the section Installed Microsoft Hotfixes – Past 90 days. List three of the hotfix IDs and the KB number:

_____

_____

_____

b. Click the link for each of the hotfixes you listed in Step a. Review the details.

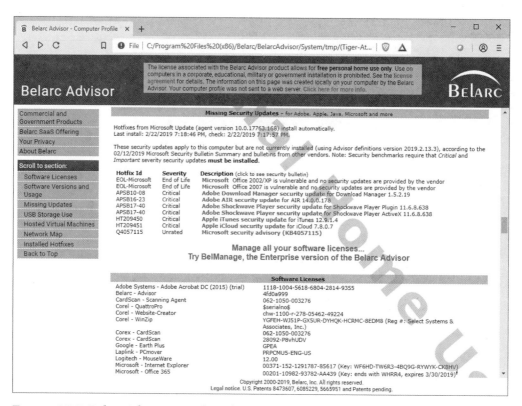

FIGURE 27-7 Belarc Advisor provides information about missing security updates.

Step 5

a. Print a copy of the report or make a PDF (if you have PDF printing or file saving support available in your browser).

b. Bring a copy of the report to class and review it with your instructor.

Lab Analysis Test

1. While browsing the Internet, Maxel has been getting a lot more pop-ups lately. He assumes he has some kind of adware on his system. What should he do to fix this?

2. Jason is working on a document when Word crashes. Which log in Event Viewer will give him more information? Which level would it be most likely identified as?

3. In the Local Security Policy applet, what does *Account lockout threshold* control?

4. What are two methods of learning more about a particular event in Event Viewer?

5. Your home computer has been receiving Windows Updates regularly, but you're not certain about security updates for third-party apps. Which portion of Belarc Advisor will check for missing updates?

Key Term Quiz

Use the following terms to complete the following sentences. Not all terms will be used.

adware

anti-malware program

chain of custody

definition file

event auditing

Event Viewer

incidence reporting

Local Security Policy

object access auditing

phishing

polymorph virus

pop-up

spam

spyware

Trojan

virus

worm

1. _____ is a type of unsolicited e-mail that usually contains hoaxes and get-rich-quick schemes.

2. A(n) _____ appears as a new window in front of whatever application you are using.

3. It is necessary to have a(n) _____ to protect your computer from viruses and other malicious programs.

4. _____ keeps track of every event that occurs on your system and assigns it a level, such as Information or Warning.

5. A piece of malicious software that gets passed from computer to computer is known most generically as a(n) _____.

Chapter 28
Operational Procedures

Lab Exercises

Being a computer technician often involves preventing problems, not merely solving them. Some of the ways that computer technicians help prevent problems include diagramming a network, making sure that power distribution and protection devices are configured correctly and are working properly, and minimizing the potential for data loss and being locked out of a computer. The exercises in this chapter are designed to help you learn and apply these skills.

 30 MINUTES

Lab Exercise 28.01: Diagramming a Network

As a CompTIA A+ technician, maintaining and upgrading networks is likely to be an important part of your job. One of the ways that you can better understand a network is by reviewing a network diagram. A network diagram provides the logical layout of the network, making it easy to identify its component parts.

Learning Objectives

In this exercise, you will create a simple network diagram using Cisco network diagram icons based on the information provided.

At the end of this lab, you'll be able to

- Understand how a network diagram works

- Locate important network components on a diagram

Lab Materials and Setup

The materials you need for this lab are

- An Internet-capable PC running Windows, macOS, or Linux for research

- Access to the www.draw.io Web site for creating diagrams

- Information about the network in the classroom (Optional)

Getting Down to Business

At first glance, a network diagram may seem quite mysterious, full of odd icons and lines. However, once you understand what the icons and lines mean, the diagram makes a lot of sense.

For purposes of this exercise, assume that the network you are going to diagram has the following components:

- One 802.11ac wireless router with integrated switch connected via Ethernet to a PC and a Mac

- Three wireless clients consisting of two laptops and one printer

Step 1   Open your Web browser and go to www.draw.io. The Draw.io Web site enables you to create XML-based flowcharts and diagrams (it was previously known as Diagramly).

    a.   When you open Draw.io, click Device in the Save diagrams to dialog box.

    b.   Click Create New Diagram.

    c.   Click Network.

    d.   Click Create.

    e.   Scroll down the shape menu in the left pane and click + More Shapes.

    f.   Scroll down in the left pane and click the Cisco checkbox, then click Apply; you will use the Cisco icons in your network.

Step 2   The example network for this exercise includes an 802.11ac wireless router, so start by adding a router to your network diagram.

    a.   Scroll down in the left pane and click the Cisco / Routers node.

    b.   Hover your mouse pointer over each of the router icons and review the type displayed in the pop-up.

    c.   Click and drag the Wireless Router icon into the workspace and place it near the center (all location instructions in this exercise are for purposes of demonstration).

Step 3   Add the computers that connect directly to the router.

    a.   Click the Cisco / Computer and Peripherals node in the left pane.

    b.   Click and drag two Laptop icons into the workspace and place them approximately as shown in Figure 28-1.

    c.   Click and drag the PC icon into the workspace and place it approximately as shown in Figure 28-1.

    d.   Click and drag the Macintosh icon into the workspace and place it approximately as shown in Figure 28-1.

    e.   Click and drag the Printer icon into the workspace and place it in the lower-right corner, below the Laptop icon.

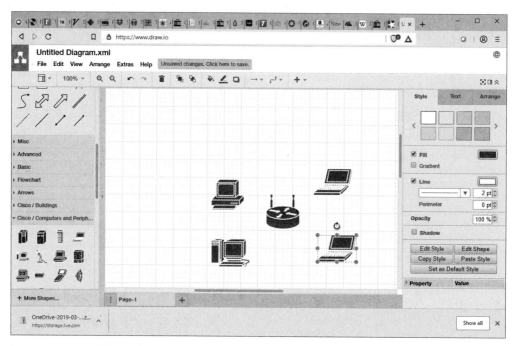

FIGURE 28-1 Adding a laptop icon to a Draw.io network diagram

Step 4 Add wired and wireless connections for the computers and printer.

a. Click the Cisco / Switches node in the left pane.

b. Click and drag the Workgroup Switch icon into the workspace and place it to the left of the Wireless Router icon, between the PC icon and Mac icon (drag the icons as needed for spacing). Even though the wireless router in the example has an integrated switch, they are considered separate devices for diagramming.

c. Scroll back up to the General shapes in the left pane.

d. Click and drag the Dashed Line icon and place it between one of the Laptop icons and the Wireless Router icon (Figure 28-2). If needed, click and drag the blue circle at each end of the Dashed Line icon to complete the connection between the Laptop icon and the Wireless Router icon. Repeat this step for the other Laptop icon and then again for the Printer icon so that each is shown connected to the Wireless Router icon via a Dashed Line icon.

e. Click and drag the Line icon and place it between the Wireless Router icon and the Workgroup Switch icon.

f. Click and drag the Line icon and place it between the PC icon and the Workgroup Switch icon. Repeat this step, placing the second Line icon between the Mac icon and the Workgroup Switch icon.

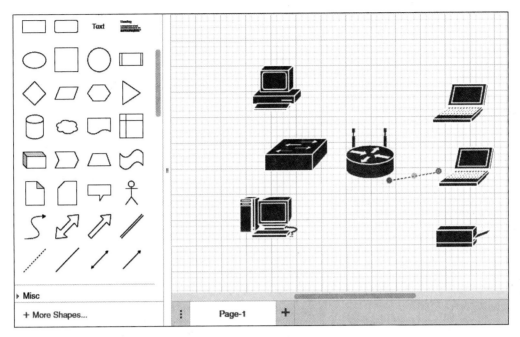

FIGURE 28-2 Adding a dotted line to the network diagram

Step 5 Save and export your diagram.

a. Click File | Save As.

b. Enter a name such as *Yourname* Network Diagram.xml (or the name provided by the instructor).

c. Click the location as directed by your instructor.

d. Follow the prompts to complete saving the diagram.

e. Click File | Export as | JPEG.

f. Click Export.

g. Enter a name such as *Yourname* Network Diagram.jpg (or the name provided by the instructor).

h. Click the location as directed by your instructor.

i. Follow the prompts to complete exporting the diagram.

j. Verify that your file has been saved and exported by starting your operating system's file manager and opening the location(s) where the file(s) are located.

k. Open the file with the default graphics file viewer on your system (see Figure 28-3).

l. Close the browser window and the file manager.

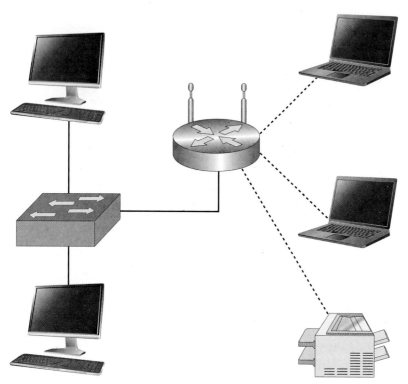

FIGURE 28-3 Viewing the exported network diagram with Windows 10's Photos app

Step 6 (Optional)   In this step, you will create a more complex network diagram. This could be a diagram of the classroom network or another network as provided by your instructor.

    a.   Use the following table to gather information about the network. Complete as much information as possible. If you can easily determine MAC and IP addresses, enter this information as well. If it is not available, don't worry about it.

Device	Connection Type	Connected To	MAC Address	IP Address	Notes

b. Review the data in the table and make sure that you know how each device connects to the network (wired, wireless, powerline adapter, repeater, etc).

c. Create a network diagram from this information using the www.draw.io Web site. Be sure to save the diagram and export it into a graphic so it can be easily viewed.

 **30 MINUTES**

Lab Exercise 28.02: Evaluating Power Distribution and Protection Hardware

Power distribution and protection hardware such as surge suppressors and battery backup units can provide a false sense of security if they are not periodically evaluated and replaced when necessary. Most surge suppressors use metal-oxide varistors (MOVs), which wear out over time. Rechargeable batteries in battery backup units will eventually fail. In this exercise, you will evaluate a typical list of power protection devices and make recommendations based on the facts provided.

Learning Objectives

In this lab, you will review information about a list of power protection devices, similar to what you might find in a typical office, and determine which ones can be kept in service or need to be replaced with units with higher capacity or better protection.

At the end of this lab, you'll be able to

- Identify surge suppressors that are unlikely to provide suitable levels of protection
- Identify battery backup units that provide too little capacity for device requirements
- Develop strategies for replacing and upgrading devices as needed

Lab Materials and Setup

The materials you need for this lab are

- A PC with Internet access
- A pencil and notepad

Getting Down to Business

In this exercise, we are assuming that the office we provide support for has had several recent power failures, some associated with thunderstorms, and some users have been reporting erratic behavior since these storms took place.

Step 1   The power protection devices you need to evaluate are listed in the following table.

Power Protection Device Type	Brand/Model #	Rated Joule Capacity (surge suppressor)	Battery VA or Wattage (battery backup)	Types of Devices Connected	Notes
Surge suppressor	Jasco SKU 37055	2160	N/A	PC Inkjet printer LCD panel External HD	Protection light is off; devices plugged into this outlet have no power. Marked UL 1449 and UL 1363.
Surge suppressor	APC Home Office SurgeArrest PH8U2	1680	N/A	PC Laser printer LCD panel	Wiring fault light is on. Marked UL 1449 and UL 1363.
Power strip	Unknown	N/A	N/A	PC Laptop LCD panel Microwave oven	One burnt socket. Cord repaired with electrical tape. Marked UL 1363.
Battery backup	Tripp Lite Internet750U	420	750 VA 450 W	Desktop PC* Laser printer* LCD panel^ External HD*	Run time of less than 10 minutes during most recent power outage.
Battery backup	CyberPower CP1350PFCLCD	1030	1350 VA 810 W	Server* LCD panel* Wireless router*	One battery has failed.

* = Connected to battery

^ = Connected to surge suppressor

Step 2 In this step, you will look up the information for each identifiable product and determine what should be done.

Jasco surge suppressor:

Company Web site: _____

What does the protection light going off indicate?

_____

What is your recommendation regarding whether to keep or replace this unit, and what is your reason?

_____

_____

APC surge suppressor:

Company Web site: _____

What does the wiring fault light coming on indicate?

_____

What is your recommendation regarding whether to keep or replace this unit, and what is your reason?

_____

_____

Power strip:

Manufacturer is unknown.

Does the power strip provide protection? Explain why:

_____

What is your recommendation regarding whether to keep or replace this unit, and what is your reason?

_____

_____

Tripp Lite battery backup:

Company Web site: _____

Does the vendor recommend connecting printers to the battery backup unit? (Perform a site search for documents if necessary.) If no, what does the vendor recommend?

_____

What is your recommendation regarding whether to keep or replace this unit, and what is your reason?

_____

_____

CyberPower battery backup:

Company Web site: _____

How many batteries does this unit use? _____

What is your recommendation regarding keeping this unit in service or replacing it, and what is your reason?

_____

_____

 30 MINUTES

Lab Exercise 28.03: Comparing Backup Methods

Backing up important information is vital to making sure a business can continue in the event of data loss or system failure. Choosing the best backup method for a particular situation is an important task you might be called upon to perform.

Learning Objectives

In this lab, you will compare file, drive, and image backup solutions.

At the end of this lab, you'll be able to

- Understand the benefits and limitations of various backup methods
- Choose the appropriate backup methods for the organization's needs

Lab Materials and Setup

The materials you need for this lab are

- A Windows PC with Internet access
- A pencil and notepad

Getting Down to Business

Backing up data enables users to have a spare copy in the event of user error (erasure or overwriting), drive failure, or system failure. Different types of backups can be used to back up data, depending on the amount of data to be backed up and the location of the systems. In this exercise, you are being asked to advise the Unlimited Widgets company about the backup needs of its users. You have been given the following outline of UW's available backup solutions.

Available backup hardware:

- 16-GB USB 3.0 flash drives
- 2-TB USB 3.0 external hard drive

Available backup software:

- Windows SyncToy
- Macrium Reflect Free Edition

Cloud storage:

- 5-GB OneDrive cloud storage account per user
- 2-GB Dropbox cloud storage account per user
- Microsoft Azure

In the following steps, you will be asked to select from these backup options (one or more) for users with different needs, and to determine whether the company needs to add additional backup options.

Step 1 One user, the Traveling Trainer, is running Windows 7 and uses her laptop to create digital photos, spreadsheets, presentations, and documents. The Traveling Trainer is out of the office approximately 70 percent of the time and provides customized training and consulting to customers. Currently, this user is creating backups on 16-GB USB thumb drives by using SyncToy. Typical backup size in a week's time is about 500 MB, so one 16-GB drive can hold over eight months' worth of backups.

The Traveling Trainer had a close call the previous month when her laptop went missing after a mix-up at a hub airport. Fortunately, the laptop was returned, along with the backup drive that she kept in the laptop bag.

Write down the URL of the Microsoft Web page for downloading SyncToy: _____

What can this user do to make sure the backup drive is not lost if her laptop is lost or stolen?

This user has a OneDrive account. How could she use it to help make her backups safer?

_____

Step 2   Another user, the Graphics Specialist, is running Windows 10 and creates digital photos and illustrations. He is in the office 100 percent of the time and is part of the production team for slideshows, videos, marketing, and training materials. Currently, this user is creating backups using Macrium Reflect Free Edition. His typical backup size in a week's time is about 2.2 GB of data because Macrium Reflect Free Edition must make full backups each time it runs, so even unchanged data is backed up each time. Actual new or edited data files are about 900 MB each week.

The Graphics Specialist had to switch to a new drive last month after filling up the first backup drive. He has been reading about different backup apps that can perform incremental backups (backing up only changed files), but doesn't want to switch to a different backup vendor.

Write down the Web site for Macrium Reflect Free Edition: _____

What upgrade options are available from Macrium Reflect that would provide incremental backups?

_____

Does Macrium Reflect offer support for Microsoft Azure? (Perform a site search to find out.)

_____

This user has a OneDrive account. Is it large enough to use for long-term storage? If not, would it be large enough after an upgrade to a Macrium Reflect edition that supports incremental backups?

_____

Step 3   Another user, the Office Maven, has just upgraded from Windows 7 to Windows 10. She is in the office 100 percent of the time and is in charge of customer and internal communications.

She has been making backups with Windows 7 Backup and Restore, and is concerned about whether she can get to old backups when she needs to. Recently, she had to recover contracts from three years ago for updating. She has just updated to a version of Windows 10 that no longer supports using Windows 7 Backup and Restore for backup.

Can the Office Maven still use Windows 7 backup files in Windows 10? If so, where is that feature located?

_____

Does Windows 10 have a built-in backup solution? If so, what is it?

_____

 **30 MINUTES**

Lab Exercise 28.04: Creating a Password Reset Disk

A lost password is always a frightening event. Fortunately, if you have a local account on your Windows computer, you can protect yourself from a brain freeze like this by creating a password reset disk. The Unlimited Widgets company's policy is to use local accounts for all users, including Windows 8.1 and 10 (Windows 7, which uses only local accounts, is also still in use). So, there's a need to protect users from their own sometimes-porous memories.

Learning Objectives

In this lab, you will learn how to create password reset disks (which can be optical discs or USB thumb drives) with Windows 7, 8.1, and 10.

At the end of this lab, you'll be able to

- Use the appropriate password reset disk creation process for each version of Windows in use

- Use the reset disk to recover from a forgotten password

Lab Materials and Setup

The materials you need for this lab are

- A Windows computer running Windows 7, 8.1, or 10; if possible, perform this task with more than one version of Windows

- A USB thumb drive of any capacity (the password reset file is only 2 KB!)

Getting Down to Business

The password reset disk is designed to help users with local Windows accounts recover from the catastrophe of being locked out of their computers without the need to contact the IT help desk for assistance. This capability is especially helpful for relatively small organizations such as Unlimited Widgets, which doesn't have 24/7/365 tech support but has some people (such as the Traveling Trainer) who are frequently out of the office visiting customers.

Step 1   Your first task is to create a local account and set up a password for it.

WINDOWS 7

    a.   Click the Start button, then click Control Panel.

    b.   Click User Accounts and Family Safety | User Accounts.

    c.   Click Manage another account.

d. Click Create a new account.

e. Type a name for the account.

f. Leave Standard user as the account type.

g. Click Create Account.

h. Click the new account icon.

i. Click Create a password.

j. Type a new password, then enter it again in the Confirm box.

k. Type a password hint.

l. Click Create password.

m. Close all dialog boxes and log out of the computer.

WINDOWS 8.1

a. If the Windows 8.1 live tiles menu is not open, click the Start button.

b. Move the mouse to the lower-right corner.

c. Click Settings.

d. Click Change PC settings.

e. Click Accounts.

f. Click Other accounts.

g. Click Add an account.

h. Click *Sign in without a Microsoft account (not recommended)*.

i. Click Local account.

j. Type a name for the account.

k. Type a password, then enter it again in the Reenter password box.

l. Type a password hint.

m. Click Next.

n. Click Finish.

o. Close all dialog boxes and log out of the computer.

WINDOWS 10

a. Open the Start menu and click Settings.

b. Click Accounts.

c. Click Family & other users.

d. Click Add someone else to this PC.

e. Click I don't have this person's sign-in information.

f. Click Add a user without a Microsoft account.

g. Type a name for the account.

h. Type a new password, then enter it again in the Re-enter box.

i. Open the Security question 1 menu and choose a question.

j. Enter the answer for this question.

k. Repeat the process with Security questions 2 and 3, choosing different questions (see Figure 28-4).

l. Click Next.

m. Close all dialog boxes and log out.

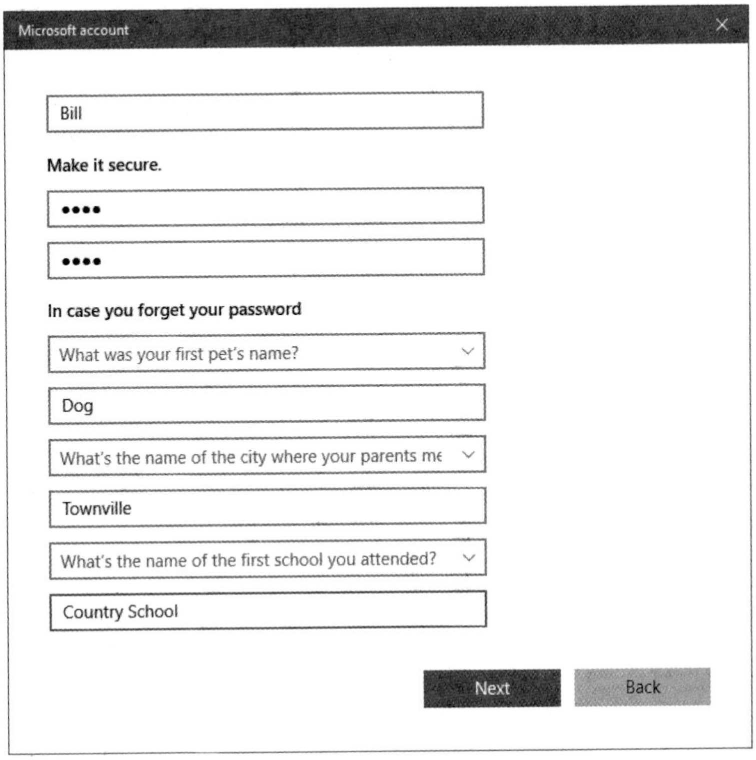

FIGURE 28-4 Selecting security questions and answers for a local account in Windows 10

> **➜ Note**
>
> Figure 28-4 says "Microsoft account" but this is an error in the edition of Windows 10 used for this lab. This dialog box is the one used to set up a local account.

Step 2   Next, log back in as the new local user and go to the Control Panel User Accounts applet, the launch point for creating the password reset disk.

WINDOWS 7

   a.   After logging in, click Start | Control Panel.

   b.   Click User Accounts and Family Safety | User Accounts.

WINDOWS 8.1

   a.   After logging in, right-click Start and click Control Panel.

   b.   Click User Accounts and Family Safety | User Accounts.

WINDOWS 10

   a.   After logging in, click Start.

   b.   Click the Search box and enter **Control Panel**.

   c.   Click User Accounts | User Accounts.

Step 3   With the User Accounts applet open, follow these steps to create the password reset disk:

   a.   Connect the USB drive or optical disc you want to use.

   b.   On the left side of the User Accounts applet, click Create a password user disk.

   c.   When the Welcome to the Forgotten Password Wizard appears, click Next (see Figure 28-5).

   d.   Select the drive from the drop-down menu and click Next (see Figure 28-6).

   e.   Enter the current password for the account and click Next.

   f.   Click Next after the Progress bar reaches 100%.

   g.   Click Finish and remove the password recovery media.

Step 4   Now, test the password recovery disk.

   a.   Log out of the computer and select the user who has a password reset disk.

   b.   Enter an incorrect password.

FIGURE 28-5 Starting the Forgotten Password Wizard

c. Click OK.

d. Click the Reset password link (see Figure 28-7).

e. In Windows 7 or 8.1, click Next. In Windows 10, you can answer security questions or click Use a password disk instead, and then click Next.

FIGURE 28-6 Selecting the removable-media drive where the password reset file will be stored

FIGURE 28-7 Preparing to start the reset password process in Windows 8.1

f. Insert the USB flash drive with the password recovery file.

g. Select it from the list of drives in the drop-down menu, then click Next (see Figure 28-8).

h. Type a new password, retype it to confirm, and type a new password hint (see Figure 28-9).

i. Click Next.

j. Click Finish.

k. Use the new password the next time you log into the account. You do not need to create a new password recovery disk.

l. Be sure to put the password recovery disk in a safe and secure location. Anyone can access the computer and reset the password by using the password recovery disk.

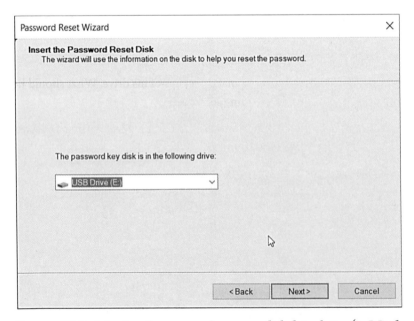

FIGURE 28-8 Selecting the password recovery disk drive letter (in Windows 10)

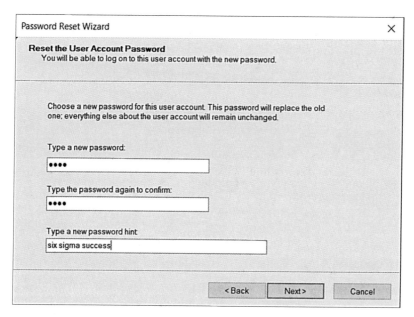

FIGURE 28-9 Creating a new password and hint (in Windows 10)

Step 5 You can remove the account if you don't need it for an actual user.

Lab Analysis Test

1. Mark has created a network diagram using Draw.io and needs to add it to a PowerPoint presentation. Which option on the File menu would provide a compatible file?

2. Kate is looking over the multi-outlet strip connected to her computer. She does not see any UL markings, but does see the brand name and model number of the multi-outlet strip. How can she find out if it's a surge suppressor or just a power strip?

3. Marvin uses the free edition of Macrium Reflect to make backups of his drive. What should he do if he wants to make incremental backups using the same software?

4. Miriam uses a Microsoft account to log into Windows 8.1. She likes the idea of using a password reset disk because she sometimes forgets her password. Can she use one?

5. Al just realized that he left his password recovery disk in the drawer of his desk when he headed out of town with his Windows 10 computer. If he forgets his password, how can he get back into his system?

Key Term Quiz

Use the following terms to complete the following sentences. Not all terms will be used.

1363	local
1449	power tap
all	surge suppressor
apps	Wi-Fi
Cisco	Windows 7
Ethernet	Windows 8.1
incremental	Windows 10

1. A network diagram often uses the _____ icon library.

2. A UL-approved surge suppressor is often marked with the UL _____ standard.

3. A backup that only backs up new or changed files is called a(n) _____ backup.

4. A password reset disk works with _____ accounts on a system.

5. As an alternative to using a password reset disk, _____ can use security questions.

Index

Symbols

Numbers

A

W